Redmine Cookbook

Over 80 hands-on recipes to improve your skills in project management, team management, process improvement, and Redmine administration

Aleksandar Pavić

[PACKT] open source*
community experience distilled

PUBLISHING

BIRMINGHAM - MUMBAI

Redmine Cookbook

Copyright © 2016 Packt Publishing

All rights reserved. No part of this book may be reproduced, stored in a retrieval system, or transmitted in any form or by any means, without the prior written permission of the publisher, except in the case of brief quotations embedded in critical articles or reviews.

Every effort has been made in the preparation of this book to ensure the accuracy of the information presented. However, the information contained in this book is sold without warranty, either express or implied. Neither the author, nor Packt Publishing, and its dealers and distributors will be held liable for any damages caused or alleged to be caused directly or indirectly by this book.

Packt Publishing has endeavored to provide trademark information about all of the companies and products mentioned in this book by the appropriate use of capitals. However, Packt Publishing cannot guarantee the accuracy of this information.

First published: February 2016

Production reference: 1190216

Published by Packt Publishing Ltd.
Livery Place
35 Livery Street
Birmingham B3 2PB, UK.

ISBN 978-1-78528-613-1

www.packtpub.com

Credits

Author
Aleksandar Pavić

Reviewer
Jijesh Mohan

Acquisition Editor
Aaron Lazar

Content Development Editor
Priyanka Mehta

Technical Editor
Siddhesh Patil

Copy Editor
Priyanka Ravi

Project Coordinator
Izzat Contractor

Proofreader
Safis Editing

Indexer
Monica Ajmera Mehta

Graphics
Disha Haria

Production Coordinator
Conidon Miranda

Cover Work
Conidon Miranda

About the Author

Aleksandar Pavić began his first project as a student at the Faculty of Technical Sciences, Novi Sad, Serbia where he developed Technical Faculty's first website. He later assembled a web team and graduated with BScs in computers sciences and information technology, and an MSc in product lifecycle management at the same university.

Acting mainly as a project manager and sometimes as a developer or team leader, Aleksandar made the following notable projects possible: student nourishment IS and ERP with smart cards at the University of Novi Sad, Novi Sad Farmer Market IS and ERP, E-government system of Novi Sad, including various sub-services, a web portal of the City of Novi Sad, Los Angeles-based `Usamailagent.com` packet-forwarding web-application, `Unival-logistics.com` online business system.

Currently, Aleksandar is employed as head of the IT services department at PUC Informatika, Novi Sad. He is involved in the following EU-funded Projects here: Sociotal, Weelive, and CLIPS.

Acting as an entrepreneur, he stands behind `www.redminegit.com`, cloud hosting, and Redmine implementations.

Aleksandar has two publications on Redmine. The first is a paper called "Project Management Using Open Source Internet Tools" in the fourth ICEIRD Conference,pp. 987-994, ISBN 978-608-65144-2-6. The second is "Monographic Publication - Master Thesis: Application of Project Management Software to Science and Educational Processes", published in Proceedings of Faculty of Technical Sciences 04/2014, ISSN 0350-428X, COBISS.SR-ID 58627591.

While participating in projects, he acts as an open source evangelist, and he advocates usage of lean methodologies backed up by Redmine as the management software of choice.

Aleksandar uses various management skills, such as, project management, product and service management, ISO 27000 and ITIL, Scrum and Agile methodologies, on a daily basis. He is also proficient in PHP, CakePHP, Ruby, Ruby on Rails, JavaScript, Bootstrap, C#, jQuery, Apache, Linux, Ubuntu, CentOs, Nginx, Phusion Passenger, Node.js, HTML5, Canvas, CentOS, Windows Servers, IIS, MySQL, PostgreSQL, and Microsoft SQL Server.

> This book would not be possible without my lovely wife who understands that working on my laptop in a Wi-Fi cafe bar while being on summer vacation is sometimes necessary to accomplish a notable result. Thanks to professors Bojan Lalic and Nenad Simeunovic from the University of Novi Sad with whom I started my project management quest. Thanks to all my colleagues, clients, and partners for using Redmine and understanding that work needs to be planned and organized because without them I wouldn't know what to write about.
>
> Of course, a special thanks to Jean-Philippe Lang and rest of Redmine's contributors for their efforts to maintain and improve Redmine as an open source product over last 10 years. Another special thanks to the people at Packt Publishing for all their hard work and providing me with an opportunity to express myself as international author and to give back to open source community by making Redmine a more credible and well-known product.

About the Reviewer

Jijesh Mohan is a computer science engineer with over 10 years of experience as a full stack developer. As an active evangelist of Redmine since 2009, Jijesh has been a passionate supporter of the Redmine community and has authored multiple plugins. His expertise ranges across several technologies, such as Ruby on Rails, Golang, ReactJS, and AngularJS.

www.PacktPub.com

Support files, eBooks, discount offers, and more

For support files and downloads related to your book, please visit www.PacktPub.com.

Did you know that Packt offers eBook versions of every book published, with PDF and ePub files available? You can upgrade to the eBook version at www.PacktPub.com and as a print book customer, you are entitled to a discount on the eBook copy. Get in touch with us at service@packtpub.com for more details.

At www.PacktPub.com, you can also read a collection of free technical articles, sign up for a range of free newsletters and receive exclusive discounts and offers on Packt books and eBooks.

PACKTLIB

https://www2.packtpub.com/books/subscription/packtlib

Do you need instant solutions to your IT questions? PacktLib is Packt's online digital book library. Here, you can search, access, and read Packt's entire library of books.

Why Subscribe?

- Fully searchable across every book published by Packt
- Copy and paste, print, and bookmark content
- On demand and accessible via a web browser

Free Access for Packt account holders

If you have an account with Packt at www.PacktPub.com, you can use this to access PacktLib today and view 9 entirely free books. Simply use your login credentials for immediate access.

Table of Contents

Preface	**v**
Chapter 1: Installing and Running Redmine	**1**
Introduction	2
Default installation on an Ubuntu server	3
Installing from a source on Ubuntu	7
Installation on Windows servers	11
Using Puma and IIS on Windows	16
Running with Apache as mod_fcgid	19
Running Redmine with Phusion Passenger	21
Running Redmine with Nginx and Thin	24
Installing optional requirements	29
Using custom Ruby for Redmine	31
Chapter 2: Customizing Redmine	**35**
Introduction	35
Customizing My page	36
Editing Redmine's views manually	38
Customizing modules per project	39
Extending user profiles with additional data	41
Customizing User roles	45
Creating and using User groups	47
Customizing the layout of the project entry page	49
Customizing the layout of the home page	50
Interacting with Redmine only through e-mail	52
Chapter 3: Project Management with Redmine	**59**
Introduction	60
Splitting your project into phases	60
Creating and using subprojects	62
Splitting your tasks into subtasks	66

Table of Contents

Managing issue relations	69
Creating and using template projects	72
Managing multiple projects simultaneously	74
Creating reports on spent time	77
Making sure everyone is optimally loaded with work	79
Relating between issue and time	81
Using the issue-code relation	83
Defining a roadmap to the release plan	88
Chapter 4: Improving Team Performance	**95**
Introduction	96
Keeping relevant documentation in Redmine	96
Putting the timeline to good use	98
Making sure that everyone is informed	101
Limiting access to some team members	104
Using metrics to improve team performance	106
Analyzing team performance through the code repository	110
Using the repository module to display code differences	114
Managing multicultural teams in different time zones	118
Applying advanced issue-code relationships	121
Improving Scrum meetings and backlogs	125
Chapter 5: Regular and Planned Maintenance	**129**
Introduction	129
Starting and restarting Redmine	130
Checking for active Redmine processes on the server	134
Configuring backup and recovery	138
Checking the data dirs for possible malware	142
Migrating and upgrading	145
Upgrading or migrating the database behind Redmine	147
Enhancing security	151
Upgrading Ruby safely	153
Chapter 6: Performance and System Tuning	**157**
Introduction	157
Fine-tuning new project creation	158
Tuning authentication and auto-login features	159
Tuning the workflows	161
Setting the log level	164
Getting the most from a single server	166
Scaling Redmine across multiple servers	170
Increasing file upload size	173
Integrating Redmine with Active Directory	174

Chapter 7: Integrating Redmine with Other Software — 179
- Introduction — 179
- Exporting to Microsoft Project — 180
- Using Redmine through browser plugins — 185
- Using Redmine mobile applications — 188
- Activity monitoring through Atom feed — 190
- Embedding Redmine into a web application — 192
- Using the Redmine REST API with PHP — 197
- Using the Redmine REST API with C# — 200
- Integrating with Tortoise SVN or GIT — 205
- Interacting with Redmine from Visual Studio — 208

Chapter 8: Getting the Most Out of Scripts and Plugins — 211
- Introduction — 211
- Pasting images from clipboard — 212
- Keeping track of your clients — 215
- Redmine for document management — 217
- Implementing and using reoccurring tasks — 222
- Practicing Kanban — 224
- Importing issues to Redmine — 229
- Using Redmine with Jenkins — 232
- Using the assigned issues summary e-mail — 237
- Text formatting with CKEditor — 239
- Being Agile with Agile Dwarf — 241

Chapter 9: Troubleshooting — 245
- Introduction — 245
- Where to get help and how to get help faster — 247
- Troubleshooting bundler installation — 249
- Troubleshooting Apache installations — 251
- Troubleshooting plugin installation — 254
- E-mail sending issues — 256
- Incoming e-mail parsing issues — 258
- Recovering from system failure — 260
- Tackling a delayed response from the server — 261

Chapter 10: Making the Most of Redmine — 267
- Introduction — 267
- How to convince management to use Redmine — 268
- Redmine as a Helpdesk with auto-responder — 270
- Using Redmine as a service desk platform — 275
- Improving Redmine Security for ISO 27000 — 279
- Redmine and SLA — 284

Table of Contents

KPIs inside Redmine	**286**
Using Redmine with ITIL	**289**
Index	**293**

Preface

Redmine is probably the most underused collaboration and management tool existing on the open source market for 10 years. Decision makers within corporations are often unaware of Redmine's full potential and ability to expand in all areas of business just by performing several actions inside Redmine and agreeing to several conventions within the company. Almost all departments of a company can store its documents, collaborate, coordinate, and benefit from its usage over an extended period of time because in every business it's crucial to know *who* did (or who is going to do) *what*, *when*, and *why*. So for example, in software development, one Redmine ticket within feature tracker can tell us who is going to do *what*—fulfill the client's request, such as export report to Excel; *why*—because it is the customer's request from within project A; *when*—the date when tasks were scheduled or done. Additionally, we can take a look at how it's done using issue-code relation. However, this should not just be limited to software if it's a design project, for example. Designers can also attach their design to a particular Redmine ticket/task if they use repository to store files. If it's a janitor company, then they can store photos of before and after repair, and so on.

Instead of just installing Redmine and using its features *out of the box*, this book tries to teach readers to think *outside the box*, and customize Redmine to improve user experience, customize workflows, and harness the power of its flexible design.

Choosing the right management tool can mean the difference between success and failure of a project. Flexible project management tools bend themselves to fit your needs. Whether it's a simple project communication, collaboration, or more complex project methodology, such as SCRUM, or issue-code relationship, or different methodology for each project, this book will teach you how to quickly customize Redmine for maximal business benefits and user satisfaction. It goes even further than project management and collaboration, illustrating how Redmine's flexible trackers could be used for automated recurring tasks and processes. Additionally, readers are advised to visit the book's website at `http://www.redminecookbook.com` and take a look at the blog and frequently asked questions section.

Preface

> Redmine is open source and donation supported, driven mostly by volunteers who donate their skills and time toward the project. They also need to pay for servers, computers they develop on, and so on. Consider donating to the project through the following link:
>
> `http://www.redmine.org/projects/redmine/wiki/Donors`

What this book covers

Chapter 1, Installing and Running Redmine, provides several different ways to obtain and install Redmine. It then goes on to elaborate on how to run it with different servers, including Nginx, Puma, Apache, Thin, IIS, and Phusion Passenger with MySQL or PostgreSQL on Linux servers or in a complete Microsoft environment with Microsoft SQL Server and IIS on Windows Server 2012.

Chapter 2, Customizing Redmine, covers some basic Redmine customizations, such as customizing roles, homepage, extending projects with custom fields, and so on.

Chapter 3, Project Management with Redmine, shifts more toward management. This chapter teaches readers how to achieve some basic project management routines, such as splitting projects into phases or subprojects, using template projects, tasks and sub-tasks, creating reports. It then moves toward a bit more complex stuff, such as using and forcing issue-code relationship, and defining a roadmap to the release plan.

Chapter 4, Improving Team Performance, also focuses on management and team-oriented scenarios, such as organizing and keeping project documentation inside Redmine, putting the timeline to good use, making sure that everyone is informed, improving team performance, managing teams in different time zones, and one scenario of SCRUM and Redmine usage.

Chapter 5, Regular and Planned Maintenance, is written for system administrators, and deals with recipes, such as migration, upgrade, backup, and recovery that are required for Redmine's usage in production over an extended period of time.

Chapter 6, Performance and System Tuning, mixes recipes from system administration, Redmine tuning, and management to improve Redmine's performance and user experience by providing how-tos for new project creation, workflows, auto-login features, server tuning, and integrating Redmine with Active Directory.

Chapter 7, Integrating Redmine with Other Software, teaches readers how to interact with Redmine directly from TortoiseSVN, TortoiseGIT, or Visual Studio; or to integrate your own software or website with Redmine through API; use mobile applications, and so on.

Chapter 8, Getting the Most Out of Scripts and Plugins, deals with some Redmine plugins and scripts, such as pasting images from the clipboard, implementing and using recurring tasks, practicing Kanban, being Agile, using Redmine with Jenkins, and using CKEditor.

Preface

Chapter 9, *Troubleshooting*, provides solutions to common Redmine issues, such as installations, slow responses from server, how to get help faster, troubleshooting plugin installation, and so on.

Chapter 10, *Making the Most of Redmine*, is mostly business- and management-oriented, while also keeping some interesting content for Redmine administrators, such as improving Redmine security, using and configuring service desk plugins and custom queries, and wiki security.

What you need for this book

You need Redmine installed, or a server (virtual or physical) so that you can install Redmine on it. If you are going to experiment with various recipes, then it's best to use some virtualization software, such as VMware, hyperV, or virtual box. Install a clean operating system (Linux or Windows), clone it, and start your work so that if you break something or want to try something else you don't have to start installing the operating system again, but simply clone the virtual machine.

Who this book is for

Redmine Cookbook is a part of Packt Publishing's cookbook series, grouping various Redmine related how-tos in 10 chapters. The recipes have been crafted for people who are already using Redmine or learning to use it and extend its features for better project management, some other kind of tracking, collaboration, or process management. Also, single developers or teams can benefit from various recipes that are related to code repositories, bug tracking, software project management, and Agile methodologies, such as SCRUM or Kanban.

Sections

In this book, you will find several headings that appear frequently (Getting ready, How to do it..., How it works..., There's more..., and See also).

To give clear instructions on how to complete a recipe, we use these sections as follows:

Getting ready

This section tells you what to expect in the recipe, and describes how to set up any software or any preliminary settings required for the recipe.

How to do it...

This section contains the steps required to follow the recipe.

How it works...

This section usually consists of a detailed explanation of what happened in the previous section.

There's more...

This section consists of additional information about the recipe in order to make the reader more knowledgeable about the recipe.

See also

This section provides helpful links to other useful information for the recipe.

Conventions

In this book, you will find a number of text styles that distinguish between different kinds of information. Here are some examples of these styles and an explanation of their meaning.

Code words in text, database table names, folder names, filenames, file extensions, pathnames, dummy URLs, user input, and Twitter handles are shown as follows: "`Aptitude` is a Linux package manager that comes shipped with Ubuntu."

A block of code is set as follows:

```
ssl    on;
ssl_certificate     /etc/ssl/certs/ssl-cert-snakeoil.pem;
ssl_certificate_key /etc/ssl/private/ssl-cert-snakeoil.key;
```

Any command-line input or output is written as follows:

```
sudo apt-get update && sudo apt-get upgrade
```

Preface

New terms and **important words** are shown in bold. Words that you see on the screen, for example, in menus or dialog boxes, appear in the text like this: "The next screen that you get asks you to configure Redmine automatically; choose **<Yes>**."

> Warnings or important notes appear in a box like this.

> Tips and tricks appear like this.

Reader feedback

Feedback from our readers is always welcome. Let us know what you think about this book—what you liked or disliked. Reader feedback is important for us as it helps us develop titles that you will really get the most out of.

To send us general feedback, simply e-mail `feedback@packtpub.com`, and mention the book's title in the subject of your message.

If there is a topic that you have expertise in and you are interested in either writing or contributing to a book, see our author guide at `www.packtpub.com/authors`.

Customer support

Now that you are the proud owner of a Packt book, we have a number of things to help you to get the most from your purchase.

Downloading the example code

You can download the example code files from your account at `http://www.packtpub.com` for all the Packt Publishing books you have purchased. If you purchased this book elsewhere, you can visit `http://www.packtpub.com/support` and register to have the files e-mailed directly to you.

Errata

Although we have taken every care to ensure the accuracy of our content, mistakes do happen. If you find a mistake in one of our books—maybe a mistake in the text or the code—we would be grateful if you could report this to us. By doing so, you can save other readers from frustration and help us improve subsequent versions of this book. If you find any errata, please report them by visiting `http://www.packtpub.com/submit-errata`, selecting your book, clicking on the **Errata Submission Form** link, and entering the details of your errata. Once your errata are verified, your submission will be accepted and the errata will be uploaded to our website or added to any list of existing errata under the Errata section of that title.

To view the previously submitted errata, go to `https://www.packtpub.com/books/content/support` and enter the name of the book in the search field. The required information will appear under the **Errata** section.

Piracy

Piracy of copyrighted material on the Internet is an ongoing problem across all media. At Packt, we take the protection of our copyright and licenses very seriously. If you come across any illegal copies of our works in any form on the Internet, please provide us with the location address or website name immediately so that we can pursue a remedy.

Please contact us at `copyright@packtpub.com` with a link to the suspected pirated material.

We appreciate your help in protecting our authors and our ability to bring you valuable content.

Questions

If you have a problem with any aspect of this book, you can contact us at `questions@packtpub.com`, and we will do our best to address the problem.

1
Installing and Running Redmine

In this chapter, you will learn how to install and run Redmine in different ways and on different platforms. This chapter covers the following recipes:

- Default installation on an Ubuntu server
- Installing from a source on Ubuntu
- Installation on Windows servers
- Using PostgreSQL as a database
- Using Puma and IIS on Windows
- Running with Apache as `mod_fcgi`
- Running Redmine with Phusion Passenger
- Running Redmine with Nginx and Thin
- Installing optional requirements
- Using custom Ruby for Redmine

Installing and Running Redmine

Introduction

Redmine is a project-management web application that is flexible in many ways, including its installation and running it. There are multiple configurations of web server software on which Redmine can run. These also include different operating systems, databases, and Ruby versions. Information on supported operating systems, web server software, or Ruby programming language interpreter and supported rails framework versions can be found at the Redmine website on the installation page:

`http://www.redmine.org/projects/redmine/wiki/redmineinstall`

This chapter presents recipes that are based on several common choices to install and run Redmine in production environments.

> This chapter's recipes are deliberately split between installing and running Redmine because it can be installed and run in multiple ways.

One of the most common configurations to run Redmine on is based on a Linux operating system, MySQL database, Phusion Passenger, and an Apache web server. This is the most common commercial offered by various hosting companies as a shared hosting at affordable prices. Also, there are already prebuilt virtual machine images for popular hypervisors, such as VMware or VirtualBox, that are offered by Bitnami and Turnkey Linux, which let you run Redmine simply by downloading the virtual machine image and turning it on; no configuration is required. However, such an approach may be an issue when you decide to go further with Redmine, install plugins, troubleshoot, upgrade, and so on.

If you are planning to use Redmine in your company or team, this chapter provides recipes that make sure that you have everything under control, and you will be able to migrate/upgrade, backup, fine-tune Redmine, and so on, because these may be required as time goes by.

As Redmine is flexible and can be used for different kinds of projects, you need to plan your installation carefully. If, for example, you are installing Redmine for a team of designers, they may want to attach large image files to tasks, and you need to plan the server's storage accordingly. Another scenario may be that if your company is going to use Redmine's flexible trackers as a service desk and there are going to be multiple-concurrent users, you are going to need more RAM memory and CPU power. The same goes for database configuration; Redmine will work on SQLite, but in larger production environments where performance is an issue, SQLite will present a problem.

While the recipes in this chapter provide step-by-step installation and configuration instructions, readers are encouraged to adopt them or use different operating systems and servers that may better fit their needs.

Default installation on an Ubuntu server

At the time of writing this book, the actual Ubuntu server version is 14.04 **Long Term Support** (**LTS**). So, this recipe covers installation on 14.04.3; however, things are probably not going to change much in the next few releases, and this is applicable to older versions of Ubuntu as well.

Getting ready

Make sure that you have `sudo` or `root` access to the server. If you don't have them, you may want to jump to *Installing from a source on Ubuntu* recipe, which explains how to install and run Redmine from the user's home directory.

1. First of all, make sure that your system is up-to-date by running the following commands:

    ```
    sudo apt-get update && sudo apt-get upgrade
    ```

2. Then, we need some prerequisites, such as MySQL or PostgreSQL, for the database. This recipe uses MySQL:

    ```
    sudo apt-get install mysql-server mysql-client
    ```

3. During installation of MySQL you will be asked to enter a password for the MySQL root user. Write down this password, you are going to use it later.

How to do it...

After updating your system, go ahead and try a simple install:

```
sudo apt-get install redmine-mysql redmine
```

After running this command on a blank Linux server box, you may get a large number of dependencies to install. Just click **<Yes>** or press *ENTER*.

Installing and Running Redmine

This process is going to take some time depending on your server and network capacity. The next screen that you get asks you to configure Redmine automatically; choose **<Yes>**.

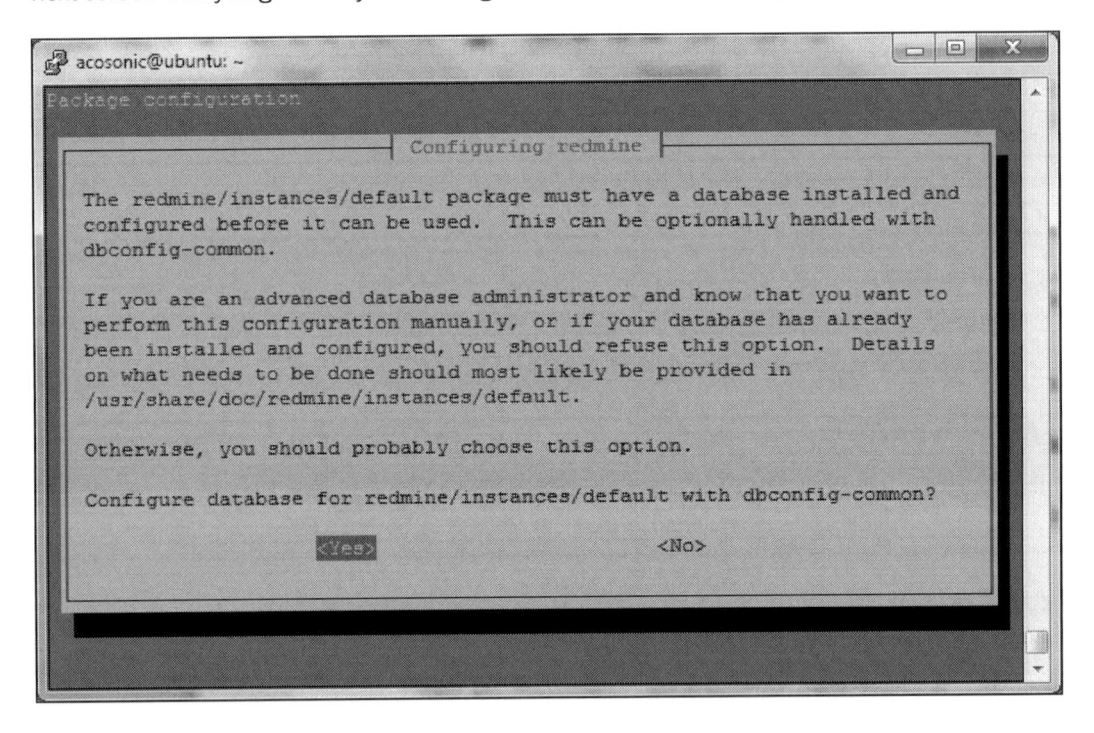

```
acosonic@ubuntu: ~
Package configuration

                    ┤ Configuring redmine ├

  The redmine/instances/default package must have a database installed and
  configured before it can be used.  This can be optionally handled with
  dbconfig-common.

  If you are an advanced database administrator and know that you want to
  perform this configuration manually, or if your database has already
  been installed and configured, you should refuse this option.  Details
  on what needs to be done should most likely be provided in
  /usr/share/doc/redmine/instances/default.

  Otherwise, you should probably choose this option.

  Configure database for redmine/instances/default with dbconfig-common?

                  <Yes>                              <No>
```

If prompted for database configuration, choose **MySQL**. On the next several screens, provide the administration password that you wrote down and the database name for your Redmine installation; then, your username and password follows, which are used by Redmine.

After providing these credentials (which you should write down somewhere safe) and waiting for the `apt-get` script to finish, you'll find your Redmine installed in the following folder:

`/usr/share/redmine`

To find out which version you installed, run the following:

`more /usr/share/redmine/lib/redmine/version.rb`

You will get something like this:

```
acosonic@ubuntu: /usr/share/redmine
require 'rexml/document'

module Redmine
  module VERSION #:nodoc:
    MAJOR = 2
    MINOR = 4
    TINY  = 2

    # Branch values:
    # * official release: nil
    # * stable branch:    stable
    # * trunk:            devel
    BRANCH = 'stable'

    # Retrieves the revision from the working copy
    def self.revision
      if File.directory?(File.join(Rails.root, '.svn'))
        begin
          path = Redmine::Scm::Adapters::AbstractAdapter.shell_quote(Rails.root.to_s)
          if `svn info --xml #{path}` =~ /revision="(\d+)"/
            return $1.to_i
          end
--More--(66%)
```

Your exact version is either *Major*, *Minor*, or *Tiny*, and in this case, it is Redmine 2.4.2 (shipped with Ubuntu 14.04.3). You will notice that the same version is used for Ubuntu versions. This rule applies for most open-software projects nowadays.

Accessing your Redmine

Installing Redmine on an Ubuntu system was easy and straightforward; however, accessing it via HTTP is not that easy and straightforward a task, and it gives you many options, as provided later in other recipes that deal with running Redmine on dedicated web server software.

To test the installation, perform the following:

1. Navigate to the Redmine installation directory:

   `cd /usr/share/redmine`

2. Run the **WEBrick** server to test the installation:

   `sudo ruby script/rails server webrick -e production`

Installing and Running Redmine

WEBrick can be used in production, but it is highly recommended that you read other recipes in this chapter and choose a more advanced and reliable solution, such as Apache or Nginx, to run Redmine.

How it works...

Apt-get installations are supposed to help administrators save time on common administration tasks. `Aptitude` is a Linux package manager that comes shipped with Ubuntu and Ubuntu-like systems; it downloads precompiled binaries and runs configuration scripts. In this case, first we update and upgrade our Ubuntu system, then we install MySQL and Redmine. Aptitude automatically installs the required dependencies and configures the system for us.

> Please keep in mind that while this may be Ubuntu's default and easy installation way, it installs Redmine to be run as a root user, and running web-applications exposed to the Internet as the root user is not a good idea. This is because as time goes by, hackers might become aware of security holes and use them to hack your entire server.

There's more...

If you want to install a newer version of Redmine than the default one that is provided in the official Ubuntu channels or you want to update an existing one, you will want to add the following repository to your system. To add it, run the following:

```
sudo add-apt-repository ppa:ondrej/redmine
sudo apt-get update && sudo apt-get upgrade
```

You must run this step first. However, the `ondrej/redmine` repository does not always keep track of the latest Redmine releases. If you want to have the latest release and easily update it, read the next recipe.

See also

For more information on **WEBrick** server take a look at its documentation at `http://ruby-doc.org/stdlib-2.0.0/libdoc/webrick/rdoc/WEBrick.html`.

Installing from a source on Ubuntu

There are two common ways to obtain a Redmine source: through **Subversion Client** (**SVN**) or by downloading the compressed source code from a website.

Also, there are two common ways to install Redmine: under a Linux user account, or system-wide. The previous recipe installed Redmine system-wide. This recipe covers the installation of Redmine under an ordinary user account in the user's home directory, *which is the recommended way to install Redmine*.

Getting ready

When downloading and installing a custom version of Redmine, make sure that you have the required prerequisites installed on your Ubuntu server. At the time of writing this recipe, the current version of Redmine is 3.2.0. You will find the list of supported prerequisites on the Redmine homepage:

`http://www.redmine.org/projects/redmine/wiki/RedmineInstall`

If you are using Ubuntu 14.04.03, then you are ready to go with Redmine 3.2.x; if you install Ruby and Rails, use the following command:

`sudo apt-get install ruby ruby-railties-4.0 ruby-dev build-essential zlib1g-dev libmysqlclient-dev`

Use the following command to check your Ruby and Rails version type:

`ruby -v`

`ruby 1.9.3p484 (2013-11-22 revision 43786) [x86_64-linux]`

`rails -v`

`Rails 4.0.2`

On the console output, you can read your versions and compare them to the supported ones listed on the Redmine website. Currently, we can confirm that we are ready to go with Redmine 3.2.0, as follows:

Installing and Running Redmine

Database configuration

You also need to have a MySQL, PostgreSQL, or SQLite database that is going to be used with Redmine. If you are creating a MySQL, or PostgreSQL database manually, *make sure that you create a UTF-8 database with a UTF-8 general_ci collation*. To create a MySQL database, perform the following:

1. Login to MySQL with a user that has sufficient privileges to create databases:

   ```
   mysql -u root -pmy_password
   ```

2. Create a UTF-8 database as follows; please keep in mind that you can choose any database name:

   ```
   CREATE DATABASE redmine CHARACTER SET utf8 COLLATE utf8_general_ci;
   ```

3. Create a user with a password (write it down in a safe place):

   ```
   CREATE USER 'redmine'@'localhost' IDENTIFIED BY 'my_password';
   ```

4. Give your user privileges, as follows:

   ```
   GRANT ALL PRIVILEGES ON redmine.* TO 'redmine'@'localhost';
   ```

How to do it...

First, let's confirm that we are not using the system as a root user by opening the console and typing the following: `whoami`

The output should be some other username than root.

Obtaining the Redmine source files

Firstly, obtain the Redmine source, either by downloading it to your computer, unpacking it, and uploading it to `/home/your_user/redmine`, or by following the methods that are illustrated next.

Downloading and extracting the Redmine source files

The `wget` tool is installed by default on the Ubuntu server; so, in order to use it to get the Redmine source, we perform the following tasks:

1. Navigate to your user's home directory by typing the following:

   ```
   cd ~
   ```

2. Utilize the wget tool to obtain a compressed Redmine source, as follows:

   ```
   wget http://www.redmine.org/releases/redmine-3.2.0.tar.gz
   ```

3. Unpack the archive:

   `tar xvf redmine-3.2.0.tar.gz && mv redmine-3.2.0 redmine`

4. Remove the downloaded archive file:

   `rm redmine-3.2.0.tar.gz`

The SVNcheckout method

Many administrators who plan to upgrade Redmine often prefer to grab the code via SVN because it allows code to be automatically updated while preserving local changes with a simple SVN update command. To use this method, perform the following steps:

1. Navigate to your user's home directory by typing the following:

   `cd ~`

2. Create a directory for Redmine, as follows:

   `mkdir redmine`

3. Check out Redmine from its official repository, as follows:

   `svn co https://svn.redmine.org/redmine/branches/3.2-stable redmine`

Redmine installation

After any of the previous methods, you should end up with the latest Redmine source in your home directory:

1. To proceed with the installation, use the following command:

   `sudo gem update && sudo gem install bundler`

   > If you are behind a proxy, the command to run `gem` commands behind a proxy is as follows:
   >
   > `gem command_name -http-proxy http://your_proxy:port`

2. Copy the default database settings to file without the .example extension:

   `cp redmine/config/database.yml.example redmine/config/database.yml`

3. Edit the database settings using your favorite editor, in this case, `nano`:

   `nano redmine/config/database.yml`

Installing and Running Redmine

4. You can edit production settings, or those for any other environment type, (for production, replace the values with your credentials):

   ```
   production:
     adapter: mysql2
     database: redmine
     host: localhost
     username: redmine
     password: my_password
     encoding: utf8
   ```

5. Now, let's run bundler from the directory from which we extracted Redmine:

   `bundle install --without development test postgresql sqlite rmagick`

6. After completing the bundler installation, you need to run several commands that are required by Redmine, as follows:

   `bundle exec rake generate_secret_token`

7. Proceed by populating the Redmine database as follows:

   `bundle exec rake db:migrate RAILS_ENV=production`

8. Load the default data, and choose a proper locale for default data:

   `bundle exec rake redmine:load_default_data RAILS_ENV=production`

9. Now, create the required directories:

   `mkdir -p tmp tmp/pdf public/plugin_assets`

10. Change permissions accordingly:

    `chmod -R 755 files log tmp public/plugin_assets`

11. Now, you can test the installation by running Redmine through a `rails server`:

    `bundle exec rails server webrick -e production -b your_server_ip`

12. Test whether Redmine is properly installed by opening the browser and typing `http://your_server_ip:3000/`. The Redmine home page should be loaded.

How it works...

This method assumes that Redmine will be installed in the user's /home/username/redmine directory. It can be used on shared hosting accounts if the Redmine prerequisites are already installed. At first, we made sure that the prerequisites were installed, then we grabbed the Redmine source either by downloading and extracting it manually or by SVN checkout. Then, we updated Ruby gems and installed bundler. Gem is a package manager for Ruby, and it is used to download and install the required Ruby libraries from the Internet. Bundler makes sure that all the gems required by an application are downloaded and installed. Then, we configured credentials for database access (in this case MySQL) and proceeded with bundling Redmine. The bundle command in *Step 5* fetches gems that are specified in Gemfile, omitting the gems that are required for development, test, postgresql, sqlite, and rmagick. Then, we called bundle exec rake generate_secret_token, which generated the hashing code that was required for cookie authentication. After this, we created database tables, and we populated them with the default data that is language/locale -dependent. The last step was to create the necessary folders and set permissions. At the end, we tested the Redmine installation with WEBrick.

See also

This recipe taught you how to install Redmine in the home directory for a user using system-wide Ruby. Take a look at the final recipe *Using custom Ruby for Redmine* if you need custom Ruby and can't tamper with the system at all (usually on shared hosting). Also, you now need a server in front of your Redmine installation. Later recipes will teach you how to use Apache, Nginx, or Puma as web-servers.

You can find alternative methods that are customized for different operating systems on the Redmine website:

http://www.redmine.org/projects/redmine/wiki/HowTos

Installation on Windows servers

This recipe teaches you how to install Redmine on Windows servers. It covers the Windows 2012 R2 Standard version and Microsoft SQL Server versions 2008 or later. However, this recipe can most certainly be applied to other Windows server versions. Also, PostgreSQL and MySQL can be used instead of **Microsoft SQL Server** (**MSSQL**).

Installing and Running Redmine

Getting ready

Make sure that the Windows server is properly installed with all the default libraries and required drivers. This recipe is based on Microsoft SQL server, and it assumes that you already have it installed. If you need to install it, make sure that you add the proper roles to the server first and include .NET 3.5 (required for SQL server 2014). Any type of MSSQL can be used (Express, Standard, Enterprise, and so on). Prepare a database named Redmine, and create a user for it. Prior to your Redmine installation, make sure that you have enabled SQL Server's TCP IP connectivity options by following the instructions that are provided here:

```
http://dba.stackexchange.com/questions/62165/i-cant-connect-to-my-servers-sql-database-via-an-ip-address
```

This will ensure that you have prepared your SQL server successfully.

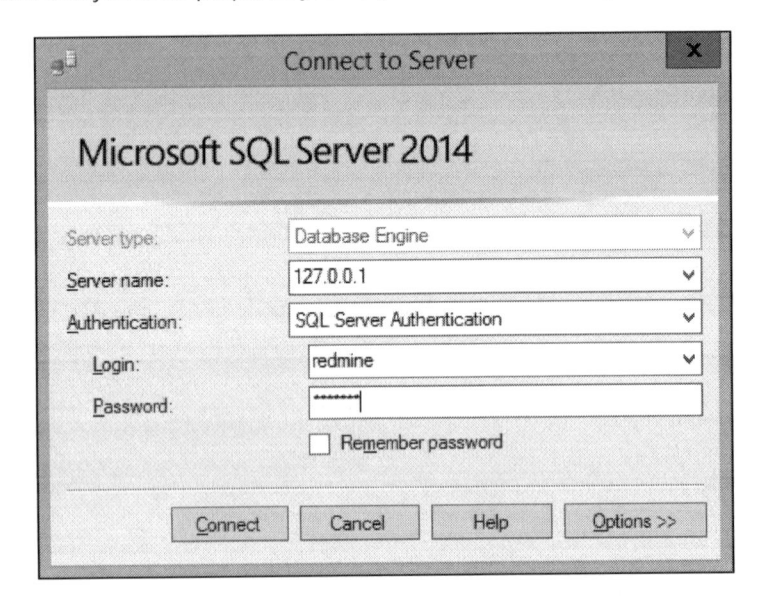

> Prior to your Redmine installation, make sure you have created the SQL server's user and database for Redmine, and that you can connect via IP with your Redmine user credentials successfully, as depicted in the previous screenshot.

How to do it...

1. First we need to install Ruby:
2. Open your browser and navigate to `http://rubyinstaller.org/`.
3. Download **Ruby 2.0.0-p645 (x64)**.
4. Right-click the Ruby installer that you downloaded and click **Run as Administrator**.
5. Proceed with the installation and make sure that you don't have any spaces or special characters in the installation path due to some potential issues with some Ruby third-party libraries. So, let's choose `C:\ruby\ruby2` as a path:

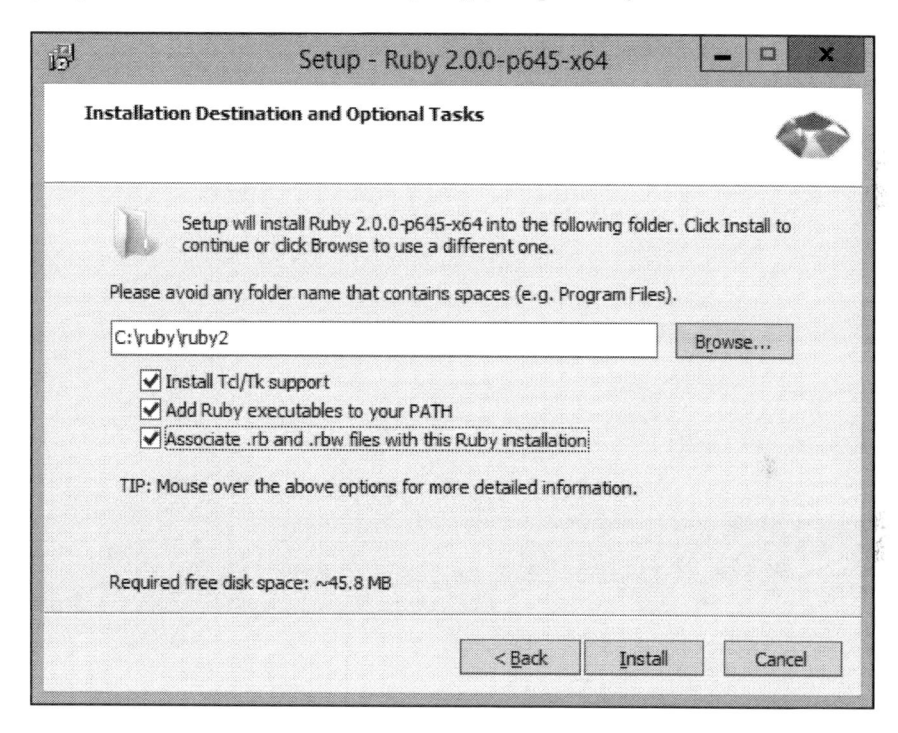

After a successful installation, in your Start menu, a new shortcut named **Start Command Prompt with Ruby** should be visible. Once clicked, you can type `ruby -v` and confirm that Ruby is successfully installed.

Installing and Running Redmine

Next, we need to install the DevKit 4.7.2 minigw 64-bit version by performing the following steps:

1. Download the file from `http://rubyinstaller.org`.

   > Make sure you are downloading the proper DevKit, it needs to match your Ruby version and system architecture: 64-bit or 32-bit.

2. Extract it to `C:\ruby\devkit`.
3. Run **Command Prompt** and navigate to `C:\ruby\devkit` by typing the following command:

   cd C:\ruby\devkit

4. Type the following command:

   ruby dk.rb init

5. Review what's initialized by typing:

   ruby dk.rb review

6. If you stumble upon a problem and get a message such as **Invalid configuration. Please fix 'config.yml.'**, then you need to edit `C:\ruby\devkit\config.yml` with Notepad and enter a line such as `C:/ruby/ruby2` so that when running `ruby dk.review`, you will get a screen like this:

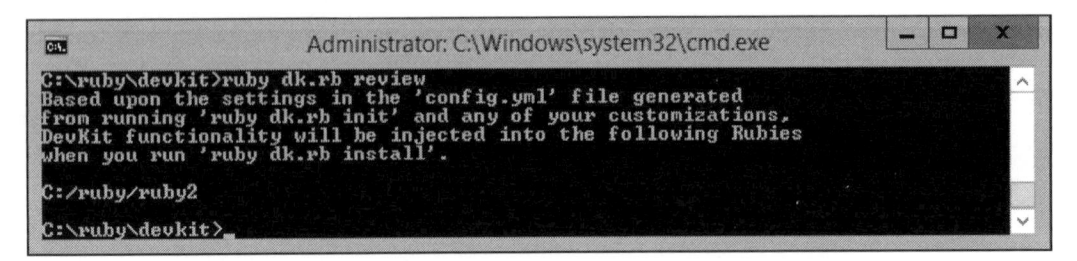

```
C:\ruby\devkit>ruby dk.rb review
Based upon the settings in the 'config.yml' file generated
from running 'ruby dk.rb init' and any of your customizations,
DevKit functionality will be injected into the following Rubies
when you run 'ruby dk.rb install'.

C:/ruby/ruby2

C:\ruby\devkit>
```

7. Type the following command:

   ruby dk.rb install

   When this is done, you will be informed that DevKit is installed.

8. Run the following:

   devkitvars.bat

9. Update `gem`, as follows:

   gem update

10. Install `bundler` by typing the following:

    `gem install bundler`

11. Download and extract Redmine to `C:\ruby\redmine`

> This recipe uses Redmine 3.1.0, which is tested with this recipe, but probably newer versions will also work.

12. Rename `C:\ruby\redmine\config\database.yml.example` to `database.yml`.

13. Edit `C:\ruby\redmine\config\database.yml`. You will find the MSSQL sample configuration at the bottom of the file, but it's enough just to edit the first production configuration in `database.yml` so that it looks like this:

    ```
    production:
      adapter: sqlserver
      database: redmine_db
      host: 127.0.0.1
      username: redmine_ms_sql_user
      password: "redmine_db_password"
    ```

    Replace the values in this code with configuration values that fit your server's IP address and database credentials.

14. Start the installation with bundler by typing the following command:

    `bundle install --without development test rmagick mysql postgresql`

15. Generate session storage encryption, as follows:

    `bundle exec rake generate_secret_token`

16. To create a database tables—objects, use the following code:

    `set RAILS_ENV=production`

    `bundle exec rake db:migrate`

17. Load the default data to the database. You can choose your language during or prior to this command. If you know that there is an existing translation of Redmine for the default language that you are choosing, you can set a two-letter country code by the Windows set command (https://en.wikipedia.org/wiki/ISO_3166-1_alpha-2):

    `set REDMINE_LANG=rs`

    `bundle exec rake redmine:load_default_data`

Installing and Running Redmine

18. Test the installation by typing the following:

    `bundle exec rails server webrick -e production`

If everything is okay, you should get a screen that looks like this:

```
C:\redmine3>bundle exec rails server webrick -e production
DL is deprecated, please use Fiddle
=> Booting WEBrick
=> Rails 4.2.3 application starting in production on http://localhost:3000
=> Run `rails server -h` for more startup options
=> Ctrl-C to shutdown server
[2015-08-03 08:54:12] INFO  WEBrick 1.3.1
[2015-08-03 08:54:12] INFO  ruby 2.0.0 (2015-04-13) [x64-mingw32]
[2015-08-03 08:54:12] INFO  WEBrick::HTTPServer#start: pid=3356 port=3000
```

After this, Redmine should be accessible via `http://localhost:3000`.

How it works...

For a Windows installation to work, we need a proper Ruby version and a Microsoft SQL server. It is not obligatory to use the Microsoft SQL Server, but this recipe uses it just from the perspective of trying to stick with Microsoft technologies. First, we set up a blank database and user for Redmine on the MSSQL server, and we make sure that it is working and able to connect via TCP/IP correctly. After this, we download and install a precompiled binary Ruby and DevKit that fits our chosen Ruby version. Then, we update Ruby gems and install `bundler`. After downloading and configuring database parameters for Redmine, we proceed by bundling Redmine, generating a session store token, and populating the database. After this, our installation is done, and we can test it with WEBrick.

See also

Now that you have Redmine successfully installed, running it requires a different recipe. To run Redmine on Windows, there are a few options that you can use, such as Apache + Fcgi, Nginx, or Puma.

The next recipe *Using Puma and IIS on Windows* is a very nice and flexible way to run Redmine.

Using Puma and IIS on Windows

Puma is advertised as a small and fast server. It is derived from Mongrel, which is an open source web server written in Ruby by Zed Shaw. It can serve Redmine on its own, or behind Nginx, Apache, or IIS. Puma can be run and installed in a user's home directory or system-wide.

Getting ready

First, install Redmine as explained in the previous recipe.

Then, we need the OpenSSL Developer Package (this contains header files and binaries), which can be downloaded from `http://packages.openknapsack.org/openssl/openssl-1.0.0k-x64-windows.tar.lzma`. Considering that we followed the previous recipe precisely, if you need a different SSL version, you can obtain it from `https://www.openssl.org`. Now, perform the following steps:

1. Download `http://packages.openknapsack.org/openssl/openssl-1.0.0k-x64-windows.tar.lzma` and copy it to `C:\ruby`.
2. Create a folder, `openssl`, in `C:\ruby` and copy the downloaded OpenSSL lzma archive here.
3. Run cmd and navigate to `C:\ruby\openssl` by typing the following: `cd C:\ruby\openssl`. Extract the content of the archive by typing:

   `bsdtar --lzma -xf openssl-1.0.0k-x64-windows.tar.lzma`

> If `minigw` bin from `devkit` is not added to path, you must specify full folder in order to execute `bsdtar`, and it would look somewhat like this:
> `c:\ruby\devkit\mingw\bin\bsdtar.exe --lzma -xf c:\ruby\openssl\openssl-1.0.0k-x64-windows.tar.lzma`

4. You should end up with OpenSSL files extracted in `C:\ruby\openssl`.

How to do it...

Once you have installed Redmine and its prerequisites, as explained in this recipe, proceed by installing the Puma server by typing the following:

`gem install puma -- --with-opt-dir=c:\ruby\openssl`

Testing Puma

This recipe assumes that your Redmine is installed, as explained in the, *Installation on Windows servers recipe*.

Run the following command from Redmine's directory in the command prompt:

`puma -e production -p 3000`

Installing and Running Redmine

You should get a screen that looks like the following:

```
Administrator: C:\Windows\system32\cmd.exe - puma -e production -p 3000

C:\redmine>puma -e production -p 3000
*** SIGUSR2 not implemented, signal based restart unavailable!
*** SIGUSR1 not implemented, signal based restart unavailable!
*** SIGHUP not implemented, signal based logs reopening unavailable!
Puma starting in single mode...
* Version 2.12.2 (ruby 2.0.0-p645), codename: Plutonian Photo Shoot
* Min threads: 0, max threads: 16
* Environment: production
DL is deprecated, please use Fiddle
* Listening on tcp://0.0.0.0:3000
Use Ctrl-C to stop
```

Navigating to `http://127.0.0.1:3000` on your browser should open Redmine screen.

Configuring Puma to start with Windows

To have your Puma server started automatically with Windows, perform the following steps:

1. Create a file, `pumastart.bat`, in `C:\ruby` with the following contents:

    `cd C:\redmine`

    `start /min puma -e production -p 3000 -t 8:32`

2. Then go to **Server Manager** | **Tools** | **Task Scheduler** | **Create a Task**.
3. Check the **Run whether user is logged or not**, **Run with highest privileges**, and **Hidden** checkboxes.
4. Then in **Actions**, go to **New** | **Start a program** and find `pumastart.bat`.
5. On the **Triggers** tab, click **New** and choose **Begin the task: At startup** (located in the top dropdown).

Configuring IIS

You should add an IIS role to your server and install the following two add-ons to IIS. You can install them directly from the Microsoft website.

You can get the URL Rewrite from `http://www.iis.net/download/URLRewrite` and the reverse proxy from `http://www.iis.net/download/ApplicationRequestRouting`.

1. Open **IIS Manager**.
2. Navigate to the website that you want to use as a Redmine proxy.
3. Click the **URL Rewrite** icon.
4. Right-click **inbound rules list.**
5. Select **Add Rule** and choose **Reverse proxy.**
6. Add an **Inbound rule** with the following: `127.0.0.1:3000`.

Chapter 1

If your Puma server runs after clicking **OK**, you should be able to type `http://localhost` or whatever your server name is and you will get the Redmine welcome screen.

How it works...

At first, we needed some prerequisites to install Puma because the `gem` to install Puma compiles it on your machine, and it requires proper OpenSSL library headers and binaries to compile. This is the reason why OpenSSL and dev tools are required. Then, the Puma installation is tested just by typing `puma -e production -p 3000`. To ensure that Puma starts after the Windows server restarts, Task Scheduler is used, and it schedules Puma to start on boot through a BAT file. In a bat file, `command -t 8,32` tells Puma to start with a minimum of 8, and a maximum of 32 threads. You can adjust these values to fit your configuration. After this, we installed two Microsoft original modules to the IIS server and added a reverse proxy rule to forward all requests to `127.0.0.1:3000` where the Puma server is listening. We used the default IIS site, but this rule works with any or multiple IIS sites.

There's more...

This recipe can be easily adopted to use Puma behind Nginx or Apache on both Windows and Linux systems. Also Thin or Unicorn can be used instead of Puma.

See also

Check out the Puma website for updates, additional configurations and fine-tuning:

`http://puma.io/`

Running with Apache as mod_fcgid

The `mod_fcgid` module is a high-performance alternative to `mod_cgi` and handles all requests for programs (such as Ruby) that need to be executed on the server. This recipe may not be a very popular choice due to the fact that many standalone Ruby servers such as Thin, Puma, and Phusion Passenger now exist. However, it may be required, and it's very reliable and relies only on Apache and Ruby executables.

Getting ready

- Install Redmine as explained in *Installing Redmine from a source on Ubuntu* to the home directory.
- Install Apache and `mod_fastcgid` by typing the following:

    ```
    sudo apt-get install apache2 libapache2-mod-fcgid
    ```

Installing and Running Redmine

How to do it...

Once the prerequisites are installed, and Redmine is confirmed as working with WEBrick, then navigate to `/home/youruser/redmine/public` and type the following commands:

```
cd /home/youruser/redmine/public
mv dispatch.fcgi.example dispatch.fcgi
chmod 755 dispatch.fcgi
mv htaccess.fcgi.example .htaccess
```

Create a new virtual host for Apache, or edit the default host. We will create a new host called `redmine.yoursite.com`:

```
sudo nano /etc/apache2/sites-available/redmine.yoursite.com
```

Enter the following contents:

```
<VirtualHost *:80>
        ServerName redmine.yoursite.com
        DocumentRoot /home/youruser/redmine/public
        <Directory /home/youruser/redmine/public >
                Options Indexes ExecCGI FollowSymLinks
                Order allow,deny
                Allow from all
                AllowOverride all
        </Directory>
        ErrorLog /var/log/apache2/yoursite_error.log
        CustomLog /var/log/apache2/yoursite_access.log combined
</VirtualHost>
```

Enable your new website and restart Apache:

```
sudo a2ensite redmine.yoursite.com
sudo service apache2 restart
```

After restarting, your Redmine should be ready and accessible through `http://redmine.yoursite.com` provided DNS is set properly or at least hosts file for testing purposes.

How it works...

At first, we installed `mod_fcgid` for Apache, then we prepared `dispatch.fcgi`; `.htaccess`, `dispatch.fcgi` is used by `mod_fcgid` through Apache and Ruby to run Redmine. `htaccess` tells Apache what to do with `dispatch.fcgid`. After this, we created a new virtual server for Apache. This may be done through an Apache management tool, such as Webmin for example, but then the value needs to be entered through an entry form or edited like we did from the command line in this recipe. After creating a virtual server, we enabled it and tested Redmine.

There's more...

If you get an error such as, **Rails application failed to start properly**, try some of the troubleshooting recipes from *Chapter 9, Troubleshooting* (the *Troubleshooting Apache installations* section.)

See also

The official mod_fcgid website is `http://httpd.apache.org/mod_fcgid/`.

More on Apache administration can be found at `https://httpd.apache.org/docs/2.2/vhosts/name-based.html`.

Running Redmine with Phusion Passenger

Phusion Passenger is a Ruby application server that was originally designed to run web applications (such as Redmine) that were built on the Ruby on Rails framework. Nowadays it has evolved, and besides Ruby applications, it supports Python and Node.js, making it a good candidate for various use cases.

This recipe is written for the Ubuntu 14.04 server.

Getting ready

Make sure that you have Apache and `passenger` installed:

```
sudo apt-get install apache2 libapache2-mod-passenger
```

Installing and Running Redmine

How to do it...

To configure Passenger, perform the following steps:

1. Open `/etc/apache2/mods-available/passenger.conf` with your favourite editor, or use nano:

   `nano /etc/apache2/mods-available/passenger.conf`

2. Add the following line: `PassengerDefaultUser www-data`.

3. So, your `passenger.com` will look something like this:

   ```
   <IfModule mod_passenger.c>
     PassengerRoot /usr/lib/ruby/vendor_ruby/phusion_passenger/locations.ini
     PassengerDefaultRuby /usr/bin/ruby
     PassengerDefaultUser www-data
   </IfModule>
   ```

   > If you are using a different Ruby version installed via RVM, update the paths accordingly. Also replace `www-data` with your user.

   Please keep in mind that `PassengerDefaultUser` can be entered in your virtual server's config file, which you may need to edit manually for installations on shared hosting.

4. Create a symbolic link to the Redmine `public` folder from a web server's root folder like this:

   `sudo ln -s /usr/share/redmine/public /var/www/html/redmine`

5. This link assumes that you installed Redmine through `apt-get`. If this is not the case and you installed it somewhere else such as `/home/user/redmine`, then you must adjust your links according to your Redmine installation and www root, which may look something like this (for example):

   `ln -s /home/user/redmine/public /home/user/public_html/redmine`

6. Make sure that `passenger` is enabled in Apache:

   `sudo a2enmod passenger`

7. Modify `/etc/apache2/sites-available/000-default.conf` by typing the following:

   `sudo nano /etc/apache2/sites-available/000-default.conf`

8. Add the following content near other `Directory` sections; if there are none, just make sure it's added before closing the `</VirtualHost>` line:

   ```
   <Directory /var/www/html/redmine>
       RailsBaseURI /redmine
       PassengerResolveSymlinksInDocumentRoot on
   </Directory>
   ```

9. Install `bundler` by typing the following:

   ```
   sudo gem update && sudo gem install bundler
   ```

10. Finish the installation and restart Apache:

    ```
    sudo touch /usr/share/redmine/Gemfile.lock
    sudo chown www-data:www-data /usr/share/redmine/Gemfile.lock
    sudo service apache2 restart
    ```

After restarting Apache, your Redmine installation should be ready to access by going to `http://your_server/redmine`.

How it works...

First, you installed Apache web server and Phusion Passenger as a Ruby application server, which runs as an Apache module. Then you edited Apache's configuration file for Passenger by adding the default user to be www-data. After this, we created a symbolic link from Redmine's public directory to the web server's root directory. Then, we edited the virtual server's config to serve this particular directory with two Redmine-related configs – `RailsBaseURI/redmine`, —which tells Ruby on Rails to access Redmine via the `/redmine` subfolder, and `PassengerResolveSymlinksInDocumentRoot` tells Passenger to follow symlink to find a Rails application through the symlink path. Instead of this, you could have written the following:

```
PassengerAppRoot /usr/share/redmine/
```

Redmine would work the same way.

There's more...

The best way to run Redmine or any other web-exposed software is to run it as a restricted user from its home directory and adjust Apache or any other web server to serve data from this directory. Running Redmine as a subdomain such as `http://redmine.yoursite.com`, is done by creating an ordinary subdomain, and an Apache virtual host file for this subdomain with the settings that are provided in this recipe.

Installing and Running Redmine

See also

If you stumble upon an error such as 403 (forbidden), error 500, or if you see Ruby code on the screen or the Passenger error screen, but you have followed the preceding steps exactly, refer to *Troubleshooting Apache installations* section in *Chapter 9, Troubleshooting*.

If you need to run Redmine as sub-uri, then take a look at `http://www.redmine.org/projects/redmine/wiki/HowTo_Install_Redmine_in_a_sub-URI`.

Running Redmine with Nginx and Thin

Nginx (pronounced Engine X) is an HTTP and reverse-proxy server with generic TCP proxying features. It is known for its stability, speed, and security. As such, it's often chosen by many web server and Redmine administrators. Thin is *a fast and very simple Ruby web server*. Combining these two servers provides additional flexibility and scalability in configuration. However, you are free to test/adjust this recipe and use any other server such as Puma or Unicorn instead of Thin.

Getting ready

Install Redmine from a repository, as explained in the *Installing Redmine on Ubuntu* recipe. If you are using Windows, then install Redmine by following the Windows installation recipe.

How to do it...

First, install Nginx and Thin by typing the following:

```
sudo apt-get install nginx thin
```

As we are using Ubuntu, the Aptitude installer will install Nginx and its required libraries for us, perform basic configuration, and start it. To test that it is installed and working correctly, navigate to your server's IP and you should see Nginx's welcome screen:

Welcome to nginx!

If you see this page, the nginx web server is successfully installed and working. Further configuration is required.

For online documentation and support please refer to nginx.org.
Commercial support is available at nginx.com.

Thank you for using nginx.

Configuring thin

To configure thin, it is better to perform the following commands as root, so we type the following:

```
sudo su
```

Then, we type one big line (explained later):

```
thin config --config /etc/thin1.9.1/redmine.yml --chdir /usr/share/redmine --environment production --socket /var/run/redmine/sockets/thin.sock --daemonize --log /var/log/thin/redmine.log --pid /var/run/thin/redmine.pid --user www-data --group www-data --servers 1 --prefix /redmine
```

Create the required directories, as follows:

```
mkdir /var/run/redmine /var/run/redmine/sockets/ /var/run/thin/ /var/log/thin/
```

```
chown www-data:www-data /var/run/redmine/sockets/ /var/run/thin/
```

```
nano /etc/logrotate.d/thin
```

Enter the following content to `nano`:

```
/var/log/thin/*.log {
        daily
        missingok
        rotate 52
        compress
        delaycompress
        notifempty
        create 640 root adm
        sharedscripts
        postrotate
                /etc/init.d/thin restart >/dev/null
        endscript
}
```

We need to make sure that thin will work properly after restart. To ensure this, we edit `/etc/init.d/thin` by typing `nano /etc/init.d/thin`.

We then add the following just before `DAEMON=/usr/bin/thin`:

```
pre-start script
    mkdir -p -m0755 /var/run/redmine
    mkdir -p -m0755 /var/run/redmine/sockets
    mkdir -p -m0755 /var/run/thin
```

Installing and Running Redmine

```
        chown www-data:www-data /var/run/redmine/sockets
        chown www-data:www-data /var/run/thin
    end script
```

Configuring Nginx

Add a new server to Nginx by typing the following:

nano /etc/nginx/sites-available/redmine

Add the following content that is updated to fit your server name needs:

```
    upstream redmine_thin_servers {
      server unix:/var/run/redmine/sockets/thin.0.sock;
      # Add additional copies if using multiple Thin servers
      #server unix:/var/run/redmine/sockets/thin.1.sock;
    }

    server {

      listen   80; ## listen for ipv4
      listen   [::]:80 default ipv6only=on; ## listen for ipv6

      # Set appropriately for virtual hosting and to use server_name_in_
    redirect
      server_name    localhost;
      server_name_in_redirect off;

      access_log   /var/log/nginx/localhost.access.log;
      error_log    /var/log/nginx/localhost.error.log;

      # Note: Documentation says proxy_set_header should work in location
      #       block, but testing did not support this statement so it has
      #       been placed here in server block
      include /etc/nginx/proxy_params;
      proxy_redirect off;
      # Note:  Must match the prefix used in Thin configuration for
    Redmine
      #         or / if no prefix configured
      location /redmine {
        root    /usr/share/redmine/public;

        error_page 404   404.html;
        error_page 500 502 503 504   500.html;

        # Uncomment below lines if using HTTPS
```

```
        # Note1:   Change $host to SSL CN if multiple host names used
        # Note2:   Adjust prefix, if different in Thin Redmine config
    #rewrite ^/redmine/login(.*) https://$host$request_uri permanent;
        #rewrite ^/redmine/my/account(.*) https://$host$request_uri
    permanent;
        #rewrite ^/redmine/my/password(.*) https://$host$request_uri
    permanent;
        #rewrite ^/redmine/admin(.*) https://$host$request_uri permanent;

        try_files $uri/index.html $uri.html $uri @redmine_thin_servers;
    }

    location @redmine_thin_servers {
      proxy_pass http://redmine_thin_servers;
    }
}
```

Enable the Redmine site under Nginx:

`ln -s /etc/nginx/sites-available/redmine /etc/nginx/sites-enabled/redmine`

Configuring Redmine for sub-uri

Using `nano`, open `routes.rb`, as follows:

`nano /usr/share/redmine/config/routes.rb`

Add the following line to Redmine's config file:

    Redmine::Utils::relative_url_root = "/redmine"

Add this line just above the line that looks like this:

    RedmineApp::Application.routes.draw do

Testing the installation

Restart both servers and test the installation:

`service thin restart`

`service nginx restart`

Now, navigate to your server's IP or `domain/Redmine`, and Redmine's initial screen should await you.

Installing and Running Redmine

How it works...

First, we performed a Redmine installation on an Ubuntu system, as explained in the recipe *Installing Redmine on an Ubuntu server*. Then, we installed the required servers: Thin and Nginx. Thin is a dedicated Ruby apps server, and Nginx is a dedicated web and reverse-proxy server. This way, we have multilayer architecture, allowing us to have, for example, one Nginx and multiple thin instances. In this case, it is connected through a Unix socket but more advanced versions of TCP upstream can be used to run multiple servers on multiple machines and load-balance this way.

Line `thin config --config /etc/thin1.9.1/redmine.yml --chdir /usr/share/redmine --environment production --socket /var/run/redmine/sockets/thin.sock --daemonize --log /var/log/thin/redmine.log --pid /var/run/thin/redmine.pid --user www-data --group www-data --servers 1 --prefix /redmine` uses the thin server to create config file.

- `--config` tells us where to put the generated file and under which name
- `--chdir` tells us which dir to use to start the thin server
- `--environment` tells us about the Rails environment
- `--socket` tells us the unix socket file path in `/var/run`
- `--daemonize` to run server as Unix daemon
- `--log` tells us location where to dump log file
- `--pid` is the unix pid file
- `--user` and `--group` under which Unix user and group to run the server
- `--servers` (how many servers to run)
- `--prefix` tells us under which prefix to run it
- `--servers` (tells how many servers to run) for managing concurrent requests (if you put more than one, then the Nginx configuration needs to follow number of the servers specified in this command)
- `--prefix` can be omitted if you want Redmine not to run as sub-uri (Nginx configuration also needs to be updated if using SSL)

After this, we create the necessary folders, set permissions, and add thin to logrotate. Nginx is already there, so we only add thin.

There's more...

You can use this recipe to set up Nginx and Thin on Windows; the only difference is Windows can't be daemonized. You need to start thin manually; set up a batch or registry file to do it. Also, the TCP port should be used instead of a Unix port.

Redmine can be forced to use SSL all the time through Nginx configuration. To do so, uncomment the SSL lines in Nginx config and copy and paste the server section, set the listen ports to 443, and add the path to your SSL key and certificate:

```
ssl    on;
ssl_certificate    /etc/ssl/certs/ssl-cert-snakeoil.pem;
ssl_certificate_key    /etc/ssl/private/ssl-cert-snakeoil.key;
```

See also

A comparison of Ruby web servers can be found at:

http://www.madebymarket.com/blog/dev/ruby-web-benchmark-report.html

Installing optional requirements

Redmine uses several optional components that may be required in some use-case scenarios. This recipe will download multiple libraries from the Internet. Do not use/download unnecessary software if you don't know what it does or just to have green lights in Redmine if you are not planning to use it. Every piece of software on the Internet-connected `server/software` is a potential security hole, especially if exposed through a web app such as Redmine.

How to do it...

Installing optional components is operating system-dependent. This recipe covers the installation of requirements on Ubuntu.

ImageMagick and rmagick

ImageMagick is a software suite to create, edit, compose, or convert bitmap images. It can read and write a variety of formats and be used from within third-party applications, such as Redmine, to perform various tasks on the images uploaded or generated by users.

To install `ImageMagick` on Ubuntu, simply type the following:

`sudo apt-get install ImageMagick libmagickwand-dev`

It will download and install a significant number of libraries that are required by `ImageMagick`.

If you have already installed Redmine and want to add the rmagick gem after installation, use the following command. It can be used for a fresh install as well:

`bundle install --with rmagick --without development test postgresql`

Installing and Running Redmine

Installing SCM binaries

Redmine uses several SCM binaries so that it can track code-issue relation in most of the popular **Source Control Management** (**SCM**) scenarios. Don't confuse this with Software Configuration Management.

On Ubuntu, installing all supported SCM binaries is extremely simple. Just open up a terminal and type the following:

```
sudo apt-get install subversion darcs mercurial cvs bzr git
```

After installation, restart your Redmine and navigate to **Administration | Settings | Repositories**.

You should get a screen that looks similar to this:

Enabled SCM	Command	Version
☑ Subversion	✓ svn	1.8.8
☑ Darcs	✓ darcs	2.8.4
☑ Mercurial	✓ hg	2.8.2
☑ Cvs	✓ cvs	1.12.13
☑ Bazaar	✓ bzr	2.7.0
☑ Git	✓ git	1.9.1
☐ Filesystem		

You can configure your SCM commands in config/configuration.yml. Please restart the application after editing it.

The green check sign and version number indicates that the repository client binary is installed and usable.

How it works...

Redmine is a complex **Ruby on Rails** (**ROR**) application that utilizes a wide variety of Ruby libraries that are required for Redmine to perform various tasks, such as exporting to PDF, connecting to a repository or manipulating images. In this recipe, we covered the installation of ImageMagick and its development libraries, which are optional but required. For example, SCM binaries are used and can be configured on a per-project basis, so you can track multiple repositories on different servers and on different SCM platforms.

There's more...

Subversion along with Git is really popular and widely used by many developers and teams. Redmine can create repositories for you automatically. Additional recipes and how tos can be found at the bottom of Redmine wiki HowTos:

`http://www.redmine.org/projects/redmine/wiki/HowTos`.

Using custom Ruby for Redmine

While Windows is without a Ruby interpreter and it needs to be manually installed, Linux distributions usually have Ruby in a base package or a web server package. This recipe teaches the user how to install and run Redmine with a custom Ruby interpreter, which can be used if Redmine needs a different Ruby version or if you can't install Ruby system-wide.

Getting ready

First, you need to install **Ruby Version Manager** (**RVM**). To use it, you need to have some basic build tools installed on your Linux box. If it's a shared hosting server, most likely these tools are already installed; if they are not, then ask root administrators to install basic build tools or look for another server where you can get sudo or root access.

Preparing for Ubuntu servers

Log in to your server and run the following command:

`curl -SSL https://rvm.io/mpapis.asc | gpg --import -`

Open your `.gemrc` file and add the following:

`gem: --no-rdoc --no-ri`

You can do this with `nano`:

`nano ~/.gemrc`

If `curl` is not installed or available for some reason, you can download a curl binary from `http://curl.haxx.se/download.html` and execute the same command just by adding `./` in front of it.

If the Ubuntu server is freshly installed, you are probably going to need some basic build tools such as make. To install them, type: `sudo apt-get install build-essential`.

Installing and Running Redmine

Preparing for Cent OS servers

For Cent OS, you don't need to import repository keys, but you probably need to install development tools that are required to compile some gems. To install prerequisites, run the following command:

```
yum groupinstall -y development
```

RVM installation

Once we have performed the necessary preparation steps, we start by downloading and installing RVM with this command:

```
curl -L get.rvm.io | bash -s stable
```

This will install the latest stable version of RVM; to start using it, type:

```
source ~/.rvm/scripts/rvm
```

After this command you can check which version of RVM is installed by typing the following:

```
rvm -v
```

How to do it...

Once we have installed RVM, we use it to install the required Ruby version.

First, we ensure RVM is working properly after installation by typing the following:

```
rvm reload
```

Then, we install a custom Ruby version; at the time of writing this book it is 2.2.1, which is supported by Redmine 3.X versions:

```
rvm install ruby-head
```

Then, we proceed with the Redmine installation, as explained in the recipe, *Installing from a source on Ubuntu*.

After this, running Redmine with Passenger, you need to add the following line to your virtual server's configuration:

```
PassengerRuby /home/your_user/.rvm/gems/ruby-2.1.0/wrappers/ruby
```

Replace `your_user` and the Ruby version with your actual username; text after PassengerRuby is actually an output of the following command:

```
which ruby
```

After this, reload Apache. If you are on a shared hosting, Apache probably reloads automatically once your server's virtual configuration is edited; if you have root access, you need to reload it manually.

Redmine should now work, if it's not working or throwing some errors, try looking at *Chapter 9, Troubleshooting*.

How it works...

First, we installed **Ruby Version Manager** (**RVM**) and its required prerequisites, which is usually a set of basic build tools that are required to compile some binary packages on Linux systems. Then, we used RVM to install a custom version of Ruby. RVM lets users have multiple Ruby versions on the system and switch to the default Ruby among them. However, most users are probably going to need only one custom Ruby version available in their home directory, which is going to be used by Redmine. Once Ruby was installed, we proceeded with the Redmine installation from the source by following the recipe *Installing from a source on Ubuntu*. Then, we configured Phusion Passenger and Apache by following the recipe *Running Redmine with Phusion Passenger* but with one variation: we needed to tell Phusion Passenger which Ruby version to use to run Redmine installed in our custom home directory.

There's more...

You can experiment with different RVM and Ruby versions and have multiple Redmines installed on the same server by following this recipe. This can also be used to upgrade Redmine without ruining your server if you need the system Ruby version to be used by some other applications. In this case, create a new user, install Redmine under this user's home directory, and migrate data from your old installation. Or just copy the whole directory and perform an upgrade also by upgrading the old database.

See also

If you need to use a different version of RVM for some reason, follow the tutorials available on RVM's website: `https://rvm.io/rvm/install`.

2
Customizing Redmine

This chapter covers the following Redmine customization features:

- Customizing My page
- Editing Redmine's views manually
- Customizing modules per project
- Extending user profiles with additional data
- Customizing User roles
- Creating and using user groups
- Customizing the layout of the project entry page
- Customizing the layout of the home page
- Interacting with Redmine only through e-mail

Introduction

Now that you have successfully installed and run Redmine, let's focus on customizing Redmine's functionality, workflows, and user experience. Recipes are based upon the English translation of Redmine. However, unless templates are modified, user interface elements should stay the same in all languages, except if Arabic is chosen, in which case Redmine displays the screen in RTL manner. Translations of Redmine are done well, and you won't have trouble using these recipes when they are translated to your or your user's languages.

> Redmine's layout is flexible and can be influenced by custom themes, so the position of **User Interface** (**UI**) elements on screen may be different from theme to theme.

Customizing Redmine

Customizing My page

In Redmine, **My page** is a feature that can be personalized for each user individually. My page is intended to be customized and used as a shortcut or dashboard, letting users organize a visual layout on their own in order to help them be more productive.

How to do it...

To customize **My page** perform the following actions:

1. Click the **My page** link that is located at the top right corner next to **Home**.
2. After navigating to **My page**, click **Personalize this page**, located on the right-hand side of the browser window below the search box.

The following picture shows a blank **My Page**; the arrow on right side points to the **My page block** drop-down list:

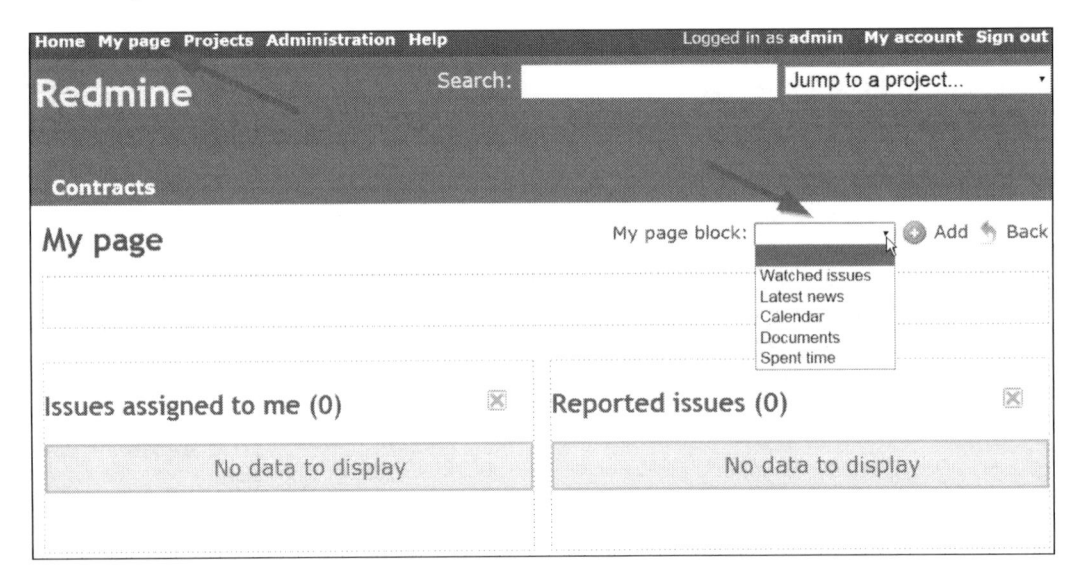

My page blocks contain the following blocks: **Issues assigned to me**, **Reported Issues**, **Watched issues**, **Latest news**, **Calendar**, **Documents**, and **Spent time**.

To add some of these blocks, choose the block that you like and click **Add**. After this, you will be able to drag this block in one of three designated areas that are displayed as dashed outbox in the following image:

Chapter 2

My page				My page block: [▼] ⊕ Add ↶ Back

Calendar ☒

Sunday	Monday	Tuesday	Wednesday	Thursday	Friday	Saturday
10	11	12	13	14	15	16

Issues assigned to me (122) ☒

#	Project	Tracker	Subject
440	example.com	Bug	Uncompleted Registration (Resolved)
376	example.com	Bug	Error in "back"

Watched issues (54) ☒

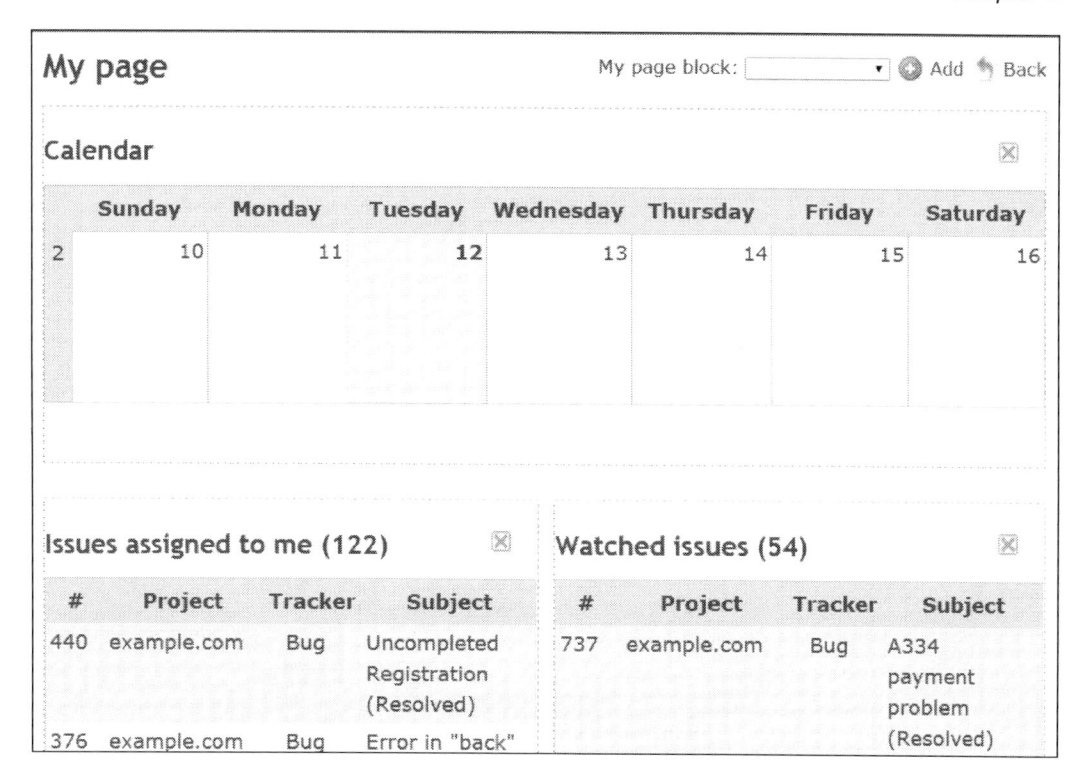

#	Project	Tracker	Subject
737	example.com	Bug	A334 payment problem (Resolved)

How it works...

This feature combines several of Redmine's features in one page. To achieve this, it lets users organize content blocks in one of three designated placeholders outlined by dashed lines, which serve as anchors for drag and drop blocks added through the drop-down menu.

There's more...

My page's layout and functions can be edited by editing Redmine's view files or by some of the Redmine plugins that are intended to do this.

See also

The plugin found at `https://github.com/Undev/redmine_my_page_queries` is a Redmine plugin, adding a **Saved Queries** block to **My page**.

Customizing Redmine

Editing Redmine's views manually

In its essence, Redmine is a Ruby on Rails web application, and it's open source. This means that you can edit its code, distribute it, or do anything else, as long as it complies with GNU General Public License v2 (GPL). So, for this recipe, we are going to add a company logo to the top left just below the top navigation row that contains **Home** and other links.

Getting ready

Make sure that you have access to the files and folders of your working Redmine installation.

How to do it...

Adding a company logo can be done in two ways. One is to customize the CSS theme and the other is to edit the base template manually. To edit the base template and add a logo or some other content, which will be visible on all pages, open `/app/views/layouts/base.html.erb` in your favorite code editor and find a line that looks like this:

```
<h1><%= page_header_title %></h1>
```

Replace it with the following content:

```
<!--<h1><%= page_header_title %></h1>-->
    <img src="<%= Redmine::Utils.relative_url_root %>/images/logo.png" style="top-margin: 15px; left-margin: 15px;"/>
```

Save the file, upload your logo to `/public/images`, and name it `logo.png`. Restart Redmine, and you should see the logo on Redmine:

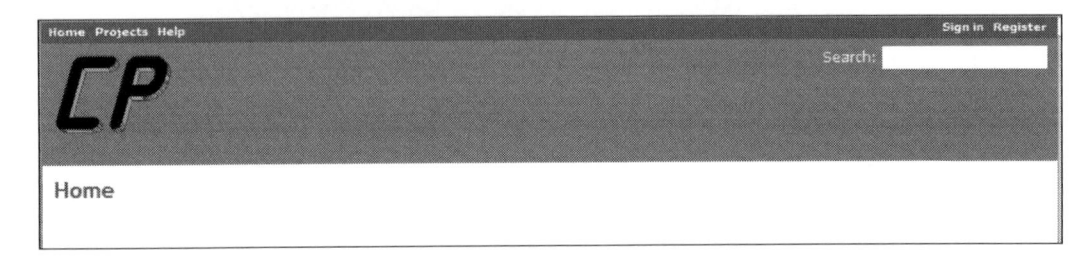

The alternative method would be to edit `/public/stylesheets/application.css`. Fi find a line that looks like `#header {min-height:5.3em;margin:0;background-color:#628DB6;color:#f8f8f8; padding: 4px 8px 20px 6px; position:relative;}`, and add your logo as a background image.

38

How it works...

As Redmine is a web application, it produces HTML code as the end result of its execution. In this recipe, we edited Redmine's source files that are used to render HTML content.

There's more...

You can also customize Redmine's terminology by editing the language files that are located in `/config/locales/`. So, for example, it's possible to use some different term, such as card instead of issue. Simply edit the `en.yml` file and replace all occurrences of issue that you don't like. The same goes for various kinds of alerts or messages from the system.

See also

Ruby on Rails tutorials, and the Redmine Developer Guide can be found at `http://www.redmine.org/projects/redmine/wiki/Developer_Guide`.

Additional customizations can be achieved through following plugin:

`https://github.com/alexandermeindl/redmine_tweaks`

Customizing modules per project

Ensuring that flexibility comes first, Redmine's projects are flexible in the sense of modules. So, modules that are going to be used in a project can be chosen on a *per-project* basis.

Getting ready

Make sure that your Redmine user has permissions to create and edit projects.

How to do it...

Modules are chosen immediately at the formation of a new project or later in the **Project Settings** tab. Please keep in mind that your users will see modules only if their roles are granted permission. To create a new project and choose modules for it, perform the following steps:

1. Click the **Projects** link at top left of the screen in the main Redmine menu.

Customizing Redmine

2. After this, click **New project**, and you will get a screen that looks like the following:

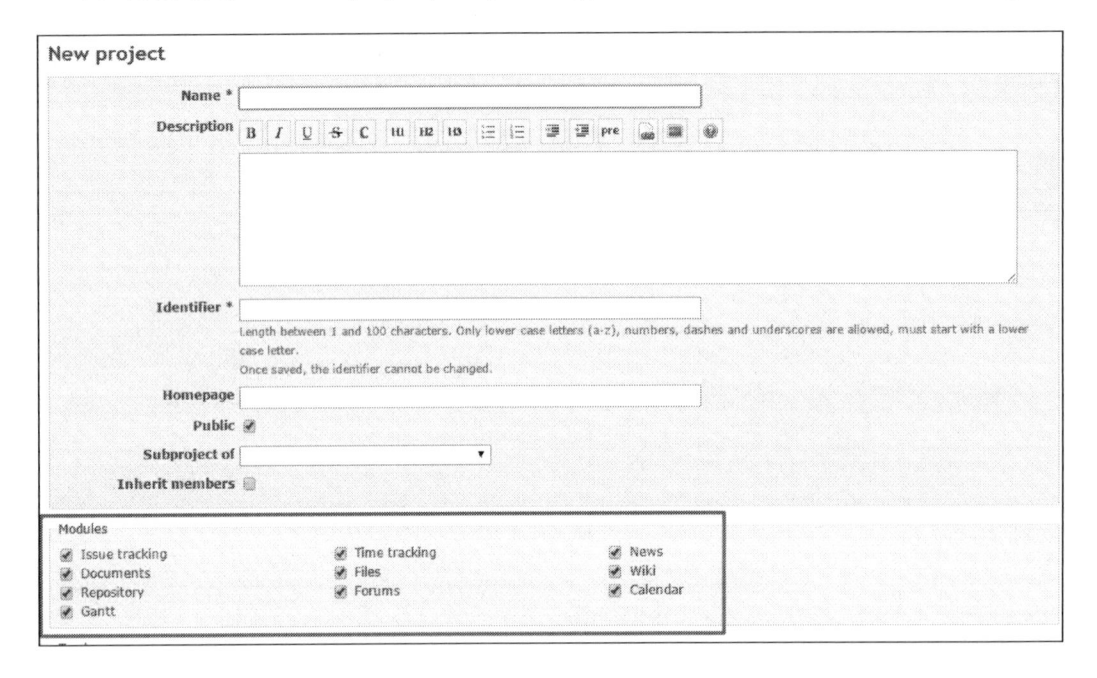

Just below the required project details section is a **Modules** section with checkboxes and module names. To turn the module on and off, just tick or untick the checkbox.

Existing projects

Modules can be activated or deactivated even for existing projects. If your user has proper permissions, you should be able to see **Settings** in the main project menu. Once clicked, the **Modules** tab should be visible, which displays the modules screen with module on/off checkboxes and a **Save** button.

How it works...

This feature enables modules such as **Documents** or **News** to be used on a *per-project* basis, meaning that each project can but does not have to use any of the modules available in the Redmine system. From a technical standpoint, settings about each project are stored in the database and can be edited either through **New project** or **Project Settings** from inside Redmine. Once a module is ticked, it is displayed in a main menu for that particular project, as displayed in this image:

Chapter 2

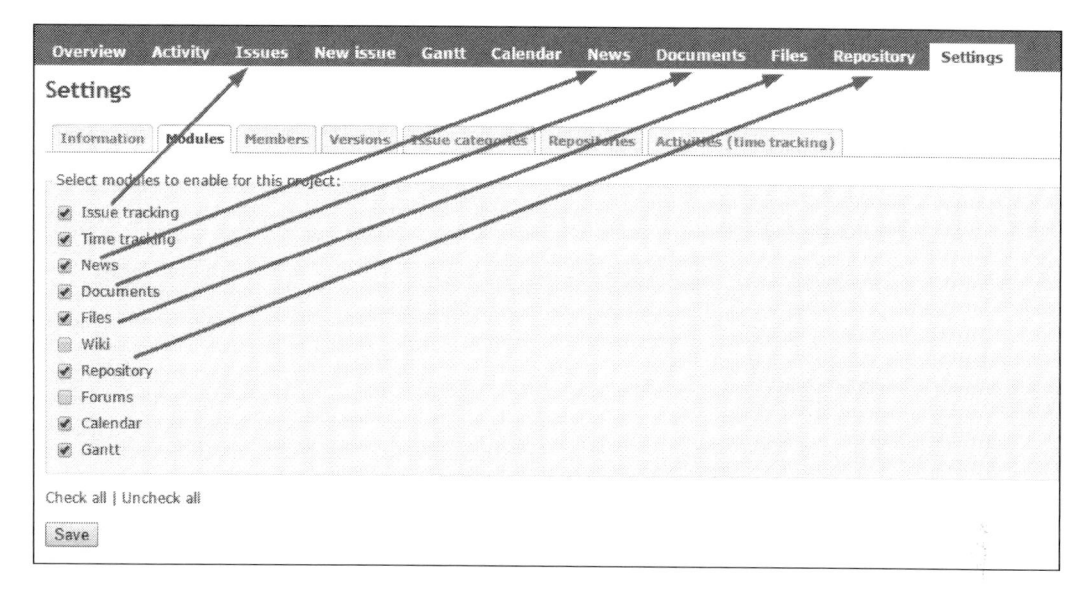

[Screenshot of Redmine Settings → Modules tab showing checkboxes for: Issue tracking, Time tracking, News, Documents, Files, Wiki, Repository, Forums, Calendar, Gantt; with arrows mapping modules to main menu items. Check all | Uncheck all. Save button.]

Once unticked, the module disappears from the project's main menu.

> Module-related data stays in the database after the module is deactivated. It will become visible once the module is active again.

There's more...

Some plugins may be displayed as a module and turned on or off on this same page on a *per-project* basis.

Extending user profiles with additional data

In the spirit of flexibility, Redmine lets users customize various objects inside the application. The objects can be: *user, group, project, activity, version, document, spent time, issue priority*, or *document category*. This recipe applies to any object.

> The custom fields feature is extremely important. It lets users customize Redmine to fit various purposes.

Customizing Redmine

For example, you can change the type of tracker from *Bug* to *Virtual server* and extend this tracker with custom fields, such as *RAM* or *Disk size*, and keep track of your virtual servers. Then, you can use filtering features to find all the servers using Windows or any other custom fields that you figured out you need in your Redmine implementation.

Getting ready

Make sure that you have administrative permissions on the Redmine system. If you have them, the **Administration** menu item will be visible at the top left, prior to the **Help** link.

How to do it...

To create new custom field for User, perform the following steps:

1. Click **Administration**, then click **Custom fields**, and click **New custom field**.
2. Select **Users** and click **Next**. The **New custom field** entry form should be displayed, as follows:

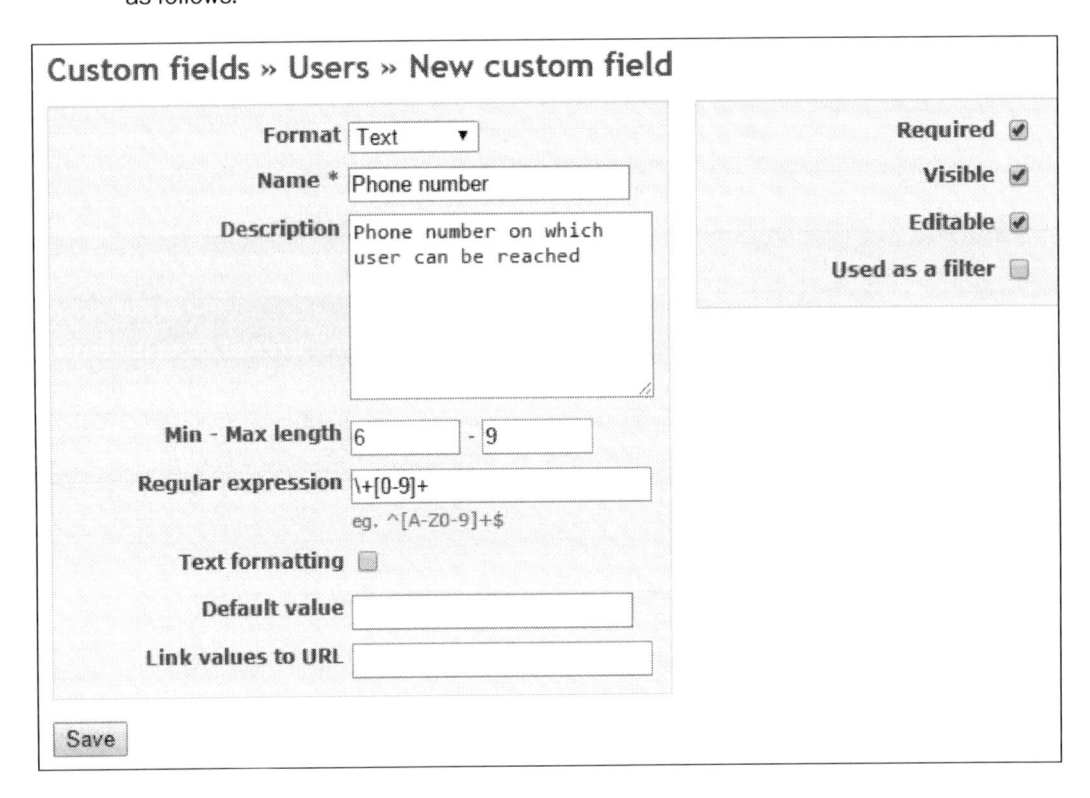

Custom fields » Users » New custom field

Format	Text
Name *	Phone number
Description	Phone number on which user can be reached
Min - Max length	6 - 9
Regular expression	\+[0-9]+
	eg. ^[A-Z0-9]+$
Text formatting	☐
Default value	
Link values to URL	

Required ✓
Visible ✓
Editable ✓
Used as a filter ☐

[Save]

3. Choose a type of field from the **Format** drop-down. The name of the field, in this case, is **Phone number**, but this can be *birth date, educational degree, home address*, or whatever you need. Fields such as **Min-Max** and **Regular expression** depend upon the format of the custom field. Options on the right, such as **Required**, **Visible**, **Editable**, or **Used** as a filter are type independent.
4. Click the **Save** button at the bottom of the form.

Test custom fields by navigating to **My account**. You should get the **Phone number** field, as displayed in the following image, and it is a required field:

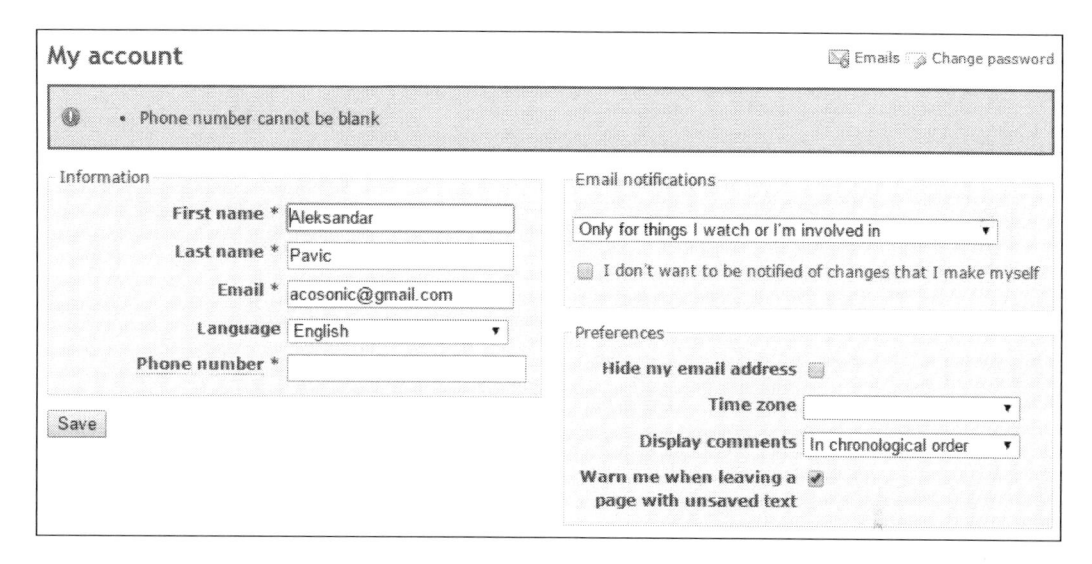

From now on, every new user added to Redmine, existing users trying to modify their account, or an administrator trying to modify their account, will have to enter a **Phone number** as it is a required field. Redmine won't let them save changes or register unless a properly formatted value is entered to the **Phone number** field.

How it works...

This feature extends built-in Redmine objects with custom fields. Technically, it works by adding custom attributes related to objects that are represented by tables in the database, and data is managed through various forms used in many places inside the Redmine application. From the management side, this feature works by adding a new value to built-in Redmine objects. Particularly in this recipe, we extended the `User` object with a new required field called **Phone number**, and we made it a mandatory field that needs to satisfy certain rules that are defined by a regular expression and min-max characters, as displayed in *Step 3* of the *How to do it...* section. Later, we demonstrated how this field is used on **My account**.

Customizing Redmine

There's more...

This recipe can be applied to projects, activities, and issues, as explained at beginning of the recipe. If you are extending issues with additional fields and tick the **Used as a filter** option, then your custom field will be displayed in the **Issues Filters** form, as displayed in the following screenshot:

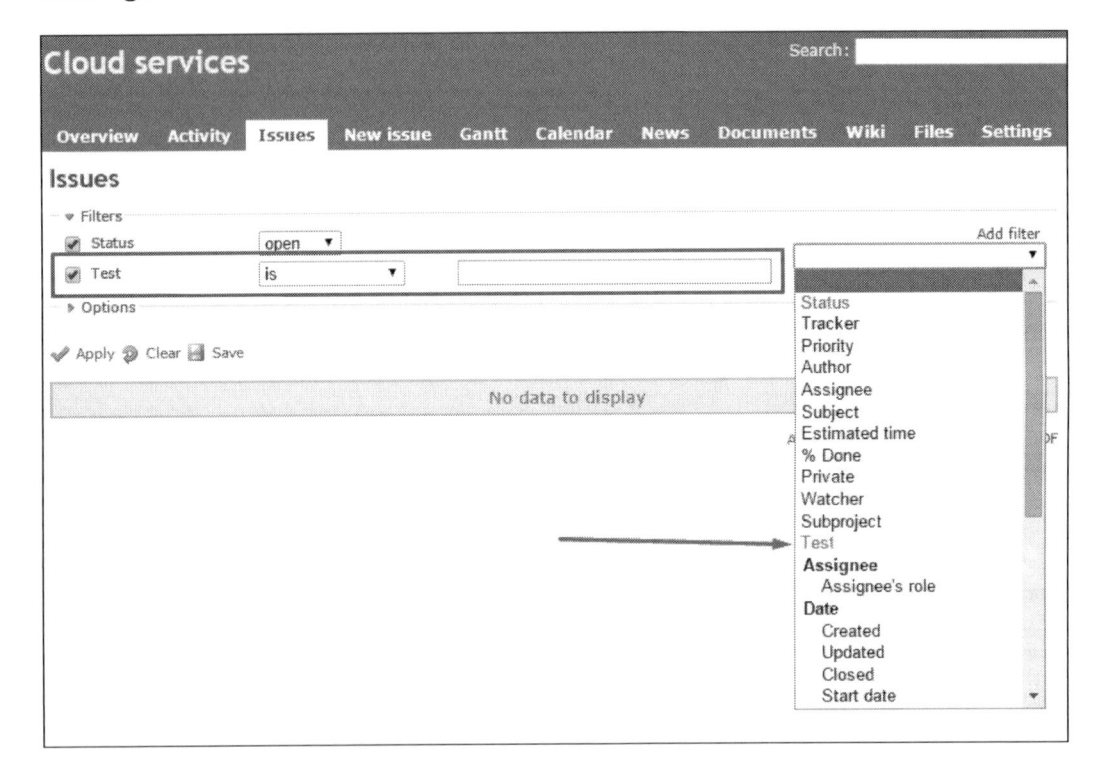

Here, **Test** is a custom field that is created for **Issues**.

See also

Refer to the recipes in *Chapter 10, Making the Most of Redmine*.

Chapter 2

Customizing User roles

User roles can be customized, and one user can be, for example, Manager on one project and Developer on another. Role customization is reflected in privilege customization.

Scenario: we are going to create a new role, called Collaborator, that has the same permissions as Manager, but the only difference is that Collaborator can't create new issues.

Getting ready

Make sure you have administrator permissions in Redmine.

How to do it...

Navigate to **Administration | Roles and Permissions**. Once clicked, the **Roles and Permissions** initial form is loaded. From here, you can customize existing roles, add new ones, or take a look at **Permissions report**. To create a new role, we are going to copy the **Manager** role by clicking the **Copy** button. Once clicked, the **New role** form will be visible with **Name** of the role starred as a required value. Enter the Collaborator name value and tick boxes as displayed in the following image:

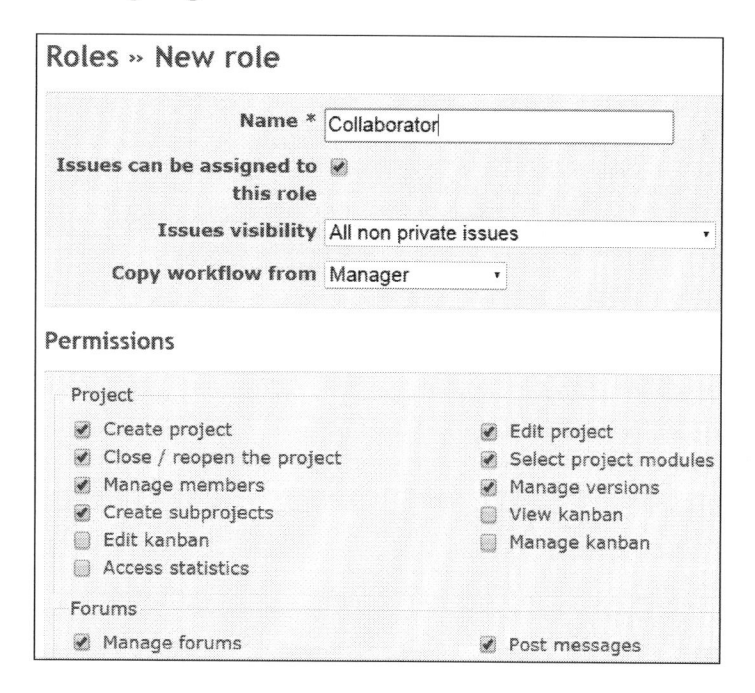

Roles » New role	
Name *	Collaborator
Issues can be assigned to this role	☑
Issues visibility	All non private issues
Copy workflow from	Manager

Permissions

Project
- ☑ Create project
- ☑ Close / reopen the project
- ☑ Manage members
- ☑ Create subprojects
- ☐ Edit kanban
- ☐ Access statistics
- ☑ Edit project
- ☑ Select project modules
- ☑ Manage versions
- ☐ View kanban
- ☐ Manage kanban

Forums
- ☑ Manage forums
- ☑ Post messages

Once you have created a new role, it becomes available to be used on new and all available projects.

45

Customizing Redmine

How it works...

Roles are customized on a *per-module* basis, meaning that each role has its own permissions set for a particular module. In this recipe, we created a new role that was based on an existing role with the difference that the new role can't add, delete, copy, or edit issues. This is achieved by cloning the existing role, entering a new name, and choosing **Per module permissions** on the **Permissions** group of the **New role** form. Per module permissions are grouped with group sections having the same name as the module; so, for example, the **Forums** module is displayed immediately under **Projects** with permissions such as **Manage forms** or **Post messages**.

There's more...

Permissions for issue statuses and transition of statuses are set on the **Workflow** part of the **Administration** menu. To adjust them, navigate to **Administration | Workflow**, choose **Role** and the type of tracker that you are editing permissions for, and click the **Edit** button. *By combining Roles and Workflows, you can achieve fine-grain security and workflow control for various kinds of Redmine implementations, ranging from standard project management to complicated ITIL scenarios.* One of these fine-grain controlled accounts can be an account for your client. Sometimes, companies, project managers, or project teams need to have their client access some of the project details, such as reports, submitting bugs, or creating requests. In some software development and project management methodologies such as Scrum or XP, it is encouraged to engage the client's participation in all phases of the project. To achieve this goal, it is best to create a special role with fine-grain access/edit/view permissions for your client, so you don't compromise potential information that might harm your relation with the client. If you have multiple clients, good practice when choosing roles for a client is to forbid the client from seeing all Redmine users by choosing **Members of visible projects** under **Users visibility** on the **New role** form. Also, projects should not be public in this case.

See also

Check out some third-party plugins, which introduce new functionality to role management. Some of these are **Global Roles** (https://www.redmine.org/plugins/global_roles), which introduce global roles for users, and the **Roles Shift** plugin (https://www.redmine.org/plugins/role_shift), which makes it possible to configure roles at a per-project level.

Chapter 2

Creating and using User groups

The User groups feature can reflect a logical or some different kind of physical organization of your company. If this is large, you may want to spend some time thinking about how to organize groups. Your company may have multiple office locations, so as an example scenario, you may have a London office and be able to assign issues to the group called London office. Afterwards, everyone in the London office will get the notification e-mail and a worker named John Doe can take the task and immediately start to work on it.

Getting ready

Before creating User groups, make sure the following is done:

- Make sure that you have administrator permissions in Redmine
- First, create users that you are going to assign to the groups

How to do it...

To create User groups, perform the following steps:

1. Navigate to the **Administration** menu.
2. Then click **Groups**. Groups display screen will appear with the **New group** button located at the top right.
3. Click this and enter the name for the group London marketing office.
4. Click **Create**, then click on the group name, and a screen like the following screenshot should appear:

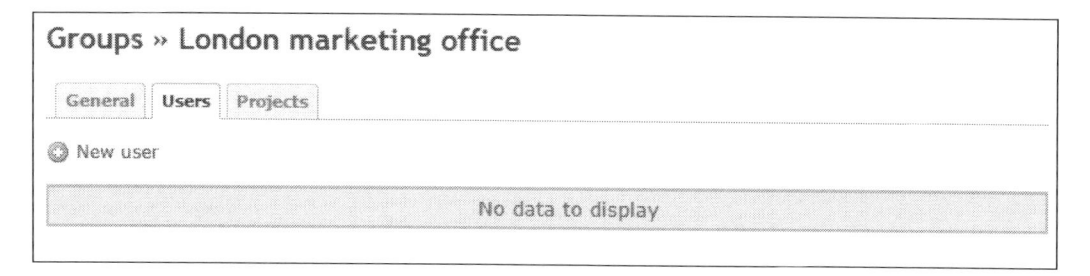

```
Groups » London marketing office

  General   Users   Projects

  New user

                    No data to display
```

47

Customizing Redmine

5. Now click **New user** and tick the checkboxes next to the users that you want to have in this group. Click **Add**, and the screen should look similar to the following screenshot:

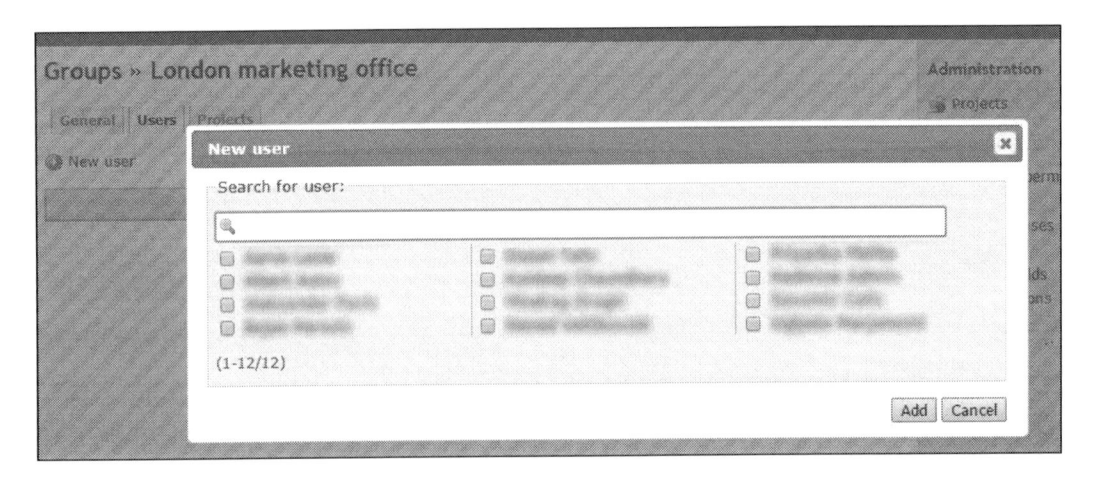

On the **Projects** tab, you can choose projects from a tree-like list and the **Roles** that your group will have on these projects.

How it works...

Redmine lets the same users belong to multiple groups. So, for example, one user can belong to the group London Office, and at the same time belong to the group Network Administrators. This feature lets you have various kinds of virtual organizations inside your Redmine system.

There's more...

Groups can also have custom attributes assigned; so, for example, London office can have the attributes *address*, *telephone*, or *working hours* added to the group.

See also

Refer to the recipe *Extending user profiles with additional data* to see how to extend objects inside Redmine with custom attributes.

Chapter 2

Customizing the layout of the project entry page

If built-in customizations don't fit your needs and you need to edit Redmine's views manually for some reason, this recipe will show you how to make **New project** private in Redmine, and how to remove the **Homepage** field on the **New project** creation form.

Getting ready

Make sure that you have access to your working Redmine installation.

How to do it...

To accomplish the goal of making the project private by default by having the checkbox at the project creation form unchecked by default in Redmine, you need to navigate to **Administration | Settings | Projects**. Untick the **New projects are public by default** checkbox, and click **Save**.

To hide the **Homepage** textbox and label, use your favorite code editor with Ruby highlight, navigate with the file browser or via the command line to your Redmine installation folder, open `redmine/app/views/projects/_form.html.erb`, find the line containing `<p><%= f.text_field :homepage, :size => 60 %></p>`, and delete it. Restart Redmine and make sure that the creation of new projects change is reflected, as in the following screenshot:

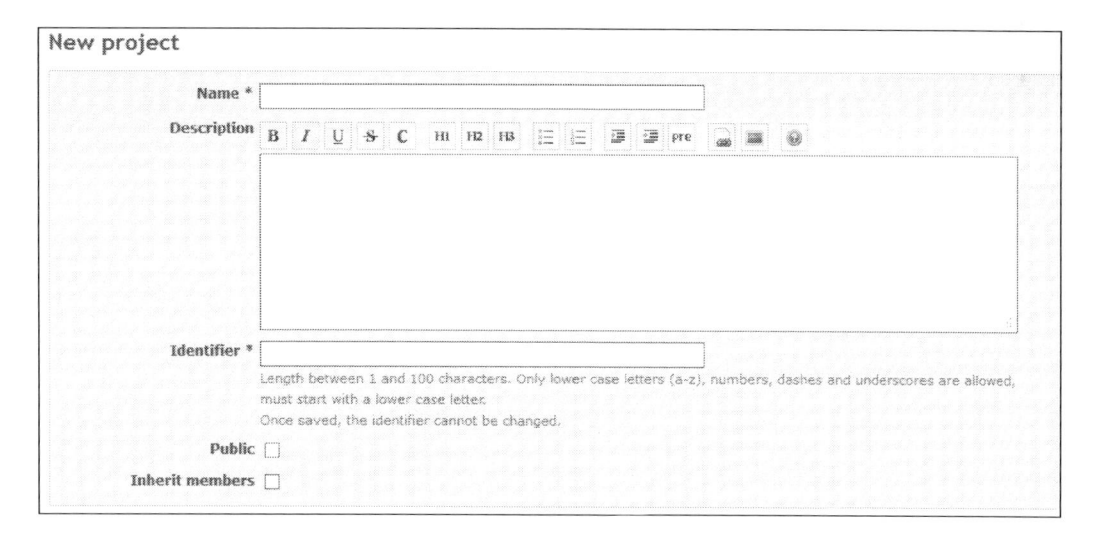

Customizing Redmine

How it works...

What we did here is deliberately combine built-in Redmine feature customization with code editing customization so that you learn to seek for built-in customizations before reaching out for the code editor. Therefore, first, we navigate to the **Settings** menu and disable the active checkbox for projects to be public. So, from now on, without restarting Redmine on a new project entry form, the **Public** checkbox will be unchecked by default. After this, we used a code editor and edited the `app/views/projects/_form.html.erb` file by removing the line that displays the **Homepage** field, and restarted Redmine to reflect this update.

There's more...

If you need to change the **Issue entry** form or any other form, you can use this same principle. Just find the view files that you need to edit, make the customization, restart Redmine, and view your change.

See also

Refer to the *Starting and Restarting Redmine* recipe from *Chapter 5, Regular and Planned Maintenance*.

Customizing the layout of the home page

The Redmine home page, also accessible from the first link at the top right of the default Redmine theme, can be customized from inside the system. It can contain links to Redmine tutorials, YouTube videos, your company page, or any kind of Textile/Markdown formatted content.

Getting ready

Make sure that you have Redmine administrator permissions.

How to do it...

Navigate to **Administration** | **Settings** | **General Tab** and edit **Welcome text**:

Chapter 2

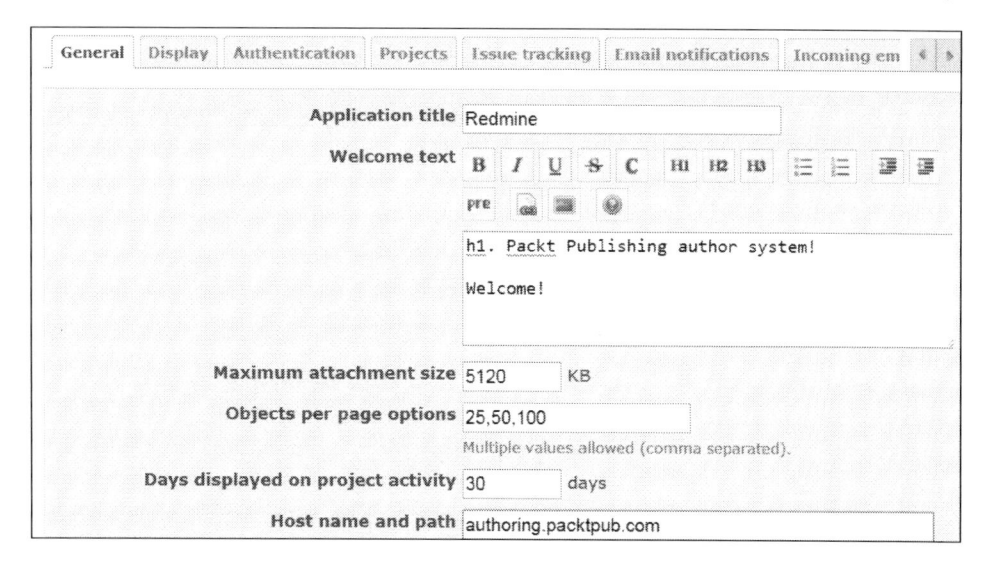

[Screenshot of Redmine General settings tab showing Application title: Redmine, Welcome text with formatting toolbar and content "h1. Packt Publishing author system! Welcome!", Maximum attachment size: 5120 KB, Objects per page options: 25,50,100, Days displayed on project activity: 30 days, Host name and path: authoring.packtpub.com]

Any content entered here will be displayed on the **Home** page, or when the **Home** link is clicked. After you enter or edit content, click **Save** at the bottom of the form, and click the **Home** link at the top. Your homepage will look like the following screenshot:

[Screenshot of the [PACKT] Publishing home page showing the Packt Publishing logo and heading "Projects, books and processes at Packt Publishing" with text "Welcome to Packt Publishing management system, here you can find..."]

The Packt logo and content that we added is visible on the Home page, for all users.

Customizing Redmine

How it works...

Redmine has built-in features to customize the content of the homepage. The home page is publicly visible by visitors if **Authentication required** is not ticked under **Authentication settings**. The home page is the first page that the user gets after logging in to Redmine. This recipe utilized the built-in homepage editor to add the Packt publishing logo and some introduction text to the homepage.

There's more...

Additional customizations of the home page could be achieved by editing its view template or theme. You can also customize which page your users get after login through third-party plugins, such as the *Landing page* plugin, available at http://www.redmine.org/plugins/landing_page. Another plugin worth mentioning is RedmineTweaks, available on https://github.com/alexandermeindl/redmine_tweaks. Once you follow it's installation procedure steps, it can be accessed through **Administration** | **Plugins** | **Redmine Tweaks** | **Configure** From there, you will be able to customize various other layouts, like **Global** sidebar, **Overview** page, add new Menu items to Redmine menus, etc.

See also

Check out the *Textile formatting* guide from Redmine help.

Interacting with Redmine only through e-mail

If your company is large or for some other reason you need to have some users interact with the Redmine system only through e-mail, this feature is very useful. It enables your users to either create new tasks/issues by e-mail or respond to existing issues by replying to e-mail messages that are emitted by Redmine. As such, it enables all kinds of logical organizations of your business. For example, you can have users submitting support requests by e-mail, and operators processing their requests through Redmine, which is extremely useful in various kinds of helpdesk departments.

Getting ready

The first thing that you need to do is open an account for Redmine on your e-mail server. It can be redmine@yourdomain.com or any other username, just make sure it's the same username that Redmine is using when sending e-mails. It does not have to be the same, but it's preferred that it be the same to avoid ambiguities that different e-mail accounts can cause.

Once your Redmine account is opened on your e-mail server, rename the `/config/configuration.yml.example` as `/config/configuration.yml` and edit it according to the settings for the account that you just created for Redmine. You can test these settings through the **Administration** menu. If you navigate to the **Administration | Settings | E-mail notifications** tab, there is a **Send test e-mail** hyperlink at the bottom right, as displayed in the following screenshot:

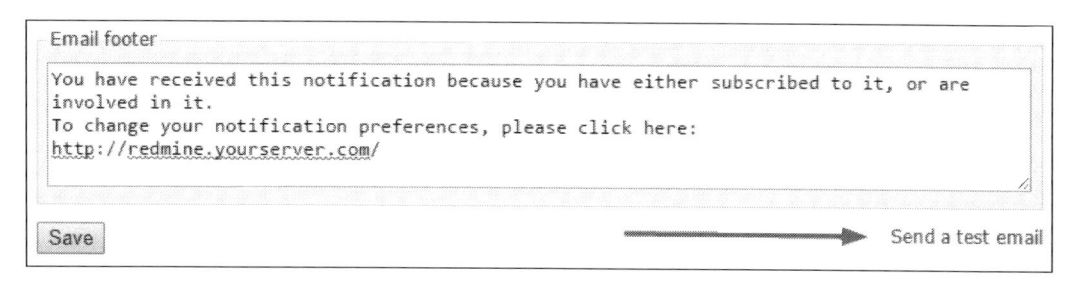

Once you have made sure that e-mail emission is working, you can proceed with configuring incoming e-mail interaction.

How to do it...

Redmine can receive incoming e-mails in two different concepts or three different settings. Basically, it is a server push or client pull. This recipe explains the client pull method because not all users have the luxury or knowledge to tamper with **Mail Transfer Agent** (**MTA**) software.

Linux users

The steps that Linux users should follow are as follows:

1. Create a shell script file, named `fetch_e-mail.sh`, in the `/extra` subfolder of your Redmine installation, with the following content:

   ```
   #!/bin/bash
   cd /var/www/redmine
   rake redmine:e-mail:receive_pop3 RAILS_ENV="production" host=your_e-mail_server username=redmine password=redmine
   ```

2. Replace the `host`, `username`, and `password` variables with the ones that fit your e-mail server and Redmine account credentials.

3. Log in or sudo to the user under which Redmine is running, and create a Unix **CRON** (**Command Run On**) job by typing the following in shell:

   ```
   crontab -e
   ```

   Then, enter the following contents:

   ```
   5 * * * * /var/www/redmine/extra/fetch_e-mail.sh
   ```

53

Customizing Redmine

> Keep in mind to replace /var/www/redmine in steps 1 and 3 with a path to your redmine installation root folder if it is different, for example like /home/my_user/redmine

Windows users

The steps that Windows users should follow are as follows:

1. Create a batch file, called `fetch_e-mail.bat`, inside the `/extra` directory of your Redmine installation, with the following content:

   ```
   rake redmine:e-mail:receive_pop3 RAILS_ENV="production" host=your_e-mail_server username=redmine password=redmine
   ```

2. Replace the `host`, `username`, and `password` variables with the ones that fit your e-mail server and Redmine account credentials.

3. Start a **Task scheduler**, hold the Windows key, then press *R*, type `Taskschd.msc` on the right side, and choose **Create Task**. Type a name for your task, optionally a **Description**, and choose either **Network service** or **Local service** as a user account under which to run the task. Also, tick the bottom **Hidden** checkbox:

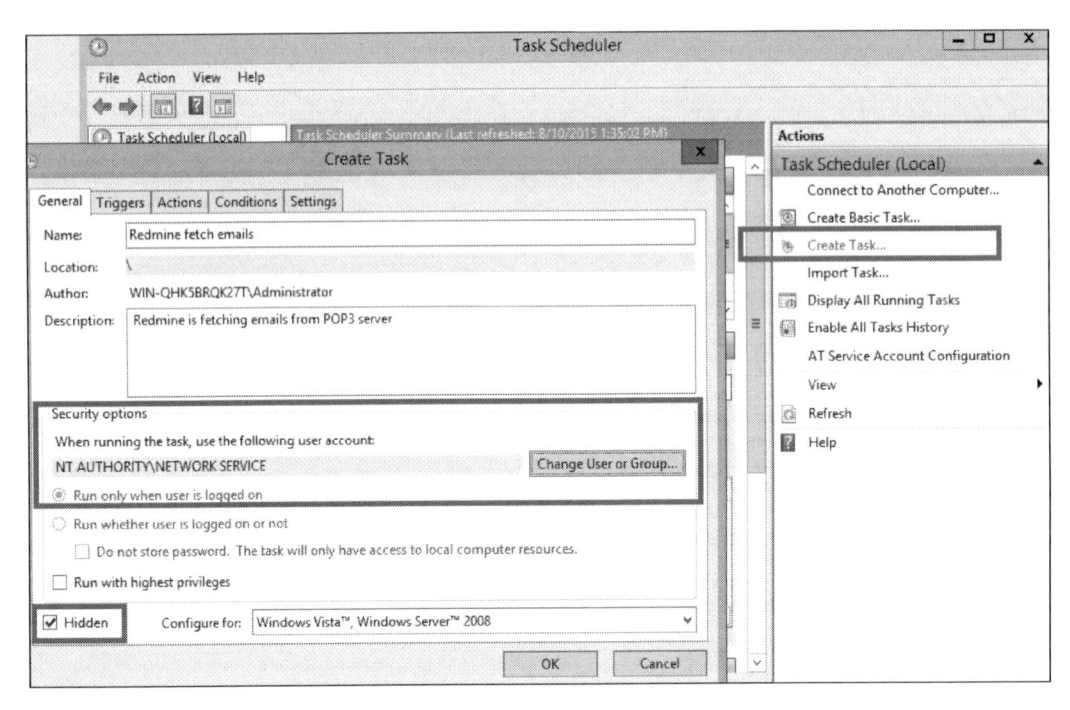

4. Next, on the **Triggers** tab, make the task run every **15 minutes**, or **5** if you need it more frequently:

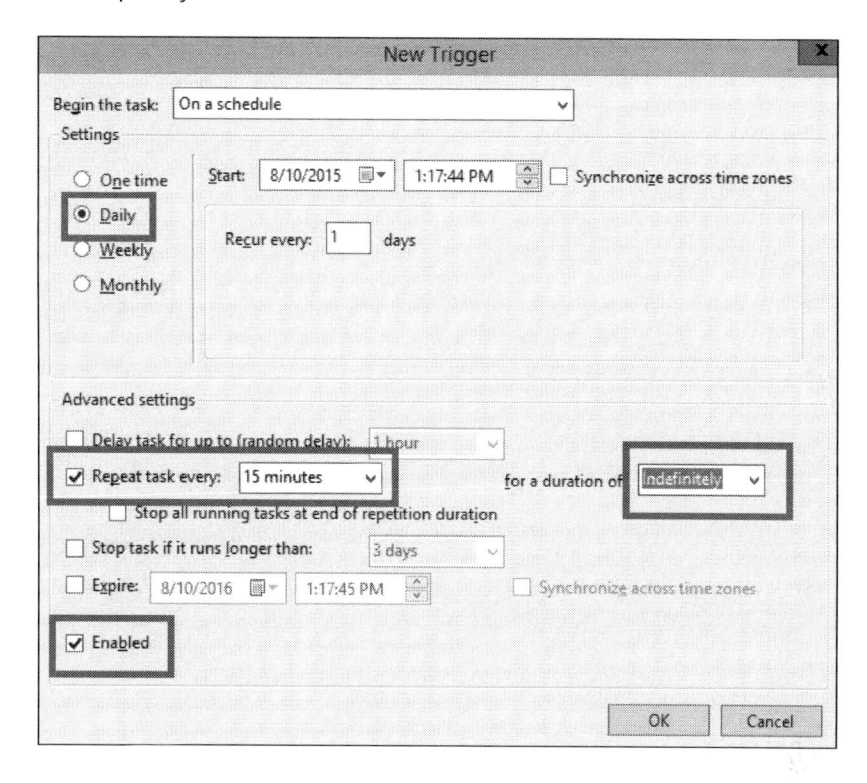

5. Finally, on the **Actions** tab, click **Browse**, and find the `.bat` file that we created. On the **Start in** section, type the `root` folder of your Redmine installation:

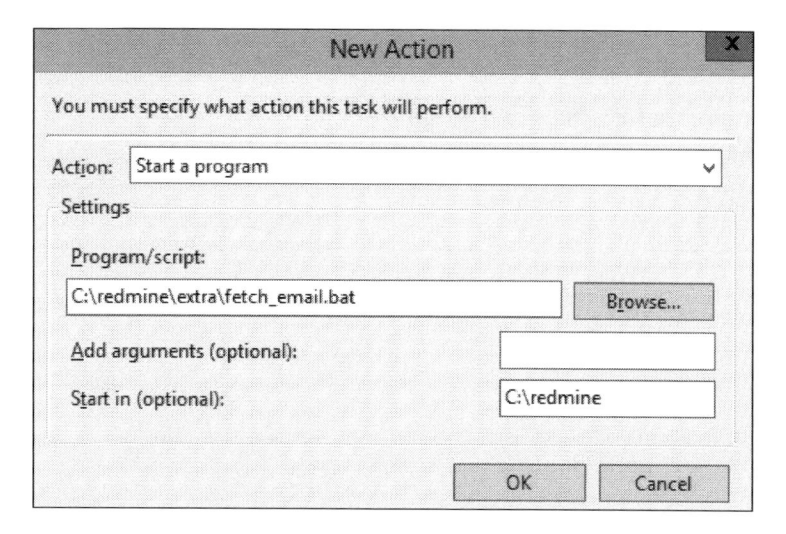

Customizing Redmine

How it works...

This recipe is implementing a POP3 client pull method. Basically, Redmine is doing what most desktop e-mail clients do: it checks for incoming e-mails every 15 minutes. What we have done for both Windows and Linux is create a shell script, and add a job to the system scheduler to be run in the given time period. In both cases, we are running a rake task with POP3 access parameters to your server, which parses incoming e-mails, and if properly parsed, it creates new Redmine issues or adds comments to existing ones.

There's more...

Under the **Incoming e-mails** tab in **Administration | Settings**, there are additional options available, which let you truncate e-mails after certain lines. For example, if your company uses *signatures*, or you need to truncate the quoted part when replying to e-mails, then just add the delimiter that your company's e-mail client is using, and the reply part won't be visible in issue updates:

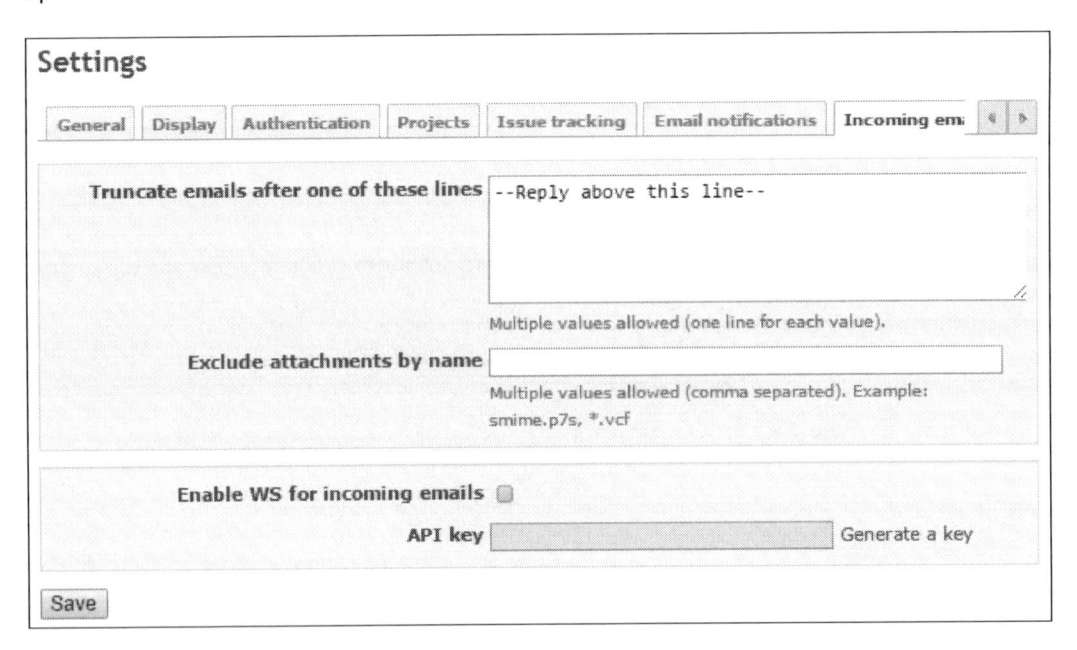

The **Exclude attachments by name** feature lets you exclude attachments, such as VCF (contact files), or signatures/logos, to be added to your issues when e-mails are parsed.

See also

Redmine's official incoming e-mail configuration page can be found at the following location:

`http://www.redmine.org/projects/redmine/wiki/RedmineReceivingE-mails`.

3
Project Management with Redmine

This chapter focuses on the following management techniques using Redmine:

- Splitting your project into phases
- Creating and using subprojects
- Splitting your tasks into subtasks
- Managing issue relations
- Creating and using template projects
- Managing multiple projects simultaneously
- Creating reports on spent time
- Making sure that everyone is optimally loaded with work
- Relating between issue and time
- Using the Issue-code relation
- Defining a Roadmap to the release plan

Introduction

In the previous chapters, we focused mainly on the technical side of Redmine, how to install and run it, and how to customize it. This chapter focuses on the management benefits of using Redmine in software-development-related projects and some generic project management scenarios. Please keep in mind that Redmine is a *flexible project management tool*, and that it's open source-featuring hundreds of plugins. So, if it does not fit your project management needs *out of the box*, then most likely there is an elegant and easy way to customize it for your requirements. This can be done either by adjusting some of its flexible features or by installing some third-party plugin. Also, another aspect of Redmine's flexibility means that you do not have to manage each project in the same way. For example, some projects have trackers, and some do not; some can be managed with one methodology, others with different ones. Redmine is built from the ground up to adapt to your project management needs by keeping flexibility in mind.

Splitting your project into phases

Sometimes, it is important to group project-related tasks into work packages or phases. One possible scenario in a non-IT related project would be, for example, *Development of a new road system*. In such a case, the first phase of the project would be expropriation of land, preparation of soil, building the road, and building the support infrastructure. Moreover, each of these phases has an independent task that is specific to that phase of the project. In IT projects, phases may vary from those strictly based upon some software development methodology, to more product-oriented phases, which include marketing, advertising campaigns, and so on, depending upon the nature of the project. Phases or work packages in IT and general project management may be grouped either by functionality, by the nature of tasks (development, design, and marketing,) or by some kind of phase that is based on schedule, payment, or product releases.

Getting ready

Make sure that you have permissions to tamper with project settings in Redmine. You need to have a project to which phases are going to be applied.

How to do it...

Open the project in Redmine that you want to split into phases, and perform the following steps:

1. Click **Settings** in the main menu.
2. Click the **Versions** tab.
3. Click the **New version** button;

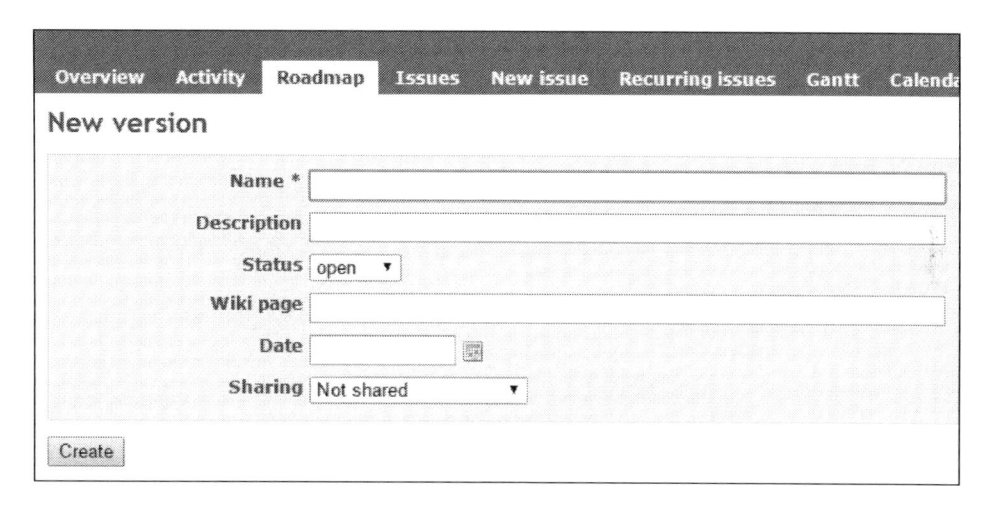

4. Enter a name of a version; for example, `Phase 1 - Land expropriation`; enter the **Description**, **Status**, **Wiki page**, **Date**, and **Sharing** optional fields.
5. Click **Save**.

The new version is going to be available while adding issues. When used this way, Version is not mandatory field. After you assign issues to versions, such as `Phase 1`, `Phase 2`, and so on, you can click the **Roadmap** tab on the main window to get a quick view of your phases and tasks that are assigned to each phase. A different approach to listing and creating reports on tasks in a specific phase would be through issue-filtering options:

1. Click **Issues** in the main project menu.
2. On the right-hand side in **Add filter**, choose **Target version**.
3. Choose which target version you want and click **Apply**. Alternatively, you can click different filtering options and choose **Group by Target** version.

Project Management with Redmine

How it works...

Redmine has a built-in version feature with an issue-tracking module. This recipe creates a new version and instructs users to assign versions while adding new tasks. After this, we utilize issue filtering to create reports on tasks and versions.

There's more...

Different approaches to splitting project into phases using built-in features would mean that you create a custom field for issue for all trackers or a specific tracker. Name the custom field `Phase` and add several items to the drop-down list. Then, when adding new tasks, choose **Phase** from the drop-down list. You can then utilize filtering features to display which issue belongs to which phase.

See also

Versions can have their own custom fields; refer to the recipe *Extending user profiles with additional data* to see how to create custom fields. The recipe *Managing multiple projects simultaneously* gives instructions about saved issue filtering. *Roadmap to the release plan* has examples on how versions can be used in software development.

Creating and using subprojects

In the previous recipe, we explained how to split project in to versions/phases or work-packages. Now, we are going to split project into subprojects. The decision to split a project into subprojects or group tasks in versions is a matter of organization and management. From Redmine's standpoint, if you break some tasks into multiple projects as a subproject of one parent project instead of versions (phases), this will mean that you will have additional flexibility in defining modules and roles on each subproject. From a management role's usability standpoint, you are still going to be able to filter issues almost in the same way as if you were using versions.

Using subprojects can be a great way to organize your projects into a tree-like structure. If your company is large, and you want to manage projects from different departments through one unique location, Redmine can prove itself useful. Another scenario in which we need subprojects is when different vendors are working on different parts of the project (such as web applications and mobile apps).

Chapter 3

Getting ready

Make sure that you have proper permissions to create and manage projects. Also, make sure that you already have tasks, plans, and teams to be engaged on your subprojects.

How to do it...

We are going to create a sample project structure for a large company, which will look like this:

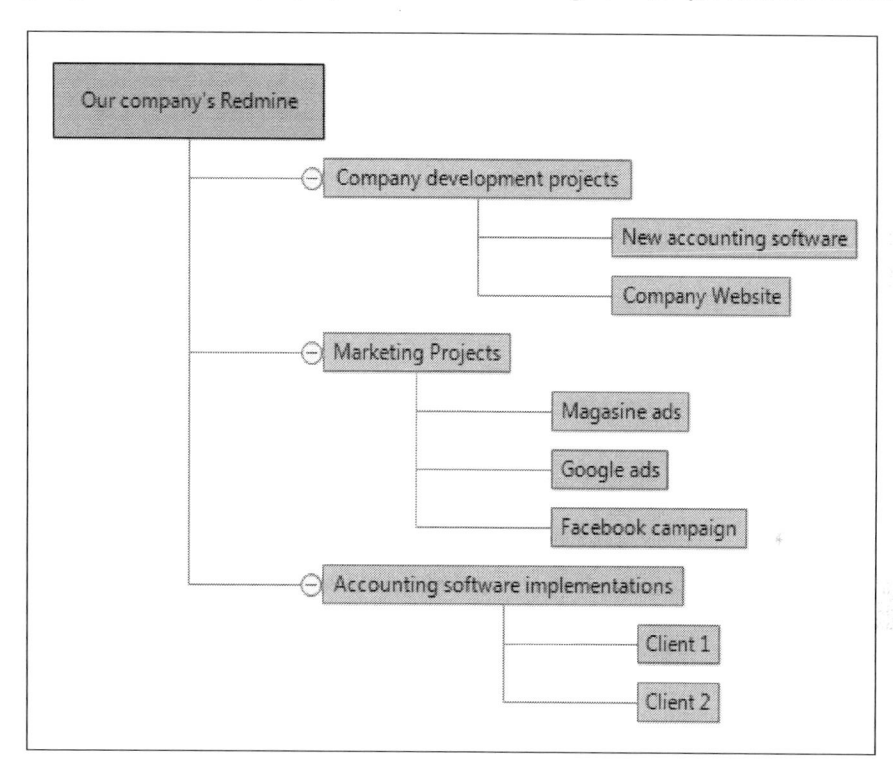

```
Our company's Redmine
├── Company development projects
│   ├── New accounting software
│   └── Company Website
├── Marketing Projects
│   ├── Magasine ads
│   ├── Google ads
│   └── Facebook campaign
└── Accounting software implementations
    ├── Client 1
    └── Client 2
```

To achieve such a tree-like structure, the following steps need to be repeated for each project/subproject:

1. Create a new parent project, in this case called `Company development projects`, and do not pick any modules if they are not required, for example, the `files` module may be required, or news. Click **Projects** in Redmine's top menu.

2. Click the **New project** button.

Project Management with Redmine

3. Enter the project name, uncheck **Modules**, and click the **Create and continue** button:

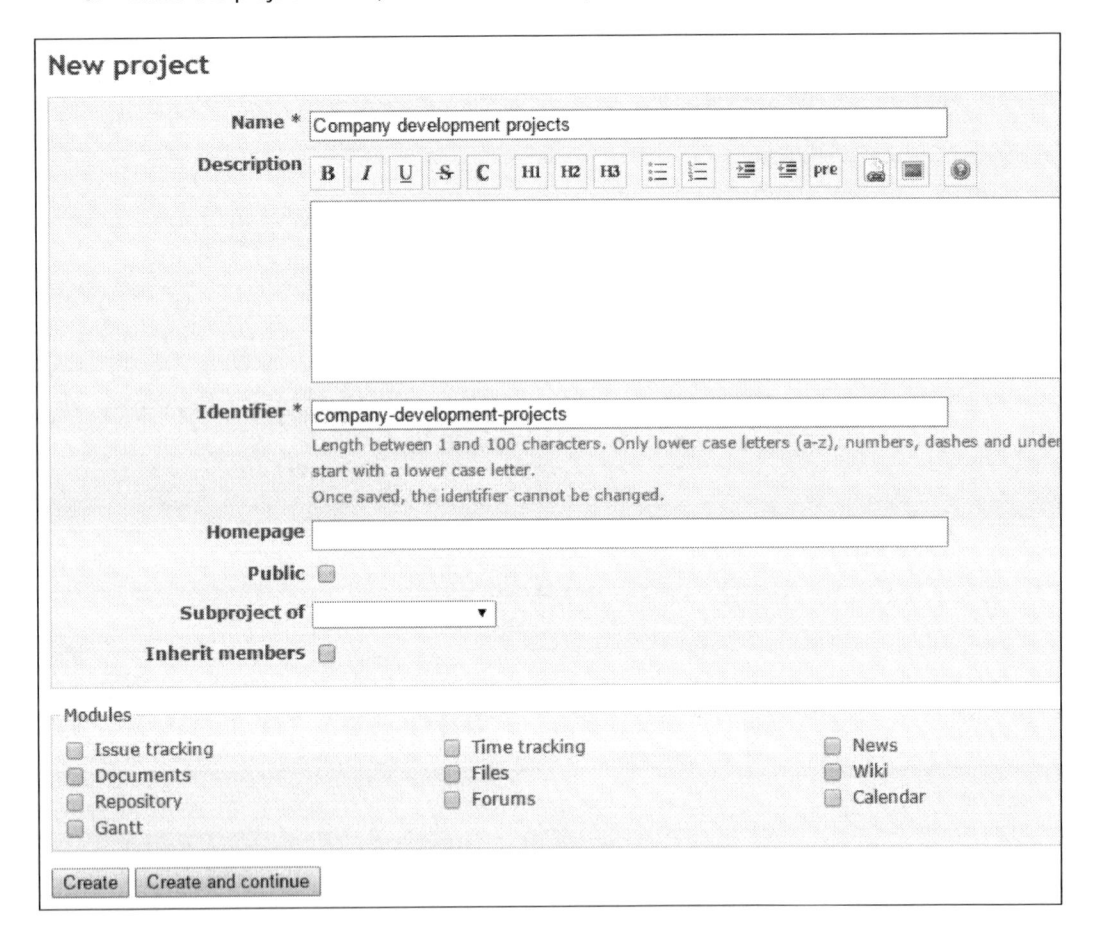

New project

- **Name *** Company development projects
- **Description** [B I U S C H1 H2 H3 ≡ ≡ ≡ ≡ pre 🖼 ▪ ◎]

- **Identifier *** company-development-projects
  Length between 1 and 100 characters. Only lower case letters (a-z), numbers, dashes and under
  start with a lower case letter.
  Once saved, the identifier cannot be changed.
- **Homepage**
- **Public** ☐
- **Subproject of** [▼]
- **Inherit members** ☐

Modules
- ☐ Issue tracking
- ☐ Documents
- ☐ Repository
- ☐ Gantt
- ☐ Time tracking
- ☐ Files
- ☐ Forums
- ☐ News
- ☐ Wiki
- ☐ Calendar

[Create] [Create and continue]

---

4. Enter the name and details of the new project or subproject in the same form as in the previous screenshot, and if it is a subproject, choose its parent project from the **Subproject of** dropdown menu.

5. Once completed, our tree-like structure will look like this:

How it works...

Redmine supports multiple projects with an unlimited number of subprojects. This feature lets us organize our projects into a tree-like structure. In order to achieve such a tree-like organization, we need to group projects in some logical units. In this recipe, we analyzed a sample company that develops and implements accounting software. For its purposes, we created three top-level projects called `Accounting software implementations`, `Company development projects`, and `Marketing projects`. Then, for each of these top-level projects, we created subprojects.

There's more...

When we are listing and filtering the parent project's issues, it will display the issues from the child projects as well by default.

> If you made a mistake while entering project data into Redmine, or you already have a mess in your projects, do not worry. Projects and subprojects in Redmine can be reorganized by clicking the **Settings** tab and choosing the proper parent project in a **Subproject of** dropdown.

Splitting your tasks into subtasks

It is good practice to group tasks per feature or job, which consist of several tasks. Splitting tasks into subtasks makes the project more clean looking and well organized. In addition, having projects clean and organized increases your chances of delivering the project on time and within budget.

How to do it...

Assuming that you have project tasks prepared on paper, in an electronic document, or in your mind, the first thing to do is create a standard Redmine issue with a type of **Feature**, **Task**, or any other custom issue type that you customized, which will serve as a parent task:

1. On the parent task that you just created, click the **Add** link:

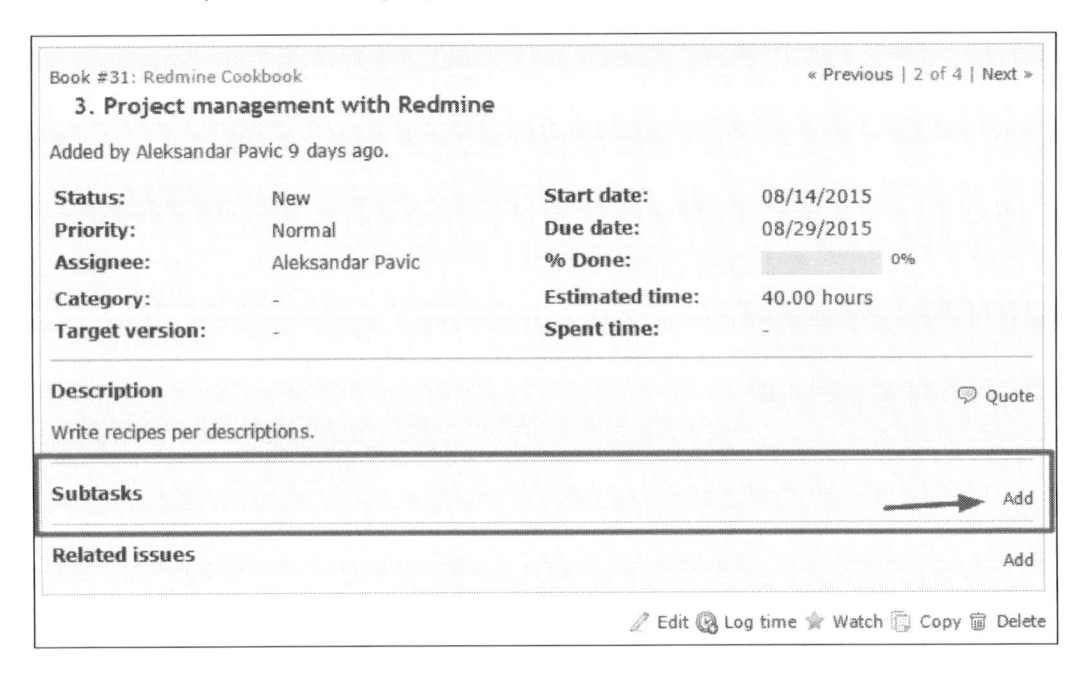

   ```
   Book #31: Redmine Cookbook                                « Previous | 2 of 4 | Next »
   3. Project management with Redmine
   Added by Aleksandar Pavic 9 days ago.

   Status:          New                    Start date:       08/14/2015
   Priority:        Normal                 Due date:         08/29/2015
   Assignee:        Aleksandar Pavic       % Done:                      0%
   Category:        -                      Estimated time:   40.00 hours
   Target version:  -                      Spent time:       -

   Description                                                              Quote
   Write recipes per descriptions.

   Subtasks                                                         →    Add

   Related issues                                                         Add

                                   Edit  Log time  Watch  Copy  Delete
   ```

2. The **Issue** entry form will open up. Fill it with your issue details. If you are adding more sub-issues in a row, click **Create and continue**. A new **Issue entry** form will load with the **Parent task** field's value preloaded:

Chapter 3

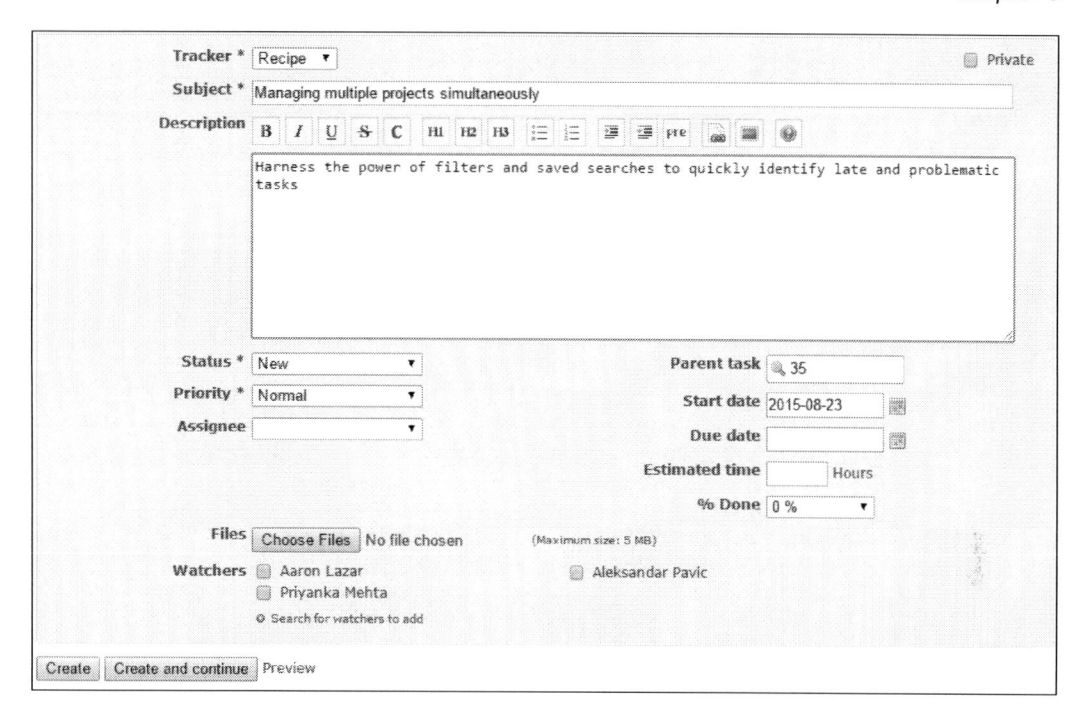

3. When you are done entering subtasks, navigate to your parent issue, and you will be able to see all of this issue's subtasks with their progress bars and statuses. The following image shows **Subtasks** of a software development project with multiple levels of subtask:

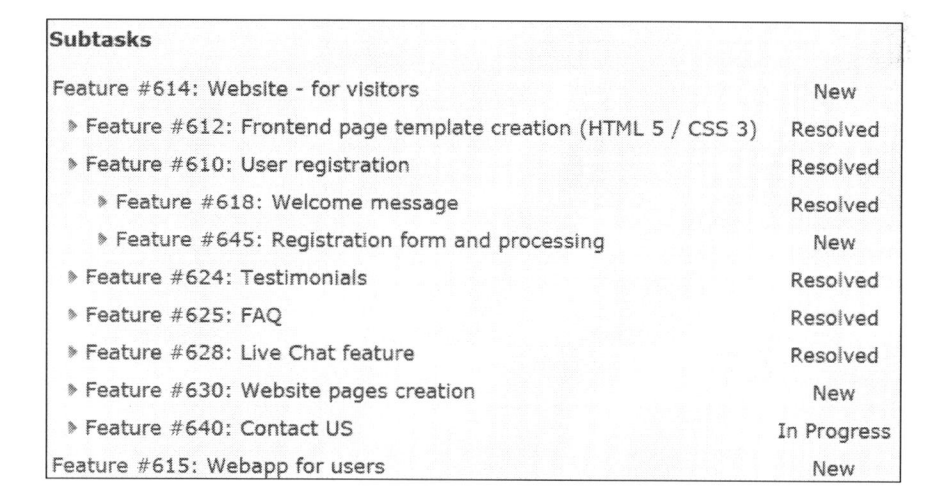

Subtasks	
Feature #614: Website - for visitors	New
▸ Feature #612: Frontend page template creation (HTML 5 / CSS 3)	Resolved
▸ Feature #610: User registration	Resolved
▸ Feature #618: Welcome message	Resolved
▸ Feature #645: Registration form and processing	New
▸ Feature #624: Testimonials	Resolved
▸ Feature #625: FAQ	Resolved
▸ Feature #628: Live Chat feature	Resolved
▸ Feature #630: Website pages creation	New
▸ Feature #640: Contact US	In Progress
Feature #615: Webapp for users	New

Project Management with Redmine

How it works...

Redmine's issue system and database design allow projects to have trackers of different kinds. Each tracker or issue can have multiple sub-issues without depth limitation. Considering this, we simply follow our natural project's task breakdown structure and enter tasks into Redmine with their accompanying subtasks through the **Issue entry** page. Once tasks are entered, subtasks of each task are displayed under the subtasks section when the issue with subtasks is displayed.

There's more...

Redmine's Gantt module displays projects with subprojects, tasks, and subtasks in a tree layout. PDF and PNG exports of Gantt charts also follow this layout. To display a Gantt chart of your tasks and subtasks, just click on **Gantt** in the main project menu:

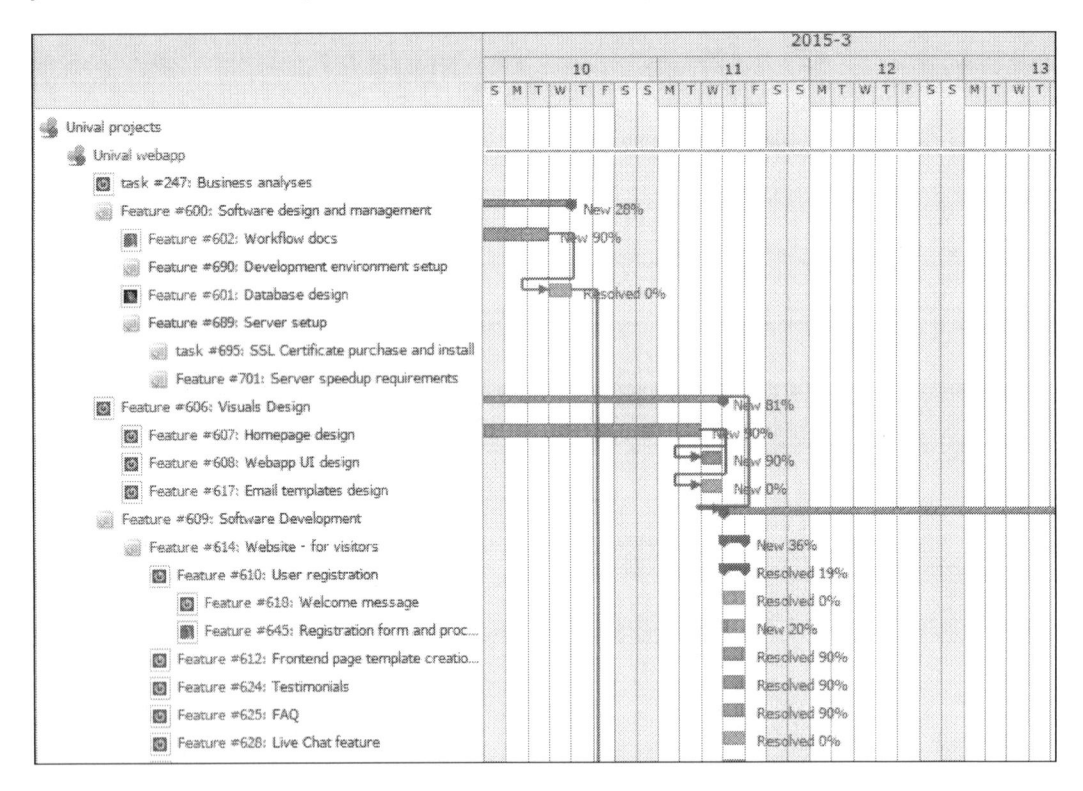

Please keep in mind that Redmine is meant to be flexible, so instead of Features, Tasks, and Bugs, you can track tasks/subtasks of just about anything. So, instead of Features/Tasks/Bugs, you can have Cleaning/Repair/Purchase. Moreover, they can be schedule-related and clearly visible on a Gantt chart.

Chapter 3

Managing issue relations

Issue relations help managers and teams to get a clear picture of how a particular task or issue affects other tasks and the ultimate outcome of the project. If a task that precedes 10 other tasks has to be delayed, then all related tasks need to be delayed as well, having a possible impact on the project's delivery date. If a task breakdown structure of a project is properly done, then all task relations can be entered in Redmine, and the impact on one task can be easily and quickly measured. Luckily, Redmine has issue relation features built in, which automate modification of start/end dates among related issues. This recipe is going to teach you how to set relations and modify start-end dates automatically.

How to do it...

The best way to relate tasks chronologically is to start adding tasks to Redmine in chronological order. The first task that you enter in Redmine should have start and end dates properly set, reflecting the real start and end dates of the task. For other tasks that are *preceded by it*, you do not have to choose proper start and end dates, just a proper length of the task, because once a schedule relation is entered, Redmine will automatically set dates for you. To enter the precedes by relation once you have entered a task in Redmine, perform the following steps:

1. View the task.
2. Click **Add** in the **Related issues** section.
3. Choose **Follows** from the dropdown menu.
4. Enter the ID of the preceding issue, and the optional delay time in days.
5. Click the **Add** button:

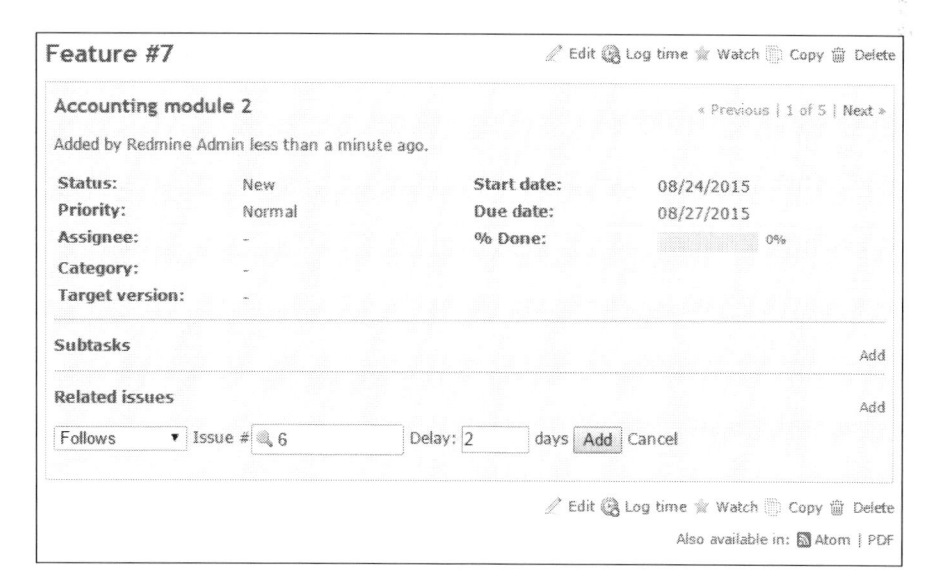

69

Project Management with Redmine

6. Once you click **Add**, the issue title should be automatically displayed.

> Date changes won't occur until you refresh the page.

7. Once the page is refreshed, automatic date updates will be visible, as displayed in the following screenshot:

Related issues — Add

Follows (2 days) Feature #6: Accounting module 1   New   08/24/2015   08/26/2015

History

Updated by Redmine Admin 2 minutes ago   #1

- **Due date** changed from *08/27/2015* to *09/03/2015*
- **Start date** changed from *08/24/2015* to *08/31/2015*
- **Follows** *Feature #6: Accounting module 1* added

How it works...

Redmine covers the following issue relationships:

- Parent-child relationships: This is explained in the *Splitting your tasks into subtasks* recipe.
- **Related to**: This covers any kind of issue relationship.
- **Duplicates** and **Duplicated by**: These are used when two issues relate to the same task or bug; if issue B duplicates issue A, closing B will leave A open but closing A will automatically close B.
- **Blocks** and **Blocked by**: These are used when one task can't be done because another task needs to be resolved and used to identify problems. If issue B blocks A, A can't be closed until issue B is closed.
- **Precedes** and **Follows**: These are used to display and organize tasks chronologically.
- **Copied to** and **Copied from**: These are used when an issue needs to be copied to a new issue for some reason.

In this recipe we covered the *Precedes* and *Follows* relationship with automatic start-end date altering features by creating the *Follows* relation between issues #6 and #7.

70

Chapter 3

There's more...

Issue relationship is visible on the Gantt chart module and can be toggled through options, as displayed in green box in this screenshot:

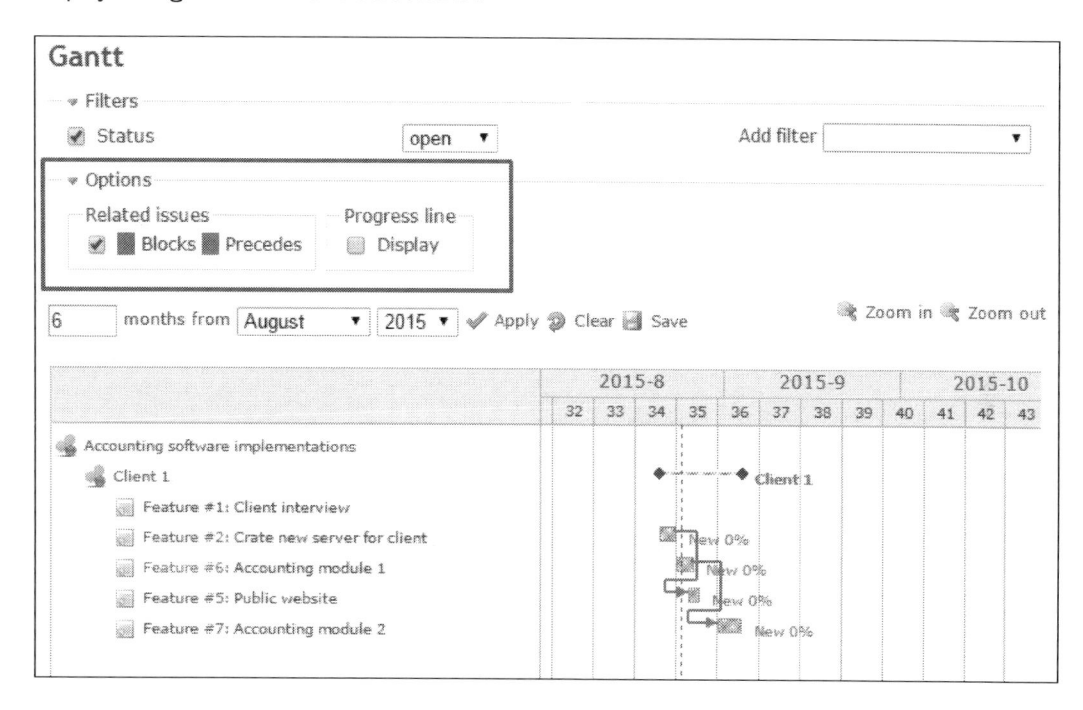

In the preceding Gantt chart, you can see a blue line indicating the schedule relation between **Feature #6** and **Feature #7**, which means that **Feature #7** follows **Feature #6**. **Feature #5** is blocked by **Feature #2**, which is displayed with a red arrow. Unchecking the **Related Issues** checkbox will simply hide the blue and red arrows from the Gantt chart.

See also

Refer to the official Redmine Issue wiki for details about Issue relations at http://www.redmine.org/projects/redmine/wiki/RedmineIssues.

Project Management with Redmine

Creating and using template projects

If you often work on similar projects, such as *creating a website*, *organizing the promotion of...*, or *building a house for ...*, then this feature can help you significantly reduce the time spent on starting a new project.

How to do it...

Probably the best way to have template projects is to create a top-level project for template projects or create *Template project* in your projects tree. Template projects should be just like a normal project with all common tasks defined and assigned. In the next image, you can see a sample tree where the template is a subproject of another type of project or a subproject of the root project called **Template projects**:

```
Projects
Accounting software implementations
    ★ Client 1
    Client 2
    ★ Template Client implementation project
Template projects
    Template Client implementation project
    Website project
```

In order to create a new project from an existing project, perform the following:

1. In the main Redmine menu, choose **Administration**.
2. Choose **Projects**.
3. Click **Copy**.
4. A **New project** form will appear with the description prefilled and copy options at the bottom of the form, allowing you to customize which project data are going to be copied:

Chapter 3

```
Copy
  ☑ Members (4)
  ☑ Versions (0)
  ☑ Issue categories (0)
  ☑ Issues (8)
  ☑ Custom queries (0)
  ☑ Forums (0)
  ☑ Wiki pages (0)

  ☐ Send email notifications during the project copy

  [Copy]
```

5. Once you have customized what is going to be copied in new project, click the **Copy** button and wait for a while until Redmine finishes copying the project.

How it works...

Redmine has a built-in copy feature, which copies the project with all its data from standard Redmine modules, such as *Wiki*, *Forum*, and *Issues*. In this recipe, we used this feature to achieve the goal of having template projects for common recurring projects, such as building a website for a customer.

There's more...

If you need to move projects across different Redmine instances and don't want to manually copy and paste tasks or tamper with the database, there are plugins and third-party tools that can perform the job for you. One of them is http://www.redmine.org/plugins/issue_importer_xls, which will let you import tasks into a newly created project, and if you even have to move projects across different project management software tools, you can use http://www.taskadapter.com/.

See also

Refer to the recipe *Creating and using subprojects* for instructions on how to create and use subprojects, and how to organize Redmine projects in a tree-like structure.

Project Management with Redmine

Managing multiple projects simultaneously

As you have learned so far, Redmine has features to manage multiple projects in a flexible way. You can have different users or the same users with different roles on each project, every project can use some or all of Redmine's default modules, and each project can use different trackers. Managing multiple projects simultaneously can be exhausting, and without proper tools this can lead to project failure, unsatisfied clients or team members. Luckily, Redmine has a built-in feature called queries to help you battle the *Project management triangle*. In this recipe, we are going to create a custom query that shows which tasks are due in the current week, grouped on a per-project basis.

How to do it...

There are two types of queries: public and private. Any user can use public queries, and private ones are visible only to the user that created them. To create a query that displays tasks due this week on all projects, follow these steps:

1. In the main menu, choose **Projects**.
2. On the right-hand side of the Projects title, click **View all issues**.
3. In the **Filters** section, check **Status**, and on the first dropdown from the left-hand side, choose **is not**; on the second drop-down, choose **Closed**.
4. In **Add filter** on the right-hand side, choose **Due date,** and the **Due date** checkbox will appear below **Status** on the left-hand side.
5. In the **Due date** dropdown, choose this week.
6. Click **Options** below the **Due date** checkbox and choose **Projects** on the **Group results by** dropdown:

Chapter 3

7. Click the **Save** button.
8. A new form called **New query** will appear with additional customization options in the **Name** field. Enter the title for your query; for example, `All projects - this week`:

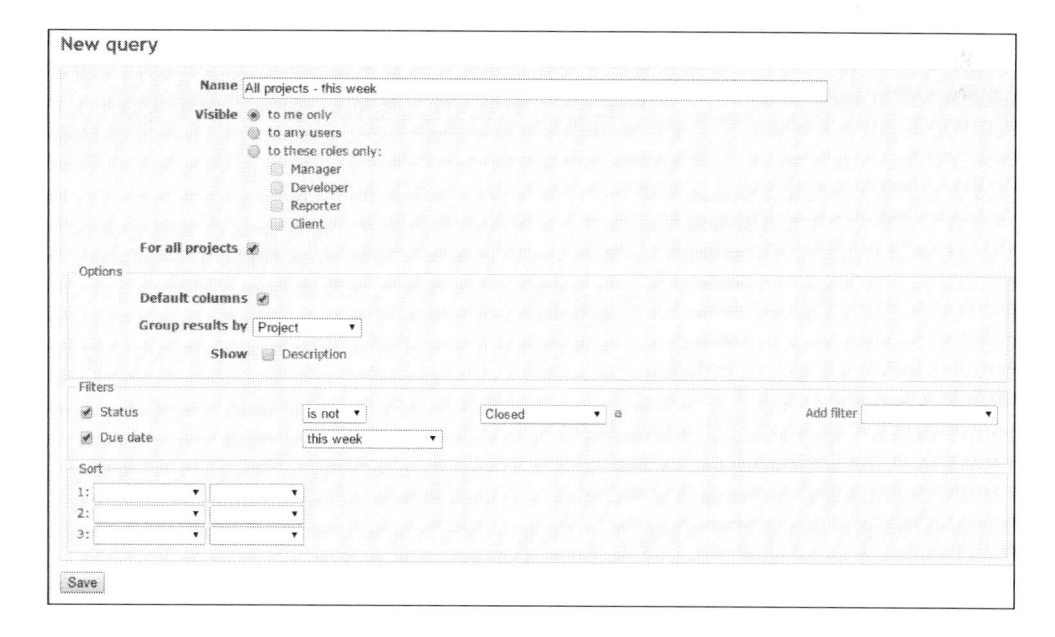

75

Project Management with Redmine

9. Customize additional filtering, sorting, and visibility options and click **Save**.

Once these steps are complete, your query should be visible on the right sidebar in the standard Redmine theme.

Once saved, navigate back to the home page, and click on the filter in the sidebar, and you should get an overview of all opened issues that are due this week on all your projects:

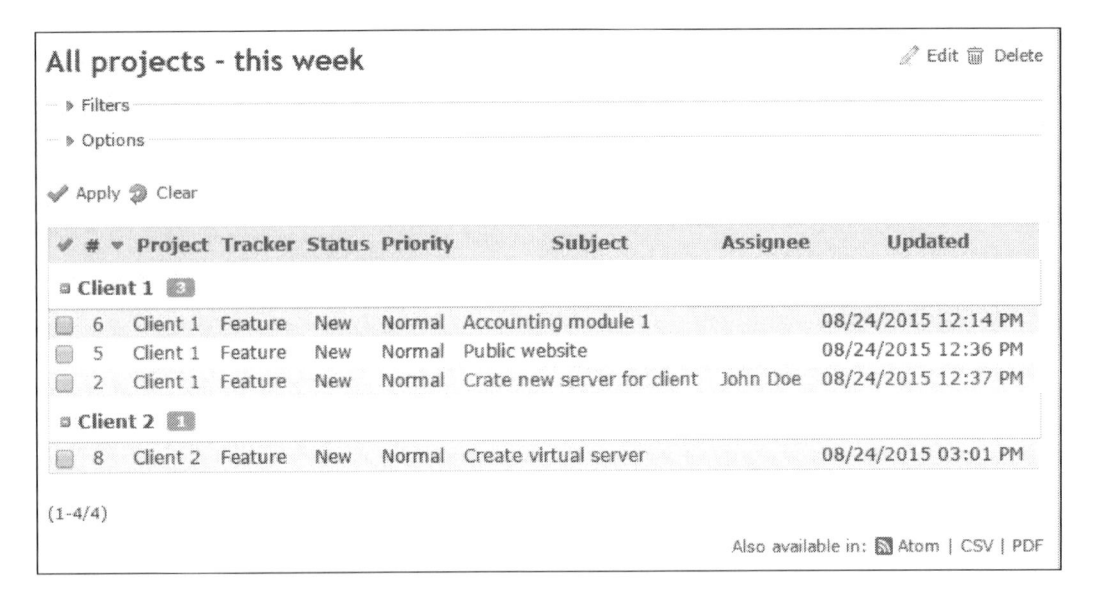

All projects - this week

▶ Filters
▶ Options

✔ Apply   Clear

✔	# ▼	Project	Tracker	Status	Priority	Subject	Assignee	Updated
Client 1 [3]								
☐	6	Client 1	Feature	New	Normal	Accounting module 1		08/24/2015 12:14 PM
☐	5	Client 1	Feature	New	Normal	Public website		08/24/2015 12:36 PM
☐	2	Client 1	Feature	New	Normal	Crate new server for client	John Doe	08/24/2015 12:37 PM
Client 2 [1]								
☐	8	Client 2	Feature	New	Normal	Create virtual server		08/24/2015 03:01 PM

(1-4/4)

Also available in: Atom | CSV | PDF

How it works...

Redmine has powerful issue-filtering features that can be saved as a *custom query*.
This recipe teaches you to use saved queries so that you can manage multiple projects simultaneously. It creates a saved query with particular filtering options, which when clicked displays issues that are filtered based on a saved search. A query can be related to one project or used globally, displaying issues for all projects, which can be useful if you are managing more than one project at a time. On an underlying Redmine system, each saved custom query creates a new row inside the queries table in the Redmine database.

There's more...

Besides saved queries and Modules, Calendar and Gantt also have multiproject and filtering features. Both can be accessed by the following steps:

1. Click **Projects** in the main menu.
2. Click **View all issues**.
3. On the right sidebar, click **Calendar** or **Gantt**.
4. Apply filters to display issues that you need.
5. If you click on **Gantt and Calendar**, and then click on saved query, it will apply saved filters and display only filtered issues.
6. Saved queries are also available for export in CSV, PDF, or by Atom feed. This means that you can have Outlook or Thunderbird, or any other feed reader fetch the saved query for you or your client and automatically check them.

> Atom feeds in combination with saved queries can significantly contribute to your company's Redmine adoption. For example, you can get notifications on your smartphone if atom feed is updated (change occured in tasks, covered by your saved search).

See also

The project management triangle definition can be found at the following location:

`https://en.wikipedia.org/wiki/Project_management_triangle`.

Creating reports on spent time

Redmine comes with a powerful filtering engine for time logs. Accessing time logs has multiple entry points. In addition, reports can be done on many bases. This recipe will elaborate on how to display the following reports, how much time each user spent on the project per month, and how to export a detailed time log.

How to do it...

To display how much time each user has spent working per month on the project, perform the following steps:

1. Click **Overview** in the main project navigation bar.
2. On the right sidebar under **Spent time**, click **Report**.

Project Management with Redmine

3. On the **Report** tab, choose **Month** under the **Details** dropdown, and on the **Add dropdown**, choose **User**:

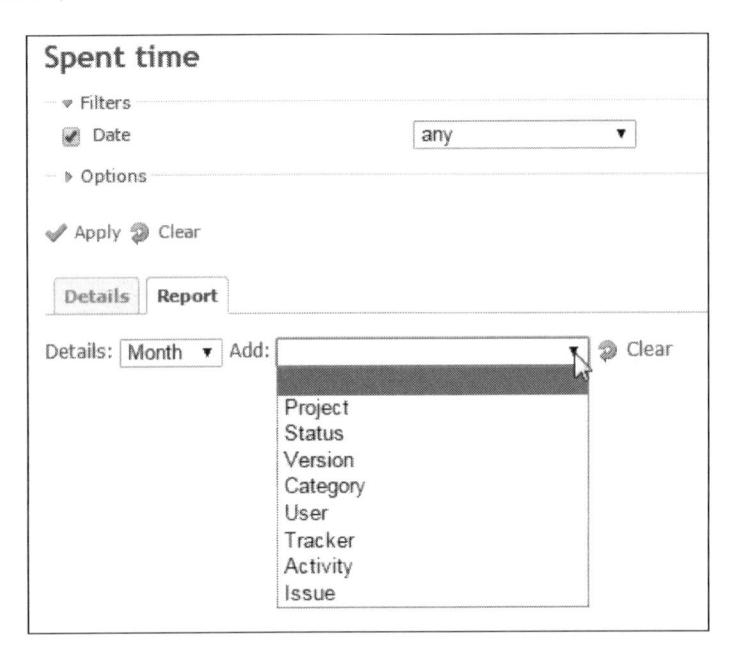

    ![Spent time screenshot showing Filters, Date any, Options, Apply/Clear, Details/Report tabs with Details: Month, Add dropdown showing Project, Status, Version, Category, User, Tracker, Activity, Issue]

4. Under the **Filters** section, you can choose the **Date** range, display only one **User**, or filter the report on various criteria offered in the **Add filter** dropdown on the right-hand side. We are going to choose **This year** under the **Date** option.

5. Click **Apply**, and you will get a report that looks like the following screenshot:

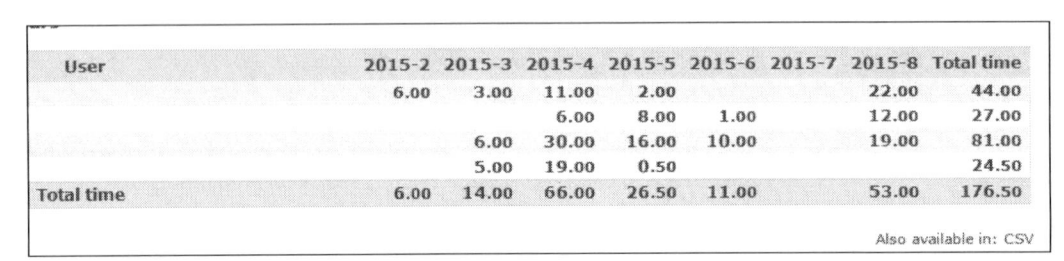

User	2015-2	2015-3	2015-4	2015-5	2015-6	2015-7	2015-8	Total time
	6.00	3.00	11.00	2.00			22.00	44.00
			6.00	8.00	1.00		12.00	27.00
		6.00	30.00	16.00	10.00		19.00	81.00
		5.00	19.00	0.50				24.50
Total time	6.00	14.00	66.00	26.50	11.00		53.00	176.50

Also available in: CSV

6. The **Details** tab offers a report on details about how time was spent, available with specific filters. To see the total time spent per issue, choose **Issue** on the **Report** tab.

> You need to click on the **Clear** button before adding new conditions under the **Report** tab, or you will get a combined report!

Chapter 3

How it works...

Redmine features a powerful reporting engine that is capable of filtering entered details about spent time, filtered according to various criteria. In this recipe, we used it to display some of the filtering capabilities, which enabled us to achieve a management goal to: see how much time each team member spent on a particular project per month. Feel free to experiment with filtering options to achieve your own goals.

There's more...

Reports on time can be exported as CSV data. This can then be imported in to Microsoft Excel or some other software and manipulated for various purposes, such as payment on a monthly basis to each developer, based on how many hours each developer spent on that project.

Making sure everyone is optimally loaded with work

To achieve a goal of having everyone optimally loaded with work, you can use different approaches. This recipe will try to give you one possible insight into how much time is planned to be spent in a given period so that you can balance the load of tasks among team members.

Getting ready

For this recipe, you need to have a project in Redmine and tasks planned to be done in the future. They can be already assigned, but this is not necessary.

How to do it...

As time goes by, developers and workers in general are completing tasks, sometimes before ETA completion dates and sometimes after. To maintain an accurate state of your projects and to make sure everyone is optimally balanced with work, the best practice would be to have tasks updated by team members so that they can edit the ETA and completion date, or you could do this for them after a daily meeting, for example. To see how many estimated hours each team member has for the next 14 days, perform the following:

1. Click **Issues** in the main project menu.
2. On **Status**, choose **open**.
3. Add the **Due date** filter, choose **in the next**, and type `14 days`.
4. Under **Options**, select the columns that you need to display.

Project Management with Redmine

5. Group results by choosing **Assignee**.
6. The end result should look like the following screenshot:

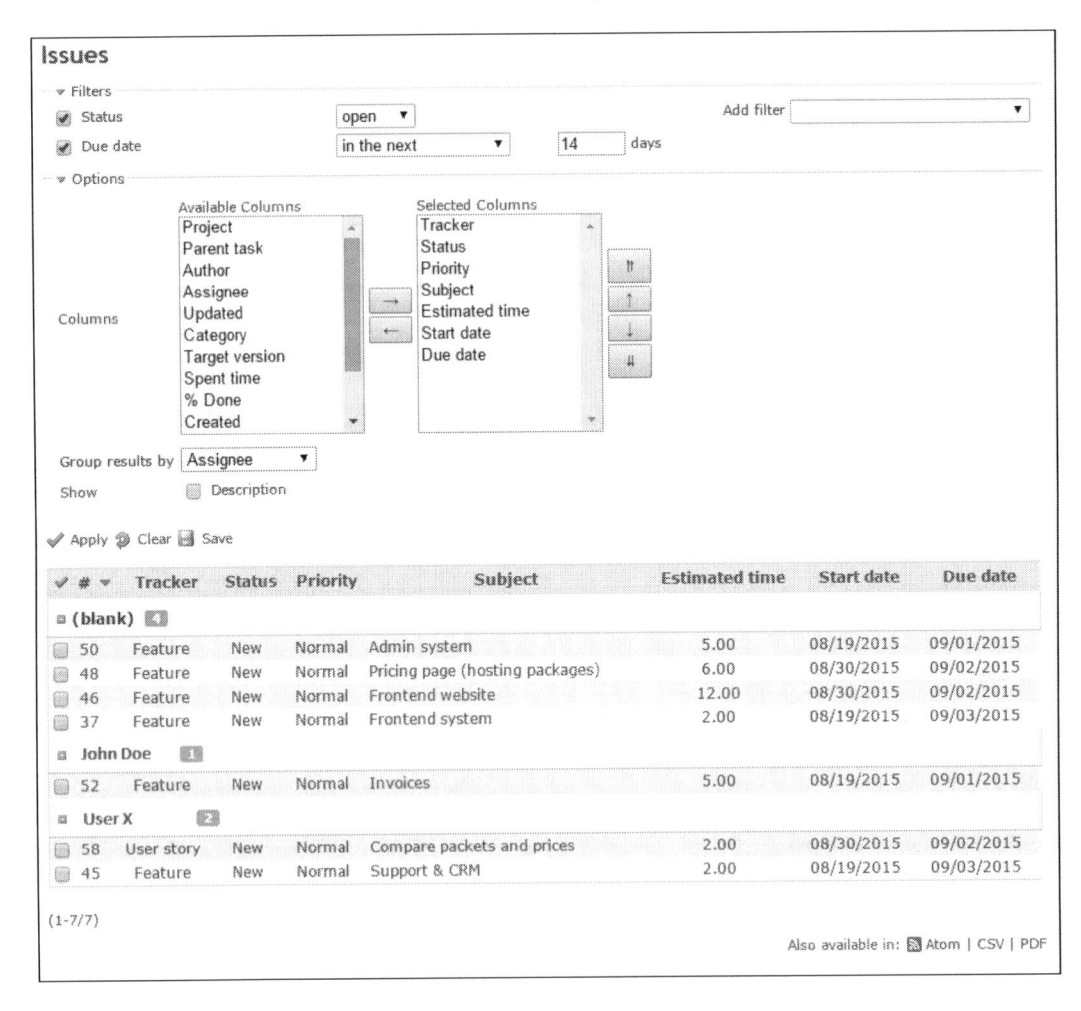

✓	#	Tracker	Status	Priority	Subject	Estimated time	Start date	Due date
	(blank)							
☐	50	Feature	New	Normal	Admin system	5.00	08/19/2015	09/01/2015
☐	48	Feature	New	Normal	Pricing page (hosting packages)	6.00	08/30/2015	09/02/2015
☐	46	Feature	New	Normal	Frontend website	12.00	08/30/2015	09/02/2015
☐	37	Feature	New	Normal	Frontend system	2.00	08/19/2015	09/03/2015
	John Doe							
☐	52	Feature	New	Normal	Invoices	5.00	08/19/2015	09/01/2015
	User X							
☐	58	User story	New	Normal	Compare packets and prices	2.00	08/30/2015	09/02/2015
☐	45	Feature	New	Normal	Support & CRM	2.00	08/19/2015	09/03/2015

(1-7/7)

Also available in: Atom | CSV | PDF

7. Below **Filters** and **Options**, you can see a report with the estimated time grouped by assignee.

How it works...

We utilized the filtering capabilities of the **Issues** module to create a report on how much each user is estimated to work on a per-task basis for the upcoming 14 days. Instead of **Due date**, you could choose different options to plan for a specific range of dates, and you can choose different columns to be displayed in the report, according to your specific needs.

Chapter 3

There's more...

Various plugins can help you get a feeling for how your team is performing. Just look for the keywords workload, schedule, planning, and resource on Redmine's official plugin list.

Relating between issue and time

Having estimated time and spent time properly logged per issue in Redmine may be very important in your organization. Whether you are a software development company paying developers on an hourly basis, or a service desk company that needs to measure various **Key Performance Indicators** (**KPIs**), this recipe will teach you how to log and edit time per issue manually and from the source control management systems.

How to do it...

To log time manually on a per-issue basis, perform the following tasks:

1. Navigate to the particular issue by any of these entry points: My page, search, issue list, direct URL, Gantt, and so on.
2. Click the **Log time** icon.
3. The **Spent time** entry form will appear:

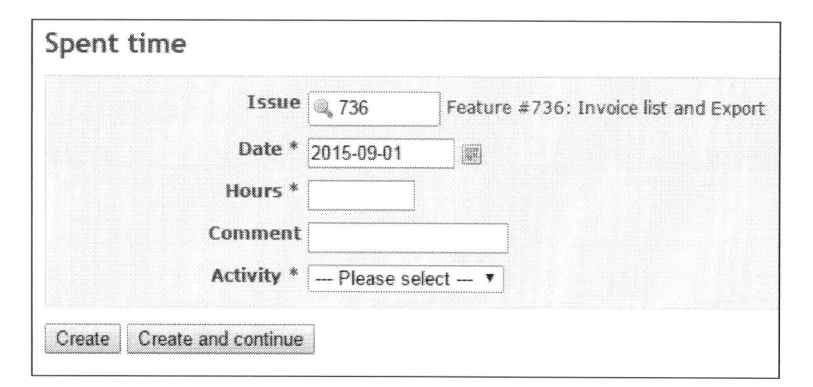

   ```
   Spent time
              Issue  736           Feature #736: Invoice list and Export
             Date *  2015-09-01
            Hours *
           Comment
          Activity *  --- Please select --- ▼

   [ Create ] [ Create and continue ]
   ```

4. Enter how much time you spent on particular date, an optional comment, and a mandatory **Activity**.
5. Click **Create** or **Create and continue**.
6. **Create and continue** will keep opening the **Spent time** form until you click **Create**, which will lead you to issue with the **Spent time** field populated with entered values.

81

Project Management with Redmine

To edit time already entered, there are also multiple entry points, either through detailed time logs, as explained in previous recipes, or by clicking on **Spent Time** on the issue itself.
Users can edit their own time logs only if they have permission to do this.

So, editing a time log can be done by clicking on the Pencil icon, as displayed in the following screenshot:

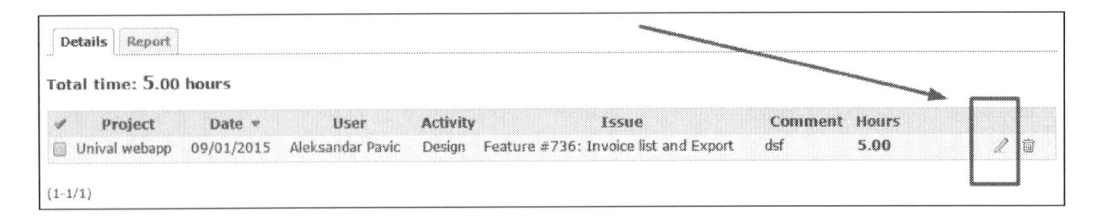

	Project	Date ▼	User	Activity	Issue	Comment	Hours		
✓	Unival webapp	09/01/2015	Aleksandar Pavic	Design	Feature #736: Invoice list and Export	dsf	5.00	✏	🗑

Details | Report
Total time: 5.00 hours
(1-1/1)

Once clicked, a normal time entry form with prepopulated dates will appear. Just edit the log and click **Save**.

How it works...

Redmine keeps time logs on a per-issue basis with attributes such as date, comment, type of activity, and spent time in hours. In this recipe, we used Redmine's built-in time logging and editing features. The goal of efficient time logging can be achieved by different means. There are various plugins and third-party tools that connect through the Redmine API and let users log time more efficiently.

There's more...

Spent time per issue can be logged via commit messages from your favorite SCM tool that is supported by Redmine. To log time via a commit message, first you need to make sure that Redmine is configured to properly log time by performing the following actions:

1. In the main menu, choose **Administration**.
2. Choose **Repositories**.
3. Enable time logging and choose default activity:

Chapter 3

Referencing and fixing issues in commit messages	
Referencing keywords	refs,references,IssueID
	Multiple values allowed (comma separated).
Allow issues of all the other projects to be referenced and fixed	☐
Enable time logging	☑
Activity for logged time	Development ▼

To log time from commit messages, you need to follow proper conventions; for example, if we want to commit 5 hours to issue **736**, the message will look like this: " **refs #736, 5h00**". After clicking on repository in the main menu and getting back to issue **736** or time logs, if your Redmine is not set to automatically update repository, you will see the time logged.

See also

Refer to the *Using the issue-code relation* recipe to learn how to configure source control management integration. Redmine's official time logging page can be found at http://www.redmine.org/projects/redmine/wiki/RedmineTimeTracking.

Using the issue-code relation

Issue-code relation is a great tool to achieve a goal of knowing *who did what, when, and why* in the source code of your project. The perfect scenario would be that each of your features is nicely described, documented, and each code revision (not too many of them) is clearly related to a feature. Let's say that 10 years after the project is done, a client asks for several modifications to the software, and after a simple Redmine search, you immediately know who developed these features initially, and you re-engage them to make the newly requested modifications, saving time, money, and nerves that you would spend without it.

> Issue-code does not have to relate only to software projects; it can be applied to any kind of project involving the usage of version management system that is supported by Redmine.

Getting ready

Make sure that you have Redmine installed with **Enabled SCM** for a version control management system that you prefer to use. If you don't have, for example, a CVS system, take a look at the *Installing optional requirements* recipe from *Chapter 1, Installing and Running Redmine*.

Project Management with Redmine

The project on which we are going to use Issue-code relationship needs to have one or more repositories configured. To add repository to project, perform the following:

1. Click the **Settings** link in the main menu.
2. Click the **Repositories** tab.
3. Click **New Repository** at the bottom left.
4. From the **SCM** drop-down menu, choose the repository type that you are adding (**Subversion**, **Darcs**, **Mercurial**, **CVS**, **Bazaar**, or **Git**).
5. Tick the **Main repository** checkbox if there are going to be multiple repositories.
6. Enter a URL and credentials in the remaining form fields.
7. Click **Create**.
8. After following the preceding steps, the project menu item called **Repository** should appear.

How to do it...

As you made sure that repository integration is properly installed, you can navigate to Redmine settings to check or tweak integration keywords, or workflow.

Configuring per-tracker workflows

Redmine can support complex integration workflows that are configurable per tracker type, *Issue, Bug, and Feature*, supporting the custom tracker that you have defined. To configure Issue-code relations and create workflows, perform the following:

1. In the main menu, click **Administration**.
2. Click **Settings**.
3. Choose the **Repositories** tab; the repository integration form is located at the bottom. Choose **Tracker**, **Fixing keywords**, **Applied status**, and **% Done**:

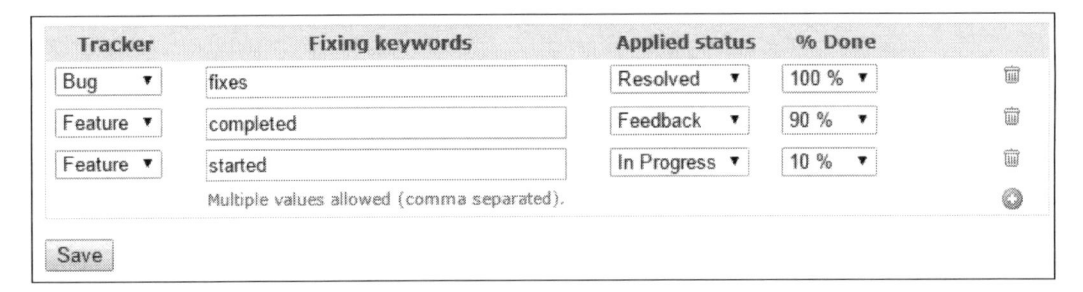

Tracker	Fixing keywords	Applied status	% Done
Bug ▼	fixes	Resolved ▼	100 % ▼
Feature ▼	completed	Feedback ▼	90 % ▼
Feature ▼	started	In Progress ▼	10 % ▼
	Multiple values allowed (comma separated).		

Save

Using the issue-code relationship via source-control

Once we have configured workflow and added repository to our project, we can start using SCM commit messages to update issues. To do so, when you or developers are done with some work, you or they should form a commit message according to the following rules:

- `#ISSUE_ID FIXING_KEYWORD`, where Issue ID is Issue ID that is provided by Redmine once Issue is created
- `FIXING_KEYWORD` is a keyword that we defined in a previous section of this recipe

So, for example, if we want to set some issue as **Resolved** and it's status to 100%, considering that we configured keywords as we did in the previous section, our commit message would look similar to fixes #3. This change is automatically visible on the issue page and the repository tab. In the following screenshot, you can see that we updated the status from new to in progress and changed done to 10% with the custom keyword **writing**:

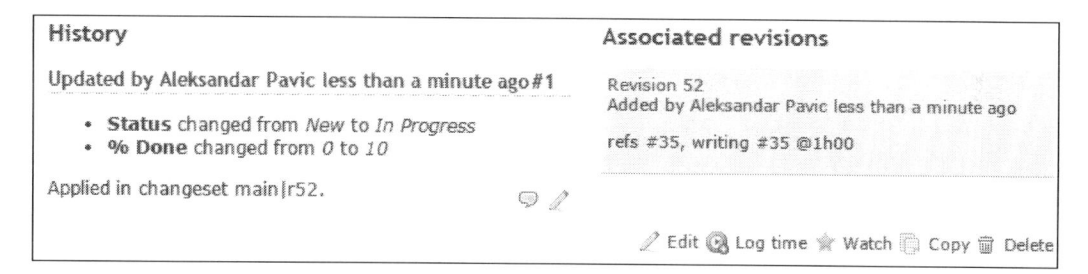

```
History                                              Associated revisions

Updated by Aleksandar Pavic less than a minute ago #1    Revision 52
                                                         Added by Aleksandar Pavic less than a minute ago
   • Status changed from New to In Progress
   • % Done changed from 0 to 10                         refs #35, writing #35 @1h00

Applied in changeset main|r52.

                                                         Edit   Log time   Watch   Copy   Delete
```

Revision and **History of revisions** are also clearly visible in the **Repository** tab on the main project menu. **Issues**, if typed properly, are hyperlinks to the **Issue** view.

Project Management with Redmine

How it works...

Redmine has specific software codes, which communicate with repository management tool binaries, enabling it to parse the repository's commit log messages and look for certain keywords that are defined under the **Repositories** tab on the **Settings** page. By parsing these keywords, it relates an individual code revision with a particular task (issue) in Redmine. This functionality lets teams automate and speed up processes by saving time and improving process compliance. The following diagram displays how Redmine automates this process:

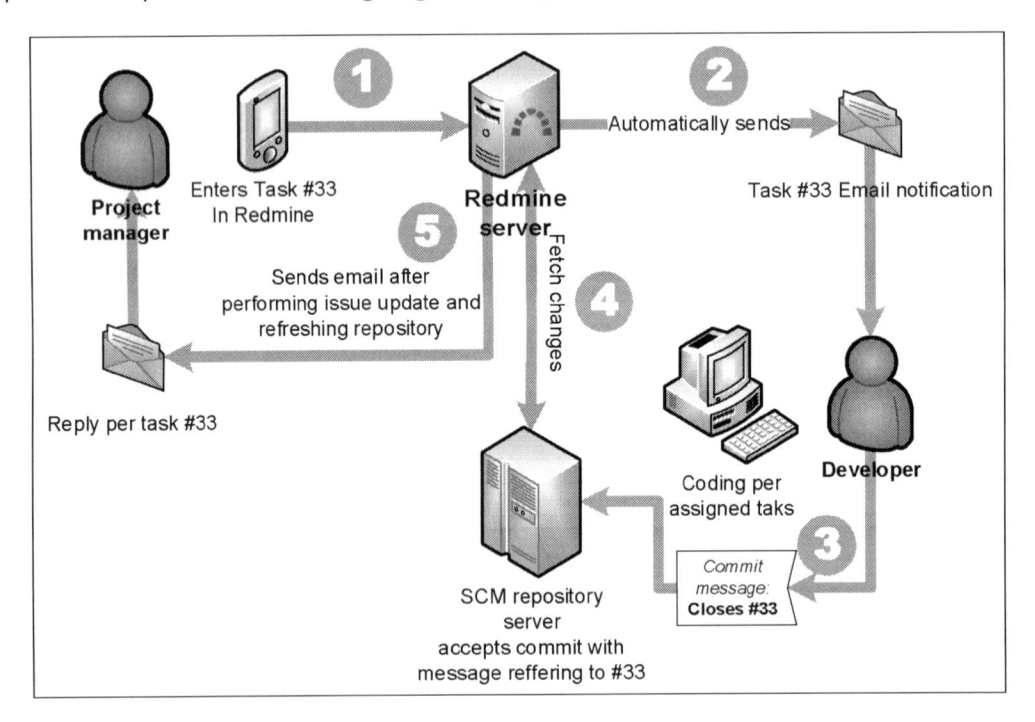

There's more...

Pre-commit hooks can force issue-code relation. For example, an SVN pre-commit hook is listed as follows, which checks for proper Redmine comment structure before letting the user commit the code:

```sh
#!/bin/sh

REPOS="$1"
TXN="$2"

SVNLOOK=/usr/bin/svnlook
```

```
LOGMSG=$($SVNLOOK log -t "$TXN" "$REPOS" | grep -e "refs #" -e
"production" | wc -c)
if [ "$LOGMSG" -le 0 ]; then echo  "Valid comments needs to have refs
#issueID." 1>&2
exit 1
fi

# Exit on all errors.
set -e
exit 0
```

To use this code you need to have Linux server hosting your SVN repositories or minigw installed on Windows servers. Make sure that you have `svnlook` installed by typing the following:

which svnlook

You should get an output like this: `/usr/bin/svnlook`. If the path output differs from this one, you need to modify `SVNLOOK` like in the preceding code. This code uses Linux-es commands `svnlook`, which is part of the SVN client package, and `grep`, which is a basic Linux console tool. The `grep` command seeks for `refs #` in SVN comments, while `SVNLOOK` forms the message that is checked with `grep`. If no message is committed, or it does not fit the proposed comment form, the pre-commit hook exits with failure, preventing the code from being committed to the repository and displaying **Valid comments needs to have refs #issueID.** on the user's screen:

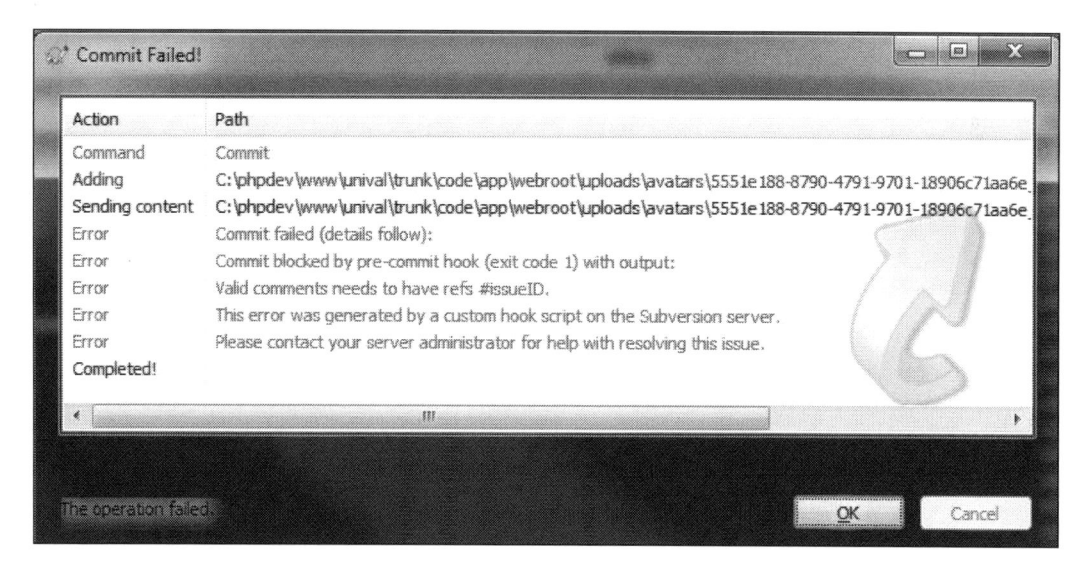

A more advanced version of pre-commit hook would be able to check whether the feature really exists in Redmine, and whether the user has rights to commit to this feature.

Project Management with Redmine

See also

Refer to the *Installing optional requirements* recipe from *Chapter 1, Installing and Running Redmine* for instructions on how to install optional requirement binaries for source code versioning management systems, such as SVN, Git, and so on.

Defining a roadmap to the release plan

Release plan is used in software development and software release lifecycles and varies depending upon the software development methodology that is used. For example, in the traditional waterfall model (Requirements => Design => Implementation => Verification => Maintenance), it is expected to release the initial software version prior to the Maintenance phase, then subsequently increase version numbers as bugs are submitted and fixed in the Maintenance phase. However, in SCRUM methodology, for example, Release plan is dictated by `tasks/features/bugs` that are organized in 30-day sprint cycles. Due to its flexibility, Redmine can support various software development and project management methodologies.

> Each software development paradigm and methodology has its own pros and cons.

For a list of current software development methodologies and their pros and cons visit the Wikipedia article `https://en.wikipedia.org/wiki/List_of_software_development_philosophies#Software_development_methodology` or find various articles and forums discussing it.

This recipe covers scenarios of using the Waterfall and Agile-Scrum models.

If you are having trouble choosing a proper software development methodology for your project, some tips are discussed next.

> The Waterfall model is better if you are doing a one-time software development project for a client.

Chapter 3

You should do this because you need to define a set of features that this software is going to have, an ETA, and bargain on the price that the client is going to pay for this set of features, as well as payment and a release schedule. Both your client and you want to minimize the *time to market* for a product. The client wants this because they want the product to be usable as soon as possible. You want this because you can start working on a new project earlier. Also, you may bargain for several payment deals, one for development, another one for new features after the initial release, and another one for maintenance and bug fixes.

> Scrum is better if you are a part of team; for example, a start-up company launching a new cloud product to the World Wide Web market.

This is a better option because your marketing, UX, and design teams would most likely come up with new ideas and features as time goes by, and you need to organize and schedule them in the order of importance.

Getting ready

Prior to entering and organizing your tasks in Redmine, be sure to conduct required meetings with clients and staff on how are you going to split tasks and come to an agreement on the roadmap to the release plan. After you reach a consensus on a plan, start managing your project in Redmine. You also need to be sure that every team member understands the processes that are defined by the methodology or your own rules that you are going to use.

How to do it...

Having a clean roadmap to release can be conducted by using the built-in versions feature that is available in issue tracker for any Redmine project. You can see the sample steps to define Scrum Sprints as follows. The procedure is the same for any methodology, and instead of user stories, you can also use different trackers depending upon the paradigm that you are going to use.

Roadmaps and versions

This is an *out-of-the-box* way without any customizations:

1. Navigate to **Settings** in the main project menu and choose the **Versions** tab.
2. Click **New Version** and enter what would be your release name; this can be something creative, such as `Precise Pangolin` for Ubuntu Linux, or just a Scrum iteration, such as `Sprint 15`.

Project Management with Redmine

3. Choose other options from the form, such as **Date**, **Wiki page**, or version visibility among subprojects:

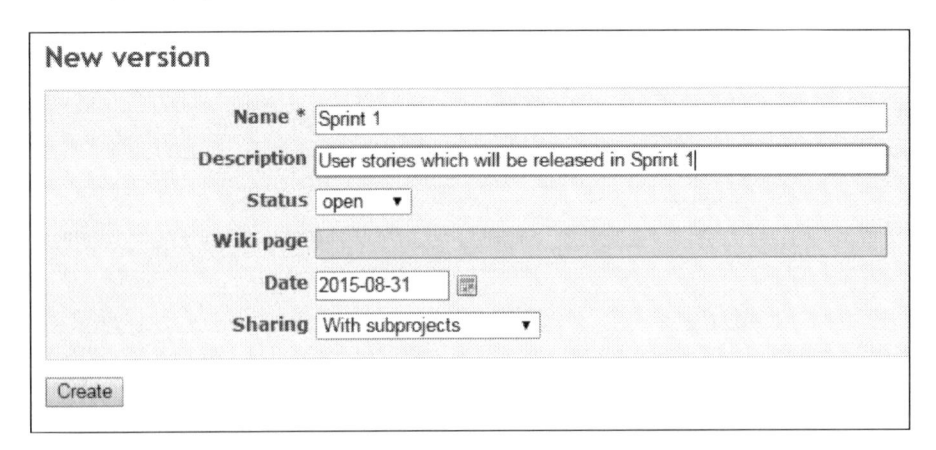

New version

Name *	Sprint 1
Description	User stories which will be released in Sprint 1
Status	open
Wiki page	
Date	2015-08-31
Sharing	With subprojects

[Create]

4. If you are entering sprints, then repeat *Step 3* and increase versions a few times depending how many months ahead you want to display in Roadmap.
5. Choose version when editing or adding a new issue.
6. To see the roadmap, click on **Roadmap** in the main project menu, and you should see clearly which issues are assigned to which version:

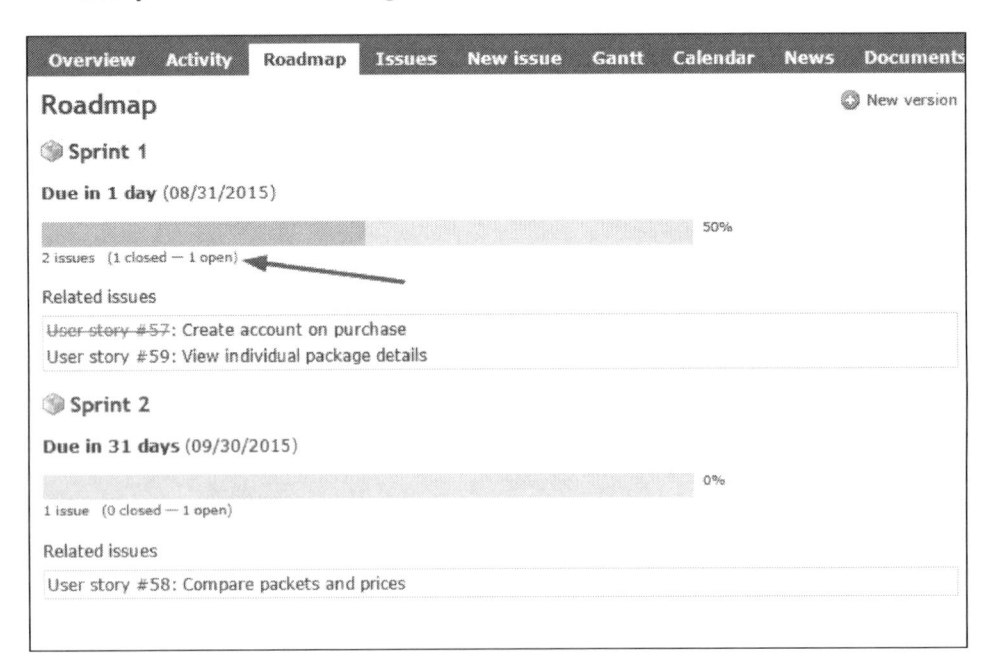

Overview Activity Roadmap Issues New issue Gantt Calendar News Documents

Roadmap   ⊕ New version

🎁 **Sprint 1**

Due in 1 day (08/31/2015)

█████████████░░░░░░░░░░░░ 50%

2 issues (1 closed — 1 open) ←

Related issues

~~User story #57~~: Create account on purchase
User story #59: View individual package details

🎁 **Sprint 2**

Due in 31 days (09/30/2015)

░░░░░░░░░░░░░░░░░░░░░░░░░ 0%

1 issue (0 closed — 1 open)

Related issues

User story #58: Compare packets and prices

Chapter 3

> **Open** and **closed** are hyperlinks to filtered issue lists for this version.

7. Click on the name of the version to see more details about that revision:

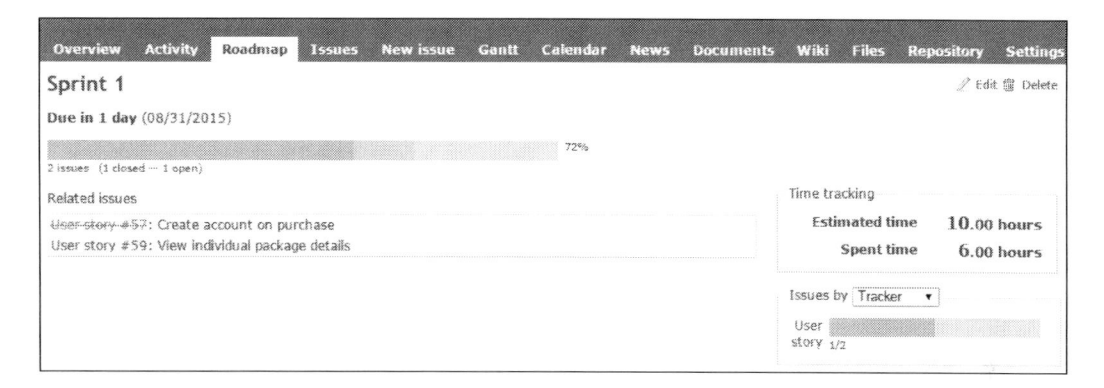

How it works...

Whether your team is playing Scrum Poker while prioritizing tasks or you have a clear roadmap defined by a contract, this feature will work for you. The feature versions/roadmaps works by creating new versions or using some methodology for prioritizing tasks like MoSCW method - `https://en.wikipedia.org/wiki/MoSCoW_method` on a per-project basis that are stored in a particular table in the database, also called versions. Users should pick versions while creating new tasks, or arranging existing tasks. Versions are a part of the Issue tracking module, and once the first version is created, a new main project menu item called Roadmap becomes visible. The **Roadmap** page displays versions with a nice progress bar and additional information regarding that particular version.

Project Management with Redmine

There's more...

Stories, tasks, and features can be organized and tracked in common Scrum way, by utilizing Redmine's custom fields feature:

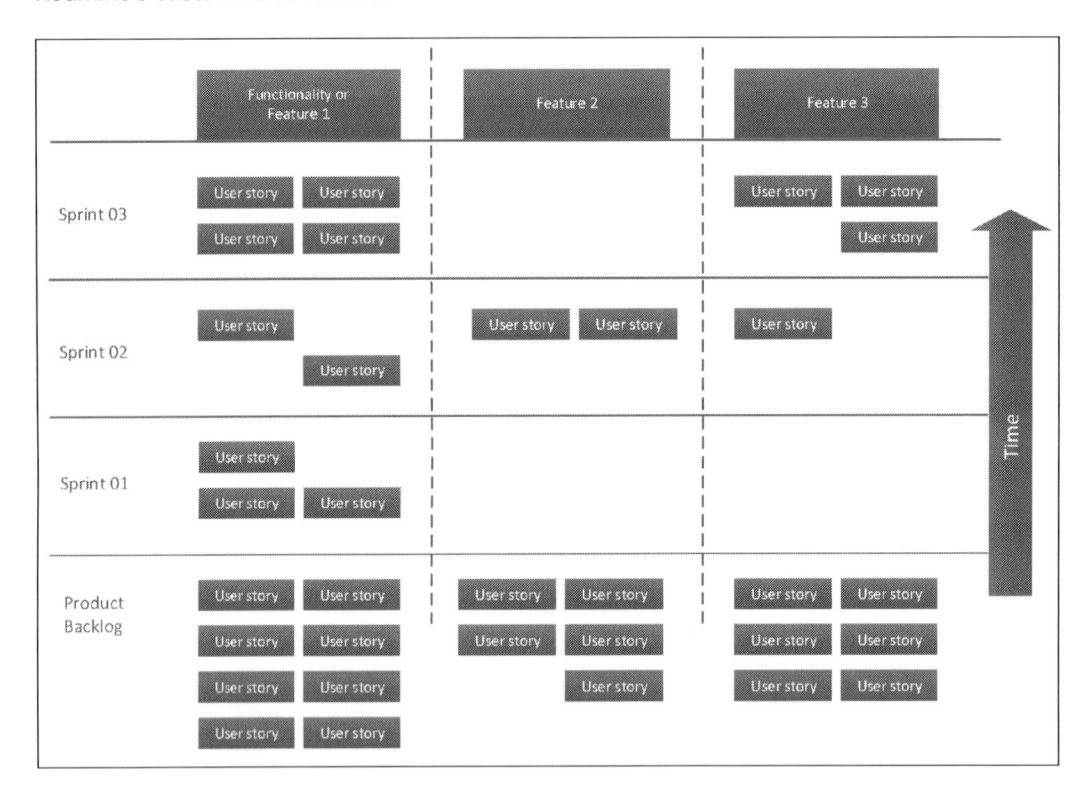

To achieve a standard Scrum workflow structure like the one in the preceding image, we can perform the following:

1. Create a tracker for **User stories**.
2. Enter new **Feature** to Redmine.
3. Choose **Add** under **Subtasks**.
4. Choose the type of tracker, **User story**.
5. Select a **Version** (Sprint) under which this is going to be released.

The Product backlog can be treated as a version-less issue, or you can create a special version, without a date, called *backlog*.

See also

Refer to *Chapter 2, Customizing Redmine* to see how to create custom trackers and workflow.

Redmine backlogs plugin can be found at `http://www.redminebacklogs.net/`. The Scrum plugin can be found at `https://www.redmine.org/plugins/scrum-plugin`.

4
Improving Team Performance

As you have already mastered Redmine and learned about some customizations and use cases, this chapter focuses on the following team-oriented scenarios:

- Keeping relevant documentation in Redmine
- Putting the timeline to good use
- Making sure that everyone is informed
- Limiting access to some team members
- Using metrics to improve team performance
- Analyzing team performance through the code repository
- Using the repository module to display code differences
- Managing multicultural teams in different time zones
- Applying advanced issue-code relationships
- Improving Scrum meetings and backlogs

Introduction

The previous chapters were focused mainly on the technical side of Redmine, how to install and run it, and how to customize it. Assuming that you have already familiarized yourself with the *bits and pieces* of Redmine, this chapter focuses on how to get the most out of customizations and improve the performance of your team by focusing on management benefits, improved user experience, and business processes.

If you are a manager managing a team of software developers or support helpdesk crew, you may wonder how to improve team performance? *The best way to improve the performance of a team is to motivate it, and Redmine should be used as a tool to motivate and boost team morale instead of strengthening control and using metrics for penalties.* You should also motivate your teammates to come up with ideas on how the management process can be improved, which customizations can be applied to Redmine, and which plugins can help improve your business processes.

Keeping relevant documentation in Redmine

While managing multiple projects, it is good practice to standardize project documentation so that managers and users don't waste time seeking information and reduce the possibility to oversee some relevant project data. For example, if your team is running multiple software projects, you can have a document called *specification that is* common to every project so that everyone knows exactly where to look for the required information. This way your teammates will save time, and it will boost confidence.

How to do it...

Redmine offers several ways to organize project documentation. To utilize the Documents module, which offers Textile formatting and attached files, perform the following steps:

1. Navigate to the **Documents** tab of the main project menu.
2. Click **Create New document**.
3. Choose **Category** from the dropdown, enter **Title**, **Description**, and attach files if required. The default upload size of attachments can be changed through **Administration | Settings | General | Maximum attachment size:**

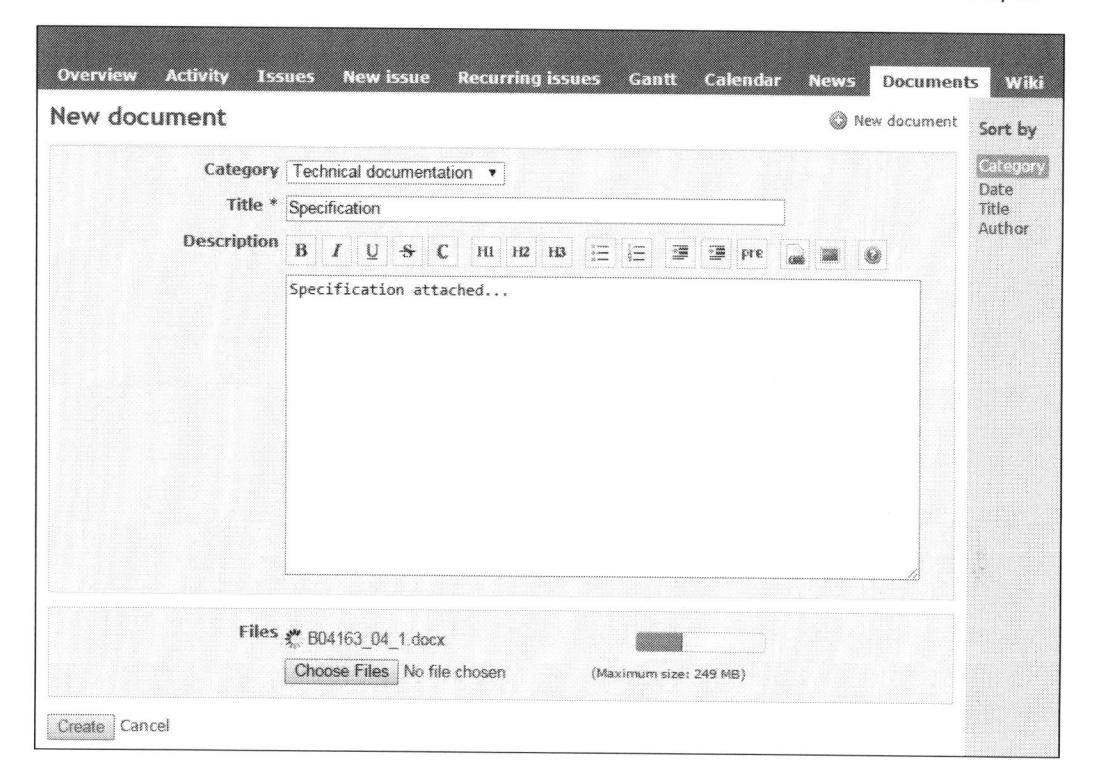

![New document form screenshot]

If you need to change the category that is offered in dropdown menu, it can be done through **Administration | Enumerations | Document Categories**; then, after clicking **New value**, a form appears allowing you to enter a name for a new document category and checkboxes indicating whether the category is active or default. In addition, on the previous screen, you can adjust the order of categories in a dropdown menu that is visible on the **New Document** tab.

How it works...

This recipe utilizes the built-in **Documentation** module that handles Textile formatted content and attachments. The **Documentation** module needs to be enabled on a per-project basis. Textile markup is chosen by default in Redmine. Apart from this, you can use Markdown formatting whose support is still experimental or no formatting at all. This can be configured by navigating to **Administration | Settings | General | Text Formatting**.

> Redmine's text engine setting is global. This means that once the Text Formatting engine is chosen, it will be used everywhere throughout the app. (News, Wiki, Documentation, Issues, and so on.)

Improving Team Performance

There's more...

The standard documentation module can be extended with plugins; one of the plugins that increases productivity is **Redmine Documents**. It provides a preview of a document in the documents tab and can be downloaded from `https://www.redmine.org/plugins/redmine_documents`.

Alternatively, the repositories and files module can be used to serve as document repositories. Some teams prefer to have their project documentation in their revision control system so that they can easily synchronize it and track changes among team members worldwide.

See also

- Refer to the Textile markup reference at `http://www.redmine.org/projects/redmine/wiki/RedmineTextFormatting`.
- Another useful extension for Documents is the DMSF Plugin, which can completely replace the default Documents module. DMSF Plugin is now open source and available at `https://www.redmine.org/plugins/dmsf`. It offers comprehensive document-management features, which may be required if your company is using some of ISO or similar business standards. To see detailed instructions on the DMSF Plugin, refer to the *Redmine for document management* recipe from *Chapter 8, Getting the Most Out of Scripts and Plugins*.

Putting the timeline to good use

After the popularization of social networks, almost every internet user is accustomed to using and following the concept of a *timeline*. Redmine comes with an **Activity** tab, which displays the overall activity of the project and subprojects in chronological order starting from the most recent events toward earlier project events reachable through pagination. The timeline also has filters and avatars that are customizable depending upon the theme that is used for Redmine. Frequent checking of project activity can give you a feel for the dynamics of your project. Is it very active or dormant? It can also help quickly identify whether some team-members are not performing as expected so that you can react early and prevent potential problems, which may endanger your desired Project outcome.

How to do it...

The **Activity** tab is mandatory for every project and cannot be switched off by default. So, as it is already there, let's try to get the most out of it.

Chapter 4

Tracking project activity

To check project activity, including the activity of all its subprojects, just click the **Activity** tab in the main project toolbar. The **Activity** view, like in the following image, will appear with sidebar filer options, offering to turn on or off some of the activities through checkboxes:

Activity
- ☑ Issues
- ☑ Changesets
- ☑ News
- ☐ Wiki edits
- ☐ Messages

[Apply]

Once filters are checked or unchecked and applied, the activity page will display the atom feed set for these filters that are available for logged in users. The Atom feed link is available at the bottom of the activity page. The feed is available on a per-project basis, so users can have their Outlook or other Atom feed clients subscribe and track project activity through their favorite feed readers.

Using gravatars

To use gravatars, the checkbox available at **Administration** | **Settings** | **Display** needs to be checked like on this screen:

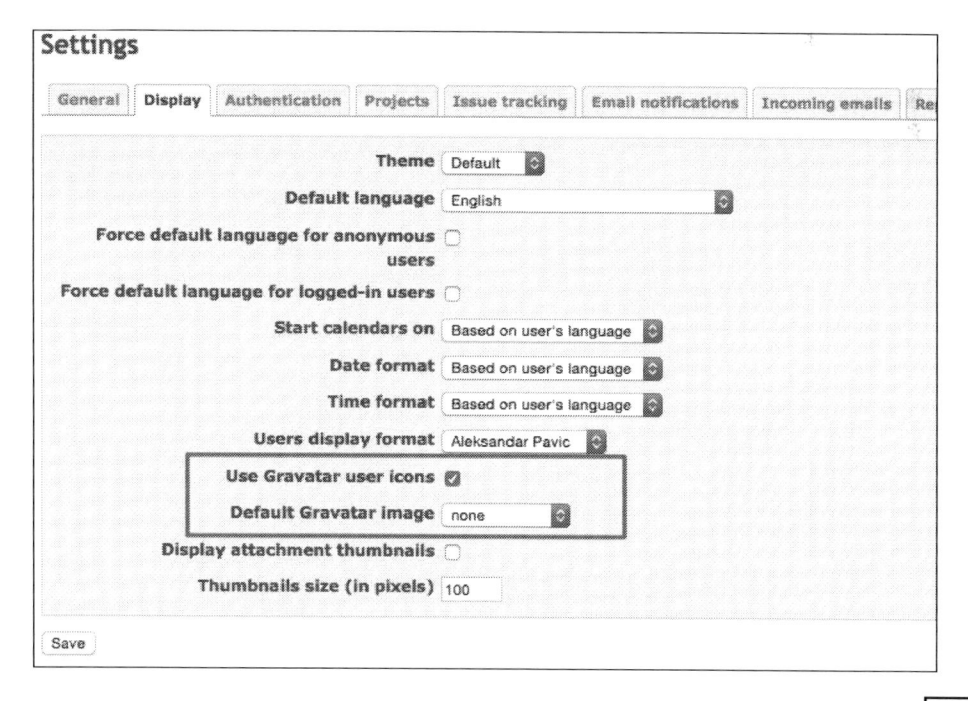

Settings

| General | **Display** | Authentication | Projects | Issue tracking | Email notifications | Incoming emails | Re

- Theme: Default
- Default language: English
- Force default language for anonymous users: ☐
- Force default language for logged-in users: ☐
- Start calendars on: Based on user's language
- Date format: Based on user's language
- Time format: Based on user's language
- Users display format: Aleksandar Pavic
- **Use Gravatar user icons: ☑**
- **Default Gravatar image: none**
- Display attachment thumbnails: ☐
- Thumbnails size (in pixels): 100

[Save]

99

Improving Team Performance

Once turned on, gravatars will start appearing on your timeline, as well as in other places, such as user profile, repository revisions, and issues.

How it works...

In this recipe, we utilize the built-in **Activity** tab, which displays project activity in chronological order. It also produces an Atom feed on a per-project basis. The **Activity** tab utilizes Gravatars. Gravatar stands for *Globally Recognized Avatars*, and this is a third-party service providing API access to various online software or desktop applications, which connect to the Gravatar API and fetch user avatars based on their e-mails. Gravatars visually improve user experience, and they improve the activity page by helping managers and team members familiarize with each other because humans are more visually cognitive-oriented and it gives more insight on who did what.

09/16/2015

11:50 AM Our webapp - Revision 813 (unimain): refs #742
Aleksandar Pavic

11:50 AM Our webapp - Revision 813 (uni): refs #742
Aleksandar Pavic

09:15 AM Website - Bug #743 (In Progress): verification card problem
Miodrag Dragić

09:13 AM Website - Bug #743 (In Progress): verification card problem
the problem when payment from validation not goes.
Miodrag Dragić

09/15/2015

> An Activity diagram can look visually appealing, but its layout might differ based upon the chosen theme for the entire Redmine system.

There's more...

The concept of a timeline is available on several places in Redmine. For example, versions offer timeline view with a progress bar (refer to the previous chapter). Gantt chart also offers a timeline view that is characteristic to a Gantt chart. Issues can be filtered in chronological order. The timeline and activity can be tracked through third-party clients, such as Outlook or some other Atom feed reader. The link to the Activity feed is available at the bottom of the activity page.

See also

- Refer to the *Activity monitoring through Atom feed* recipe from *Chapter 7, Integrating Redmine with Other Software*, for more detailed instruction on how to use Atom feeds from within Redmine and other feed readers, such as Outlook, or Thunderbird.
- As the timeline concept gained its popularity with the growth of Facebook, check out `https://zapier.com/zapbook/facebook/redmine/`. This is a Zap which lets you connect the Facebook timeline with Redmine and vice-versa.
- To create and use gravatars, register and upload a photo at `http://en.gravatar.com/`.

Making sure that everyone is informed

Information, communication, and collaboration are three words that are often heard in the project management world. Making sure everyone is informed can literally mean life and death for your project. Luckily, with proper work and process organization, Redmine can be the tool that ensures that everyone is informed in a timely manner. In this recipe, we are going to present two scenarios:

- Assigning an issue to one worker and have other workers informed about that issue and any update on it
- Assigning a task to a group of people

How to do it...

In project and process management, usually one employee or contractor is "responsible" for a task or process, even if there are several employees performing the task together. Redmine follows this practice by default and allows tasks to be assigned to a single person who is then responsible for these tasks. Additionally tasks can have watchers who are informed about any updates to these tasks. However, if you really need to assign tasks to multiple persons, Redmine allows issues to be assigned to a group.

Improving Team Performance

Assigning issues with watchers

To add a watcher to an issue, simply click on the **Add** button on the right sidebar under the **Watchers** section. Then, a search form will appear with names listed below it, alphabetically. If the user that you are trying to add is not already listed, simply start typing letters of their name or surname. Once assigned, watchers can be viewed on the right sidebar in the default theme and edited if the user has proper privileges.

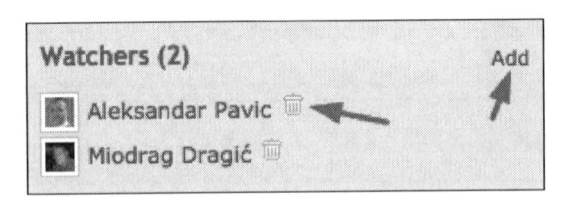

Some user roles can have issues assigned to them without knowing that there are watchers assigned to the issue. To configure this role's permissions, navigate to **Administration | Settings | Roles and permissions**, click on the Role's name, find a group box called **Issue tracking**, and configure the roles:

Assigning issues to groups

Some organizations find this feature very useful. For example in helpdesk scenarios, assigning issue to a group can shorten time required for issue to be resolved, because first available operator from a group can attend to it. While the other way, choosing watchers individually each time, increases error rate and requires much more mouse clicks. To assign an issue to a group, first create a group as explained in the *Creating and using user groups* recipe of *Chapter 2*, *Customizing Redmine* and assign it to your project. Make sure that the **Role** under which you are adding the group has the permissions that will allow issues to be assigned to this role. If this is the case, **Group** will be visible under the **Assignee** field at the bottom of the dropdown:

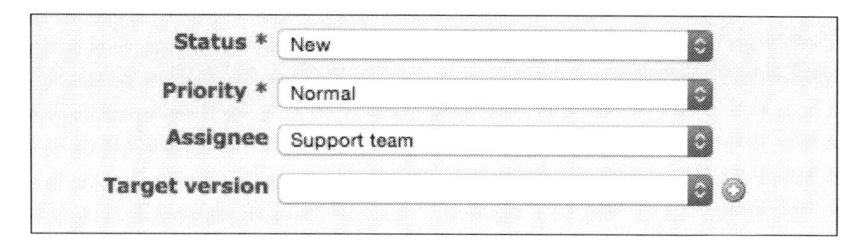

Status *	New
Priority *	Normal
Assignee	Support team
Target version	

In the preceding image, we assigned a task to the **Support team** group. Once the issue is assigned to a group, the first available technician claims the issue by choosing themselves as **Assignee**. This means that they are now responsible for this task, its status, and progress.

How it works...

This recipe utilizes built-in features to inform multiple Redmine users about assigned issues or updates to issues that they are assigned to or included in. In business process management, one employee is always responsible for a task, and other employees can be involved, participate in the task, and update its status. Redmine enables this feature by having the task assigned to one person, and other persons added as watchers. However, many organizations adopt different management practices, such as assigning a task to a group or department because it can be beneficial to their company. In such cases, once task is assigned, some user from the group should accept the issue by changing the owner from group to himself.

There's more...

The best practice to keep everybody informed is to establish some kind of routine, which will oblige workers to check their e-mail and Redmine first thing when they start work.

> E-mail notifications can be turned off completely, but it is not recommended, because it may result in slower response times, or some users overseeing important information.

Redmine also utilizes News, Wiki, Documentations, and Forum modules, which can become part of your information sharing routine.

See also

- Have a look at https://www.projectsmart.co.uk/project-communications-how-to-keep-your-team-engaged-and-informed.php, as it is a really nice article by Project Magazine on project communication, which focuses on the project management part of this recipe.

Limiting access to some team members

For some reason, you may want to limit or completely disable access to a project or certain project data or resources to certain team members. In the twenty first century, identity management and access rights are advancing to more serious levels as companies digitalize more and more of their business processes and overall data, including sensitive material that can be the subject of industrial espionage or simply should not go public. In this recipe, we are going to consider a scenario which disables access to some team members of the Redmine project, or the overall system.

How to do it...

Limiting access to a certain member can be done in several ways and depends upon the scenario that you need to perform.

Locking users

Locking users will disable their Redmine account completely, preventing them from logging in to the system. However, such users may still have access to certain resources, such as code repositories, if they are managed outside Redmine. To lock the user, simply navigate to **Administration | Users**, find the user that you want to lock, and click the lock icon to the right of username. Once unlocked, the user gets full access as they had before their account was locked. By default, only active users are displayed. If you need to display all or only locked users, use the **Status** filter above, and choose the status of users that you want to display.

Shifting roles

This is a strategy that should be used when the administrator or manager wants to upgrade or downgrade the access rights of a certain user. So, for example, you can promote a user with a **Developer** role to a **Management** role by navigating to the **Members** tab in the project's settings. From here, you can simply click **Edit** near the user name and tick the checkbox near the role name that you wish to add or remove for that user on that particular project:

Chapter 4

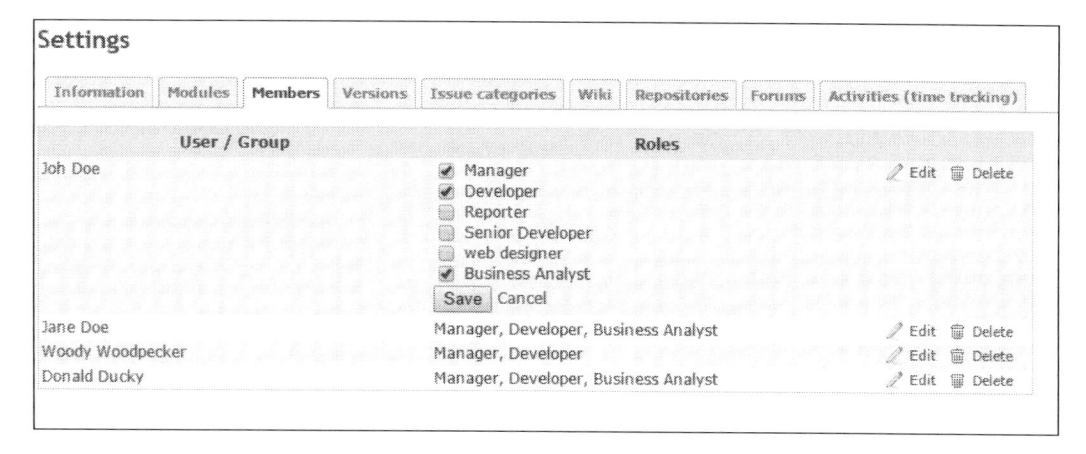

Settings								
Information	Modules	**Members**	Versions	Issue categories	Wiki	Repositories	Forums	Activities (time tracking)

User / Group	Roles		
Joh Doe	☑ Manager ☑ Developer ☐ Reporter ☐ Senior Developer ☐ web designer ☑ Business Analyst [Save] Cancel	✎ Edit	🗑 Delete
Jane Doe	Manager, Developer, Business Analyst	✎ Edit	🗑 Delete
Woody Woodpecker	Manager, Developer	✎ Edit	🗑 Delete
Donald Ducky	Manager, Developer, Business Analyst	✎ Edit	🗑 Delete

Deleting user accounts

This feature is also available, but it should not be used, unless you have created a user account by accident and there are no issues assigned to this user. Deleting accounts does not delete all references and tasks assigned to the user, but it creates trouble if you need to add the same user back to the system again. It is also managed by navigating to **Administration | Users**.

How it works...

Redmine has built-in roles and a permission system for user accounts, identities, and fine-grain per module, per-project control of privileges. This recipe utilizes built-in features to limit access or shift roles. In any case, you should plan your project's roles carefully and assign privileges to roles and roles to members, wisely.

There's more...

If you are using Active Directory or some other LDAP provider, then disabling or limiting access to Redmine is controlled through the external LDAP admin tool.

See also

- Refer to `https://www.redmine.org/plugins/redmine_ldap_sync` for information on advanced syncing of LDAP and Redmine.

Using metrics to improve team performance

Team performance may vary depending upon the nature of the project, team motivation, requirements, project management, methodology, or other factors. Project metrics are also dependent upon various factors. Out of the box, Redmine offers several metrics, which may be useful. Extended metrics can be achieved through plugins, third-party tools, or custom database queries. Improving team performance would require that you already have some performance record, then you analyze it, find bottlenecks, and work on methods to improve this record.

Getting ready

You will need Redmine to be used in production for a while to gain some data so you can use metrics. This period may vary depending upon the frequency of use of your Redmine installation.

How to do it...

Built-in metrics are available for several Redmine features. Metrics can help you identify problems, bottlenecks, or ineffective personnel.

Project issue metrics

Project issue metrics are available on the summary page of that particular project. It displays real-time data, and it reflects your customizations of Redmine's trackers, priority, versions, and categories. So if you have modified issue priorities, or you renamed or added different trackers, they will be visible on this summary page. To access it, click **Issues**, then **Summary** in the right sidebar:

Reports

Tracker

	open	closed	Total
Bug	5	-	5
Feature	73	3	76
Support	-	-	-
Section	-	-	-
task	3	-	3

Version

	open	closed	Total
Phase 1 - initial launch	-	-	-
Phase 2 - good to have features	6	-	6

Category

No data to display

Priority

	open	closed	Total
Immediate	-	-	-
Urgent	-	-	-
High	-	-	-
Normal	81	3	84
Low	-	-	-

Version metrics

Version metrics is only available if milestones are defined, as explained at the beginning of *Chapter 3, Project Management with Redmine,* in the recipe, *Splitting your project into phases.* To access these metrics, perform the following:

1. Click **Roadmap** in the project's main menu.
2. Click the particular version's name.
3. View the statistics that are displayed as follows:

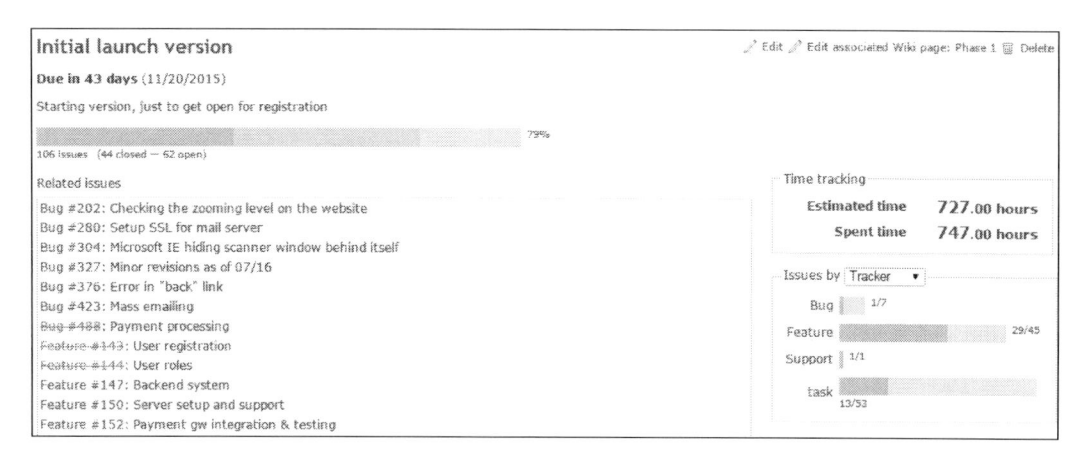

```
Initial launch version                                              Edit   Edit associated Wiki page: Phase 1   Delete
Due in 43 days (11/20/2015)
Starting version, just to get open for registration
                                                       79%
106 issues  (44 closed — 62 open)
Related issues                                             Time tracking
Bug #202: Checking the zooming level on the website          Estimated time    727.00 hours
Bug #280: Setup SSL for mail server                             Spent time     747.00 hours
Bug #304: Microsoft IE hiding scanner window behind itself
Bug #327: Minor revisions as of 07/16                      Issues by  Tracker  ▼
Bug #376: Error in "back" link
Bug #423: Mass emailing                                         Bug    1/7
Bug #488: Payment processing                                   Feature                29/45
Feature #143: User registration                                Support   1/1
Feature #144: User roles
Feature #147: Backend system                                     task
Feature #150: Server setup and support                                   13/53
Feature #152: Payment gw integration & testing
```

In the preceding image, we can clearly see that "Initial launch version" is due in 43 days, but it will most likely greatly exceed the estimated hours because it is already 20 hours more than planned, and it is still many days and many tasks away from completion. Early identification of such problems may mean the difference between success and failure. Another error that we see in the image is that tasks such as **Setup SSL for mail server** are categorized as **Bug** instead of **Task**, and **Mass e-mailing** is a feature, instead of a **Bug**.

User metrics

User metrics are available when the user profile is clicked through any of multiple entry points. This can help you quickly identify your user's activity in the system.

Time metrics

Time metric features also have multiple entry points. They are explained in more detail in the *Creating reports on spent time* recipe in *Chapter 3, Project Management with Redmine.* Time metrics are probably done with the most detailed approach as compared to other statistics and metrics featured in the default Redmine instance.

Improving Team Performance

How it works...

Redmine comes with several real-time statistics and metrics that are related to issues, projects, versions, and spent time. This recipe utilizes built-in statistics and, additionally, explains how to get advanced and custom statistics in its *There's more...* section. As Redmine is a Ruby on Rails **MVC (Model-View-Controller)** database-based web application, it stores various relational data with multiple attributes assigned to it. If you cannot find adequate statistics required for your particular problem, you can always connect directly to the database and create the required report, or create your own plugin, which will suit your needs.

There's more...

Plugins such as `https://www.redmine.org/plugins/redmine_stats` can provide valuable dashboards, which display a nice overview with charts. To add this plugin, perform the following:

1. Navigate to your Redmine installation root.
2. Download and extract or `git-clone` it to the plugins directory of your Redmine:

   `git clone https://github.com/luisfontes19/redmine_stats.git plugins/redmine_stats.`

3. Restart Redmine, as follows:

   `rm tmp/restart.txt && touch tmp/restart.txt.`

4. Give permissions to roles so that your users can see and use it by navigating to **Administrator | Roles & Permissions**.
5. Choose the role that you want to give permissions, and in the Project group tick the **Access statistics** checkbox.

If the installation is successful, you will notice the **Statistics** link in the main Redmine menu at the top:

Chapter 4

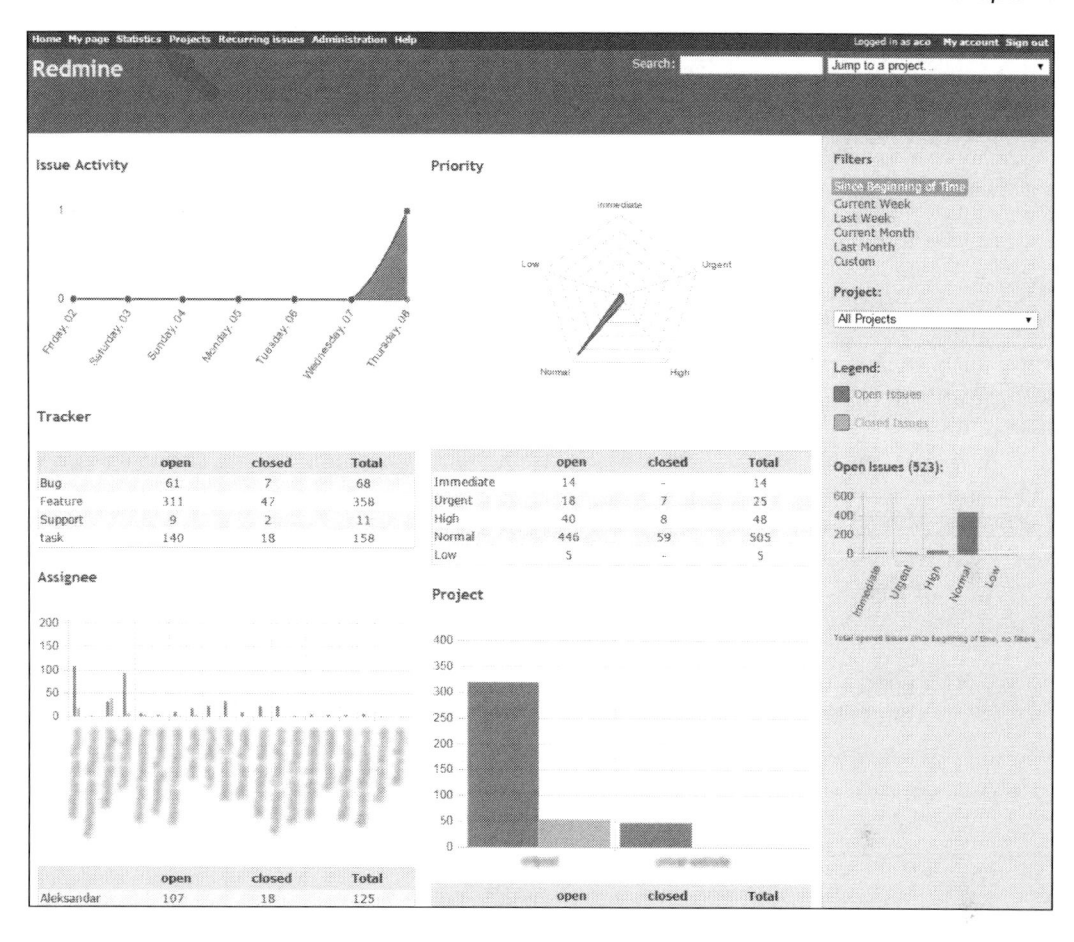

As mentioned earlier, Redmine is a database-oriented application. It is possible to use thirdparty tools to create specific reports. There are even programs that are specifically built for these purposes, such as `http://redminereports.codeplex.com/`.

See also

- Refer to the *Creating reports on spent time* recipe from *Chapter 3, Project Management with Redmine*.
- To see an excessive list of project-related statistics visit the **Center for Business Practices** (**CBP**) and download Measures of Project Management Performance and Value at `http://www.pmsolutions.com/audio/PM_Performance_and_Value_List_of_Measures.pdf`.

Improving Team Performance

Analyzing team performance through the code repository

Unfortunately, version control systems are not very widely used outside of the software development business despite the fact that today most version control systems handle binary files with ease. Also, internet speeds and storages easily handle large files. Therefore, this recipe focuses on the team performance analysis through the code repository, but it can be applied to any VCS supported by Redmine or visualization software.

This recipe assumes that you have an in-house development team working permanently on one software development project long-term. In this case, team performance analysis through the code repository can help you identify whether some team members are working less than others, or a situation where the development team is not getting enough tasks from the management team, and so on. Someone may argue that you can't have exact measurements because some tasks are more complex than others, team members have different jobs, and so on. But, as a manager, you are supposed to know and be able to understand why the code statistic is looking like that and also be able to gain valuable information from VCS statistics, which can help you organize the team better, take the load off some members, and so on.

Getting ready

You need to have a project with VCS used for several months. The repository module needs to be turned on and the repository added for a particular project that you are reviewing. To learn how to do it, check out the *Getting ready* section of the *Using the issue-code relationship* recipe from *Chapter 3, Project Management with Redmine*.

How to do it...

To view a graphical representation of your project's repository, perform the following steps:

1. Click the **Repository** tab in the project's main menu.
2. Click the statistics icon just under the **Repository** item in the main project menu that is outlined as follows:

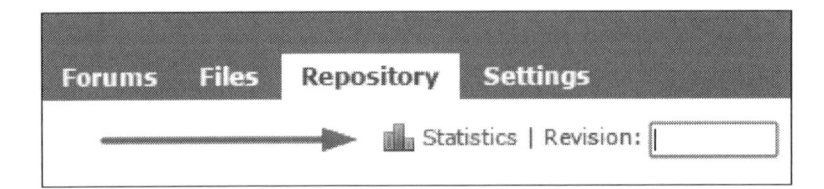

Chapter 4

3. Once clicked, you will get a diagram like below:

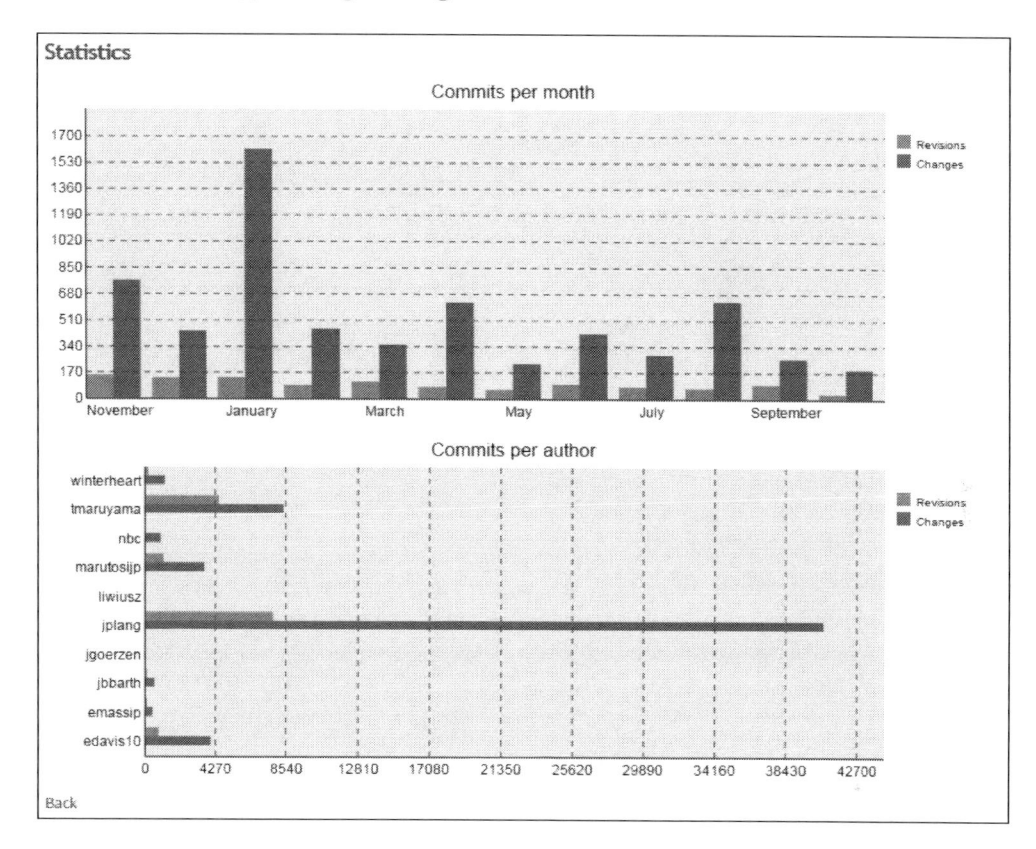

[Statistics chart showing "Commits per month" bar graph with months from November to September on horizontal axis and values from 0 to 1700 on vertical axis, and "Commits per author" bar graph listing authors: winterheart, tmaruyama, nbc, marutosijp, liwiusz, jplang, jgoerzen, jbbarth, emassip, edavis10, with values from 0 to 42700. Legend shows Revisions and Changes.]

Back

4. The preceding image is a statistic from the official Redmine repository that is accessible through www.redmine.org. The top chart represents **Commits per month**. The horizontal axis represents the months of current year, and the vertical axis represents a number of changed or added files. **Revisions** is a count of repository commits and is displayed in reddish orange. **Changes** is a count of the number of files that have changed overall and is displayed in blue.

> Statistic charts display statistics one year behind, starting from the current month.

Improving Team Performance

The bottom chart displays a number of **Changes** and **Revisions** made by each committer. In the preceding charts from the official Redmine repository, we can see that the month with the most changes was **January**, and most code revisions were done in **November**. In the bottom chart, we can see that member **jgoerzen** has very little commits. To improve team performance, it is not wise for important projects to rely only on one person. There should not be only one blue or red line sticking out too much because it means that one user does the most changes or revisions in the project. And when that user leaves the project from some reason, it will impact the project very much.

How it works...

Redmine comes with a Repository module, which offers basic statistics that are independent of the version control system. This means that repository statistics display the same type of charts regardless of baseline VCS that you use as Redmine provides the common drivers for several supported version control systems. These graphs are generated in SVG format, which may not display on older browsers, such as IE 8, or older.

There's more...

If you are not satisfied with the basic overview level charts that Redmine offers, you can try some of the third-party repository analyzing tools. The following is a result produced from the SvnStat tool, which produces a graphical representation of the SVN repository statistics. In the following table, we can see that this code repository is pretty well balanced among three developers, which can mean that tasks were equally balanced:

Author ID	Changes	Lines of Code	Lines per Change
Totals	8499 (100.0%)	1707766 (100.0%)	200.9
John	2316 (27.3%)	596763 (34.9%)	257.6
Alex	3138 (36.9%)	537343 (31.5%)	171.2
Suzy	2446 (28.8%)	460779 (27.0%)	188.3
Marina	537 (6.3%)	105103 (6.2%)	195.7
Root	26 (0.3%)	4261 (0.2%)	163.8
Sandy	28 (0.3%)	3207 (0.2%)	114.5
Unknown	8 (0.1%)	310 (0.0%)	38.7

This table was produced with the statsvn software, which is a statistical tool that is used to extract data from the subversion repository and present it in a statistical, tabular, or graphical way. Also, the following chart is produced with a similar tool, called svnstat. The top chart represents the number of commits that is spread across a 24-hour day, statistically. In the following image, we can see that the developer *Misa* is mostly active at 23:00 and 00:00, which means that we can schedule assigning tasks to this developer for a later phase in a day, or we can plan for them to continue working on some features that someone else will stop working on at 17:00 hours, for example. By analyzing such graphs, you can discover valuable information, which can help you organize your team more efficiently and, for example, deliver new features to customers in the shortest time possible:

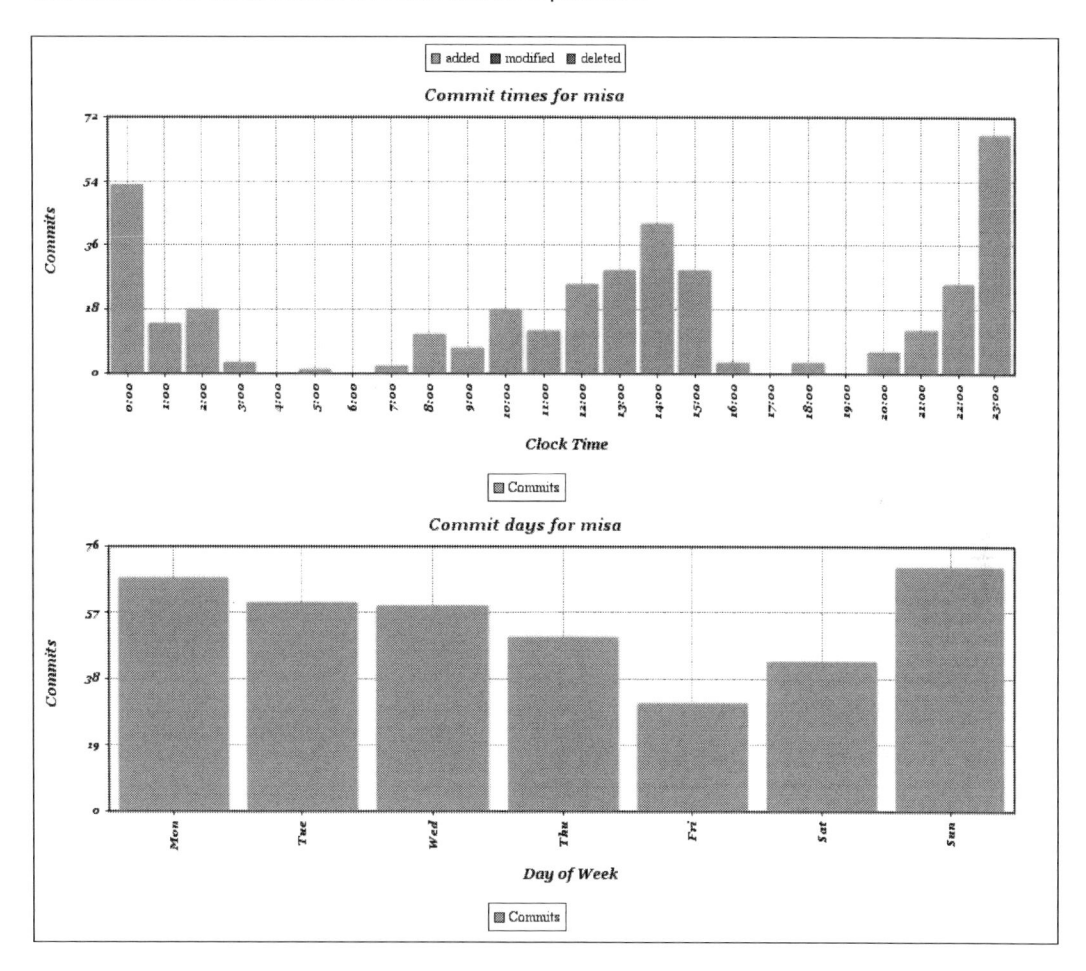

The bottom chart in the preceding image displays the frequency of commits on a weekday basis. Judging from the preceding image, you can come to the conclusion that you can assign more tasks to developer Misa on Friday as it's most likely that they will be working on them over the weekend because Sunday is their most active day.

Improving Team Performance

> Please keep in mind that every major repository management can provide statistics, and try to find the right third-party tool to help you visualize data.

See also

- You can download SvnStat from SourceForge at `http://svnstat.sourceforge.net`, and you can download StatSvn from `http://www.statsvn.org/`. More information about these particular examples can be found on the author's website under the **Blog** section at `www.redminecookbook.com/blog`

Using the repository module to display code differences

When doing software development projects, software code is an invaluable asset. Many teams prefer performing various kinds of code reviews. Redmine lets you share links with differences between source code among two commit versions with your team as simple as copying and pasting a URL where everyone can see the code. Luckily, these code review features are a built-in part of the repository module.

Getting ready

The repository module needs to be turned on and the repository added for a particular project you are going to view the code for. To learn how to do this, refer to the *Getting ready* part of the *Using the issue-code relationship* recipe from *Chapter 3, Project Management with Redmine*.

How to do it...

To see code, revision, differences, or which files were changed in particular code revision, use the following steps:

1. Navigate to the project that has a repository module turned on and the repository properly configured.

Chapter 4

2. Click the **Repository** tab, and you will get a view that looks similar to the following image:

Name	Size	Revision	Age	Author
branches		916	4 days	Aleksandar Pavic
tags		1	7 months	Aleksandar Pavic
trunk		915	4 days	dule

Latest revisions

#			Date	Author		Comment
916	●		10/09/2015 03:14 PM	Aleksandar Pavic	refs #717 - production update	
915		●	10/09/2015 03:13 PM	dule	refs #750	
914			10/09/2015 02:44 PM	Aleksandar Pavic	refs #717 - production update Lani's requests	
913			10/09/2015 01:42 PM	dule	refs #750	
912			10/09/2015 01:12 PM	dule	refs #750	
911			10/08/2015 03:10 PM	dule	refs #749	
910			10/08/2015 02:57 PM	dule	refs #749	
909			10/08/2015 02:56 PM	dule	refs #749	
908			10/08/2015 02:55 PM	dule	refs #749	
907			10/08/2015 02:55 PM	dule	refs #749	

[View differences]

View all revisions

On the upper part of image, you can see a structure of your repository; in this case, it is branches, tags, and trunk. On the lower part of the image is a list of the 10 most recent code revisions. If you need to see more revisions, click **View all revisions** that is below the **View differences** button.

Viewing the differences between two repository revisions or revisions per folder

To view code and file differences between two revisions of the whole repository or one of its sections, choose the revisions that you wish to compare by selecting the radio button next to the revision number. In the previous image, you can see two rows of radio buttons next to each other. You will notice that clicking the left button will automatically position the right radio button, one revision before the revision that you selected. In the previous image, revisions 916 and 915 are selected for comparison. Once you tick the radio buttons for the revisions that you want to compare just click **View differences**.

Improving Team Performance

To view the code differences of a particular folder

Use the following steps to view the code differences of a particular folder:

1. Navigate to this folder on a tree-like document browser. To expand folders, click the **+** sign next to the folder icon:

Name	Size	Revision	Age	Author	Comment
branches		916	4 days	Aleksandar Pavic	refs #717 - production update
tags		1	7 months	Aleksandar Pavic	Basic directory structure
trunk		915	4 days	dule	refs #750
code		915	4 days	dule	refs #750
app		915	4 days	dule	refs #750
Config		830	24 days	Aleksandar Pavic	refs #717 fixes
Console		99	6 months	misa	refs #610
Controller		913	4 days	dule	refs #750

2. Once you find the folder that needs to be compared with some previous revision, click this folder's name on the right-hand side of the folder icon. In this case, the `Controller` folder.
3. Scroll to the bottom of the page, select revisions, and click **View differences**.

Viewing differences between two versions of the same file

To view the code differences between two versions of the same file, perform the following steps:

1. Find the file in a file browser that you want to compare.
2. Click the file name.
3. Choose the left and right radio boxes next to the revision numbers.
4. Click the **View differences** button.

You will get the code differences displayed side by side, or in an inline view:

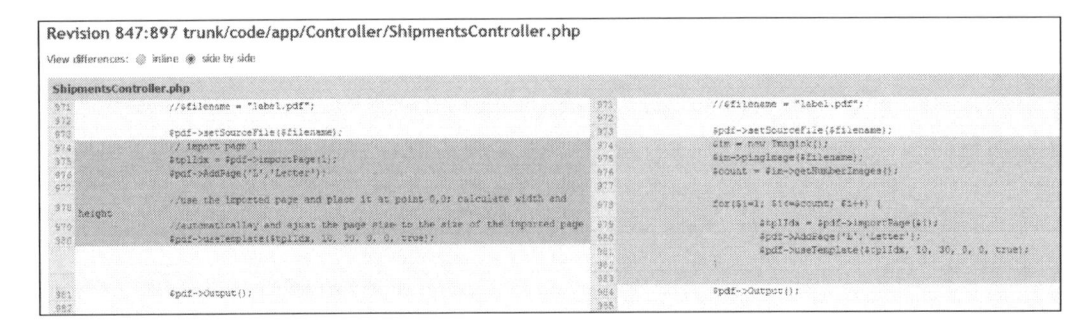

[116]

Chapter 4

On the left-hand side is a code that was in the `ShipmentsController.php` file in revision 847, and in green on the right-hand side is the code that is now in revision 897. Grey code is unchanged. The same coloring rules apply for inline differences.

How it works...

The repository module comes with useful features for file and folder revision comparisons. These features are working very well and provide a unified user interface and experience across different version control management systems, so it's more likely that you are going to use such features through Redmine, than through the specialized GUI of your VCS tool.

There's more...

While comparing the code, please note the URL of the comparison in the address bar of your browser. It will look somewhat like this: `http://redmine.mycompany.com/projects/website-backend/repository/diff/trunk/code/app/Controller/ShipmentsController.php?utf8=✓&rev=897&rev_to=847`.

Such URLs let us share the link through e-mail or chat messages, and other members can click on it and view the code differences.

Another feature that you may find useful is unified diff export of changes. Unified diff export is available at the bottom right of the compare page. Once you click the **View differences** button, it will become available. Clicking it will download the diff file to your computer, which you can later view with a text editor or other specialized software, such as Tortoise diff in the following image:

117

Improving Team Performance

See also

- Refer to the Wikipedia article on code review at `https://en.wikipedia.org/wiki/Code_review`
- If you are not satisfied with Redmine's built-in features, here is a list of specialized solutions for code review purposes that can be found at `https://en.wikipedia.org/wiki/List_of_tools_for_code_review`

Managing multicultural teams in different time zones

In the twenty first century, multicultural teams in different time zones working on the same project are common practice. This is due to the growth of outsourcing, especially if teams are working on a software product that needs to conquer the global marketplace, or you want to boost productivity by having someone working on the project 24/7.

How to do it...

Multicultural and different time zone teams can have various differences, such as work preference, language, different work approach practices, and so on. Redmine can help boost the productivity of international teams in different ways. One good practice would be to create a document with rules and instructions on what the project collaboration process should look like. Also, make sure that everyone is informed of such a document and follows the rules explained there.

Work organization

If you have a large team with international offices, then you may want to break the project into subprojects or organize the team per location-based groups. If you are organizing teams in location-based groups, such as a London office, the London office may have its project manager or team-leader role who will perform the micromanagement and further assignment of a task.

> Establish rules, such as *common language, workflows, coding standards, corporate document branding standards,* and so on.

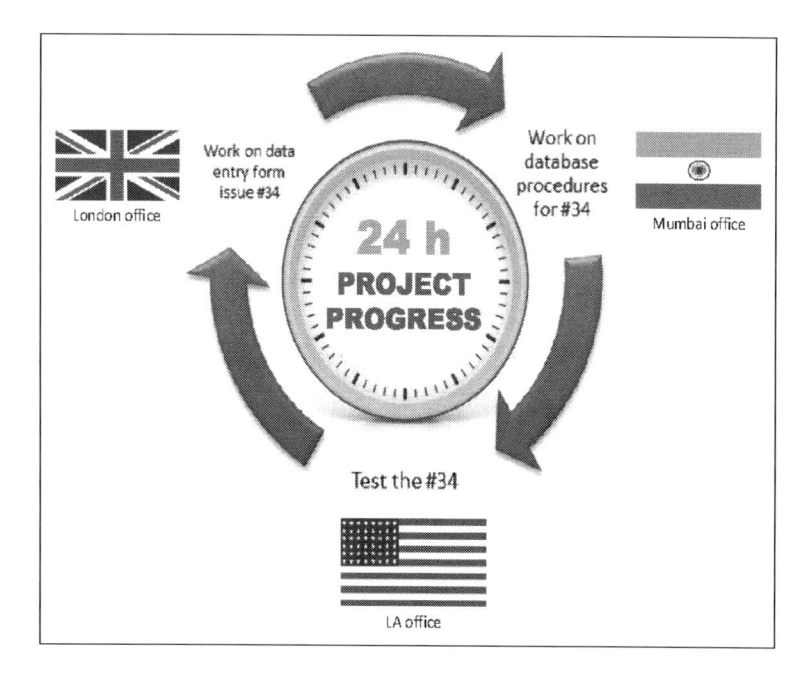

The preceding image illustrates a possible scenario of having three different teams working on a Redmine ticket 34. For detailed instructions on how to work with groups, refer to the *Creating and using user groups* recipe from *Chapter 2, Customizing Redmine*.

Setting up Redmine multilanguage and time zone features

Every user can choose their **Time zone** and **Language** settings on the **My account** page:

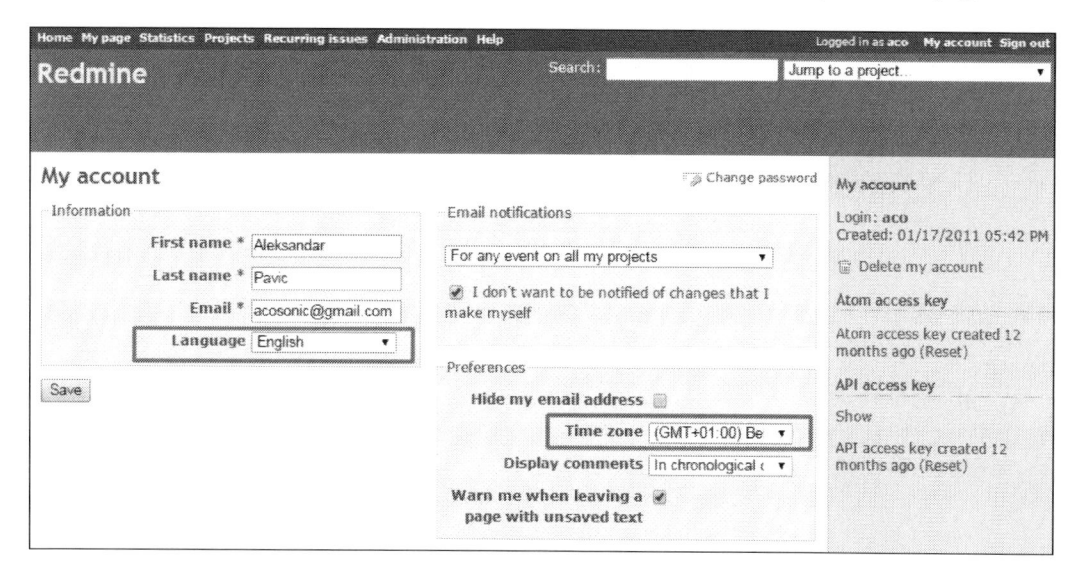

Improving Team Performance

Choosing the language will change the user interface language for that user for all pages, but sometimes plugins will stay in English because they might not be translated to the user's language.

How it works...

This recipe utilizes built-in Redmine features to boost the productivity of an international team by providing guidelines on which rules to set, and how to configure Redmine to help multilanguage teams in different time zones collaborate. Managing multicultural dislocated teams would require more strict Redmine usage routines because not updating an issue status can cause an unwanted delay on project delivery, or it can cause a possible team idle timeout due to the fact that one team may need to wait a whole day before they get a response from the dislocated team about the status of the task, which might have been done.

There's more...

If your project is software development-related, another good practice is to have a document called *Coding guidelines* explaining what the code should look like (naming conventions, braces, and so on). To make sure coding guidelines are followed, you can use some syntax or other types of code checkers, such as PHPMD, Java's PMD, or some software as a code repository pre-commit hook. So, if a submitted code does not follow the predefined set of rules, the version control system will prevent this code from being committed until the rules are satisfied. This way you will prevent multiple teams or team members from uploading poorly-formatted code, which will increase the level of collaboration and save the time required to maintain the code in the future.

See also

- Java PMD (https://pmd.github.io/) and PHP mess detector (http://phpmd.org/) both can be used as pre-commit hooks. Also refer to the next recipe, *Applying advanced issue-code relationships*, where you can see some brief instructions on how to configure post-or pre-commit hooks.

Chapter 4

Applying advanced issue-code relationships

To apply and use an advanced issue-code relationship, as explained in the *Using the issue-code relation* recipe from *Chapter 3, Project Management with Redmine*, Redmine needs to be configured to fetch changes automatically, and it requires to be triggered in some way. By default, it is done by the user clicking the repository tab. But this way, we can have significant idle time, even days or weeks, before somebody clicks on the repository tab and have Redmine automatically fetch commits, update statuses, and send e-mails, which will invoke other users to start developing their code per task, or testing it. Such a scenario is possible if you are not on a tight schedule or running some methodology, which involves clicking the repository tab on your project's main menu several times per day.

Getting ready

You will require administration privileges and access to your source control management's tool working directory. You will also probably require a root or administrator privilege for a server where the SCM tool is located.

How to do it...

Fetching changes automatically can be done in two ways. One way is to configure source control management's action once the SCM server accepts the code, and the other way is to configure cron or a scheduled task to do the same. These two concepts are called client push or server pull, respectively. Configuring SVN's post-commit hook or git's post-receive hook depends upon the operating system and SCM software. Configuring scripts for SVN or git requires the same actions:

1. Configure Redmine to accept incoming repository update requests by enabling the checkbox near **Enable WS for repository management**, which can be located by navigating to **Administration | Settings | Repositories**:

Improving Team Performance

2. Create the post-commit (SVN) or post-receive (git) files; they are usually located in subdirectory or hooks from your project's SCM working directory.

3. Give 755 permission so that everyone can read and execute this file because the script may be invoked from a different user depending upon server settings.

4. Edit the content of that file by typing the following for SVN repositories:

   nano post-commit

   You can type the following for git repositories:

   nano post-receive

5. Obtain the API key from *Step 1*, paste the following content and replace `<redmine url>` and `<API key>` with values according to your setup:

   ```
   #!/bin/sh
   wget http://<redmine url>/sys/fetch_changesets?key=<API key>
   ```

   > The preceding way works well with SVN, and GIT repositories. For GitHub repositories, you need to use the following plugin:
   > `https://github.com/koppen/redmine_github_hook`

6. Save the file with *CTRL+S*.

7. Commit some code and reference some issue ID, as explained in the *Using the issue-code relation* recipe from *Chapter 3, Project Management with Redmine*. So, your commit message should look somewhat like this: **Testing scm post-commit hook, refs #33**.

Open the issue 33 in your redmine installation, but make sure that you or somebody else didn't click the repository tab prior to you opening the issue. If your post-commit script did the job, you should see the new revision under the **Associated revisions** section on the issue page:

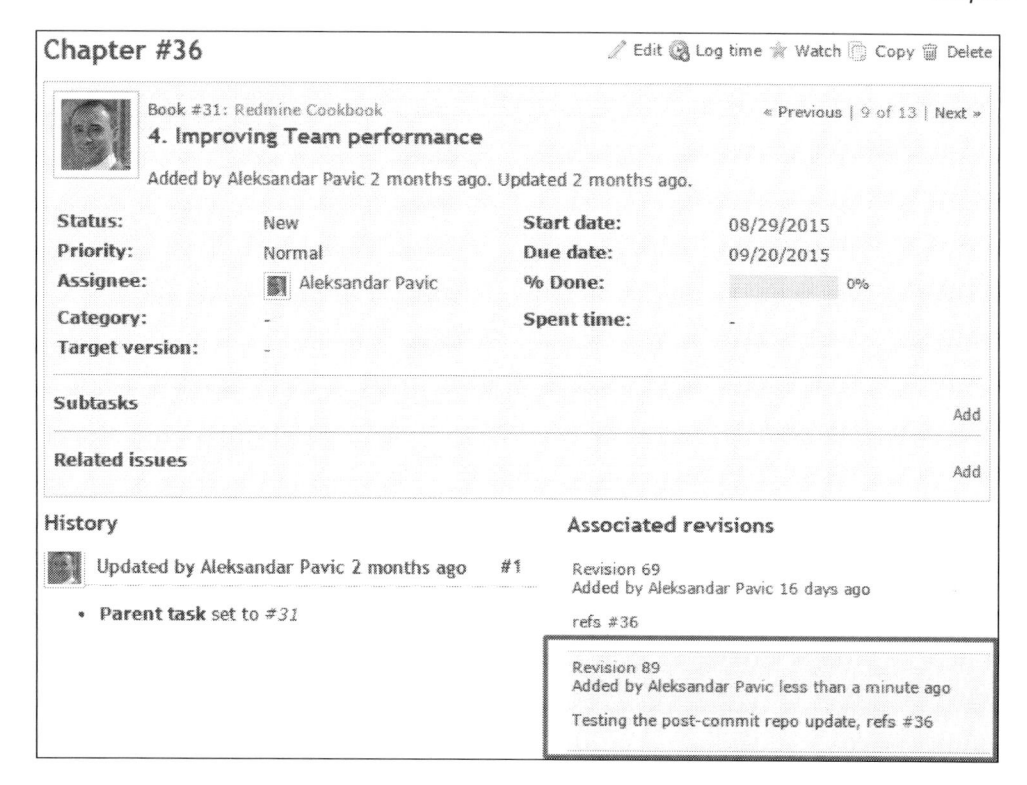

There's more...

The previously explained method is performing an update by utilizing server push, which may present a problem if there is a large frequency of commits, or if for some reason you can't edit repository postcode acceptance scripts, or if they do not work. In such cases, you can configure the client pull method by utilizing Unix's cron job, or Window's scheduled tasks. To create a cron job, perform the following steps:

1. Log in to your server as a user under which Redmine is running.
2. Navigate to the extra folder of your Redmine implementation.

Improving Team Performance

3. Create a new file called `update_repo.sh` by typing the following:

   `nano update_repo.sh`

4. Paste the following content to the `update_repo.sh` file and replace `/your Redmine` dir with the proper path, as follows:

   `#!/bin/bash`

   `#`

   `cd /your redmine dir`

   `ruby script/runner "Repository.fetch_changesets" -e production`

5. Create a cron job that will run every X number of minutes between repository update by typing the following:

   `crontab -e`

6. Paste the following contents, replace X with the desired number of minutes, and use the full path to your `update_repo.sh` script:

   `*/X * * * * /some path/extra/update_repo.sh`

Client push and server pull can also be used to notify team members on the IRC channel or Slack chat.

See also

- Refer to the *Interacting with Redmine only through e-mail* recipe from *Chapter 2, Customizing Redmine*, for instructions on how to configure and use Windows task scheduler for rake tasks. The same instructions apply for *client pull* from the *There's more* section of this recipe if you are using a Windows platform. Client pull and server push methodologies are explained at https://en.wikipedia.org/wiki/Push_technology and https://en.wikipedia.org/wiki/Pull_technology.

- The Redmine official how to on server push can be found at http://www.redmine.org/projects/redmine/wiki/HowTo_setup_automatic_refresh_of_repositories_in_Redmine_on_commit.

- For a slack plugin, visit https://www.redmine.org/plugins/redmine-slack.

Chapter 4

Improving Scrum meetings and backlogs

Scrum has been mentioned in this book in several recipes. This recipe is focused primarily on customizing Redmine to optimize the Scrum development process as much as possible.

How to do it...

The first part of this recipe is focused on meetings, and the second part to backlogs.

Saving time required to prepare for Scrum meetings

Redmine can improve Scrum meetings by helping the team be better organized prior to a Scrum meeting where every team member is intended to answer to following questions asked by the Scrum master:

- What did you accomplish yesterday?
- What will you do today?
- What obstacles are impeding your progress?

Team members can speed up their preparation by using custom issue filtering queries saved for their accounts. To see which issues you worked on yesterday, perform the following steps:

1. Click **Issues** in the project's main menu.
2. From status dropdown, choose **Any**.
3. On right-hand side from the **Add filter** dropdown, choose **Updated**.
4. From the **Updated** dropdown, choose **yesterday**.
5. On right-hand side from **Add filter**, choose **Assignee**.
6. On the **Assignee** dropdown, choose **is <<me>>**:

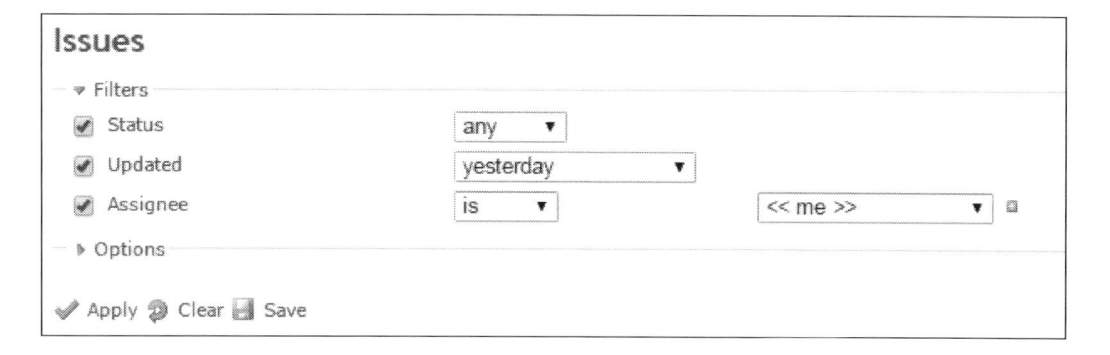

Issues			
▼ Filters			
☑ Status	any ▼		
☑ Updated	yesterday ▼		
☑ Assignee	is ▼	<< me >> ▼	
▶ Options			
✓ Apply ⟳ Clear 💾 Save			

125

Improving Team Performance

7. Click the **Save** button with floppy drive icon, a new query form will appear.
8. Fill the form, for example, the name can be **Scrum - done yesterday by me** like in the following image, **Visibility** is set to **any user**, and tick the **For all projects** checkbox. You can set up the **Sort** criteria according to your specific needs:

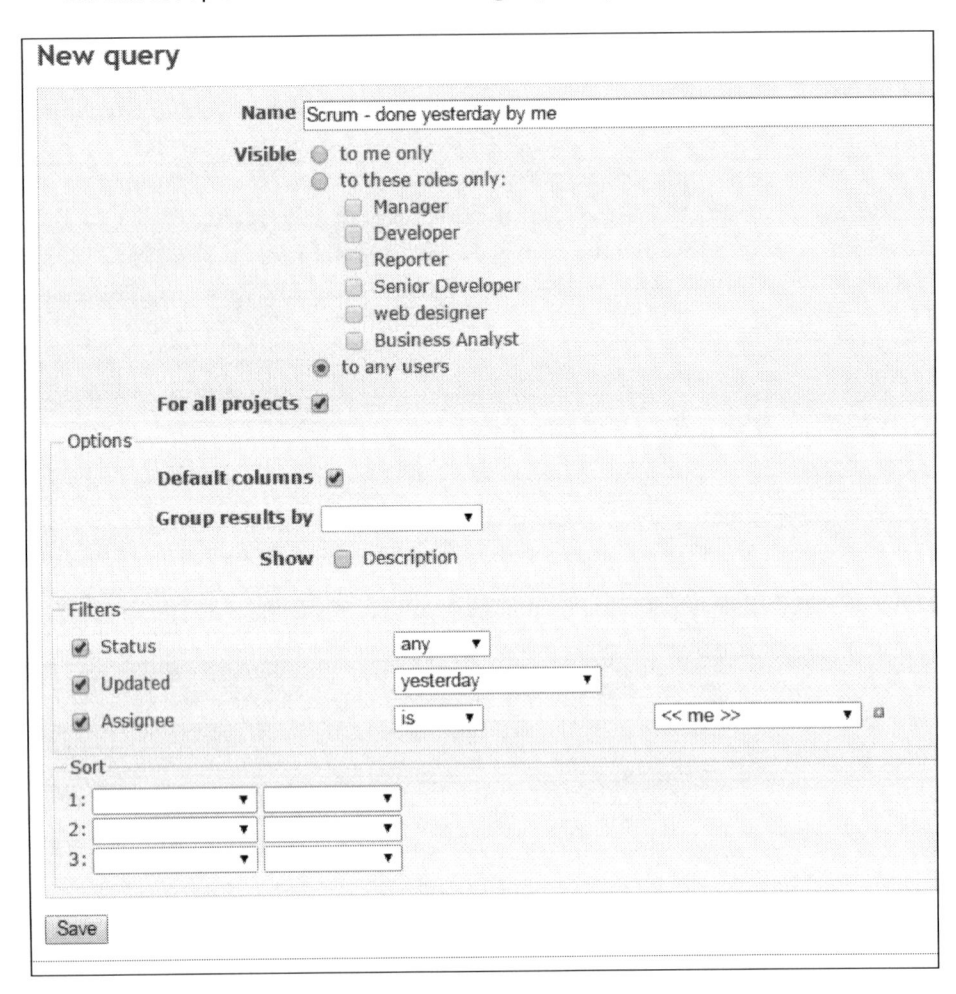

New query

Name Scrum - done yesterday by me

Visible
- to me only
- to these roles only:
  - Manager
  - Developer
  - Reporter
  - Senior Developer
  - web designer
  - Business Analyst
- ● to any users

For all projects ✓

Options
Default columns ✓
Group results by [▼]
Show ☐ Description

Filters
- ✓ Status — any ▼
- ✓ Updated — yesterday ▼
- ✓ Assignee — is ▼ — << me >> ▼

Sort
1: [▼] [▼]
2: [▼] [▼]
3: [▼] [▼]

[Save]

9. Click the **Save** button, and a new query will be visible to all users in the right sidebar.

Chapter 4

> What did you accomplish yesterday may create a problem for multi time zone teams. If one team is finishing their workday, and another team is starting, and you want to have them all on the same meeting, then they need to say what they did during the current day, and adjust their saved search accordingly by choosing **less than a day ago** from the **Updated** dropdown.

10. While team-members are answering questions, and choosing what they will work on today or tomorrow, they can use `roadmap/versions` Redmine's feature.

Improving backlogs and the overall Scrum process

In the recipe *Defining a roadmap to the release plan* in *Chapter 3, Project Management with Redmine*, we already covered one way to implement the backlogs concept to Redmine. Further improvement of the backlogs Scrum concept means installation and usage of plugins. There are several plugins but mostly poorly maintained. It is not good practice to start your Redmine implementation with an older version of Redmine simply because some plugin is not updated to support the newer version of Redmine. For this reason, a plugin simply called "Scrum" is recommended. It is actively maintained, well-documented, and can be downloaded from `https://redmine.ociotec.com/projects/redmine-plugin-scrum`.

To start using this plugin perform the following steps:

1. Follow the installation tutorial from the plugin's wiki page.
2. Once installed, restart Redmine (refer to the *Starting and restarting Redmine* recipe from *Chapter 5, Regular and Planned Maintenance*).
3. Configure this plugin simply by following the instructions from your Redmine sidebar:

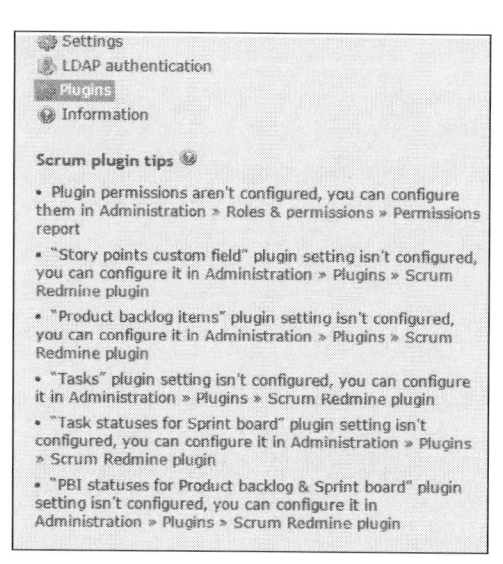

```
Settings
LDAP authentication
Plugins
Information

Scrum plugin tips

• Plugin permissions aren't configured, you can configure
  them in Administration » Roles & permissions » Permissions
  report
• "Story points custom field" plugin setting isn't configured,
  you can configure it in Administration » Plugins » Scrum
  Redmine plugin
• "Product backlog items" plugin setting isn't configured,
  you can configure it in Administration » Plugins » Scrum
  Redmine plugin
• "Tasks" plugin setting isn't configured, you can configure
  it in Administration » Plugins » Scrum Redmine plugin
• "Task statuses for Sprint board" plugin setting isn't
  configured, you can configure it in Administration » Plugins
  » Scrum Redmine plugin
• "PBI statuses for Product backlog & Sprint board" plugin
  setting isn't configured, you can configure it in
  Administration » Plugins » Scrum Redmine plugin
```

4. If you have some problems or need support, visit the *Forums* page on this plugin's URL that was provided earlier.

How it works...

The first part of this recipe utilizes built-in features from Redmine's issues module to create a saved search, which is used to help team members prepare for Scrum meetings. The second part of this recipe recommends usage of the *Scrum* plugin and explains the necessary steps to start using this plugin for more efficient Redmine usage in Scrum development methodology-related project.

There's more...

Redmine features issue relations, and one such issue relation is Blocks and Blocked by. These relations should be updated during Scrum meetings if such an event occurs. Having issue relations accurately organized can help minimize problems and maximize the chance of hitting the project's planned target release date, budget, and so on. Once the blocking issue is resolved, Redmine will update related issues automatically.

See also

- Refer to the Wikipedia article on Scrum at `https://en.wikipedia.org/wiki/Scrum_(software_development)`.

5
Regular and Planned Maintenance

This chapter targets the system administrator and focuses on tasks that are required to keep your Redmine installation healthy over an extended period of time:

- Starting and restarting Redmine
- Checking for active Redmine processes on the server
- Configuring backup and recovery
- Checking the data dirs for possible malware
- Migrating and upgrading
- Upgrading or migrating the database behind Redmine
- Enhancing security
- Upgrading Ruby safely

Introduction

In order to actively maintain production of your Redmine installation, you need to understand a few basic things, such as how the database is used, what are application and configuration files, where user submitted files are stored, and whether there are some third-party scripts or processes, such as cron jobs, running. These four know-hows are the most likely pillars of maintaining most web applications apart from knowing the ins and outs of underlying server platforms, operating systems, and the programming language or framework that the web application is built upon. This chapter provides several recipes aimed at making sure that your Redmine installation is updated and working properly.

Starting and restarting Redmine

Starting and restarting Redmine differs upon server and operating system configurations. In this recipe, we are going to cover a few of the most common configurations.

Getting ready

Make sure that you have server administration privileges.

How to do it...

As mentioned earlier, starting and restarting Redmine differs upon server configuration, so here are a few most common ways to restart Redmine.

Restarting Redmine under Phusion Passenger

To restart Redmine running under Phusion Passenger, perform the following actions:

1. Navigate to your Redmine installation folder.
2. Navigate to `app/tmp` folder.
3. Create an empty file called `restart.txt`.
4. Log in to your Redmine or refresh it.
5. Remove `restart.txt`.

Step 5 is not necessary because Phusion Passenger checks for the file's timestamp. If, for some reason, you want Redmine restarted after each request, then instead of `restart.txt`, create a file called `always_restart.txt`. However, always restarting will drastically decrease your server performance.

> If your Rails environment is set to development, then your Redmine will be restarted after each request.

Restarting Redmine on Puma

To restart Redmine running under Puma server, several options are available, either send the Puma process the `SIGUSR2` signal through a PID file or by process ID, To find your server's ID, perform the following actions:

1. Find the Puma process:

   `ps aux | grep puma`

2. Extract the PID (column 2) from the result from the parent Puma process (child processes have the parent's process PID listed at the end).

3. Send the `SIGUSR2` signal to gracefully restart Puma:

   `kill -s SIGUSR2 4242`

On Windows machines, this approach may be more preferred, due to its lack of a kill tool, so it can't send `SIGUSR2` to the process the same way like a Unix console:

1. Create a file under your Redmine's `config` folder.
2. Paste the following contents:

```
environment ENV['RAILS_ENV'] || 'production'
daemonize
workers    2 # should be same number of your CPU core
threads    1, 6
pidfile    "/var/run/puma_app1.pid" #on windows use different
folder path
```

To start Redmine with Puma, configured this way, type the following:

```
bundle exec pumactl -F config/puma.rb start
```

To restart Redmine gracefully, type the following:

```
bundle exec pumactl -F config/puma.rb phased-restart
```

To restart Redmine the hard way, type the following:

```
bundle exec pumactl -F config/puma.rb restart
```

Regular and Planned Maintenance

Restarting Redmine on another application server

Whether served under Windows or Linux operating systems, in this case, it may be impossible to restart Redmine without restarting the application server running it. Usually, this is done through a start-stop script or by killing the server's process.

How it works...

Usually, Redmine installations are hosted behind a proven and reliable web server, often hosting several websites or web applications on the same machine. Restarting the web server, usually Apache or IIS, won't do the trick. This is because Redmine runs on its own web or application server, which is proxied or called through the frontend web server:

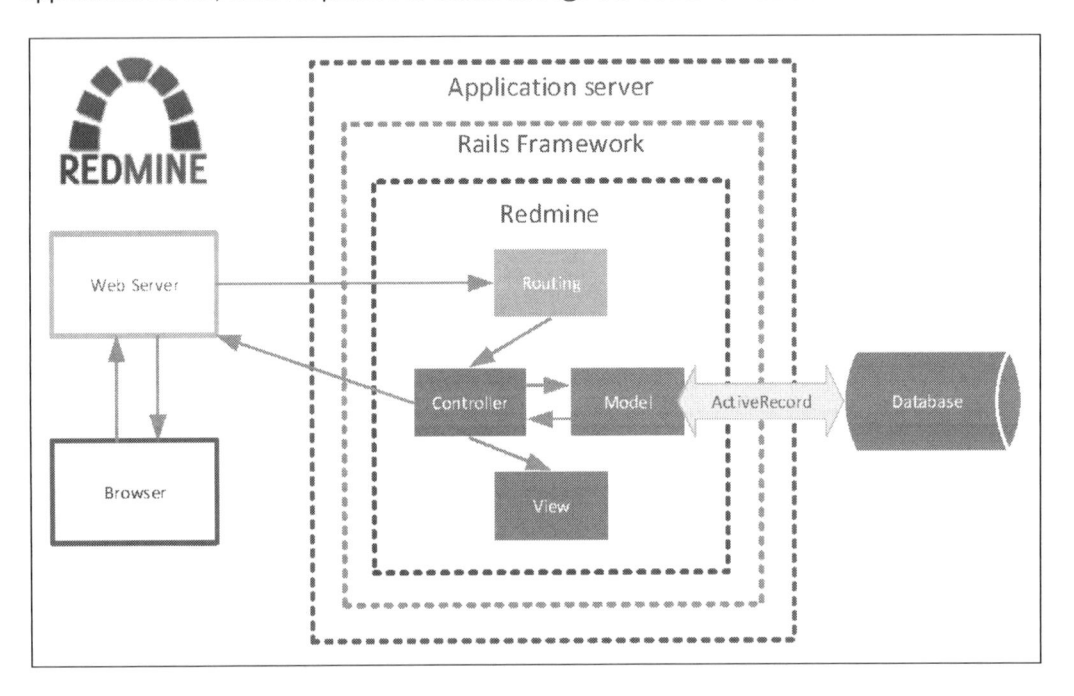

In the preceding image, you can see a logical overview of Redmine, running on the Rails framework on the application server, where **Web Server** and **Database** are displayed as separated entities.

There's more...

Rails applications such as Redmine can be deployed in multiple ways. The situation gets even more complicated when there are multiple servers deployed to perform different or, even worse, the same jobs. Multiple servers are required to be scaled. Most likely, you will not need to scale a Redmine system on more than two or three servers. The following image displays a possible layout of such a system on a virtual infrastructure:

Chapter 5

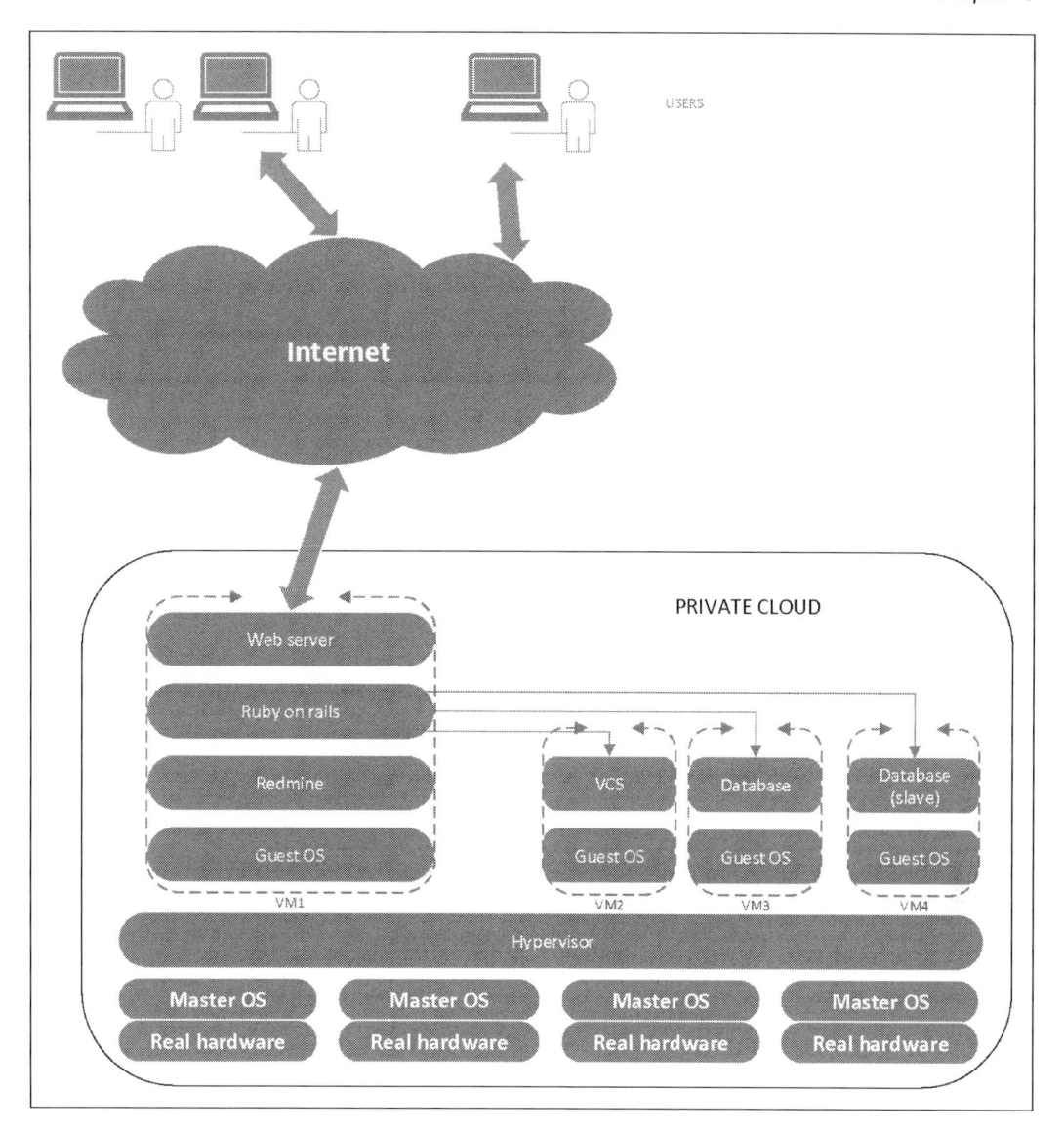

As you can see, multiple users are accessing the Web server that runs Redmine as a Ruby on Rails app where VCS is farmed out on a separate virtual machine (VM2), and Database is farmed out to two servers where one server is a slave. The whole system is running on a Hypervisor of a private cloud, which runs on multiple host computers. Such configurations usually offer additional services, such as backups, high availability, and disaster recovery.

Regular and Planned Maintenance

See also

- Refer to the Puma server guide at `https://github.com/puma/puma` and `http://ruby-journal.com/digesting-pumactl/`.
- Also refer to the Phusion Passenger guide at `https://www.phusionpassenger.com/ documentation_and_support/`.

Checking for active Redmine processes on the server

At the beginning of the Ruby programming language, the Rails framework and various servers that were capable of running web applications written in the Ruby on Rails framework had garbage and memory leaks. Back then, companies, such as Twitter and 37signals launched web applications that gained mainstream popularity and also popularized Ruby on Rails web development. However, ordinary developers did not have administrators that were experienced enough and had troubles dealing with memory leaks and server problems. So, applications were deployed with watchdogs restarting them after they hit a certain number of processes or consumed a certain amount of megabytes. Nowadays, it is less likely that such a situation will occur, but for whatever reasons, you may end up needing to inspect your server.

Getting ready

Make sure that you have server administration privileges; root privileges for Linux or Administrator privileges in the case of Microsoft Windows servers. For Microsoft Windows servers, you can download and install the Sysinternals process explorer from the following location: `https://technet.microsoft.com/en-us/sysinternals/processexplorer`.

How to do it...

Checking for active or zombie processes also differs upon platform and servers that you are using.

Checking the status of Phusion Passenger under Linux

As Phusion Passenger is the most widely-used deployment technique, here is how to check its status on Linux machines:

1. Log in to your server as a root.
2. Type the following command: `passenger-status`, and you will get a screen like this:

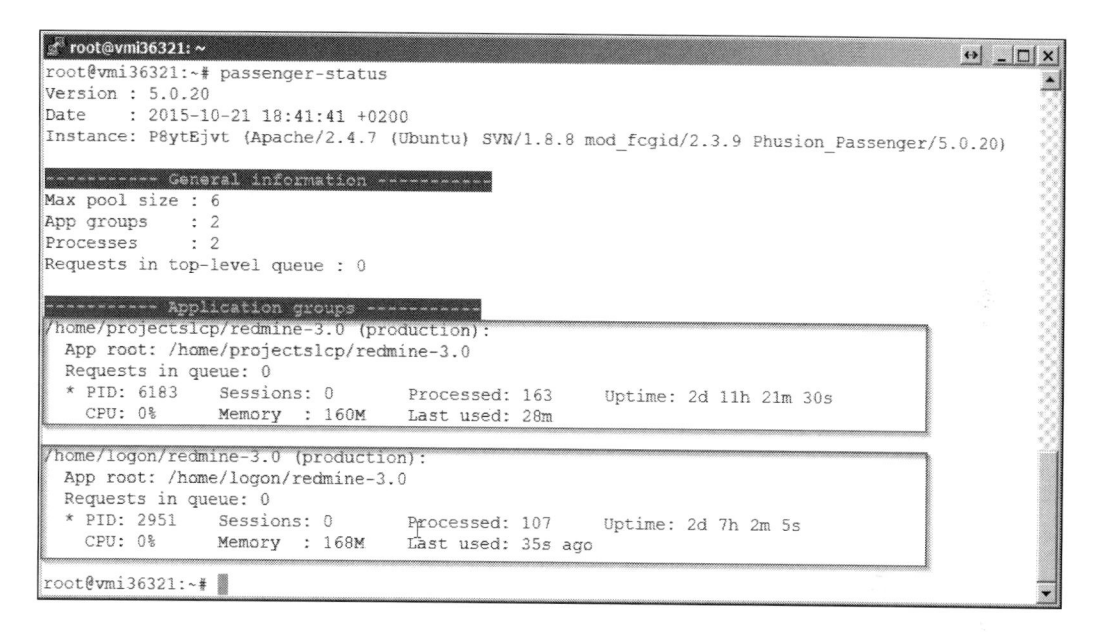

```
root@vmi36321:~# passenger-status
Version : 5.0.20
Date    : 2015-10-21 18:41:41 +0200
Instance: P8ytEjvt (Apache/2.4.7 (Ubuntu) SVN/1.8.8 mod_fcgid/2.3.9 Phusion_Passenger/5.0.20)

----------- General information -----------
Max pool size : 6
App groups    : 2
Processes     : 2
Requests in top-level queue : 0

----------- Application groups -----------
/home/projectslcp/redmine-3.0 (production):
  App root: /home/projectslcp/redmine-3.0
  Requests in queue: 0
  * PID: 6183    Sessions: 0      Processed: 163     Uptime: 2d 11h 21m 30s
    CPU: 0%      Memory  : 160M   Last used: 28m

/home/logon/redmine-3.0 (production):
  App root: /home/logon/redmine-3.0
  Requests in queue: 0
  * PID: 2951    Sessions: 0      Processed: 107     Uptime: 2d 7h 2m 5s
    CPU: 0%      Memory  : 168M   Last used: 35s ago
root@vmi36321:~#
```

The preceding screenshot shows regular passenger processes that are configured to stay in memory through the `PassengerMinInstances` value in Apache's virtual server.

> Setting the PassengerMinInstances value to at least 1 keeps Redmine preloaded in RAM, drastically increasing its performance on the first request if Redmine was not accessed for a while.

Regular and Planned Maintenance

Checking servers under Windows

On Microsoft Windows servers, you may want to inspect processes with more advanced tools, which will display details about each process, how much memory it consumes, and so on. In the following image, you can see the `sysInternals` process explorer:

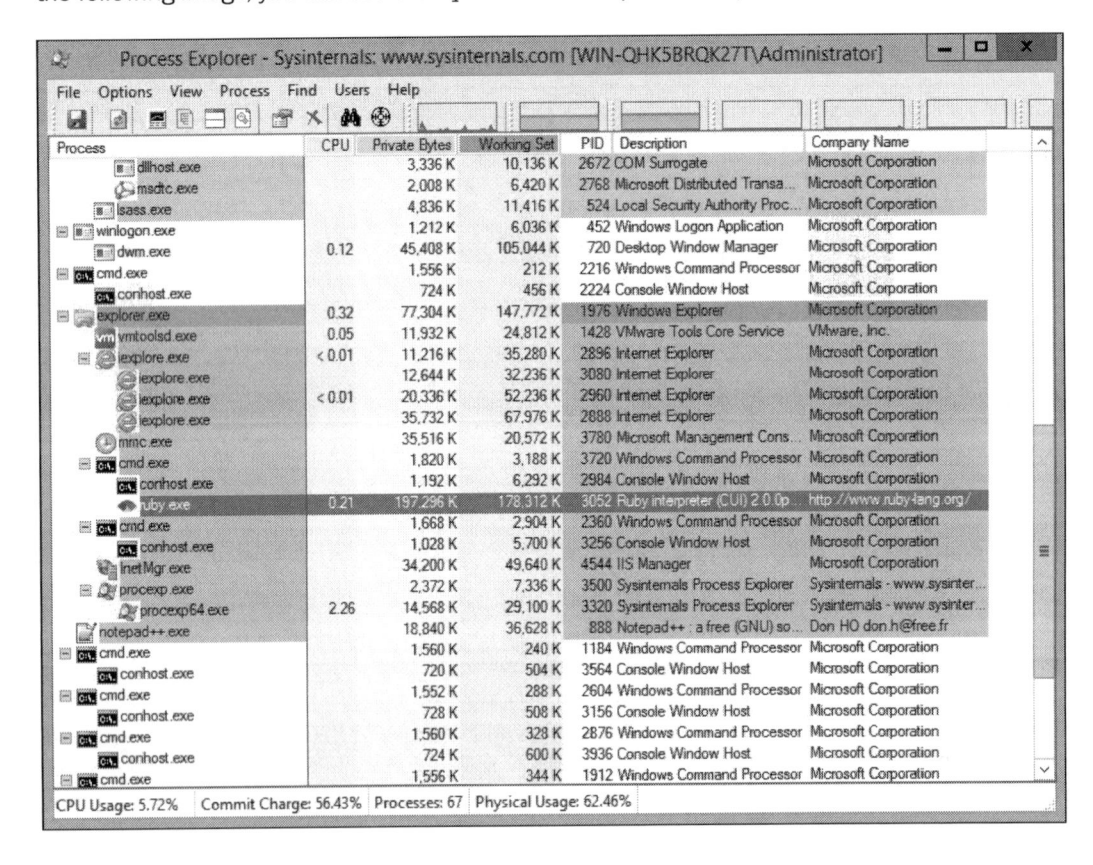

Ruby interpreter for Windows is consuming 197 MB of active RAM, which is pretty small for today's standards. This process is actually a Puma server running Redmine that is able to concurrently serve multiple requests.

How it works...

It takes some time from the user's request until the web server spawns processes of Redmine to handle the user's request. To decrease this timeout, it is common practice to configure the server to preallocate some threads so that our requests could be served faster. However, such an approach can consume memory with idle Redmine processes. Another reason why occasional inspection is required are zombie processes, which occur when a parent starts a child process and the child process ends but the parent doesn't pick up the child's exit code. The process object has to stay around until this happens. It consumes no resources and is dead, but it still exists—hence, *zombie*.

There's more...

On Linux machines, you can use more human readable and detailed commands, such as the following:

```
ps -eo size,pid,user,command --sort -size | awk '{ hr=$1/1024 ;
printf("%13.2f Mb ",hr) } { for ( x=4 ; x<=NF ; x++ ) { printf("%s
",$x) } print "" }'
```

This will display more detailed output like this:

```
root@vmi36321:~# ps -eo size,pid,user,command --sort -size | awk '{ hr=$1/1024 ; print
 x=4 ; x<=NF ; x++ ) { printf("%s ",$x) } print "" }'
         0.00 Mb COMMAND
      1119.70 Mb /usr/sbin/mysqld
      1005.61 Mb Passenger core
       550.68 Mb /usr/sbin/clamd
       520.96 Mb /usr/sbin/opendkim -x /etc/opendkim.conf -u opendkim -P /var/run/open
91@localhost -b sv
       381.38 Mb Passenger RubyApp: /home/logon/redmine-3.0 (production)
       338.51 Mb Passenger ust-router
       330.14 Mb Passenger watchdog
       317.46 Mb Passenger RubyApp: /home/projectslcp/redmine-3.0 (production)
       217.23 Mb rsyslogd
       168.13 Mb /usr/sbin/named -u bind
```

Regular and Planned Maintenance

In the preceding image, you can see that the situation with memory consumption is not exactly as it seems at first glance. So, if you don't have to, don't force your apps to be in memory unless you have RAM memory to spend, or you really need a fast response. To clarify the previous command, `ps -eo`, the ps tool displays currently active processes, switches; -eo tells us to display all processes in output format that are defined after letter o in the following format: size, pid, user, and command, then sort by size. Then, pipe this content as input to awk, which filters the content by the following pattern, enclosed by single quotes (`'`):

```
'{ hr=$1/1024 ; printf("%13.2f Mb ",hr) } { for ( x=4 ; x<=NF ; x++ ) { printf("%s ",$x) } print "" }'
```

See also

- Refer to `https://www.phusionpassenger.com/library/admin/nginx/overall_status_report.html` for more detailed instructions on passenger-status command

Configuring backup and recovery

There are multiple ways to perform a backup and recovery of your Redmine system. A good backup strategy should ensure that you can easily and quickly recover from the following:

- Hardware failure or any other type of catastrophe
- Compromised data
- Compromised software code

This recipe provides only the basic manual backup technique of the complete Redmine directory and database. You can learn about the details of Redmine backup so that you can later easily configure any backup software of your choice to perform the backup for you or simply schedule these steps.

Getting ready

Prepare your backup and recovery strategy. Is it going to be a full backup, partial backup, saving deltas of last backup, or something else? Install any backup software if necessary, such as Bacula or Amanda.

How to do it...

To have a proper backup system, you would need to store backup files for a certain amount of time, which may vary, depending upon your backup strategy. This recipe teaches you how to take a backup of Redmine's database and its full production-working directory.

Backing up the database

On Windows, if you are using MSSQL, perform the following actions:

1. Open your SQL Server Management Studio.
2. Right click on **Database**.
3. Choose **Tasks** then click **Backup** | **Back Up Database**.
4. If not already chosen, choose **Back up** to **Disk**, and add file, or edit the existing file.
5. Click **OK**.

On Linux and MySQL, perform `mysqldump` by typing the following command but replace the variables in < > and paths according to your settings:

```
mysqldump -u <username> -p<password> <redmine_database> > /path/to/
backup/redmine_db_`date +%y_%m_%d`.sql
```

Backing up files

On Windows, right-click and zip the folder with your Redmine installation. On Linux, type the following command:

```
tar czvf /path/to/backup/redmine_files_`date +%y_%m_%d`.tar.gz /path/to/
redmine/installation
```

> You can automate both backups via cron job or scheduled tasks, but make sure to automate deletion of old backups so that you don't consume too much or all of your hard drive's space.

Restoring a backup

When a full backup is taken as explained previously, simply putting the files back to their original locations, and restarting servers (Apache, Passenger, Puma, Unicorn or IIS) should do the trick.

Restoring a database

On Windows servers with an MS SQL server, perform the following actions:

1. Right click on databases and choose **Restore**.
2. On the **General** page, use the **Source** section to specify the source and location of the backup sets to restore.
3. Choose **Device**, click **Add**, and find your backup file.

Regular and Planned Maintenance

On Linux machine, type the following command, replacing the variables and dates according to your settings:

```
mysql --user=<username> --password=<password> <database> < /path/to/backup/redmine_db_15_10_23.sql
```

Restoring files

Simply place files back in their original location, for example, `/home/myuser/redmine`:

1. Copy the files here to the following location:

   ```
   cp /path/to/backup/redmine_files_15_10_23.sql /path/to/original/location
   ```

2. Uncompress and untar files, as follows:

   ```
   tar xvfz redmine_files_15_10_23.tar.gz
   ```

> Don't forget to restart your web server and application server once the restore has been performed.

How it works...

Backup is all about planning and strategy. Backup of Redmine can be done in several ways depending upon what are you trying to achieve. As mentioned at the beginning of this chapter, you can backup the whole system or some of its components, such as database, applications, configuration files, user submitted files, and third-party scripts. Of course once you make your backup system, make sure your restoration procedure works, by testing it.

There's more...

Backup is one piece of the puzzle. If your organization is serious about using Redmine 24/7 then you may want to consider some of the **High-Availability** (**HA**) options. One way to achieve this goal is with properly configured network equipment and virtual machine hypervisor in addition to the two separate data centers that are ideally located on two different continents.

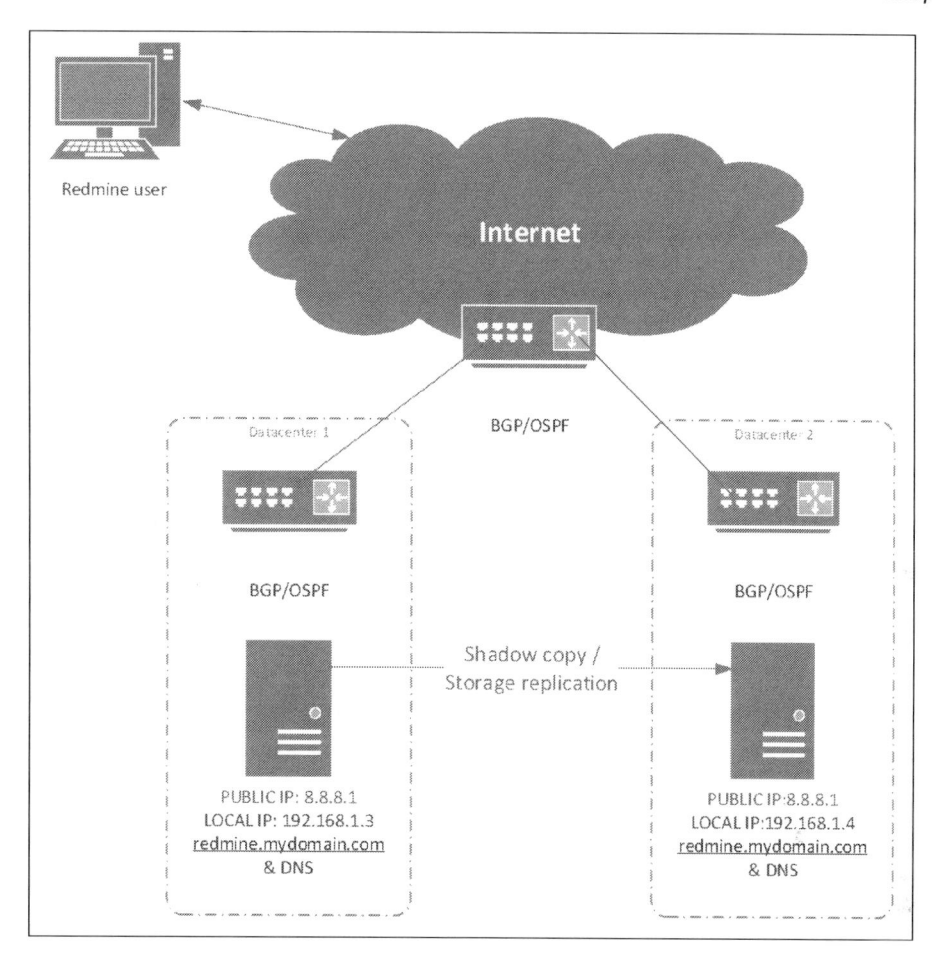

In the preceding image you can see the logical structure of Redmine running in HA mode on a virtualization clustering system, such as **VMW**are, Xen, HyperV, or any other system that is advanced enough to perform required HA routines. The most important part of this scheme is networking the equipment configuration in such a way that routers react if, for some reason, data center one becomes unavailable and reroute all traffic to data center two where the virtualization cluster comes in to place, activating the virtual machine in data center two. Theoretically, you can achieve HA where you will lose only one ping and data center two will become available. Once DC1 is recovered, you can manually trigger routines and make traffic route to DC1 as it were before the disaster.

Regular and Planned Maintenance

See also

- To choose your backup strategy and learn about backup, visit `https://en.wikipedia.org/wiki/Backup`.
- For information on how to achieve high availability with two XEN servers visit `https://www.howtoforge.com/the-perfect-load-balanced-and-high-availability-web-cluster-with-2-servers-running-xen-on-ubuntu-8.04-hardy-heron`.

Checking the data dirs for possible malware

As Redmine allows users to upload any kind of attachment to issues, documents, and files, it is possible that some users will upload a file infected with a computer virus, or malicious code inside a Word macro document. This recipe will show you a few tricks to avoid such an unwanted scenario.

Getting ready

The first thing that we need to do is to install an open source antivirus called clamav.

Linux machines

To install clamav on Linux, perform the following steps:

1. Install antivirus components by typing the following on Ubuntu:

   `apt-get install clamav`

2. Schedule an antivirus database update by typing the following:

   `crontab -e`

3. Add the following content:

   `05 00 * * * freshclam`

Windows users

To install clamav on Windows, perform the following steps:

1. Download the executable file from `http://sourceforge.net/projects/clamav/files/latest/download`
2. Install to a certain directory `C:\clam`.
3. Add the directory to the system PATH variable by navigating to **My Computer | Properties | Advanced system settings | Environment variables**.

4. Initialize Clam antivirus, its update, and database by copying the config files from the `conf_examples` subdirectory to the directory where the executable files are.
5. Rename them from `.sample` to `.conf`.
6. Edit config files providing the proper paths.
7. Set up a scheduled task to run freshclam daily by opening **Server Manager**, then click **Tools** at the top right, **Task Scheduler**, **Create a Basic Task**, and choose to run task daily and command freshclam.

How to do it...

The proper way to protect your Redmine installation is to scan attachments upon upload, and then display an error message if a virus is found. A plugin which utilizes clamAV – an open source antivirus can be installed in the following way:

1. Download or `git-clone` the plugin to your Redmine's `plugins` folder, it should be named `/plugins/redmine_clam`, from https://github.com/madumlao/redmine_clam.
2. Reinstall Redmine to install the missing clamav gem by navigating to the root directory, and typing the following:

   bundle install

3. Run the plugin install scripts by typing the following:

   `bundle exec rake redmine:plugins:migrate RAILS_ENV=production`

Once installed, you should be able to see the plugin in your plugins list:

Plugins		
Clam plugin Plugin that provides a clamd scanner for file attachments http://github.com/madumlao/redmine_clam	Mark David Dumlao	0.0.1

How it works...

This recipe instructs administrators to install clamav antivirus on the server. Then, it explains how to set up regular virus detection database updates. From Redmine's standpoint, it instructs administrators to install the plugin, which is supposed to scan files, and disable their upload if they are infected. Anyway, in the *There's more...* section, you can see how to scan data directories for potential malware without a plugin.

Regular and Planned Maintenance

There's more...

If you already have a system in production running for a while, or you are migrating to a new platform, and there are multiple attachments in the system, you can run a `rake` task of the previously mentioned plugin or run the antivirus manually. To run the rake task, follow these steps:

1. Navigate to your Redmine's installation home.
2. Run the rake task by typing the following:

   ```
   rake redmine:attachments:clamdscan RAILS_ENV=production
   ```

A manual clamAV scan of user submitted files can also be triggered with the following command (without plugin installation):

```
user@host:~/redmine-3.0$ clamscan -r --bell -i .
./files/2015/10/151023111437_eicar.com.txt: Eicar-Test-Signature FOUND
./files/2015/10/151022233748_eicar.com: Eicar-Test-Signature FOUND
./files/2015/10/151023111411_eicar.com.txt: Eicar-Test-Signature FOUND

----------- SCAN SUMMARY -----------
Known viruses: 4039345
Engine version: 0.98.7
Scanned directories: 952
Scanned files: 4154
Infected files: 3
Data scanned: 35.00 MB
Data read: 26.14 MB (ratio 1.34:1)
Time: 21.711 sec (0 m 21 s)
```

In the preceding console window with command and output, you can see that clamscan found three viruses. It is actually a harmless Eicar test string that is used to confirm that the antivirus software works correctly.

See also

- The Eicar test string can be downloaded from: `http://www.eicar.org/anti_virus_test_file.htm`.

Chapter 5

Migrating and upgrading

Migrating and upgrading from version A to version B or from Linux with MySQL to Windows with **Microsoft SQL Server** (**MSSQL**) for Redmine is not a problem, as long as you have the proper tools and know-how about your database and files.

Getting ready

Make sure that you have server administration privileges.

Ensure you are running migration or upgrade in a test environment.

Follow the recipe *Configuring Backup and Recovery* to make a backup and take a snapshot of your virtual machine if possible.

Here is a checklist before performing the upgrade:

- Is your database compatible?
- Are all required plugins compatible?
- Is your operating system and web server version supported?
- Is your Ruby and Rails version supported by the Redmine version you are upgrading to?

How to do it...

To successfully migrate or upgrade Redmine, here is the usual list of items to be migrated or checked after upgrade:

- Redmine database
- Uploaded files
- Configuration files (migrated and/or updated)
- Plugins
- Scheduled cron jobs
- Custom themes

Migrating Redmine

Migration of Redmine is possible across servers (Thin, Puma, Unicorn, Passenger), platforms (Windows, Linux, Freebsd), and underlying databases, as long as you have uncorrupted data. One way or another you will be able to move it to the desired system.

Regular and Planned Maintenance

To migrate Redmine from server one to server two, follow these steps:

1. Perform the backup as already instructed in the *Getting Ready* section on server one.
2. Install Redmine on server two.
3. Restore files and plugins from the backup's files folder to the new installation's files and plugins folders, respectively.
4. Restore the database overwriting the existing Redmine database that is generated after installation.
5. Migrate cron jobs and scheduled tasks (to see cron jobs for particular users type crontab or take a look at scheduled tasks on Windows).
6. If you are migrating between different Redmine versions, you may need to run the following rake tasks:

   ```
   bundle exec rake db:migrate RAILS_ENV=production
   bundle exec rake redmine:plugins:migrate RAILS_ENV=production
   ```

Upgrading Redmine

Upgrade can be done in multiple ways depending upon your installation. If you have a checked-out working copy via SVN, or extracted, follow these steps:

1. Perform backup as already instructed in the *Getting Ready* section on server one.
2. Run the SVN update if you have installed SVN or download the new version of Redmine from: http://www.redmine.org/projects/redmine/wiki/Download.
3. Extract overwriting the old installation.
4. Run the following command:

   ```
   bundle install --without development test
   ```

5. Restart the web server.

How it works...

In both cases, migration and update, we run bundle install, which installs or updates necessary gems that are required by Redmine to run. Ruby gems are specific libraries and gem is a package manager that is used to install required gems. The gem requirement for some Ruby on Rails applications are specified in Gemfile in the application's root. In the case of update, we do not need to move these files, settings, or database. Just updating the application's code and running bundle install ensures that the application is updated with all requirements updated, considering that our server meets the requirements. In case of migration, we simply move our customized stuff into another default installation of Redmine, update the database if required, and start the server.

See also

- Refer to the list of requirements for active Redmine versions at: http://www.redmine.org/projects/redmine/wiki/RedmineInstall#Requirements
- Redmine upgrade official tutorial can be found at: http://www.redmine.org/projects/redmine/wiki/RedmineUpgrade

Upgrading or migrating the database behind Redmine

Dealing with production databases is always a risky process. Even if it's a minor upgrade from version x.01 to x.02, there is always a possibility that the database will stop working or data corruption will occur. Migrating databases also poses a data consistency risk. To avoid data loss, follow the instructions provided in this recipe, always use a test environment, and never delete backups until you are sure that the new system is working as expected, and you have a backup of your new system.

Getting ready

Before performing a database upgrade, make sure it is working with your Redmine's database drivers.

Follow the recipe *Configuring Backup and Recovery* to make a backup and take a snapshot of your virtual machine if possible.

How to do it...

To upgrade the database behind Redmine, make sure to create a backup before upgrading. As Redmine uses any of the following DBMS: MySQL, PostrgreSQL, MSSQL, and SQLite, you will need to consult your database's manual to perform an upgrade. So, from Redmine's standpoint, the update process will look as follows:

1. Check the requirements of the new database system before upgrading. You can find them on Redmine's website: http://www.redmine.org/projects/redmine/wiki/RedmineInstall#Requirements.

Regular and Planned Maintenance

2. You can see a section looking like the following image:

Supported database back-ends

- MySQL 5.0 or higher
  - make sure to install the C bindings for Ruby that dramatically improve performance. You can get them by running `gem install mysql2`.
  - Redmine 2.x is not compatible with mysql 5.7.3 (#17460). Il will be supported by Redmine 3.
- PostgreSQL 8.2 or higher
  - make sure your database datestyle is set to ISO (Postgresql default setting). You can set it using: `ALTER DATABASE "redmine_db" SET datestyle="ISO,MDY";`
  - some bugs in PostgreSQL 8.4.0 and 8.4.1 affect Redmine behavior (#4259, #4314), they are fixed in PostgreSQL 8.4.2
- Microsoft SQL Server
  - Redmine 2.x: 2008 or higher (since Redmine 2.3.0)
  - Redmine 3.x: 2012 or higher
- SQLite 3 (not for multi-user production use!)

---

3. Perform a full backup of your database system, including log files and system files, not just Redmine database.
4. Perform upgrade of the database system.
5. Run `bundle install`, it will download the gem; if it's a new version of the database, a newer version of the gem might be out as well.
6. Run the `rake` task, as follows:

   `RAILS_ENV=production bundle exec rake db:migrate`

How it works...

Redmine connects to databases through Ruby library's `gems`, such as MySQL2, and uses a database abstraction layer called *ActiveRecord*. A combination of these two lets Redmine use any database management system supported by ActiveRecord. This architecture lets us perform migrations. In the following image, the mentioned DB architecture is visually represented using vendor's logos:

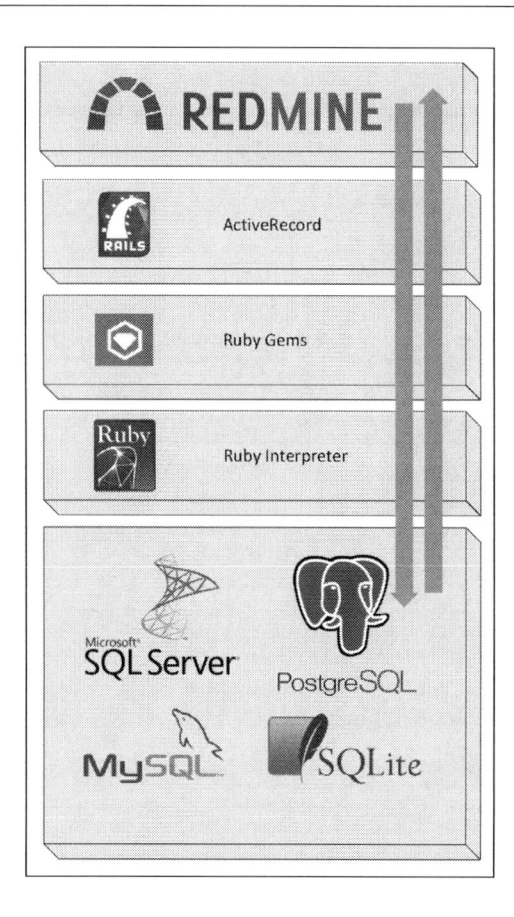

In order to write something to database from a Redmine system or read from it, logical layers of code are displayed top-down and bottom-up.

There's more...

If you are migrating a database across different **DBMS (Database Management Systems)**, you can do it with a professional tool, such as Navicat Premium, or try to use ANSI SQL.

Regular and Planned Maintenance

To move the database and data across platforms using Navicat Premium, perform the following:

1. Create connections for source and target databases MySQL and MSSQL, in this case.
2. Create a Redmine database at the target machine (Redmine database owner SA at the MSSQL machine.)
3. Choose **Tools | Data Transfer**.
4. Select the tables that you want to migrate (all) and click **Start**. Once done, you should get 0 errors and message **successfully completed**.

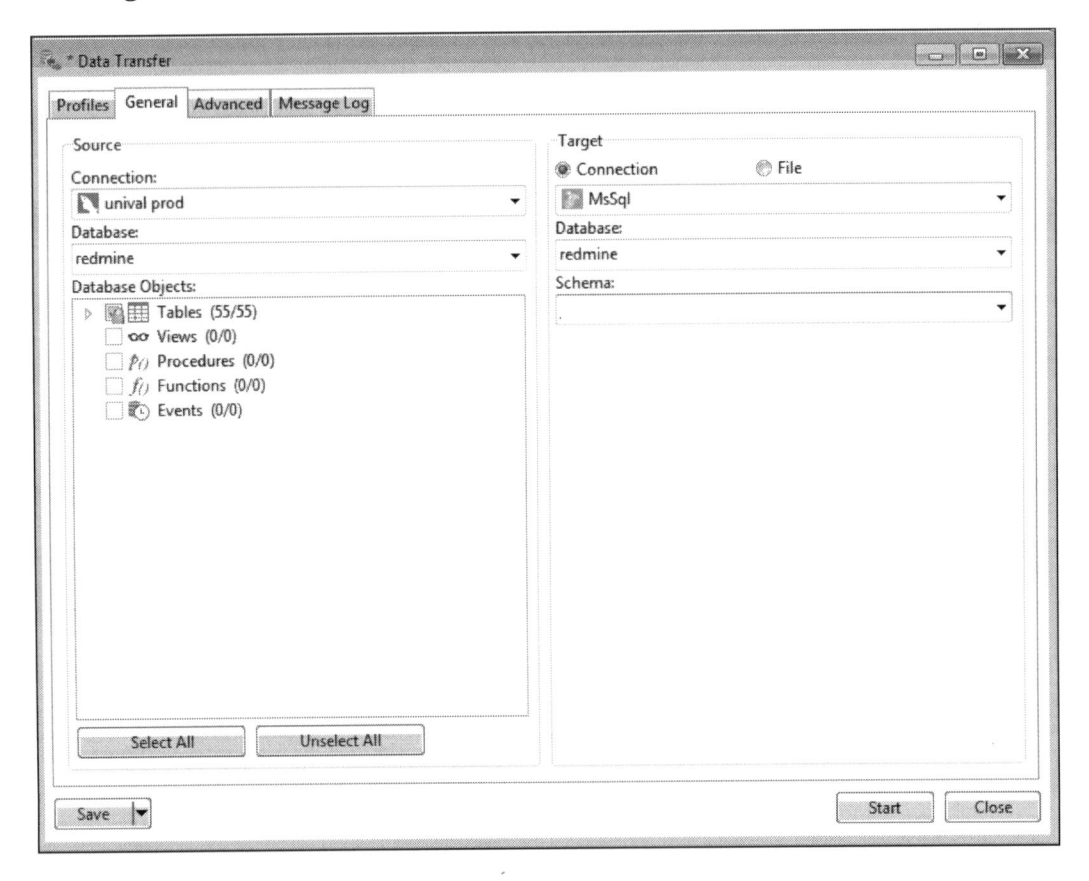

In the preceding image, you can see the data transfer screen of Navicat Premium, transferring the Redmine database from MySQL to MSSQL server.

If this does not work for you, you can try exporting the database dump in ANSI SQL, or target SQL system's format.

> MySQL can dump PostgreSQL-compatible SQL dump, as follows:
> ```
> mysqldump -u <username> -p<password>
> --compatible=postgresql <databasename> > redmine_postgresql.sql
> ```

If you are only migrating the database behind Redmine, once the migration is done you might need to re-run bundle install to ensure missing gems are installed.

See also

You have updated your server, and Redmine stopped working. What happened and why? To learn more about troubleshooting and reading logs, check out *Chapter 9, Troubleshooting*.

- Navicat Premium is available as a trial version for 14 days, and it can be obtained from their website: `http://www.navicat.com/products/navicat-premium`

Enhancing security

This recipe covers the security of the server, database, and the communication of the user's browser and e-mail communication through SSL so that no data goes unencrypted from and to a Redmine system.

Getting ready

Make sure that you have server administration privileges. Prepare self-generated or obtain proper and valid SSL certificates for your server (Apache, IIS). To generate a free, but valid, certificate and install it, follow the guidelines in the *Enhancing security* recipe of *Chapter 10, Making the Most of Redmine*.

How to do it...

To ensure maximal security of your Redmine box, follow these steps:

1. Make sure that the web server running your Redmine is running as a separate user or group from other web presentations.
2. Make sure that the server is properly updated and the root password is used only by server administrators.
3. Change root and user's administering passwords every few months.
4. Don't use the same password for database and server's user.

Regular and Planned Maintenance

5. Configure Redmine to communicate with the e-mail server through SSL (if it is on a different machine, or on shared hosting), follow the rules explained at `http://www.redmine.org/projects/redmine/wiki/EmailConfiguration`.

> If you use self-generated certificates, you may get error messages that the certificate fails. To overcome this problem, add the following line to the end of your e-mail configuration:
> `openssl_verify_mode: 'none'`

6. Make sure that Redmine runs only on SSL. To configure SSL on Apache, you should be able to configure it like any other virtual host. The same goes for IIS on Windows servers.

To ensure that Redmine runs only in SSL mode, and to redirect your users to SSL, you can do the following:

1. Navigate to your Redmine folder.
2. Open `config/application.rb` in code editor.
3. Add the following line below some other `config.something` command:

   `config.force_ssl = true`

How it works...

This recipe outlines the need for secure communication in and out of your Redmine box. Depending upon the nature of your projects, this recipe is more or less interesting. However, nowadays it's always good idea to keep all your data and communications secure.

Making sure that the web server running your Redmine is running as a separate user or group from other web presentations ensures that your Redmine instance won't get hacked or be compromised if some other part of the system is hacked. Not using the same password for database and system ensures hackers won't easily hack your database even if they got into the system. They can read the Redmine config file though. But most likely they won't be doing this, but rather try to with some automated script by usually targeting PHP websites running on some older version of some popular CMS, such as Wordpress or Drupal. Using secure e-mail and web communication ensures that your IP traffic won't be intercepted inside your LAN network, or somewhere over internet.

There's more...

For maximal Redmine security, you should not forget occasional security audits of your Redmine's projects and users. These audits should consist of the following:

- A list of users who have administrator privileges access
- Archive unused, old, or failed projects
- Compare a list of Redmine users with your company's users
- Make sure that all users use secured e-mail accounts
- Walk through projects and make sure users are assigned according to their project roles
- Make sure projects are not displayed as public if they are not supposed to be

Finally, make changes according to your findings by deleting users, changing their e-mail addresses, or roles on the project.

See also

- Monitor Redmine's security advisories page, as it will tell you which version of Redmine is vulnerable to certain security vulnerability, at https://www.redmine.org/projects/redmine/wiki/Security_Advisories.

Upgrading Ruby safely

The recommended way of safely upgrading Ruby implies that you have installed your Redmine server's Ruby using **RVM** (**Ruby Version Manager**). RVM works under both Linux and Windows. This recipe deals with a scenario where you want to upgrade the Ruby version on which your Redmine instance is running.

Getting ready

Make sure that you have server administration privileges.

Check the requirements of the Redmine version against the Ruby version on Redmine's website installation instructions, at the following URL: http://www.redmine.org/projects/redmine/wiki/RedmineInstall#Requirements.

Regular and Planned Maintenance

How to do it...

Assuming that Ruby on your server is installed with RVM, upgrading Ruby should be very easy and straightforward. RVM even lets you use multiple versions of Ruby binaries on your system.

[RVM can be installed at user level, bypassing the system-defined options]

To find out which version of Ruby your system is running, type the following as root or sudo:

`ruby -v`

You will get a message like the following:

`ruby 1.9.3p484 (2013-11-22 revision 43786) [x86_64-linux]`

Then, if you switch to some of the user accounts and type the same command, you may get a different a Ruby version as follows:

`ruby 2.2.1p85 (2015-02-26 revision 49769) [x86_64-linux]`

To see the location of Ruby used, type the following:

`which ruby`

For Ruby that was properly installed by RVM, the output will look like this:

`/home/your_user/.rvm/rubies/ruby-2.2.1/bin/ruby`

If Ruby is not properly installed, the output will most likely look like this:

`/usr/bin/ruby`

Finally, to perform a Ruby upgrade, type the following:

`rvm upgrade 2.1.1 2.1.2`

RVM lets you run multiple instances of Ruby at the same time.

This means that you can run the following commands:

`rvm install <wanted Ruby version>`
`rvm use <wanted Ruby version>`

To see the list of rubies installed by RVM, type the following:

`rvm list rubies`

How it works...

As their website states, **RVM** (**Ruby Version Manager**) is a command-line tool which allows you to easily install, manage, and work with multiple Ruby environments from interpreters to sets of gems.

In this recipe, we utilized RVM to install, upgrade, downgrade, or choose the existing Ruby installation to be the default.

There's more...

You can check which version is your RVM by typing the following:

`rvm -v`

It should give an output like this:

`rvm 1.26.11 (latest) by Wayne E. Seguin <wayneeseguin@gmail.com>, Michal Papis <mpapis@gmail.com> [https://rvm.io/]`

To see the default version of Ruby through RVM, type the following:

`rvm list default`

See also

- Refer to the RVM homepage: `https://rvm.io/`.

6
Performance and System Tuning

If you are using Redmine in production, as its usage grows, the database and the file system usage also grow, as well as CPU, and consumed memory. To make sure that your Redmine is running perfectly and all users are happy, this chapter provides several recipes:

- Fine-tuning new project creation
- Tuning authentication and auto-login features
- Tuning the workflows
- Setting the log level
- Getting the most from a single server
- Scaling Redmine across multiple servers
- Increasing file upload size
- Integrating Redmine with Active Directory

Introduction

Redmine performance is not only related to the speed of the web-server response and getting it to consume less RAM while reducing the rendering time from, for example, 128 ms to 96 ms. Optimization is also about logically tuning it to gain maximum performance from it as a project management and collaboration tool. This chapter deals with both tangible and intangible performances, which may affect your user's daily routines, increase their satisfaction, and fine-tune business processes. If you are worried about what will happen to your servers if you use Redmine on a large number of users for several years, will it be able to scale-out and how to do it, this chapter also gives you recipes about scaling Redmine up and out.

Fine-tuning new project creation

New projects can be created as per default settings when Redmine is installed and used out of the box. Most users don't become instantaneously aware of Redmine's flexibility, and Redmine is flexible in this case as well. New projects can be created with or without certain trackers, public by default, and so on. Here is how to fine-tune your project creation.

Getting ready

A Redmine administrator account is necessary in order to access the Administration menu.

How to do it...

Here is how to fine-tune your project creation. To configure a new project screen's settings, perform the following actions:

1. Go to **Administration | Settings | Projects**.
2. Choose the Project visibility option by checking or unchecking **New projects are public by default**; when unchecked, your projects will be private (only visible to project members, not visible for unauthenticated users, or users not added to the project).
3. Check or uncheck modules that you want to be active for newly created projects per default in the **Default enabled modules for new projects** section.

> Some plugins may appear here as modules, and they can be switched on/off on a per-project basis. Check the documentation while installing them.

4. To choose default trackers, tick them in the **Default trackers for new projects** section.
5. To manage which trackers will appear in the **Default trackers** section or add new trackers, navigate to **Administration | Settings | Trackers**.
6. If you want to generate sequential project identifiers, you should tick with same name option.
7. Choose **Role** given to a non-admin user who creates a project from the drop-down box.
8. To **Modify Roles**, navigate to **Administration | Roles** and edit their order, or create a role that will be visible on the Project settings screen.

How it works...

As you have learned so far, almost everything in Redmine is done with flexibility in mind, so are projects and project creation. In this recipe, we utilized built-in settings for new project creation to customize options and values that are available on the new project creation screen. In this recipe, we accessed settings that are available only to users with administrator permissions and customized the new project creation screen which can be used by any other Redmine user if its role allows it to create new projects.

There's more...

Additionally, the project creation screen can be extended with additional custom fields, which may be required in some cases. To extend the project creation screen, perform the following actions:

1. Navigate to **Administration | Custom fields**.
2. Click **New custom field**.
3. Choose the **Projects** radio button and click **Next**.
4. Create a custom field by populating the presented form.

> Ticking the **Required** checkbox will make the field a *required* field that must be filled with each newly created project!

Tuning authentication and auto-login features

Usually when there is no need for maximal security, web applications let users tick a *remember me* checkbox on the login screen which lets them log in to the application without entering a username and password each time the web application is accessed. Redmine lets you customize this feature by choosing how long users should stay logged in and offers additional authentication features.

How to do it...

To fine-tune authentication features, perform the following actions:

1. Navigate to **Administration | Settings | Authentication**.
2. Choose a setting from the **Autologin** dropdown.

Performance and System Tuning

3. If anything except disabled is chosen, the **Stay logged in** checkbox will be hidden on the **Login** screen:

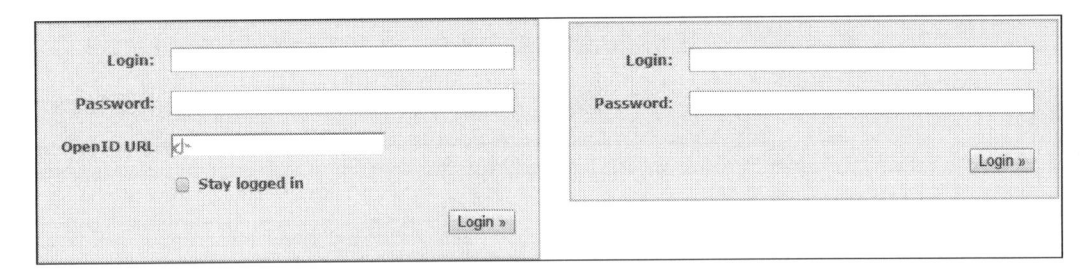

4. The options on the **Autologin** dropdown will let you choose how long a user can stay logged in without the need to enter a username and password each time the browser is opened. Once this date expires, the user will have to re-authenticate, but users can tick the checkbox again and stay logged in for another time period specified by the dropdown.

5. Additionally, newer versions of Redmine feature **Session maximum lifetime** and **Session inactivity timeout**. These settings can also be tuned in order to maximize security. Session lifetime is the maximal time after login, and inactivity will automatically log the user out.

How it works...

Redmine utilizes cookies and sessions for authentication. In this recipe, we configured these values through built-in administrative features. While this recipe may be easy, it certainly has a great impact on your end users and security. If users get logged out too fast, they may get frustrated, or they may get frustrated if they have to log in to the system too often, so it presents a delicate balance between user experience and good security.

There's more...

Additionally, faster login and better user experience can be achieved by utilizing the OpenID feature. To use OpenID, perform the following actions:

1. Navigate to **Administration | Settings | Authentication.**
2. Tick the checkbox near **Allow OpenID login and registration**.
3. It will add the **OpenID** field on your Redmine login screen.
4. To utilize OpenID further means that users who want to use it need to have their **OpenID URL** from some OpenID provider.

5. You can get the full list of providers here at `http://openidexplained.com/get`, or use `https://openid.stackexchange.com/`, which is used in this example.
6. Instruct users to grab their OpenID connection string from their OpenID provider, it usually looks like this: `http://provider_url.com/user/set-of-hexadecimal-string-values`.
7. Then they need to navigate to **My account**, and paste the OpenID string:

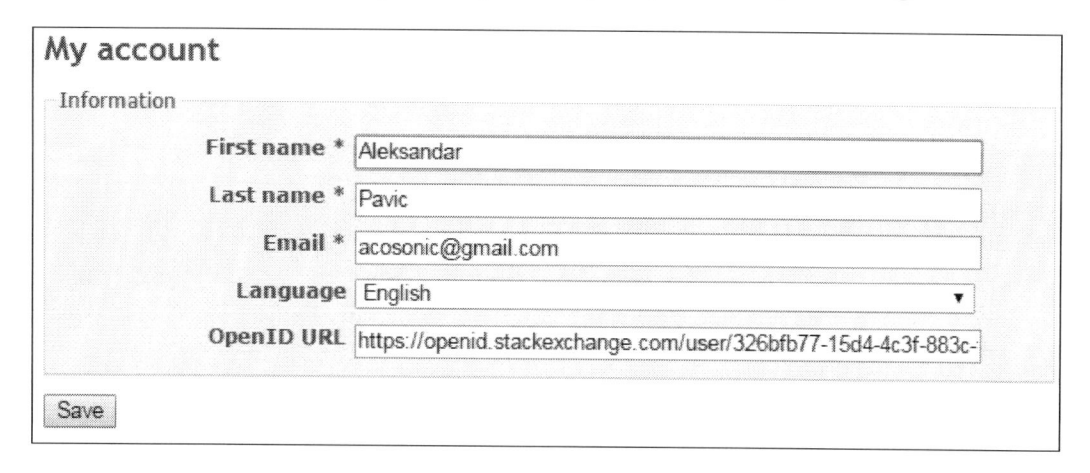

Users can benefit from a tool such as clipboard history `ClipX` with the `Sticked` plugin to keep their OpenID accessible all the time and use it during login.

See also

- Refer to the recipe, *Integrating Redmine with active directory*, to learn how to use Redmine in a corporate environment and authenticate users through Active Directory.

Tuning the workflows

The combination of Redmine workflows and permissions let you implement various workflow execution scenarios. This recipe will teach you how to fine-tune permissions that are related to workflows, trackers, and *who can change the issue state to what*.

Performance and System Tuning

How to do it...

Fine-tuning user permissions is not just about the Roles and permissions screen. Permissions relate to workflows as well. For example, Redmine let's you set up workflows in such a way that for a particular tracker (such as bug, for example), particular roles, such as **Developer**, can only change states from-to based upon given permissions. So, let's say that **Developers** are not allowed to close the issue, they can only work on the issue until it's resolved, and then only **Manager** can close the issue if tracker is a feature. This should not apply to the tracker type, **Bug**. To do this, perform the following:

1. Navigate to **Administration | Workflows**.
2. From the **Role** dropdown, choose **Developer.**
3. From the **Tracker** dropdown, choose **Feature.**
4. Click **Edit**, and a screen like the one in the following screenshot should appear:

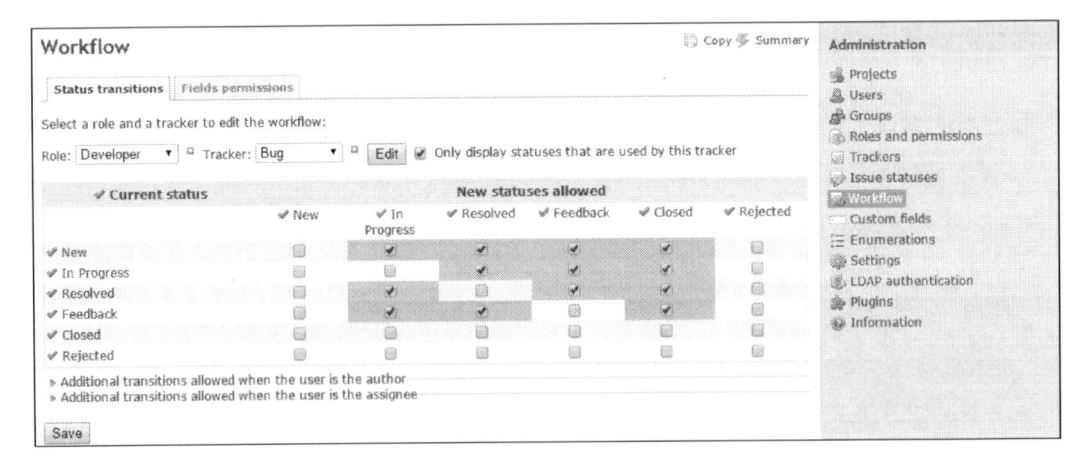

5. Untick checkboxes in the **Closed** column. So, the outcome should look like the following:

Chapter 6

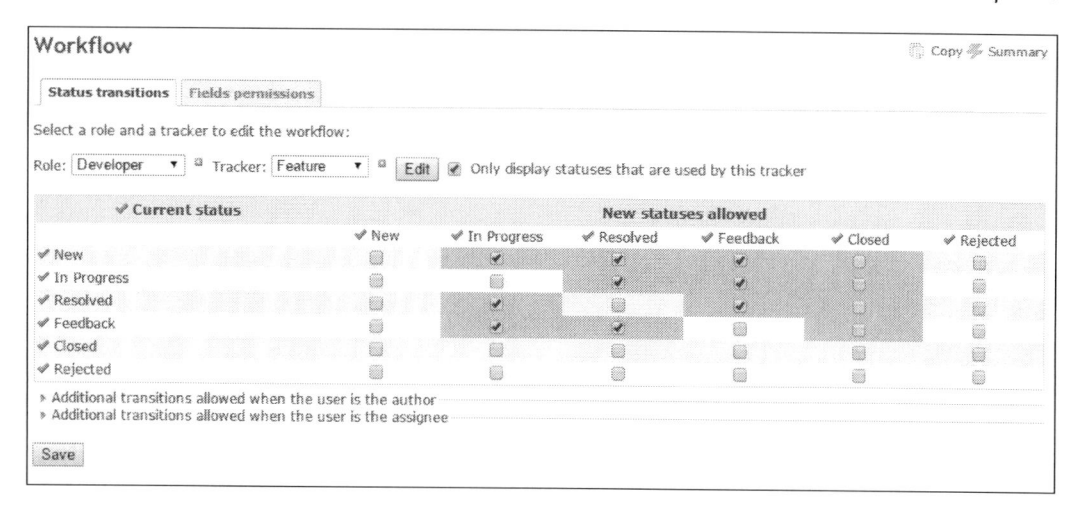

![Workflow screenshot showing Status transitions tab with Role: Developer, Tracker: Feature, and a matrix of current statuses vs new statuses allowed]

How it works...

We are utilizing built-in features of fine-grain workflow permissions and control. The **Workflow Status transitions** form lets you specify from-to transition permissions for any role and any tracker. This fine-grain control can let you map your real company business processes to Redmine based on particular roles and its permissions. On the form, once you click the **Edit** button, new statuses are displayed in vertical columns. Horizontally, are the current statuses of the issue. So, the form is actually representing a matrix of from-to states. What we have done in *step 2* and *step 3* is chosen role and tracker, in this example, the **Developer** role and the **Feature** tracker. In *step 5*, we removed (unchecked) the **Closed** status for a developer. This means that a Developer won't be able to close any feature.

There's more...

Additionally, the status transitions form lets you customize workflow even more, in such a case that a user under a particular role is **Author** or **Assignee**. In the example from this recipe, we will let the developer close the issue whose type is featured only if they are the Author, which would make sense as it's the same user that requested the feature in the first place. To do so, perform the following steps:

1. Expand the **Additional transitions allowed when the user is the author** section.

163

Performance and System Tuning

2. Check all the checkboxes in the **Closed** column:

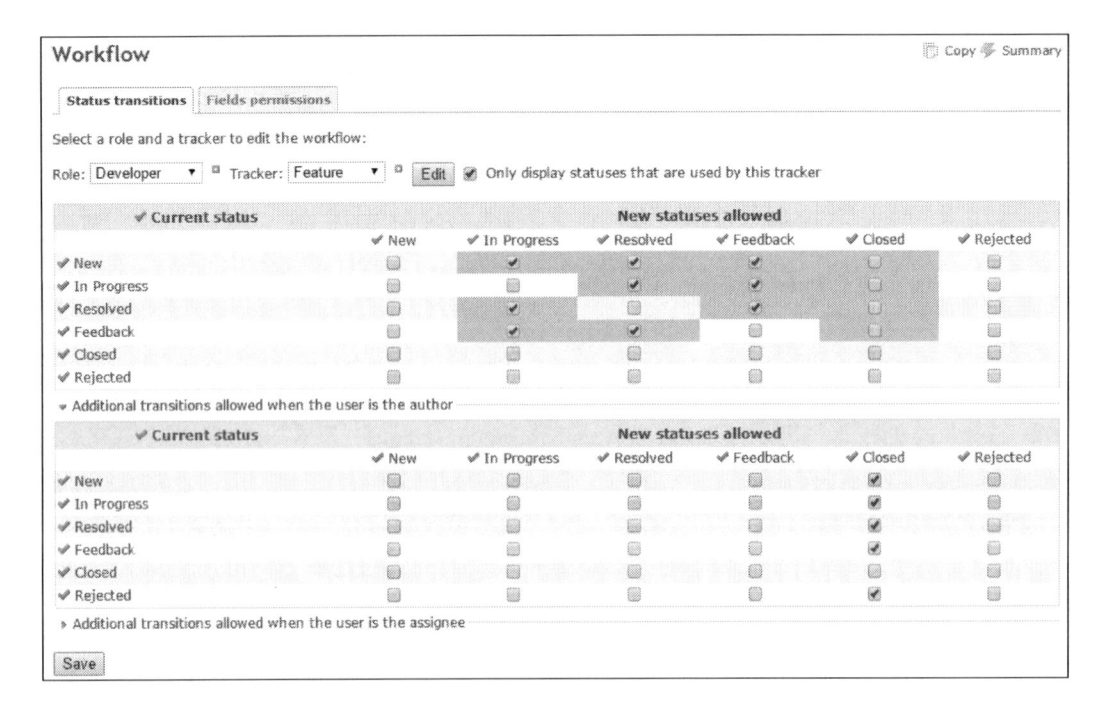

If you want developers to tamper with issue statuses only if issues are assigned to them, then uncheck all checkboxes on the topmost status matrix or copy them to the bottom form named **Additional transitions allowed when user is the assignee** by clicking checkboxes one by one.

Setting the log level

Normally, the log is the first thing to check when something goes wrong. In a production environment, until everything is working fine, you want your logs to be as small as possible and leave the smallest footprint on CPU and memory. This recipe teaches you how to tweak log-level settings in Redmine.

Getting ready

Server administration privileges are required so that you can edit configuration files from Redmine's installation folder.

How to do it...

To configure the Redmine log level, perform the following actions:

1. Navigate to the folder where your Redmine installation resides.
2. Navigate to the sub-folder `config`.
3. Create a file called `additional_environment.rb`.
4. Enter the following line:

   `config.logger.level = Logger::WARN`

5. Save the file.
6. Restart Redmine.

How it works...

Redmine relies on Ruby on Rail's `Logger` class, and can be configured according to the settings that are available from the `Logger` class. On line 4, possible values after the `=` `Logger::` are as follows:

Possible options	Description
UNKNOWN	This is an unknown message that should always be logged.
FATAL	This is an unhandleable error that results in a program crash.
ERROR	This is a handleable error condition.
WARN	This is a warning.
INFO	This is generic (useful) information about system operation.
DEBUG	This is low-level information for developers.

Any of these given values can be used, and they are sorted top-down by verbosity.

There's more...

Usually, when there are logs generated, they tend to consume too much disk space, and eventually, all disk space. If your disk quota gets full, you may end up debugging Redmine or any other web application not knowing that everything is okay with it and you should check your quota. Luckily, there are numerous ways to avoid logs filling your server's hard drives. Here is how to utilize Redmine's built-in log-rotate feature:

1. Follow the steps in the *How to do it...* section of this recipe up to *step 4*.

Performance and System Tuning

2. Add this additional line to the `additional_environment.rb` file just above the `config.logger.level = Logger::WARN` line:

   `config.logger = Logger.new('/path/to/logfile.log', 2, 1000000)`

3. Replace the `/path/to/logfile.log` file with your required path. The `Logger.new` command tells the system to put the file in the specified path, the second variable (2 in this case) tells how many files to rotate, and the third parameter is file size. Please keep in mind that the user under which Redmine is working needs to have write permission on this file.

Alternatively, you can configure log-rotate on Linux machines by creating a file, `/etc/logrotate.d/redmine`, with the following contents:

```
/home/user/redmine-3.1.1/log/production.log {
    su user user
    daily
    missingok
    rotate 7
    compress
    delaycompress
    notifempty
    copytruncate
}
```

You should replace path and user with your values. On Windows, you can use `LogRotateWin`, which can be downloaded from `http://sourceforge.net/projects/logrotatewin/`.

Don't forget that this is only application-level logging. There may be other places where logs related to Redmine rely. Such places are Apache usage logs, which can give you statistics about your system's usage. If it's a public Redmine installation, it may be a good idea to run statistics on Redmine's web server, just like you would be doing for regular website using Awstats, webalizer, or any other tool.

Getting the most from a single server

Nowadays, it is possible to have servers with 3 TB of Ram memory, 10 TB or more of SSD or SAS raid drives, 4 processors with 16 cores each and multiple network cards. Such a server should be able to serve thousands of users or virtualize many servers without even breaking a sweat. This recipe offers some Redmine speed-up techniques to minimize response times and maximize server usage.

Chapter 6

How to do it...

Whether you are purchasing a new server or already own one, here is how to allocate resources so that your application server is utilized optimally.

Step 1: Plan your usage

The first step is to determine the number of users that you want to concurrently serve without spawning new processes.

> If you preallocate too much RAM, your server might end up getting lower performance because it might start swapping too soon.

Then, you need to find the ideal ratio between application server and database. You can see a sample of a good configuration for Redmine, considering that the application server consumes most CPU and RAM, in the following image:

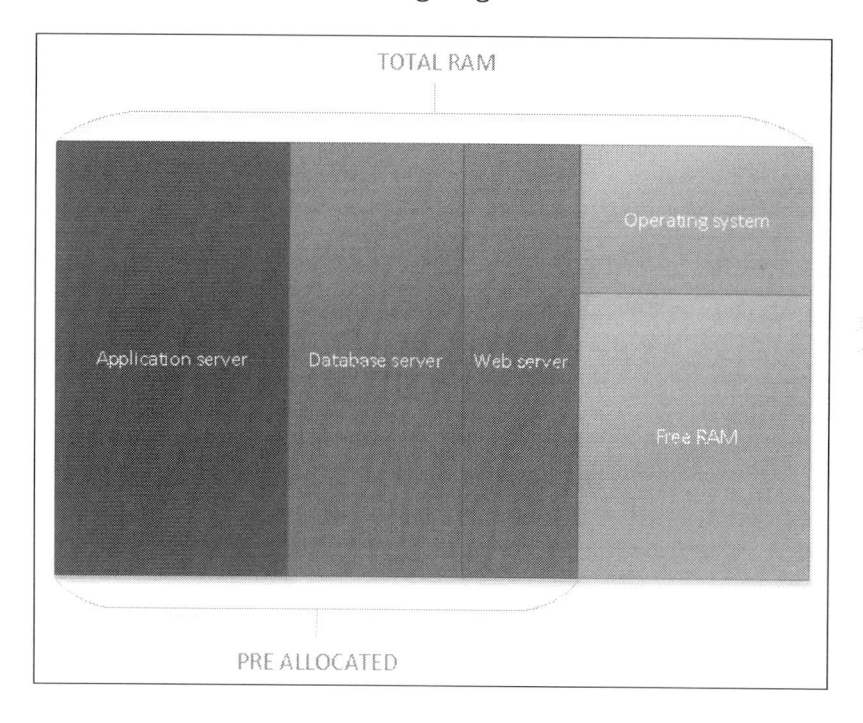

[Diagram showing TOTAL RAM divided into PRE ALLOCATED sections: Application server, Database server, Web server, Operating system, and Free RAM]

Performance and System Tuning

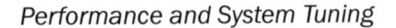

Please keep in mind that the preceding image is not a silver bullet of memory usage, it may depend upon multiple factors. The following math formula applies to Application servers as well as to Database servers:

```
Planned App/Database Server Memory Consumption =
Sum of Global Buffers + (Planned number of Connections * Per thread
memory variables)
```

The key value here is Planned number of Connections. This is actually your planned number of concurrent users. Please keep in mind that you don't have to preallocate a thread for each new user, this is only used to reduce the time required to spawn new processes while users work on the system concurrently.

To determine the number of threads, they should be calculated in the following way: one thread per connection per CPU core for best performance. Nowadays, some CPUs support even up to 8 threads per core, so you should consult your CPUs documentation to properly calculate the number of preallocated threads.

Once you have determined the number of concurrent users, you should calculate your server's RAM and thread usage, divide it by the number of servers (Application server, Database Server, Web server, and possible other servers such as version control), and configure servers accordingly.

Step 2: Increase the number of threads or processes in the memory of your application server

In *Chapter 1, Installing and Running Redmine*, we covered multiple configurations of Redmine servers. Each of them covers detailed instructions, here is how to specify memory usage options to them:

- **Phusion passenger**: This adds the value `PassengerMinInstances N`, replacing the `N` with the number of threads to your virtual host block
- **Thin**: This increases the number of servers `--servers N`
- **Puma**: This increases number of minimum, threads with option `-t min:max`

Step 3: Allocate more CPU and RAM for the database

You should consult your RDMBS configuration manual in general to calculate the optimal Database server's RAM and CPU usage.

For MySQL, the following is a list of MySQL configuration settings to increase or consider increasing. MySQL is configured or tuned through the `my.cnf` configuration file whose location might be different, but usually it's in `/etc/my.cnf` or `$MYSQL_HOME/my.cnf`.

We use the following global buffers:

```
key_buffer_size
innodb_buffer_pool_size
innodb_additional_mem_pool_size
innodb_log_buffer_size
query_cache_size
```

We use the following per thread variables:

```
read_buffer_size
read_rnd_buffer_size
sort_buffer_size
join_buffer_size
thread_stack
net_buffer_length
```

For PostgreSQL, you can use a tool such as `http://pgtune.leopard.in.ua/`, which will perform the math for you.

For MSSQL server, configuration is done through SQL Server Management Studio in the following way:

1. Right-clicking **Server**.
2. Choose **Properties**.
3. Choose the **Memory** tab, set the value for **Minimum server memory**.
4. Set the value for **Max Degree of Parallelism** (controls the number of processors that can be used to run a single SQL server statement).

How it works...

1. Depending upon your application server choice, the key is to allocate as many processes as possible. This is so that your users don't wait for the time necessary for a new process to spawn and start executing your Redmine instance code that is necessary to serve the request.
2. Each RDBMS has its own memory allocation settings, and depending upon your RDBMS and server memory limits, we are tuning the server to gain the most out of the extra memory available.

Performance and System Tuning

There's more...

You can additionally work on speeding up your Ruby interpreter by utilizing RVM patchsets. To use RVM Patchsets, you need to reinstall your Ruby, and Redmine afterwards. Considering you already have RVM installed, as explained in *Chapter 1, Installing and Running Redmine*, in the *Using custom Ruby for Redmine* recipe, here is how to install a custom patchset:

1. Run the following command:

   `rvm install 2.2.3 --patch railsexpress -n railsexpress`

2. You should replace `2.2.3` with the version of Ruby that you want to install.
3. Reload shell if required to make sure that new Ruby is used.
4. Once installed, check your Ruby version by typing the following:

   `rvm list`
   `rvm rubies`

   `=* ruby-2.2.3-railsexpress [ x86_64 ]`

   ```
   # => - current
   # =* - current && default
   # *  - default
   ```

   Where you can see that the current and default version is with the `railsexpress` patch.

5. Proceed with the Redmine installation as planned.

See also

- You can use a tool such as `http://mysqltuner.com/` to fine-tune your MySQL database or find similar tools.
- Refer to Phusion Passenger optimization tips at `https://www.phusionpassenger.com/library/config/apache/optimization/`.
- RVM patchsets homepage can be found at `https://github.com/skaes/rvm-patchsets`.

Scaling Redmine across multiple servers

It is very unlikely that you are going to need to scale Redmine very much. Needing to scale it would mean that you have hundreds or thousands of users working simultaneously on the system. However, after using Redmine intensively for several years, you might end up scaling it to improve response time.

Getting ready

Rule out the possibility that something else (such as network problems, virus, faulty hardware, or misconfiguration) is causing your server to work slowly or misbehave.

How to do it...

As you obviously made sure that you need to scale up Redmine, here is one technique on how scaling out (preferably on physical servers) can be achieved.

> If you are facing high server loads, make sure to check your network interfaces and use some advanced routing protocols, such as OSPF or BGP, to balance network traffic.

In the following image, you can see a proposed high-performance Redmine scale-out solution:

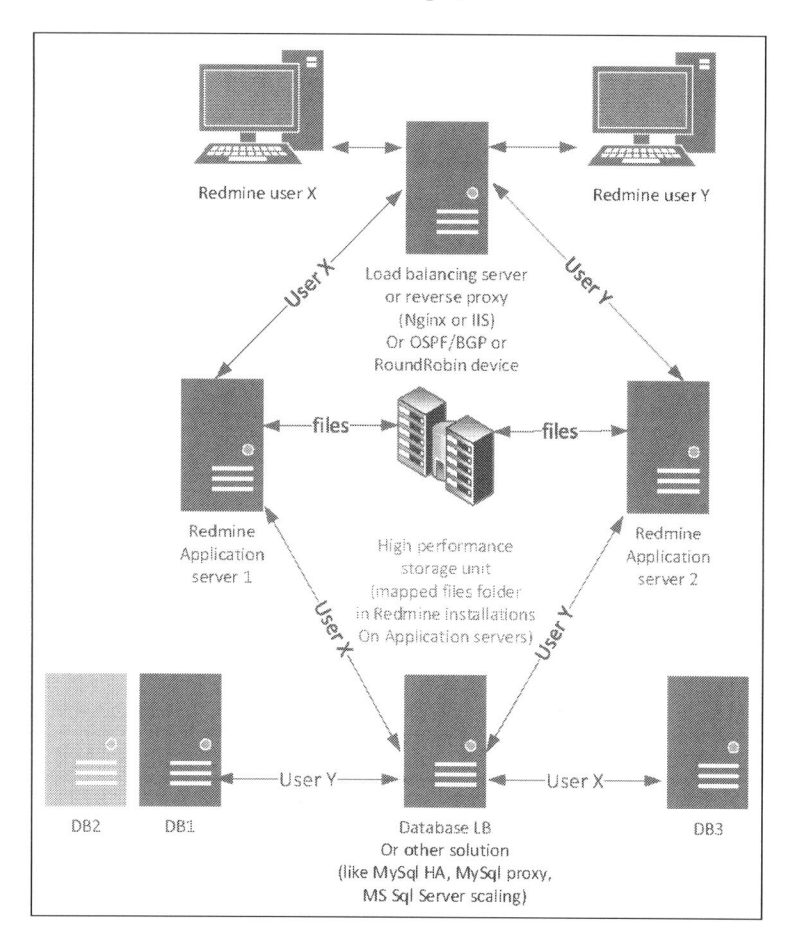

Performance and System Tuning

The proposed scheme is illustrating an example for two users only. Please keep in mind that one server can support hundreds or thousands of users before getting overloaded. To achieve the preceding infrastructure layout, you would need the following:

1. A front load-balancing or reverse-proxy server (you can use IIS or Nginx, as explained in the recipes in *Chapter 1, Installing and Running Redmine*).
2. A fast-storage unit or server where user submitted files will be located.
3. A load-balanced cluster of databases.
4. Two application servers (you can use Thin, Puma, Unicorn or even Apache with Passenger). The only specific change to this installation is to map the network drive from the storage unit.

> You can configure Redmine's `additional_configuration.rb` to use a different folder than `/files` to keep uploaded files by adding the following line: `attachments_storage_path: /var/redmine/files`
>
> For Windows, you would use the following: `attachments_storage_path: D:/redmine/files`
>
> Here D can be a mapped drive, in this case, from a storage server

How it works...

Ruby on Rails applications, such as Redmine, are stateless, meaning that they are built from the ground up to support server farms. Anyway, there are two types of scaling, scale up and scale out. In this recipe, we use the scale-out technique to balance load on multiple servers. The proposed scaling scheme has one potential limitation—it is a storage unit. For storage virtualization and scale up, there are numerous solutions. Either you are going to use some vendor-provided system from vendors, such as Netapp, EMC, HP, IBM, Dell, or FujitsuSiemens, or you are going to rely on commodity hardware and try something such as Hadoop. However, most likely, storage won't be a problem because it's only a simple file-serving request. Ruby interpreter and database would use most of your computing power in Redmine because Redmine is not optimized for any database in particular, but rather it uses ActiveRecord to enable cross-database compatibility. That is why on a proposed scale-out scheme, you can easily add new application and database servers into the array just by installing, configuring, and adding them to database and HTTP reverse-proxy servers.

There's more...

What we just discussed can be achieved on physical hardware, virtual machines, or even container based virtualizations such as Docker. If you are going to try the Docker Redmine system, it should go smoothly, and you can add new instances on demand. The only change you would need to perform on Docker installed Redmine is to mount an external or network volume to share files among instances.

Chapter 6

See also

- Official Docker Redmine can be found at `https://hub.docker.com/_/redmine/`

Increasing file upload size

File upload size can annoy your users if it's set improperly. This recipe explains how to increase file size and avoid common problems.

How to do it...

To increase file upload size, perform the following actions:

1. Navigate to **Administration | Settings | General**.
2. Configure the value of maximum attachment size in KB.
3. Click the **Save** button.
4. To check your file upload size, you can try adding a new issue, and the current file upload limit will be displayed there like in the following image:

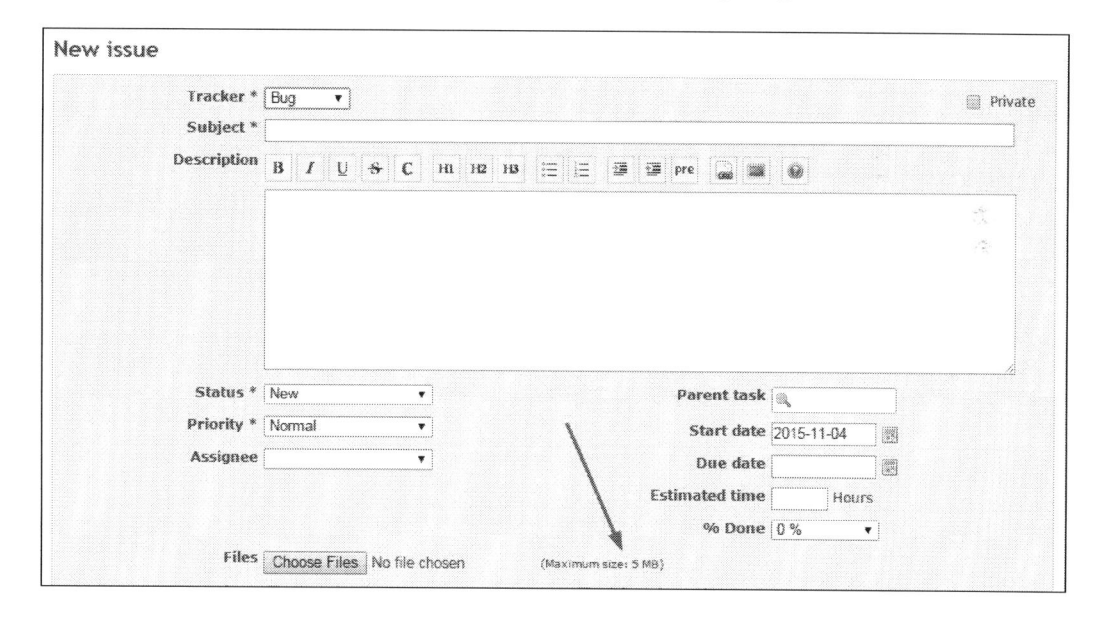

If you still face problems uploading files, check for the following limitations.

Performance and System Tuning

These will be limitations on Apache-hosted Redmine:

Check for `LimitRequestBody` in your virtual host configuration or general configuration, and `SecResponseBodyLimit` if `mod_security` is installed and used.

On Nginx look for and replace with the following desired value instead:

```
server {
  client_max_body_size 100M;
}
```

On IIS, Change the values of the following:

```
<requestLimits maxAllowedContentLength ="<length>" />
in
%windir%\system32\inetsrv\config\applicationhost.config
And
<httpRuntime maxRequestLength="8192" />
In machine.config
```

How it works...

File upload size may be limited by Redmine internally, which is easily configurable through the administration menu, or it may be limited by the web server, in which case it requires reconfiguration of the web server, and a restart. To test upload size, you can attach the file to document, issue or wiki.

See also

- If any of the preceding do not work, or produce errors, refer to *Chapter 9, Troubleshooting*.

Integrating Redmine with Active Directory

In corporate usage scenarios, companies often rely on LDAP services, such as Microsoft **Active Directory** (**AD**) for user authentication, or overall digital identity management. In this case, Redmine does not fall out from the loop, but rather it plays nice with Microsoft Domain; Active Directory or another LDAP compatible service.

Getting ready

Administrator rights are required for Redmine. They are not necessary user account used for accessing Active Directory, but preferred.

How to do it...

This is a multiple steps recipe, the first thing is to figure out details about your AD. To determine proper AD settings, perform the following actions:

1. Open Windows command line as administrator and type the following:

   `whoami /fqdn`

2. You will get a response like the following:

   `CN=pavic.aleksandar,OU=Engineering,OU=Users,DC=rmtest,DC=local`

3. Now type the following:

   `nslookup`

   You will get a response like this:

   `Default Server:  dc01.rmtest.local`
   `Address:    10.20.0.5`

4. Open Redmine and navigate to **Administration | LDAP Authentication**.
5. Click **New Authentication Mode**.
6. Fill out the form in the following way:
   - **Name**: This is the name of the authentication method, for example AD1 (indicating we are using Active Directory number 1)
   - **Host**: This is where you paste the Default Server value from the `nslookup` command, in this case, `dc01.rmtest.local`
   - **Port**: This is `389` (for LDAPS - LDAP Secure, the port is 636°)
   - **Account**: This is `Administrator@rmtest.local`

   > For some servers, you may need to use a different format, such as `RMTEST\Administrator`. Redmine only tests connectivity to the AD server, and it will give you a positive result, but users won't be able to log in if this setting is incorrect.

   - **Password**: This is the domain user's password
   - **Base DN**: This is where you paste the content from `whoami /fqdn` command, in this case, `DC=rmtest,DC=local`
   - **LDAP filter**: This filters the users from particular AD groups, in this case, `OU=Users`
   - **Timeout (in seconds)**: This is how long to wait for the AD server

Performance and System Tuning

- **On-the-fly user creation**: This setting, when clicked, will create users in Redmine.

> For this setting to work, users on AD must have the e-mail value entered. In Redmine, navigate to **Administration | Settings | Authentication** and set the value of **Self-registration** to **Automatic account activation**.

7. Fill out the **Attributes** section, as follows:
    - **Login** attribute: This is `sAMAccountName`
    - **Firstname** attribute: `givenName`
    - **Lastname** attribute: `sn`
    - **Email** attribute: `mailPrimaryAddress`

8. Click **Save**.

9. You should see a new entry under **Authentication modes**, and the buttons **Test**, and **Delete**. Click the **Test** button.

The next thing is to configure users. Are you going to create Redmine users on the fly from Active Directory, or add users manually? If users are added manually, then while adding user, you need to choose a source for its authentication under the **Authentication** section of the **New user** form:

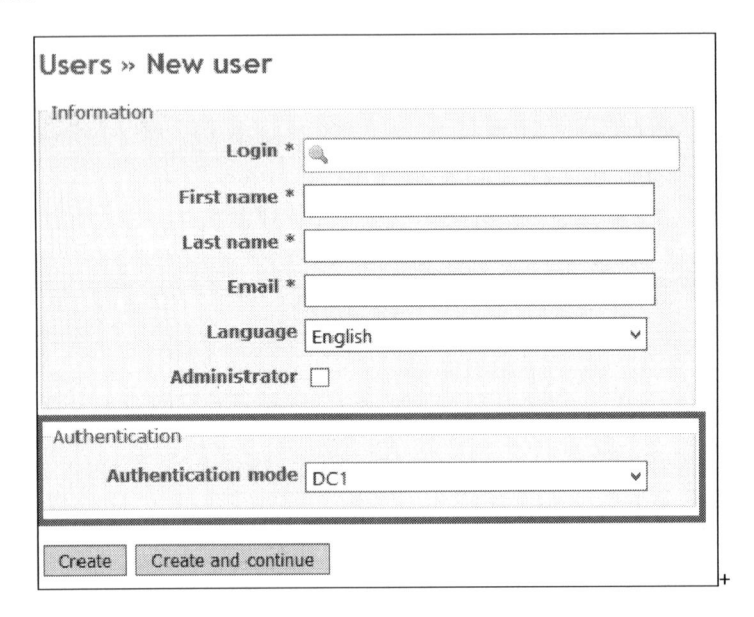

Users » New user

Login *	
First name *	
Last name *	
Email *	
Language	English
Administrator	☐

Authentication

Authentication mode	DC1

[Create] [Create and continue]

—176—

How it works...

This recipe utilizes Redmine's built-in **LDAP** (**Light Directory Access Protocol**) features to connect to Microsoft Active Directory, and allow users registered at AD, to log in to Redmine. Under the hood, this feature utilizes LDAP protocol standard, it connects to LDAP provider (such as Microsoft AD), and performs a query each time a user is trying to access the Redmine system against AD's database of users.

There's more...

Troubleshooting Active Directory authentication and connectivity issues:

Issue 1: After clicking test, you get **Unable to connect (No such address or other socket error)**. First check whether your Redmine server has connectivity to your AD server. Is it blocked by a firewall or some other network problem?

If it's command line under Windows, obtain the **PortQuery** tool from the Microsoft Website at `http://www.microsoft.com/en-us/download/details.aspx?id=17148` and in it, type the following:

`PortQry.exe -n DC1.mydomain.local -e 389  -p udp`

Replace `DC1.mydomain.local` with your domain controller. If the connection is successful, you should get a dump of AD related data.

Under Linux, perform the following:

1. Use `netcat`, you can install it if missing by typing:

   `apt-get install netcat`

2. Type the following command:

   `nc -v DC1.mydomain.local 389`

   If this is successful, you will get a connection successful message.

Issue 2: Connection to AD is successful, but you are not able to log in to Redmine. Most likely, your username entered at *Step 6* is not properly entered, or the password is wrong. To test proper settings for user account login, try using the following tool: `http://ldaptool.sourceforge.net/`. It is a cross-platform tool, so the instructions to use it are the same. To test your AD connectivity, perform the following actions:

1. Start the `ldaptool`.
2. Click **File | Configurations | New**.

Performance and System Tuning

3. On the first tab, **Configuration**, enter the name of the configuration.
4. On the second tab, **Server**, enter the IP or hostname of your **Domain Controller**.
5. Then, on the third tab, **Connection** enter the same values that you entered in Redmine, **Base DN**, **User DN** is the username of the user that should be used to pull AD users, and its password. Usually, it's DOMAIN\User or User@DOMAIN.
6. Once entered, click **Open**

Then, you should see an entry on the left sidebar, double-click it, and you should get the details of your AD listed. If not, most likely, you misconfigured the user. Try different settings until you find the proper ones. The following is a sample of properly configured ldap tools:

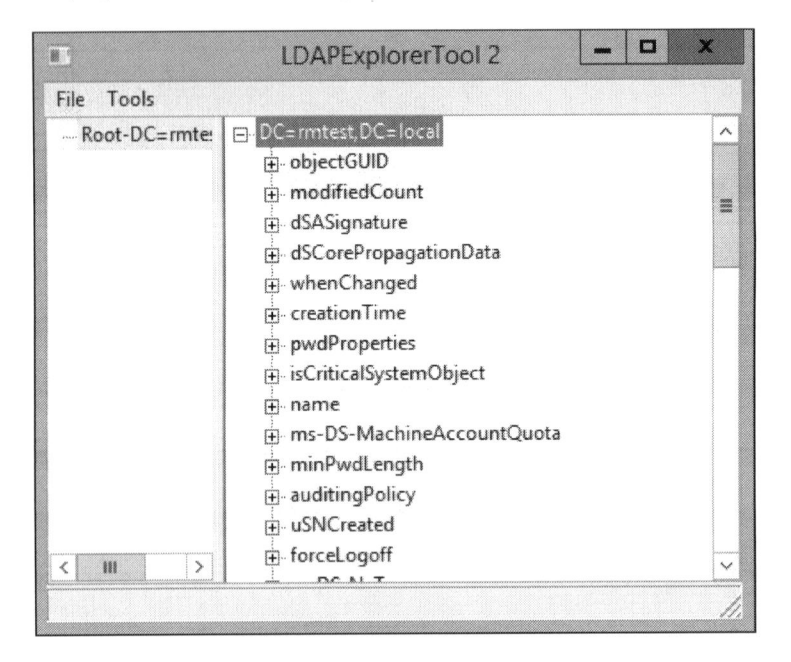

```
LDAPExplorerTool 2
File  Tools
 Root-DC=rmte:    DC=rmtest,DC=local
                    objectGUID
                    modifiedCount
                    dSASignature
                    dSCorePropagationData
                    whenChanged
                    creationTime
                    pwdProperties
                    isCriticalSystemObject
                    name
                    ms-DS-MachineAccountQuota
                    minPwdLength
                    auditingPolicy
                    uSNCreated
                    forceLogoff
```

Here you can see values pulled from the rmtest domain, indicating that our username and password work, and it will most likely work in Redmine.

See also

- Refer to *Chapter 9, Troubleshooting*, to debug problems if they occur.

7
Integrating Redmine with Other Software

The recipes in this chapter are related to Redmine's integration with other software, as follows:

- Exporting to Microsoft Project
- Using Redmine through browser plugins
- Using Redmine mobile applications
- Activity monitoring through Atom feed
- Embedding Redmine into a web application
- Using the Redmine REST API with PHP
- Using the Redmine REST API with C#
- Integrating with Tortoise SVN or GIT
- Interacting with Redmine from Visual Studio

Introduction

Redmine is built with flexibility in mind. Its design and the good web application development framework (Ruby on Rails) that it is based upon provide it with ability to integrate with various software products in different ways. Such integrations can help developers, managers, or any kind of team member to integrate their favorite work environment or mobile devices with Redmine. Usually, it is done through Redmine API, and this chapter teaches readers how to use some of Redmine's popular third-party tools and create basic applications that connect to Redmine for purposes such as creating Redmine issues from your ERP software, web portal, or even a website contact form for CRM purposes.

Integrating Redmine with Other Software

Exporting to Microsoft Project

If, for some reason, you need to import a Redmine project into Microsoft Project 2013, this recipe teaches you how to export Redmine issue data and import it to a Microsoft Project. Please keep in mind that Redmine-exported data can be used or imported in other software capable of CSV or Excel import.

Getting ready

Prepare Microsoft Project to open legacy file formats:

1. Start Microsoft Project and create a new blank project.
2. Go to **File | Options**.
3. Choose **Trust Center**.
4. Click the **Trust Center Settings** button.
5. Choose the **Legacy Formats** tab.
6. Choose **Allow loading files with legacy or non-default file formats**.
7. Close dialog boxes by clicking **OK**.

How to do it...

The first step is to export data from Redmine to a CSV file. To do it, perform the following steps:

1. Click on **Issues** in the main project menu.
2. Expand **Options**:

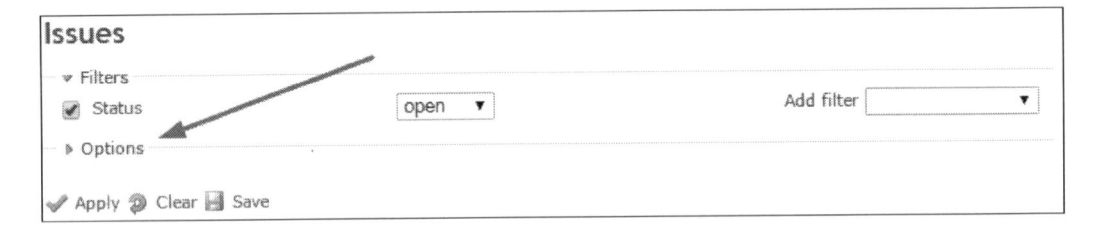

3. Choose and order the fields:

Chapter 7

[Screenshot of Issues filter page showing Available Columns, Selected Columns with annotations: "1. Choose and order columns" and "2. Save as Ms Project Export filter"]

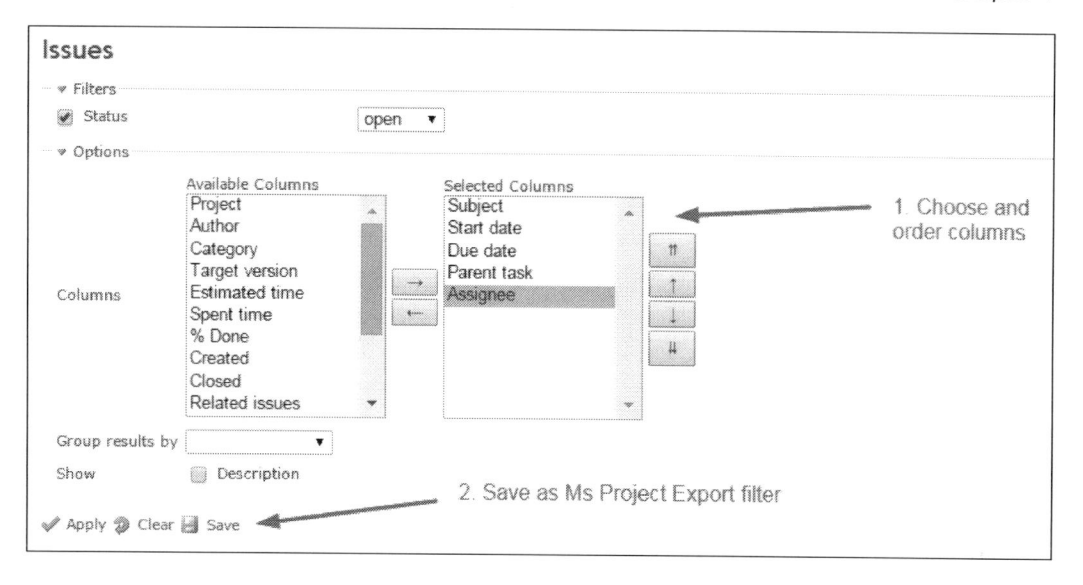

4. Save this as a new saved search for all projects so that you can reuse it later and for other projects if required. Click on the **Save** button.
5. Enter the **Name** field value, for example, MS Project Export, tick the **For all projects** checkbox, and click **Save**. Your saved query will be visible in the sidebar.
6. You should be redirected to the filtered issue page again. At the bottom of the page click **CSV**.

The second step is to import data to Microsoft Project. To achieve this, follow these steps:

1. Run Microsoft Project (2013, in the following image) and choose **New from Excel Workbook**:

[Image: New from Excel workbook icon]

Integrating Redmine with Other Software

2. In the open dialog, choose **CSV** file type:

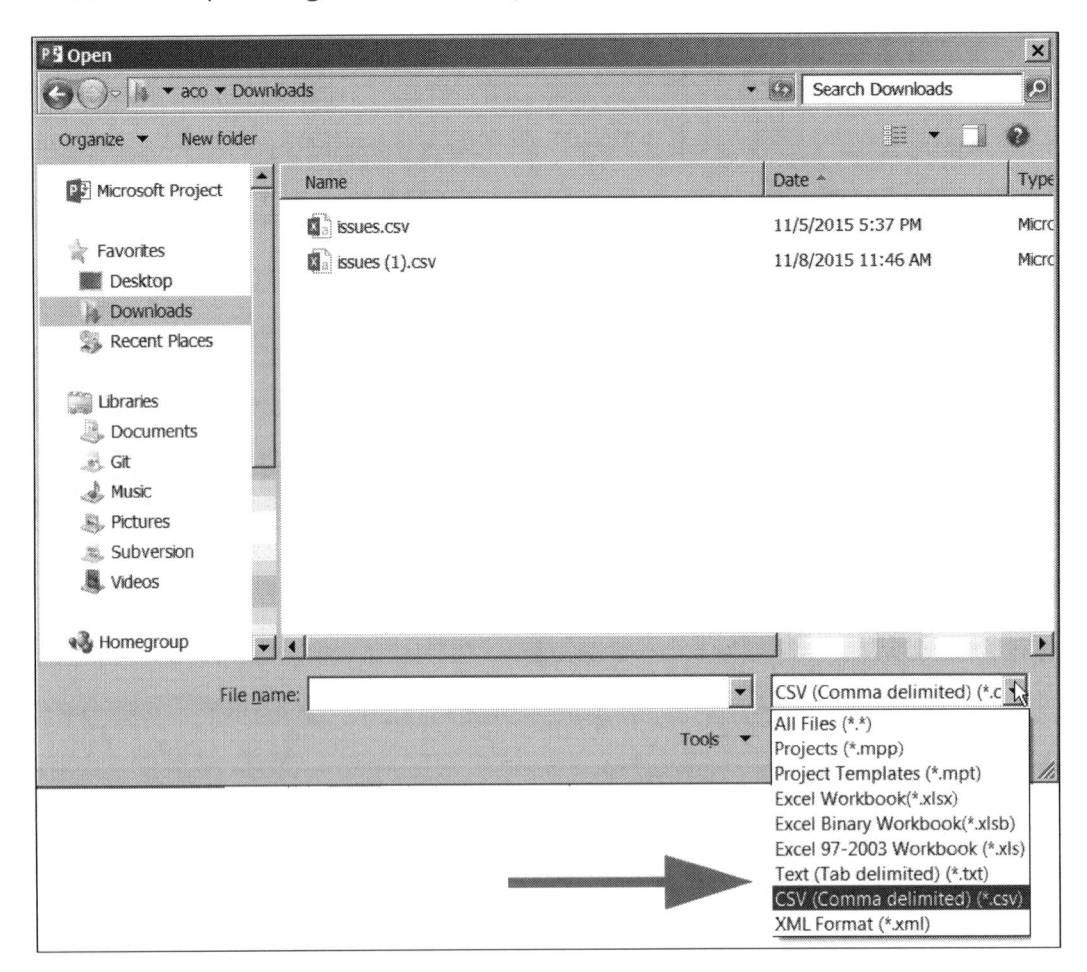

3. The **Import wizard** will show up, choose **Next**.
4. Leave **New map** selected, and click **Next**.

5. On **How do you want to import this file** leave **As a new project**, and click **Next**.
6. On the following screen, choose **Tasks**, tick the **Import includes Headers**, and for **Text delimiter,** enter comma, and click **Next**:

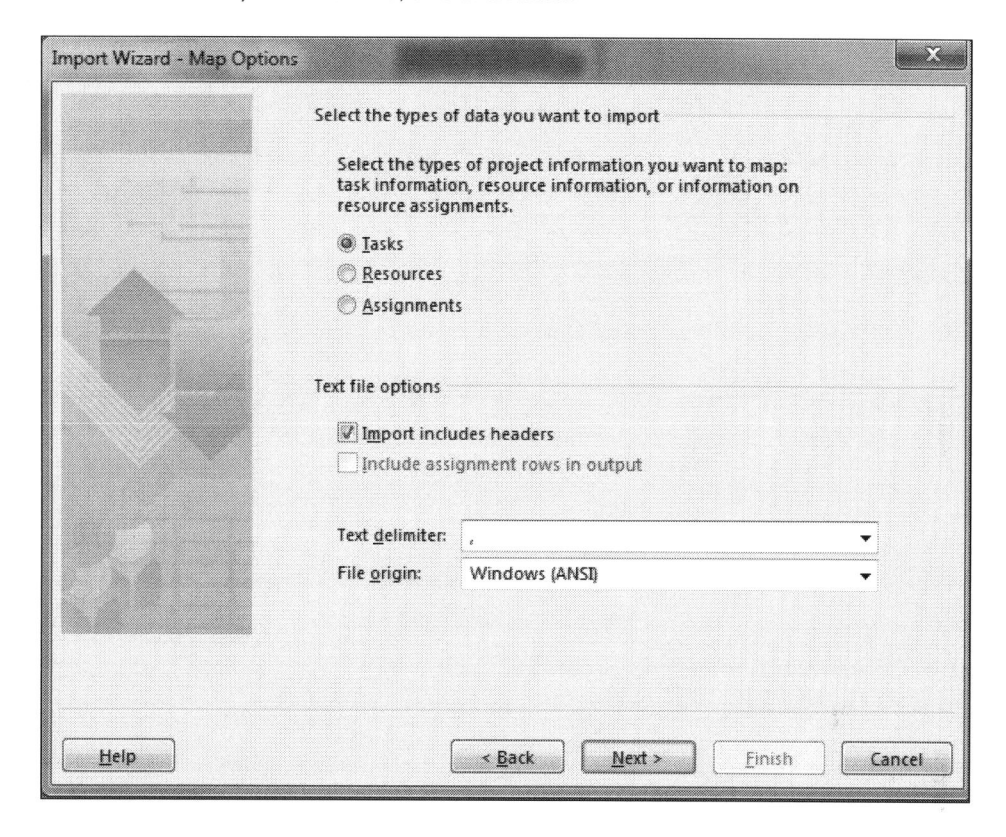

7. Perform field mappings, `# => Unique ID, Subject => Name, Start date => Start, Due date => Finish, Assignee => Resource Name`, and click **Finish**.

Integrating Redmine with Other Software

> You can quickly find the Project's field name by typing the first letters to Microsoft Project field.

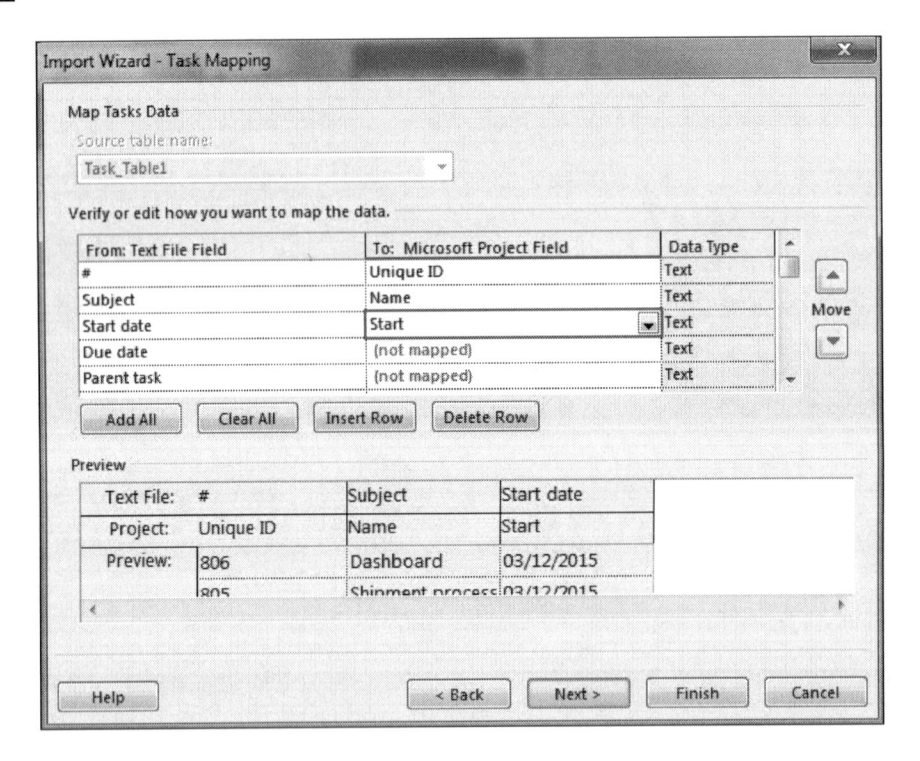

Once complete, your Redmine tasks will be imported to Microsoft Project, where you can perform various operations on these tasks. You can take a look at what the imported project might look like in the following image:

If you are not satisfied with the imported results, try experimenting in Redmine; or import your data to Microsoft Excel first and then perform actions on data, such as date formatting, if it's not properly imported to Project.

How it works...

This recipe utilizes Redmine's Issue filtering and CSV export features in order to create a CSV file that is compatible with Microsoft Project. At first, we prepare Microsoft Project to be able to import files because a CSV file is treated as a legacy file format. Then, we perform filtering of Redmine issues and export them to CSV. The last part is importing them to Microsoft Project by following the import wizard and mapping field names.

There's more...

Microsoft project's tasks can hold various attributes, just like Redmine's. In order to maximize compatibility, you can customize Redmine fields and change your Redmine project management process. One such tweak could be the creation of a custom field called Predecessors because Redmine does not allow export of Issue relations per type, but rather, it exports all issue relations under one field.

Using Redmine through browser plugins

As Redmine is a flexible **REST (Representational State Transfer)** web application. It is logical that there is going to be various third-party applications and even browser plugins that are aimed at making your daily work more pleasing. As there are multiple browser plugins related to these tasks, this recipe utilizes the one that, at the time of writing this book, has the most ratings on the Google Chrome extensions market.

How to do it...

Google Chrome extensions are usually downloaded and installed through the browser itself from Chrome marketplace. To access it, perform the following:

1. Access the **Redmine Issues Checker** extension from Konrad Dzwinel by typing the following URL: `https://chrome.google.com/webstore/detail/redmine-issues-checker/cmfcfjopbfmekonldgghddhkphapbpek?hl=en-US`.

Integrating Redmine with Other Software

2. Click the **Add Extension** button and click **Add Extension** again if requested. The extension should install, and a gray Redmine logo with question mark should be installed with a notification about its successful install:

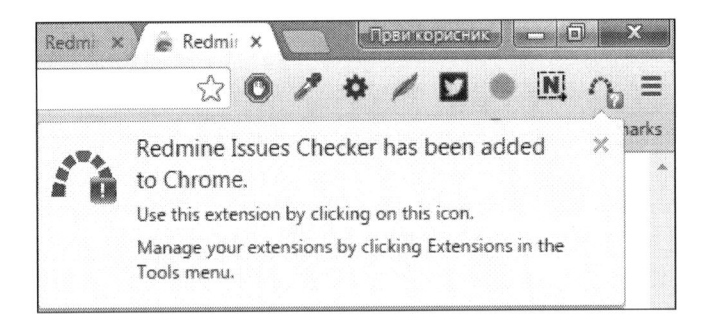

3. Right-click the icon and choose **Options**. A form with Redmine login details should appear, like in the following screenshot:

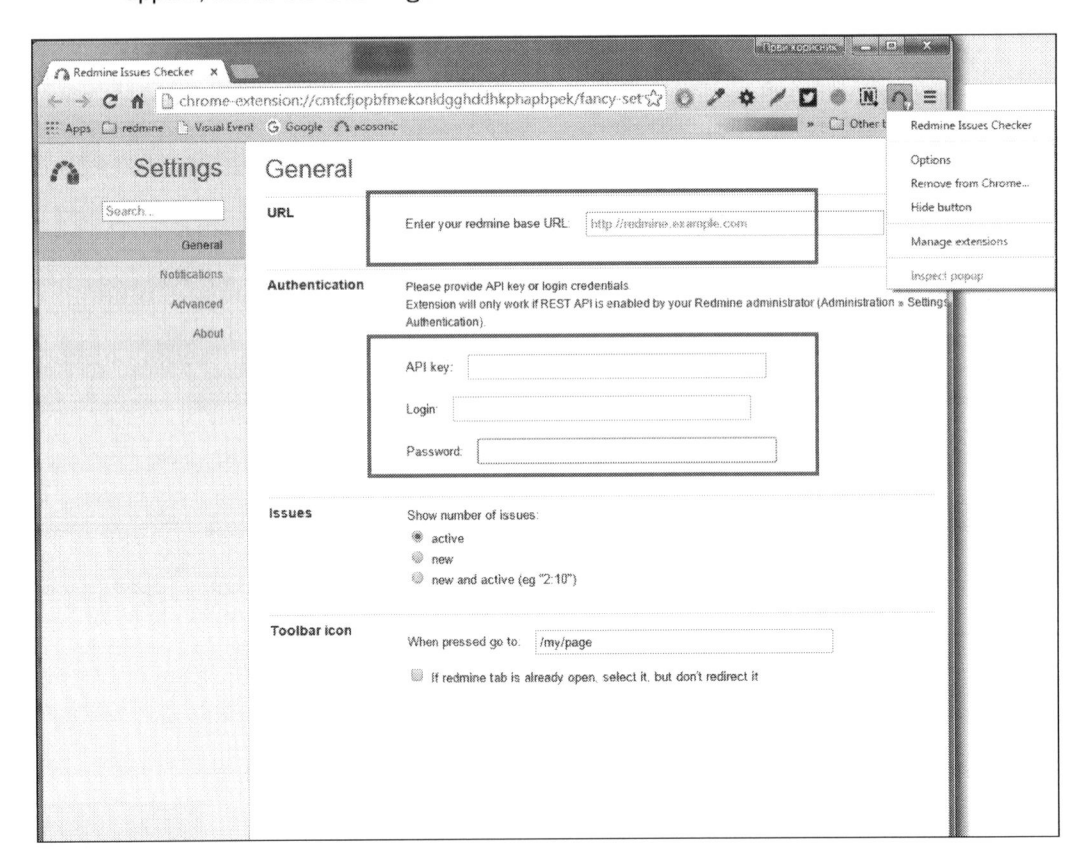

4. Fill in the details outlined in the preceding image. The first line is a Redmine **URL**; the second one is an **API Key**, and your Redmine **Login** and **Password**. To get your API key, perform the following:

    - Log in to Redmine.
    - Click **My account** at the top right.
    - In the right sidebar, click **Show** under the API access key section. Your key should look like the following image:

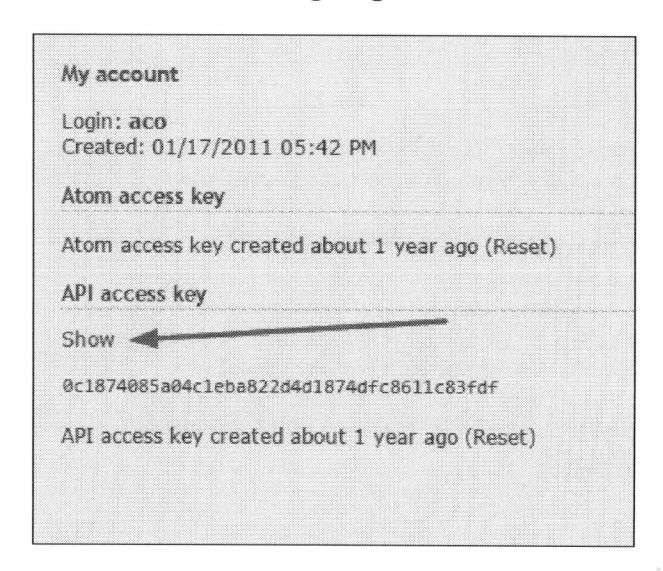

    ```
    My account

    Login: aco
    Created: 01/17/2011 05:42 PM

    Atom access key

    Atom access key created about 1 year ago (Reset)

    API access key

    Show  ◄
    0c1874085a04c1eba822d4d1874dfc8611c83fdf

    API access key created about 1 year ago (Reset)
    ```

5. Once configured, this extension will alert you when there is a new issue in Redmine, and clicking this will take you to your page. You can also configure different pages or options, through options.

How it works...

This plugin connects to Redmine through the API, and displays notifications.

There's more...

You can experiment with various Redmine extensions and plugins. To find them, just type Redmine in the **Search** field in the Chrome marketplace, which can be accessed directly from Google Chrome by typing: `https://chrome.google.com/webstore/category/extensions?hl=en-US`

Using Redmine mobile applications

Nowadays, smartphone application marketplaces are saturated with almost any term from everyday language. The same situation is with Redmine. In marketplaces, there are several applications that utilize Redmine API for easier touchscreen interaction with your favorite project management application. Choosing the right app for you is a matter of preference.

Getting ready

Prepare a smartphone, tablet, or another Android device.

How to do it...

This recipe uses Android RedminePM - Redmine Client App for showcase purposes only.

> Please keep in mind that there are multiple Redmine smartphone applications for every modern smartphone OS platform that are available from Android, IOS, and Windows marketplaces.

Application installation

Log in to Google marketplace with the same account that you use on your android device, and perform the following actions:

1. Navigate to `https://play.google.com/store/apps/details?id=jp.co.projectmode.redminepm`.
2. Click the **Install** button.
3. Choose your device if there are multiple choices and click **Install** once again.

Application configuration

Once the icon is installed, touch it like any other application, and then perform the following steps:

1. Navigate to **Settings | Add account**.
2. Enter your Redmine URL and your account details on the provided form.
3. Click **Save**.

Chapter 7

Once installed and configured, you will be presented with a screen which shows your projects. Clicking some of them opens a screen with issues like in the following image:

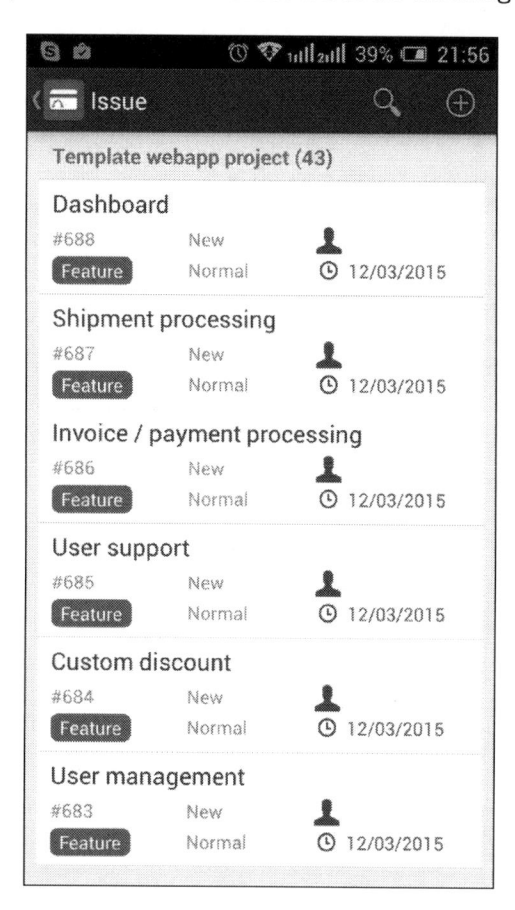

> Every application has its own features or pros and cons. It is probably best if you try some of them before deciding which one you or your team are going to use.

How it works...

Redmine API enables it to be used through any internet connected devices, and the appearance of various free or open source applications for smart mobile devices is a natural thing as the popularity of Redmine grows. In this recipe, we installed and configured one of many android applications on the market.

Integrating Redmine with Other Software

There's more...

Besides applications to interact with Redmine projects, issues, and other modules, on the market, you can find specialized time-tracking applications. These may come in handy if you are a software developer, or paid by the hour for any other type of work and the time is calculated through Redmine.

See also

Check out Google Play, iTunes store, and Windows marketplace for other Redmine applications for smartphones and tablets.

Activity monitoring through Atom feed

Sometimes, executives do not want or do not have enough time to interact with Redmine on a daily basis, or they just want to be informed about the status of certain Redmine projects or tasks, usually through their mail clients with Atom feed features.

Getting ready

This recipe uses Microsoft Outlook 2013.

How to do it...

The first thing is to determine what you are going to display in the Atom feed. For example, you want to track all open issues where the tracker is a bug on some project. To do this, perform the following steps:

1. Navigate to **Issues.**
2. Apply a filter aimed to display only new bug issues.
3. Find the Atom feed icon at the bottom of the page, right-click it, and choose **Copy Link**.
4. Start Outlook 2013.
5. Navigate to **File | Account Settings | RSS Feeds**.
6. Click **New**.
7. Paste the copied link and click **Add**.
8. Click **OK**.
9. Click **Close**.

Your RSS feed should be visible in Outlook:

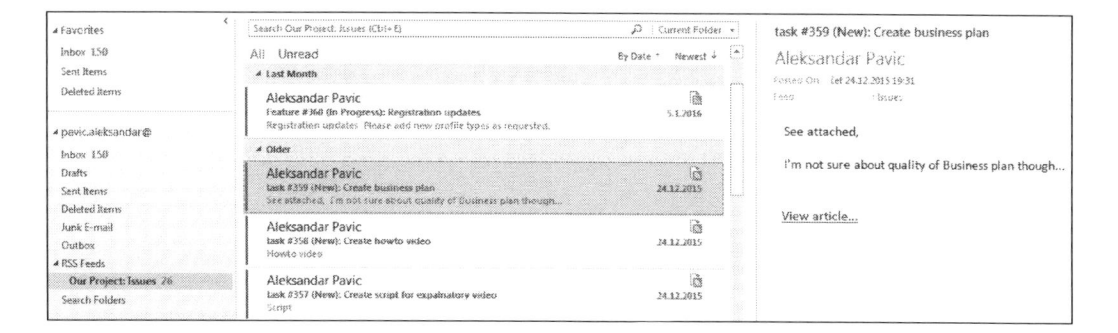

Clicking **View article** opens the browser and takes you to this issue's page in Redmine.

> Instead of Bugs, Features, and Support, you can add your own tracker, such as Customer Inquiry.

This way, for example, a company CEO or product development manager can track all new complaints from their usual work environment, which may help them make daily decisions according to most recent events.

> Timely responses can help preserve your customer.

How it works...

In Redmine, there are multiple points that can be tracked through Atom feed. Whether you are going to track saved searches, news, or activity, look for the Atom icon at the bottom of the page and use your favorite Atom feed reader to track updates.

Atom feed integration utilizes built-in Atom feed features, and links already contain your Atom access key, which can be reset if required through the **My Account** page.

See also

Refer to the *Putting the timeline to good use* recipe in *Chapter 4, Improving Team Performance*.

Integrating Redmine with Other Software

Embedding Redmine into a web application

There may be numerous reasons why would you want to display complete Redmine, or part of it as a part of some other website, for example, a corporate intranet portal, such as SharePoint, or some dashboard. In this scenario, you are going to learn how to display Redmine reports on time spent on particular projects in this current year, and hide the headers, leaving only real-time reports.

Getting ready

A Redmine administrator account is necessary. To prepare Redmine for these steps, the first thing to do is administration settings preparation:

1. Navigate to **Administration | Settings | Authentication**.
2. Uncheck the **Authentication required** checkbox.

> This will leave your public projects browsable by unauthenticated users.

3. Navigate to the project settings of the project that you want to access– **Project | Settings | Information**.
4. Tick the **Public** checkbox.
5. Click the **Save** button.

The second thing to do is due to the same origin policy. If your Redmine is hosted on a different domain, then in the website you are trying to embed it into:

1. Navigate to your Redmine installation folder, subfolder `/app/controllers`.
2. Open your `application_controller.rb` in text editor.
3. Add the following code:

```
#********** Begin Custom Code **************
  after_filter :embed_set_access_control_headers
  def embed_set_access_control_headers
    headers['Access-Control-Allow-Origin'] = '*'
    headers['Access-Control-Allow-Methods'] = 'POST, GET, OPTIONS, PUT'
    headers['Access-Control-Max-Age'] = "1728000"
  end
#********** End Custom Code **************
```

In the `before_filter` section (usually at the top of the file)

4. Restart Redmine.

> In line headers `['Access-Control-Allow-Origin'] = '*'` of the preceding code, you should replace * with the URL of the website that you are allowing access to Redmine. The star character allows access to every IP address on the internet.

How to do it...

Once you have made sure that prerequisites are done, here is how to generate a report, for example, how many hours each user spent in the current year on a project:

1. Log out from Redmine.
2. Navigate to the project that you want to use.
3. In the right sidebar on the project's homepage click **Report**.
4. In the topmost dropdown choose **this year**; in the bottom dropdown choose **User**. The **Details** dropdown should be already set to **Month**:

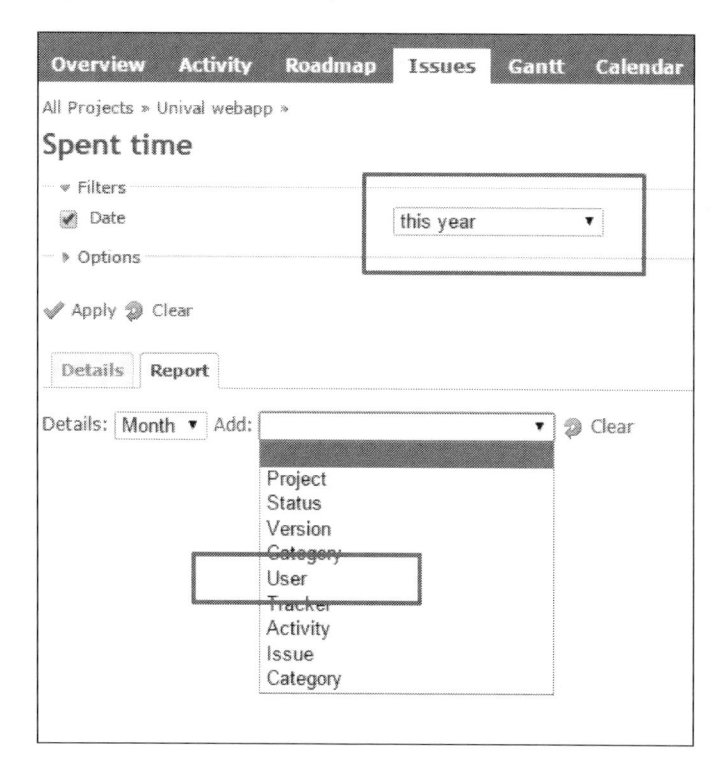

5. Copy the URL from the address bar to the clipboard.

6. The next part is embedding the URL of the report to your site or portal. You can find sample HTML or Javascript code, which embeds the preceding generated report to an HTML page, as follows:

```html
<html>
<head>
<style>
#if1 .contextual,#if1 .breadcrumb, #if1 #query_form, #if1 .other-formats {display: none;}
</style>
<script src="https://ajax.googleapis.com/ajax/libs/jquery/2.1.3/jquery.min.js"></script>
</head>
<body>

<h1>Your website...</h1>
<div id="if1"></div>

<script type="text/javascript">
$(function() {

$("#if1").load("http://redmine.mydomain.com/projects/website-backend/time_entries/report?utf8=%E2%9C%93&f%5B%5D=spent_on&op%5Bspent_on%5D=y&f%5B%5D=&columns=month&criteria%5B%5D=user #content");

});

</script>
</body>
</html>
```

7. In the preceding code, you have performed access control origin, and if the other settings were done right it should produce output like in this example:

Your website...

Spent time

Total time: 233.00 hours

User	2015-2	2015-3	2015-4	2015-5	2015-6	2015-7	2015-8	2015-9	2015-10	2015-11	Total time
Aleksandar Pavic	6.00	3.00	11.00	2.00		4.00	22.00	5.00			53.00
Miodrag Dragić			6.00	8.00	1.00		12.00	12.50	3.00	1.00	43.50
Tatić Dušan		6.00	30.00	16.00	10.00		19.00	5.00	26.00		112.00
Savomir Ćelić		5.00	19.00	0.50							24.50
Total time	6.00	14.00	66.00	26.50	11.00	4.00	53.00	22.50	29.00	1.00	233.00

To troubleshoot issues with this recipe, turn on the development console of your browser (usually the F12 key). One possible message in your console may look like *No 'Access-Control-Allow-Origin' header is present on the requested resource*. This means you have not performed the *Getting Ready* step properly.

How it works...

This is a complicated recipe due to the fact that you need to modify `application_controller.rb` in order to overcome browser-introduced same origin limitation. To make this work, first we had to disable the obligatory Redmine authentication, then make the project public. After this, we modified `application_controller` in such a way to allow the CORS request from our website to Redmine. In the second part of this recipe, we generated a sample report, and then created an HTML file, which includes a jQuery library, and loads part of the Redmine report. At the top of the file, notice the style element, which hides unwanted parts of the Redmine report.

There's more...

This recipe considers that there is no authentication. If you want to preserve authentication, there are two methods that you can use to preserve it. One is to develop a script that will perform authentication before doing the Request. Another is to have a copy of the database and another instance of Redmine, which will be used for these purposes. Here is a sample PHP file that you can use on your website or intranet portal, which performs three requests (first, request to grab the authenticity token; second, request to log in; and third, request to grab the file that you want to display on your website). Please keep in mind that you need to extract data and hide elements in this case. To use this file, make sure that you have `curl` installed on your server and replace configuration variables at the top of the file:

```php
<?php
#settings
$username = "user";
$password = "pass";
$redmineUrl = "http://redmine.yourdomain.com/";
$requestUrl = "http://redmine.yourdomain.com/projects/website-backend/time_entries/report?utf8=%E2%9C%93&f%5B%5D=spent_on&op%5Bspent_on%5D=y&f%5B%5D=&columns=month&criteria%5B%5D=user";

# First call gets hidden form field authenticity_token and session cookie
$ch = curl_init();
$sTarget = $redmineUrl."login";
curl_setopt($ch, CURLOPT_URL, $sTarget);
curl_setopt($ch, CURLOPT_SSL_VERIFYPEER, false);
curl_setopt($ch, CURLOPT_SSL_VERIFYHOST, false);
```

```php
curl_setopt($ch, CURLOPT_USERAGENT, $_SERVER['HTTP_USER_AGENT']);
curl_setopt($ch, CURLOPT_RETURNTRANSFER, true);
curl_setopt($ch, CURLOPT_COOKIEFILE, "/tmp/redmine.txt");
curl_setopt($ch, CURLOPT_REFERER, $redmineUrl."login");
$html = curl_exec($ch);

# parse authenticity_token from html response
preg_match('/<input name="authenticity_token" type="hidden" value="(.*?)" \/>/', $html, $match);

$authenticity_token = $match[1];

# set post data
$sPost = "username=$username&password=$password&authenticity_token=$authenticity_token&back_url=".$redmineUrl;

# second call is a post and performs login
$sTarget = $redmineUrl."/login";
curl_setopt($ch, CURLOPT_URL, $sTarget);
curl_setopt($ch, CURLOPT_POST, true);
curl_setopt($ch, CURLOPT_POSTFIELDS, $sPost);
curl_setopt($ch, CURLOPT_FOLLOWLOCATION, true);
curl_setopt($ch, CURLOPT_RETURNTRANSFER, false);
curl_setopt($ch, CURLOPT_HTTPHEADER, array("Content-type: application/x-www-form-urlencoded"));

curl_exec($ch);
curl_setopt($ch, CURLOPT_URL, $requestUrl);
curl_setopt($ch, CURLOPT_RETURNTRANSFER, false);

# display server response
$redmineResponse = curl_exec($ch);
echo $redmineResponse;
curl_close($ch);

?>
```

See also

Refer to the CORS Request explanation at https://en.wikipedia.org/wiki/Cross-origin_resource_sharing.

Using the Redmine REST API with PHP

The REST API is widely used by third-party applications. This recipe teaches you how to use a basic PHP application that connects to Redmine. For this example, we are going to create a sample app that submits issue to a project. Such applications can be used, for example, on website contact forms, and initiate a support or CRM request.

Getting ready

Before you begin, research ready-made examples and libraries that you can use in your project.

This recipe assumes that you know either PHP, HTML or C# (Windows forms).

How to do it...

One of Redmine's PHP libraries that updates often is kbsali's library, which can be forked or downloaded from `https://github.com/kbsali/php-redmine-api`.

To create your first Redmine app, perform the following steps:

1. In your `www-root`, create a folder called `phprmtest` (short for PHP Redmine test).
2. Download and extract `php-redmine-api` library to `phprmtest`.
3. Create a file called `test.php`.
4. Paste the following contents, replacing the values in the PHP section of the code to fit your Redmine URL, username, password, project ID, and user IDs:

   ```
   <html>
   <head>
   <title>RM Test</title>
   </head>
   <body>

   <form action="test.php" method="post" class="smart-green">

     <h1>Contact Form<span>Please fill all the texts in the fields.</span></h1>
     <p>
     <?php
     if(isset($_REQUEST['subject'])) {
     require_once 'lib/autoload.php';
   ```

Integrating Redmine with Other Software

```php
    $client = new Redmine\Client('http://redmine.yoursite.com',
'user', 'pass');

    $test = $client->api('issue')->create(array(
       'project_id' => 'webapp2',
       'subject' => $_REQUEST['subject'],
       'description' => $_REQUEST['message'],
       'assigned_to_id' => 3,
       'watcher_user_ids' => array('13','18'),
    ));
    if(isset($test->id)) print '<div class="success">Your message was sent successfully!</div>';
    else print '<div class="error">There was error sending Your message!</div>';
}
?>
    <label>
      <span>Subject:</span>
      <input id="name" type="text" name="subject" placeholder="Redmine issue title">
    </label>
    <label>
      <span>Message :</span>
      <textarea id="message" name="message" placeholder="Redmine description"></textarea>
    </label>
    <label>
      <span> </span>
      <input type="submit" class="button" value="Send">
    </label>
  </p>
</form>
</body>
</html>
```

5. Open the `test.php` in your browser. This is usually `http://localhost/phprmtest/test.php`, and you should get a form like this:

Chapter 7

Contact Form
Please fill all the texts in the fields.

Subject:
Redmine issue title

Message :
Redmine description

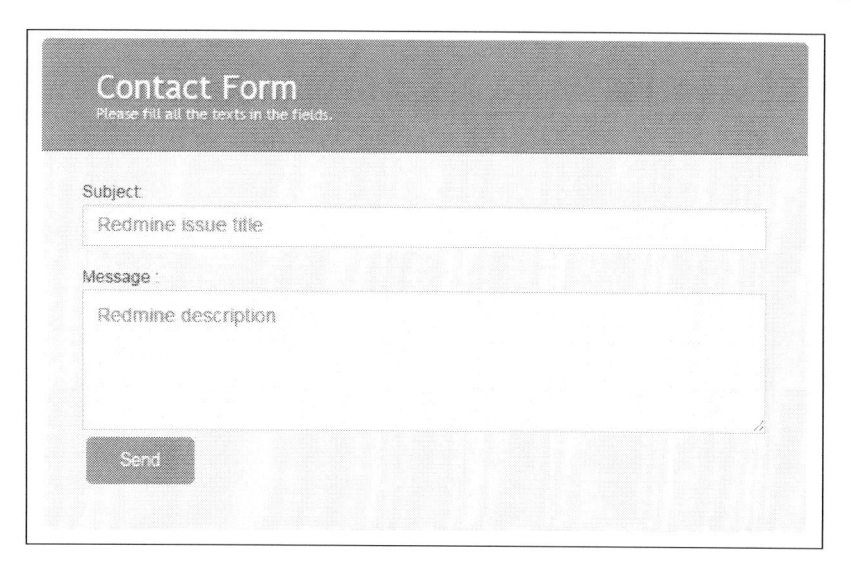

Send

6. Fill the form values and click **Send**.
7. You should get a **Your message was sent successfully!** message, and a new issue should be visible in Redmine under your project.

> This recipe shows only basic stuff. For the full features of Redmine API and the library's capabilities, read the documentations and look for more examples.

How it works...

This recipe utilizes Redmine's REST API and a third-party library made for PHP. First, we downloaded or git cloned kbsali's Redmine PHP library, from `https://github.com/kbsali/php-redmine-api`, extracted it, and created a sample test file. This file consists of an HTML form and a PHP part. We created a sample contact form, which creates, new issue in Redmine. To explain the code in more detail, `require_once 'lib/autoload.php'` includes all necessary Redmine API libraries and presents them to your application's scope. `$client = new Redmine\Client('..` creates a new object that opens a connection to your Redmine API. Then, `$client->api('issue')->create(` tells the API to use the endpoint issue, and method create takes the array as a parameter with issue-related data.

There's more...

If you are using Drupal or some other CMS or Framework, search for ready-made modules or plugins that you can use. One such example is the Drupal module that is available at `https://www.drupal.org/project/redmine`.

Integrating Redmine with Other Software

Using the Redmine REST API with C#

This recipe creates a basic C# desktop application that enables a user to select a project from a drop-down list, and then create a new issue in Redmine, taking the data from the form's fields.

Getting ready

You need Microsoft Visual Studio 2013 Community Edition or newer.

How to do it...

To create C# client for Redmine, we either need a ready-made C# library, or access to the Redmine API directly and parse responses, which is much more complicated. To create a sample C# app, follow these steps:

1. Start Visual Studio and create a new project, choose **Windows Forms Application**:

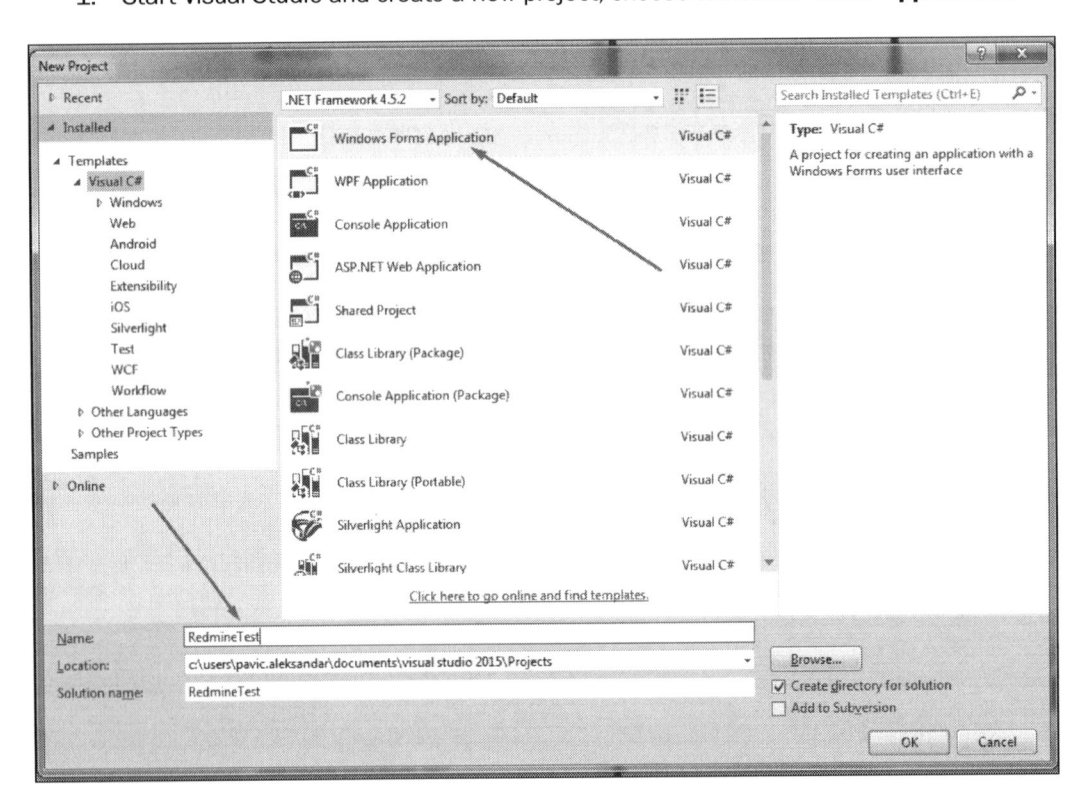

Chapter 7

2. Name it **RedmineTest** and click **OK**.

3. Download from the Internet the `https://github.com/zapadi/redmine-net-api` library or use NuGet to install the Redmine package. To install via NuGet, follow these steps:

    - Right-click **References** in **Solution Explorer** and click **Manage NuGet Packages**.
    - In the **Search box** type Redmine and press **Enter**.
    - Choose the latest version and click **Install**:

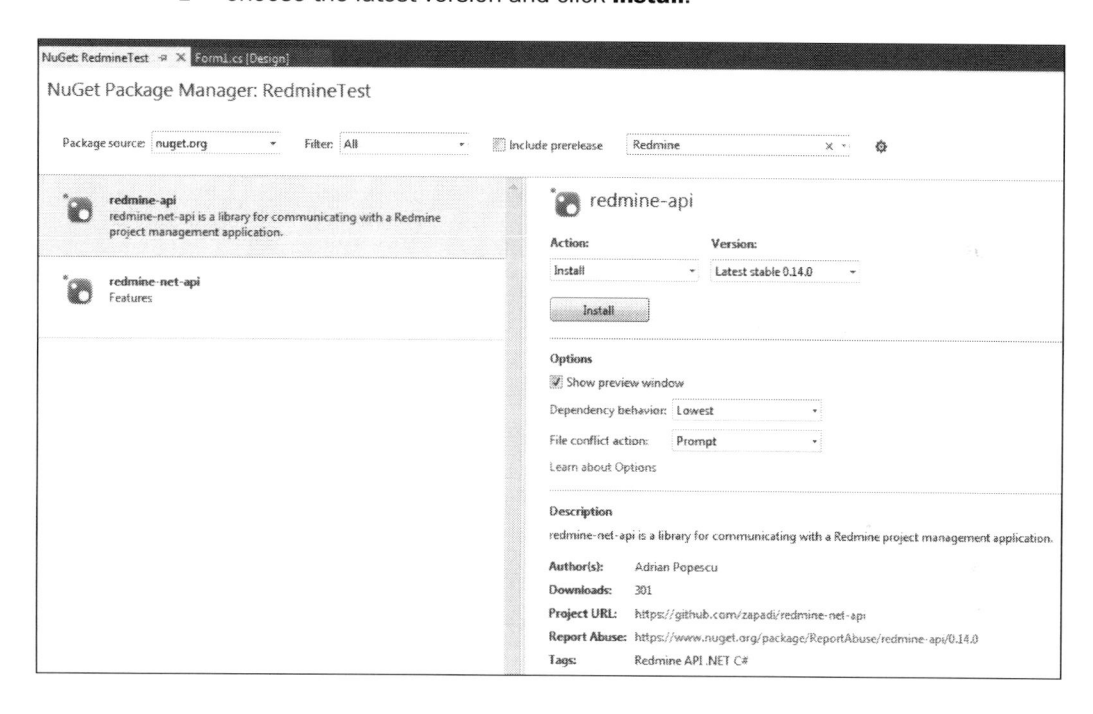

4. Drag the elements from **Toolbox** to the form to create a layout similar to this:

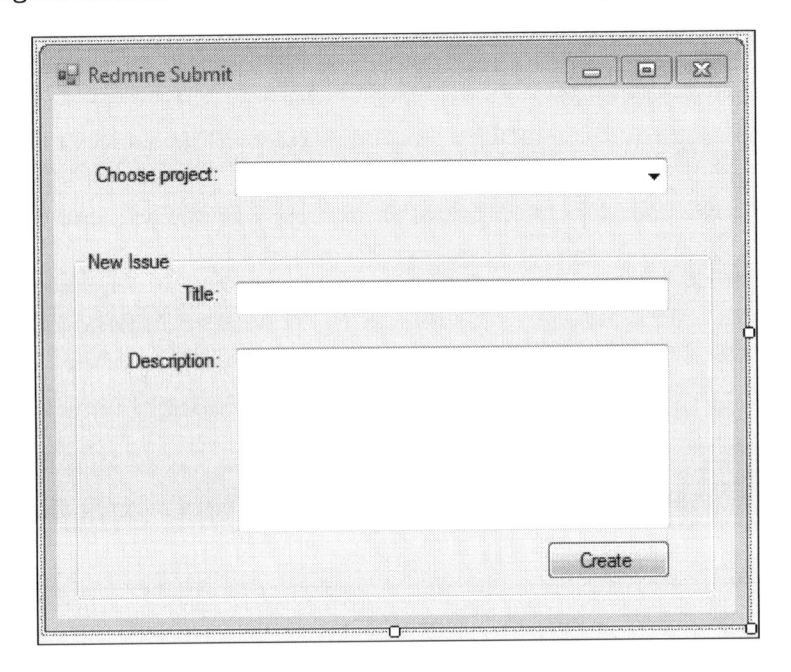

5. Use the following code for the form, and update names of form elements, if required, and your Redmine credentials:

```
using System;
using System.Collections.Generic;
using System.ComponentModel;
using System.Data;
using System.Drawing;
using System.Linq;
using System.Text;
using System.Threading.Tasks;
using System.Windows.Forms;
using System.Collections.Specialized;
using Redmine.Net.Api;
using Redmine.Net.Api.Types;

namespace RedmineTest
{
    public partial class Form1 : Form
    {
        private string host = "http://redmine.yoursite.com";
```

```csharp
        private string apiKey =
"0c1874085a04c1eba822d4d1874dfc8611c83fdf";

        public Form1()
        {
            InitializeComponent();
        }

        private void Form1_Load(object sender, EventArgs e)
        {
            var manager = new RedmineManager(host, apiKey);

            var parameters = new NameValueCollection {  };
            foreach (var project in manager.GetObjectList<Project>
(parameters))
            {
                ComboboxItem item = new ComboboxItem();
                item.Text = project.Name;
                item.Value = project.Id;
                comboBox1.Items.Add(item);
            }

        }

        private void button1_Click(object sender, EventArgs e)
        {
            ComboboxItem item = comboBox1.SelectedItem as
ComboboxItem;
            if (item != null) {
                var manager = new RedmineManager(host, apiKey);
                var newIssue = new Issue { Subject = textBox1.
Text, Description = textBox2.Text, Project = new IdentifiableName
{ Id = item.Value } };
                manager.CreateObject(newIssue);
            } else
            {
                MessageBox.Show("Please choose project!");
            }
        }
    }

    //just a helper function for combo box...
    public class ComboboxItem
    {
```

Integrating Redmine with Other Software

```
            public string Text { get; set; }
            public int Value { get; set; }

            public override string ToString()
            {
                return Text;
            }
        }
    }
```

6. Debug or run the example by entering the data, clicking create, and checking for this issue in Redmine.

How it works...

This recipe utilizes Redmine's REST API, and C# library, available from `https://github.com/zapadi/redmine-net-api` or via the NuGet package manager for Visual Studio. At first, we created an empty Windows forms application, then added the Redmine .NET API library. After this, we created some basic fields on the form and adjusted the example code. To explain the code in more detail, `using Redmine.Net.Api;` and `using Redmine.Net.Api.Types;` are namespaces of the Redmine .NET library. The `private string host = "http://redmine.yoursite.com";` and `private string apiKey = "0c1874085a04c1eba822d4d1874dfc8611c83fdf";` variables are the Redmine configuration settings that are based upon your configuration. The rest of the API interaction is performed through manager object, for which you can get intellisense suggestions or search for more methods in the library's documentation and source code.

There's more...

The same library can be used for ASP or other types of C# projects.

See also

You can find the source codes of Redmine Desktop clients, some of them done in C# at Redmine homepage `http://www.redmine.org/projects/redmine/wiki/ThirdPartyTools`.

Chapter 7

Integrating with Tortoise SVN or GIT

TortoiseSVN and TortoiseGIT integrate Redmine tasks in to their user interface through a plugin. This recipe explains how to install and configure the required plugin.

Getting ready

You need to download and install TortoiseSVN or TortoiseGIT from their websites: `https://tortoisesvn.net/` or `https://tortoisegit.org/`.

How to do it...

To start using the Tortoise SVN Redmine plugin, perform the following steps on client machines:

1. Download the TurtleMine plugin from `https://github.com/jlestein/turtlemine` and build it in Visual Studio, or download the compiled versions from `http://www.redminecookbook.com/turtlemine`.
2. Install the TurtleMine plugin.
3. Open Windows Explorer, navigate to your SVN project, right-click to open the Tortoise SVN menu, and choose **Tortoise SVN | Settings**.
4. Choose **Issue Tracker Integration**.
5. Click **Add**:

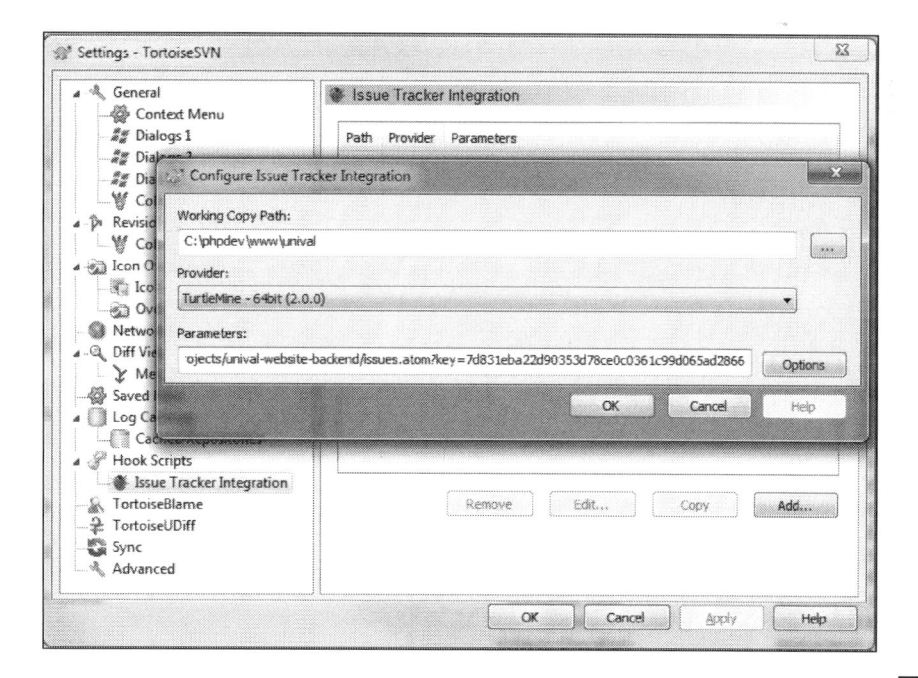

Integrating Redmine with Other Software

6. On the **Working copy** path, find SVN project that you want to use Redmine for, and click **Select Folder**.
7. On the **Parameters** field, paste the value of your project's issue list, and **Atom** feed:

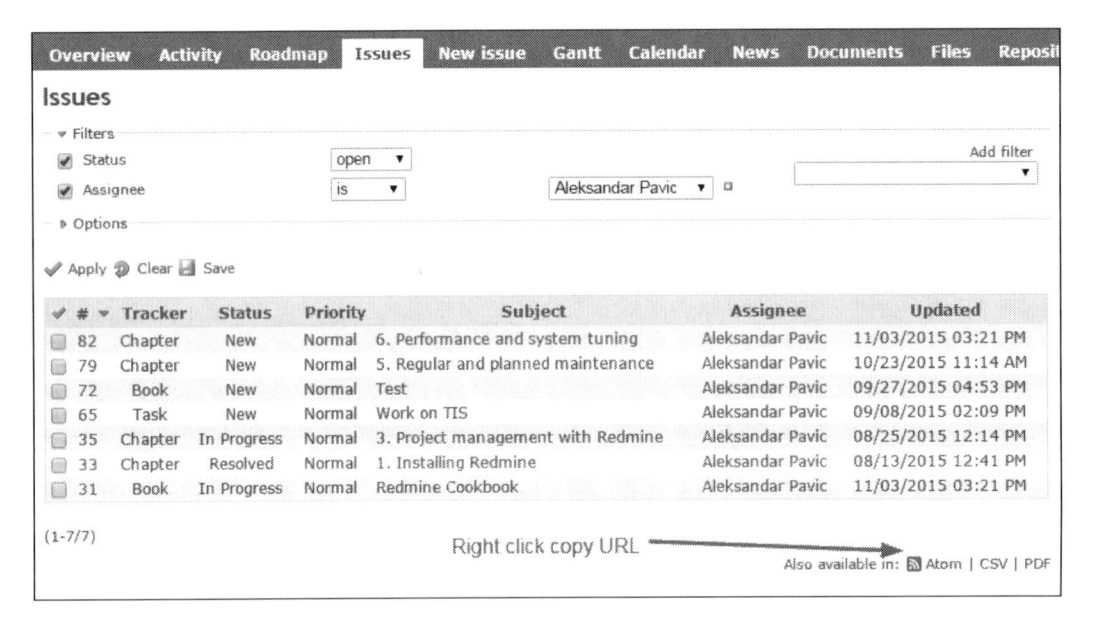

#	Tracker	Status	Priority	Subject	Assignee	Updated
82	Chapter	New	Normal	6. Performance and system tuning	Aleksandar Pavic	11/03/2015 03:21 PM
79	Chapter	New	Normal	5. Regular and planned maintenance	Aleksandar Pavic	10/23/2015 11:14 AM
72	Book	New	Normal	Test	Aleksandar Pavic	09/27/2015 04:53 PM
65	Task	New	Normal	Work on TIS	Aleksandar Pavic	09/08/2015 02:09 PM
35	Chapter	In Progress	Normal	3. Project management with Redmine	Aleksandar Pavic	08/25/2015 12:14 PM
33	Chapter	Resolved	Normal	1. Installing Redmine	Aleksandar Pavic	08/13/2015 12:41 PM
31	Book	In Progress	Normal	Redmine Cookbook	Aleksandar Pavic	11/03/2015 03:21 PM

(1-7/7)

Right click copy URL

Also available in: Atom | CSV | PDF

8. Navigate to **Options | Test**. You should get a **Success** message box if test is successful.
9. Click **OK**.
10. Right-click in Windows Explorer on your project's working copy and **do svn commit**.
11. Click the **Redmine issues** button, and you should get a screen that looks like this:

Chapter 7

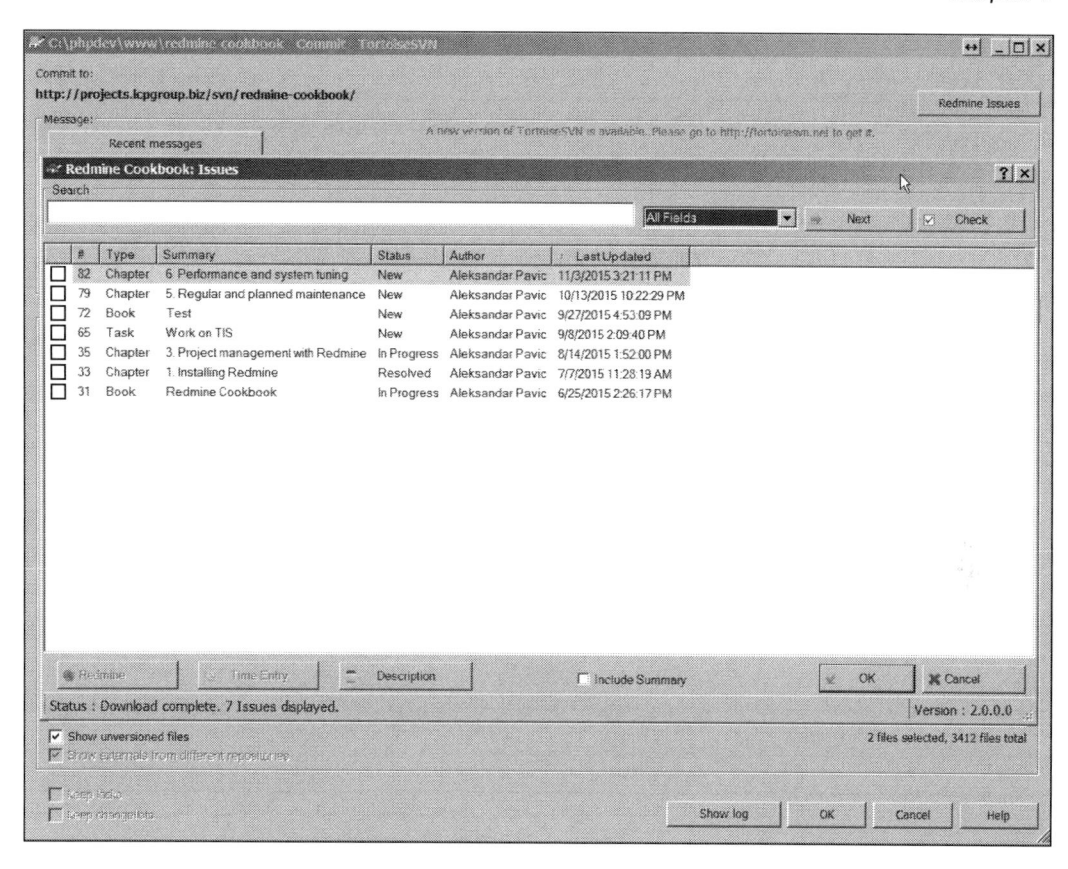

12. Check one or multiple items and click **OK**.
13. On your commit message, you will get a message that looks like this (Issue **#82**, **#79**).

How it works...

In this recipe, we used a third-party plugin for TortoiseSVN. At first, we installed the plugin, configured it by selecting the SVN working copy, and pasting the issues Atom feed.

> You can create an Atom feed with custom issue query, such as selecting only bugs or by any other criteria.

Integrating Redmine with Other Software

Once configured, this plugin is used like a hook and adds a Redmine issues button to Tortoise's commit screen. It reads issues from the Atom feed, provides several features, such as opening Redmine forms in the browser on click, providing issue details, or creating the commit message for you.

> The plugin works both for TortoiseSVN and TortoiseGIT, in the same way as described previously.

Interacting with Redmine from Visual Studio

Integrating Redmine tasks into Visual Studio can help programmers get a better user experience, and improve effectiveness, as everything is integrated in their known environment. Most likely, developers will not even need to log in to Redmine, unless they have something to comment on tasks. Everything depends on the team's workflow organization.

Getting ready

A Redmine administrator account is necessary and Visual Studio 2010-2013.

Make sure that **Administration | Settings | Enable REST web service** is checked.

How to do it...

To integrate Redmine with Visual Studio, either install vsix from the Visual Studio Gallery or download and install it directly from `https://redminetasklist.codeplex.com`. So, to start using this excellent plugin, the flow should look like this:

1. Download and install the plugin.
2. Navigate to **Tools | Options**.
3. Select **Redmine Task List** in Tree view.
4. Enter values for Redmine's user values **username**, **password**, and **URL**:

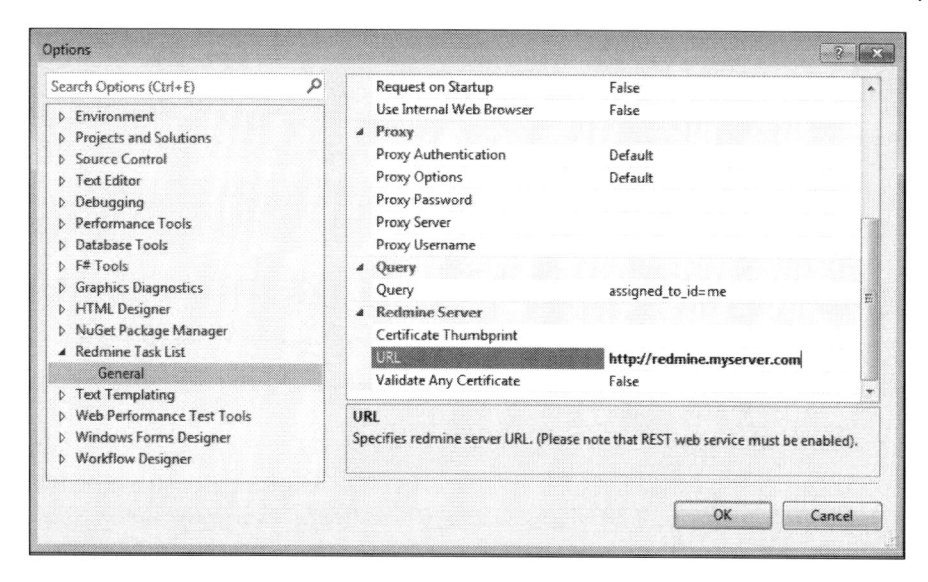

To start using the plugin, follow these steps:

1. Turn on the task list by navigating to **View | Task list**.
2. Turn on **Redmine toolbar**.
3. Pull data from Redmine, either from the toolbar icon or by navigating to **Tools | Get Redmine Tasks**:

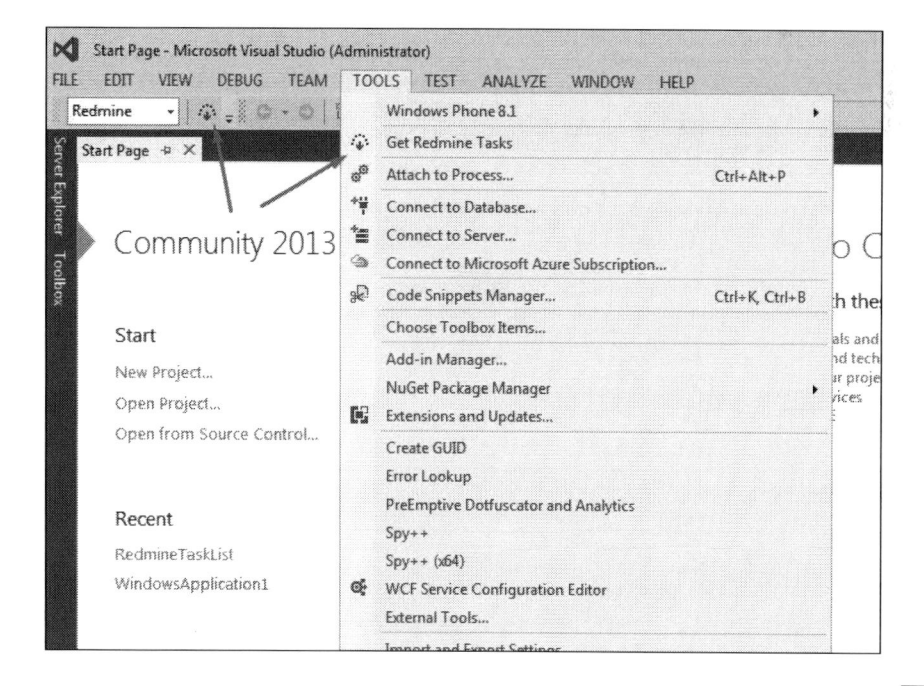

Integrating Redmine with Other Software

Once pulled, you should see tasks in the task list, which is just an ordinary Visual Studio window that can be docked, pinned, and so on:

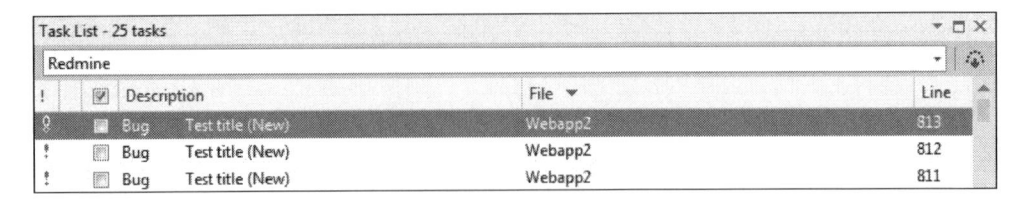

!		Description		File ▼	Line
?	■	Bug	Test title (New)	Webapp2	813
!	▫	Bug	Test title (New)	Webapp2	812
!	▫	Bug	Test title (New)	Webapp2	811

To sort issues by a per-project basis, click **File**, and it will sort and group them.

How it works...

This recipe installs a ready-made plugin for Visual Studio, versions 2010-2013, which gathers issue details from Redmine and displays them in Visual Studio's native Windows environment. After download and installation, it can be used on a per-project basis or configured to integrate the whole visual studio with Redmine, which is a result of the previous recipe steps.

There's more...

To use the plugin on a per-project basis, follow these steps:

1. Right-click on your project in solution explorer and choose **Redmine Settings**.
2. Set your Redmine log in credentials and query the URL for project details. To get query URL, just cut the `http://your_redmine_url` from address bar when you create the file in Redmine:

```
Redmine Task List Connection Settings
▲ Authentication
   Password              ••••••••
   Username              aco
▲ Query
   Query                 set_filter=1&%5B%5D=status_i
▲ Redmine Server
   Certificate Thumbprint
   URL                   http://redmine.myserver.com
   Validate Any Certificate    False

Certificate Thumbprint
Specifies certificate thumbprint used for validation.
                                   OK    Cancel
```

You can connect to multiple different Redmine instances on the basis of every project.

8
Getting the Most Out of Scripts and Plugins

The recipes in this chapter are related to scripts and plugins which extend Redmine's functionality, as follows:

- Pasting images from clipboard
- Keeping track of your clients
- Redmine for document management
- Implementing and using reoccurring tasks
- Practicing Kanban
- Importing issues to Redmine
- Using Redmine with Jenkins
- Using the Assigned issues summary e-mail
- Text formatting with CKEditor
- Being Agile with Agile Dwarf

Introduction

This chapter deals with scripts and plugins, which come with Redmine or are developed by a third party. When it comes to Redmine plugin installation, the procedure is usually the same:

1. Download, SVN checkout, or git-clone the plugin to the `plugins` folder. This chapter assumes Git checkout as a default instruction.

Getting the Most Out of Scripts and Plugins

> When dealing with opensource software and plugins, such as in Redmine's case, if a plugin is not updated for a while (several months or years), but the software that the plugin is made for is updated frequently, the situation that might happen is that a plugin is not working with the most recent version of software it is made for. Due to open source and social nature of its development, it is very likely that somebody else, apart from the original author, has forked the original repository and keeps maintaining it. In such cases, search for a more recent fork of the original plugin through GitHub, or other social coding interfaces.

2. Run bundle install to collect missing gems.
3. Migrate the database.
4. Restart Redmine.
5. Enable or configure the plugin on a per-project or global basis.

> Recipes are written for the Linux console, to use or test them under Windows, just replace the Linux commands with appropriate Windows commands. Also, replace cron jobs with appropriate scheduled tasks.

Pasting images from clipboard

Installing this plugin can increase productivity drastically and reduce the time required to take a screenshot, save it as a file, upload it to Redmine, and then add it as an image.

Getting ready

You need server administrator permissions and git installed on the server.

How to do it...

In order to start using this, paste images from the clipboard plugin following these steps:

1. Navigate to your Redmine home directory:

   ```
   cd path/to/redmine
   ```

2. Type the following:

   ```
   git clone git://github.com/credativUK/redmine_image_clipboard_paste.git plugins/redmine_image_clipboard_paste
   ```

3. Run bundle install to install missing gems.

    `bundle install`

4. Next migrate the bundle as follows:

    `bundle exec rake redmine:plugins:migrate RAILS_ENV=production`

5. Restart Redmine by typing the following:

    `rm tmp/ && touch tmp/restart.txt`

6. Once you have performed these steps, open Redmine in your browser and navigate to **Administration | Plugins** and the plugin should be visible:

7. Test your plugin by pressing print screen and pasting your image to view issue or by dragging it:

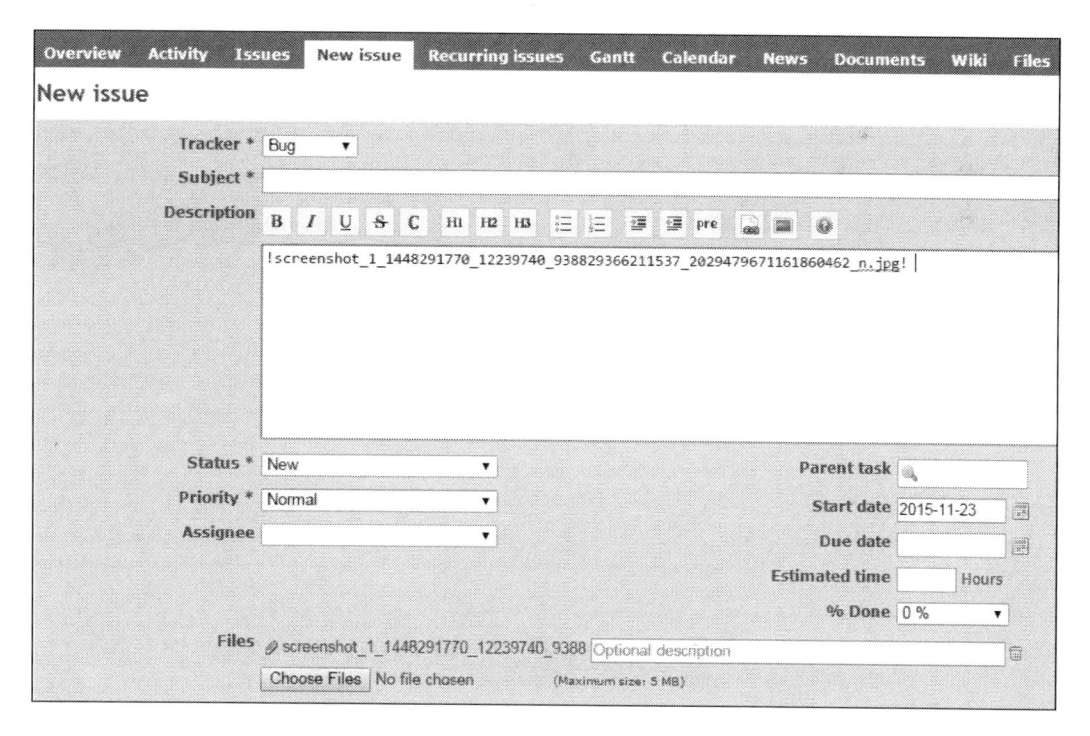

Getting the Most Out of Scripts and Plugins

How it works...

In this recipe, we installed a Redmine plugin, which lets users paste an image file from the clipboard or drag and drop it directly in to a new issue, comment, wiki page, or document. Installation is standard and done like any other Redmine plugin.

> The plugin may not work on some browsers; paste will only work with WebKit compatible browsers (Chrome, Safari), but drag and drop should be supported by most modern browsers including Firefox and IE.

There's more

Alternatively, you can use different plugins, such as `https://github.com/peclik/clipboard_image_paste`, which will let you edit images pasted from the clipboard. After installation, when you try to create a new issue, there is a small **Add picture from clipboard** link, which when clicked opens an editor that can crop pasted images:

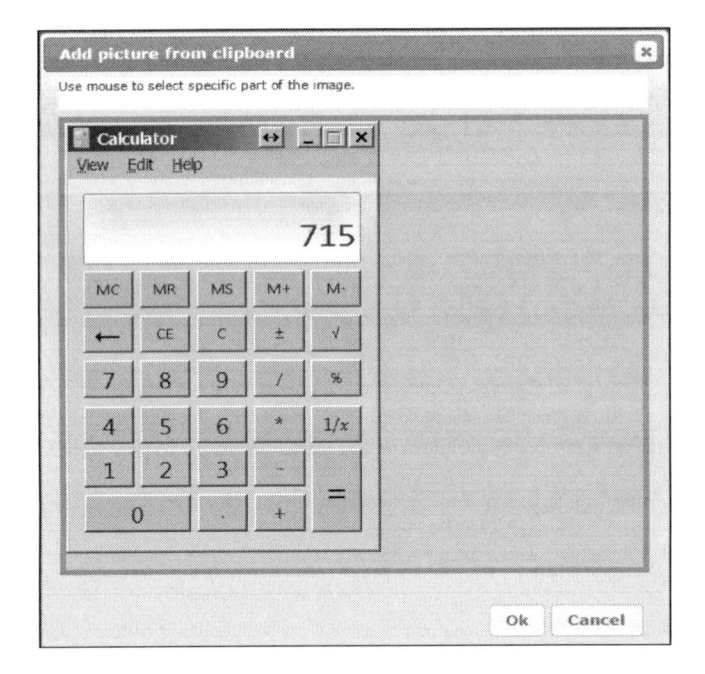

> File upload via drag and drop works since the Redmine 2.3 version. It does not create a !...! part unless it's an image file.

Keeping track of your clients

Redmine offers multiple ways to manage clients. Either create a special role called client and expand it, or use some plugins, like the one described in this recipe. Considering this, if you are following Redmine's main use-case scenario of managing multiple projects simultaneously, it is good practice to install clients plugin, and be able to quickly find client's contact details.

How to do it...

To start using this plugin, follow these steps:

1. Navigate to your Redmine installation root.
2. Grab the latest version from GitHub, by typing the following:

    ```
    git clone https://github.com/splbio/customer_plugin.git plugins/customer_plugin
    ```

    > Do not confuse this fork of the plugin with the original Eric Davis-es repository which is unmaintained, on GitHub https://github.com/edavis10/redmine-customer-plugin/tree/master because the original version is incompatible with Redmine 3.0 and later.

3. Install missing gems:

    ```
    bundle install
    ```

4. Migrate the database:

    ```
    rake redmine:plugins:migrate RAILS_ENV=production
    ```

5. Restart Redmine by typing the following:

    ```
    rm tmp/restart.txt && touch tmp/restart.txt
    ```

Getting the Most Out of Scripts and Plugins

6. Once Redmine is restarted, you should see the plugin installed and visible in the main menu as **Customer List**. Click it and click **New**, you will get a form to enter customer details like in the following screenshot:

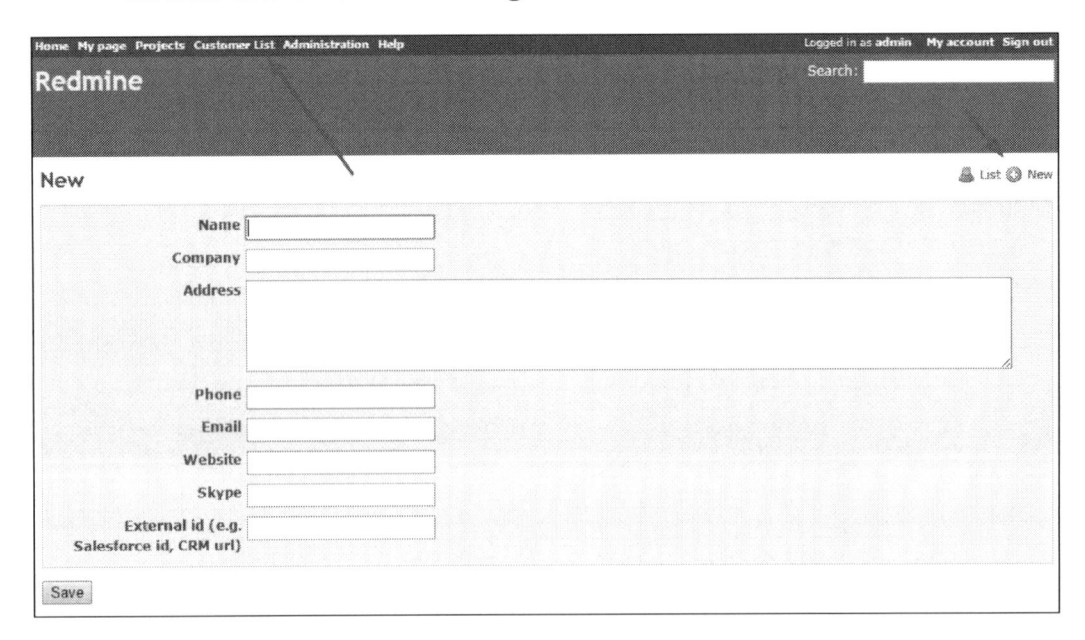

The customer module needs to be turned on for new and existing projects once it's installed. To assign a customer to a project, follow these steps:

1. Navigate to the main project's menu **Settings | Modules** and tick **Customer Module**.
2. Click the **Assign** button and choose **Customer** from the drop-down menu.

After this plugin is successfully installed and the customer assigned, you should see a list of your customers assigned to a project when the customer button is clicked in the main project menu:

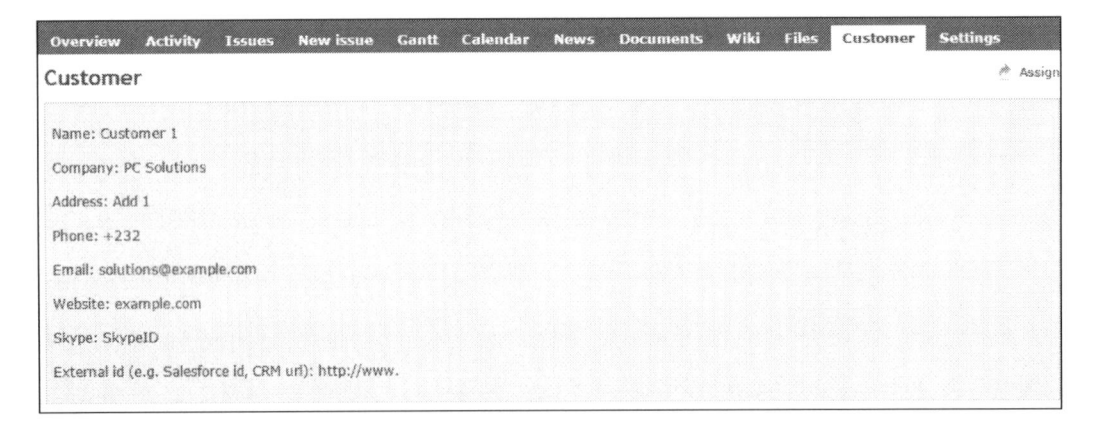

How it works...

The Redmine customer plugin extends the functionality of Redmine providing customer details that can be attached to a project. It installs just like any ordinary Redmine plugin, and once installed it needs to be turned on a per-project basis.

See also

If you need more complex customer details, there are different plugins available, and it is possible to create accounts for clients on Redmine and extend them with additional data, refer to *Chapter 2, Customizing Redmine*.

Redmine for document management

Redmine ships with a built-in documents module. Some users may not find this module satisfying their needs. In such cases, there are modules that improve this document's module functionality, or completely replace it. One such module is the Document Management System Features module.

Getting ready

If you want to use document-indexing and search features on the server, you need to install some additional software and libraries. To do this, open the console and type the following:

```
sudo apt-get install libxapian-ruby1.9.1 xapian-omega libxapian-dev xpdf
antiword unzip catdoc libwpd-0.9-9 libwps-0.2-2 gzip unrtf catdvi djview
djview3 uuid uuid-dev
```

> This recipe is crafted for the Ubuntu server. The Microsoft Windows version probably can be achieved using minigw or cygwin.

How to do it...

Once you have installed pre-requisites, if you are willing to use them to index, proceed with the installation of DMSF plugin by following these steps:

1. Open the console and navigate to your Redmine installation root.
2. Clone the git repository, as follows:

    ```
    git clone https://github.com/danmunn/redmine_dmsf.git plugins/redmine_dmsf
    ```

3. Run the following:

   ```
   bundle install -without development test
   ```

4. Run the database migration code:

   ```
   bundle exec rake redmine:plugins:migrate RAILS_ENV="production"
   ```

5. Restart Redmine as follows:

   ```
   rm tmp/restart.txt && touch tmp/restart.txt
   ```

Once this plugin is installed, it needs to be configured, and its roles and workflow need to be set up.

> Redmine DMSF does not modify the features of the standard documents module, but it can import documents from the standard module. To do this, type in the console:
>
> ```
> rake redmine:dmsf_convert_documents project=test RAILS_ENV="production"
> ```

To start using this plugin on your documents depending upon your plans of usage, you may need to prepare workflows for your documents (for example, Manager needs to approve the project status report, or change in business process). To do this, follow these steps:

1. Navigate to **Administration | Approval workflows**.
2. Click **New approval workflow**.
3. Enter a name for the new workflow.
4. Click **Create**.
5. Click the workflow's name on **Approval workflows**.
6. Click **New step**, select users that need to approve the document in a workflow, and choose **AND** or **OR**, as a rule for approval:

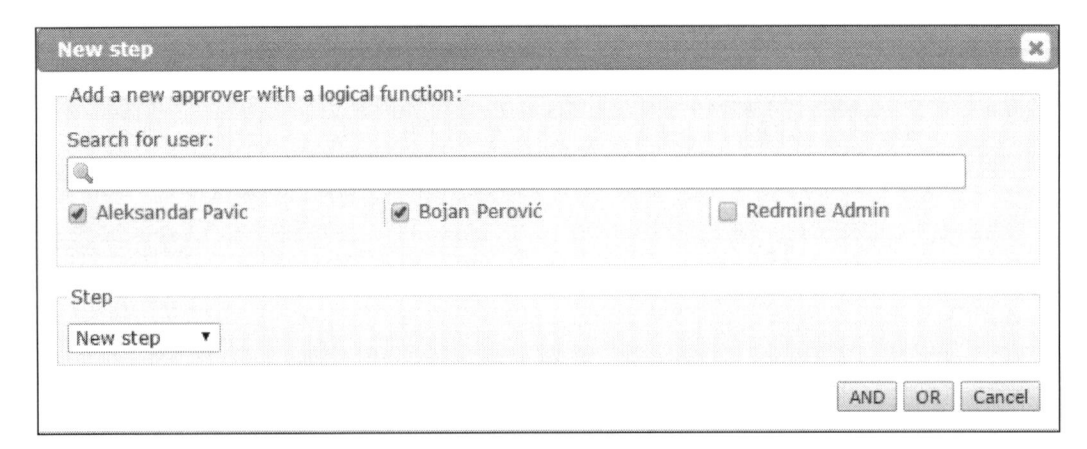

Chapter 8

Repeat the previous process to create workflows to fit all your business process needs.

To actually start using this plugin, follows these steps:

1. Enable it on a per-project basis while creating a new project or through the project's main menu by navigating to **Settings | Modules**.
2. On the project's main menu, you will see the menu item called DMSF, which when clicked opens a screen that displays the main document management features screen:

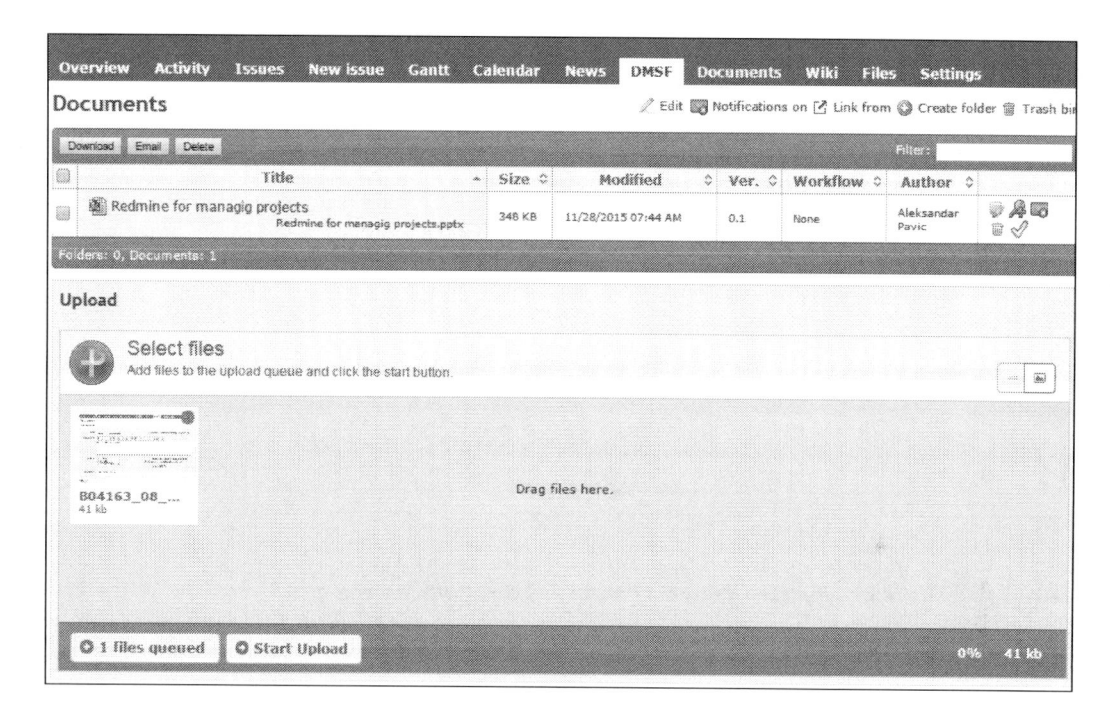

3. To upload one or multiple documents, just drag them to the designated area or click the **Add files** button and then **Start Upload**.

Getting the Most Out of Scripts and Plugins

4. After upload, when it is complete, you will be presented with a metadata entry screen where you can choose document revisions, add descriptions, and provide comments:

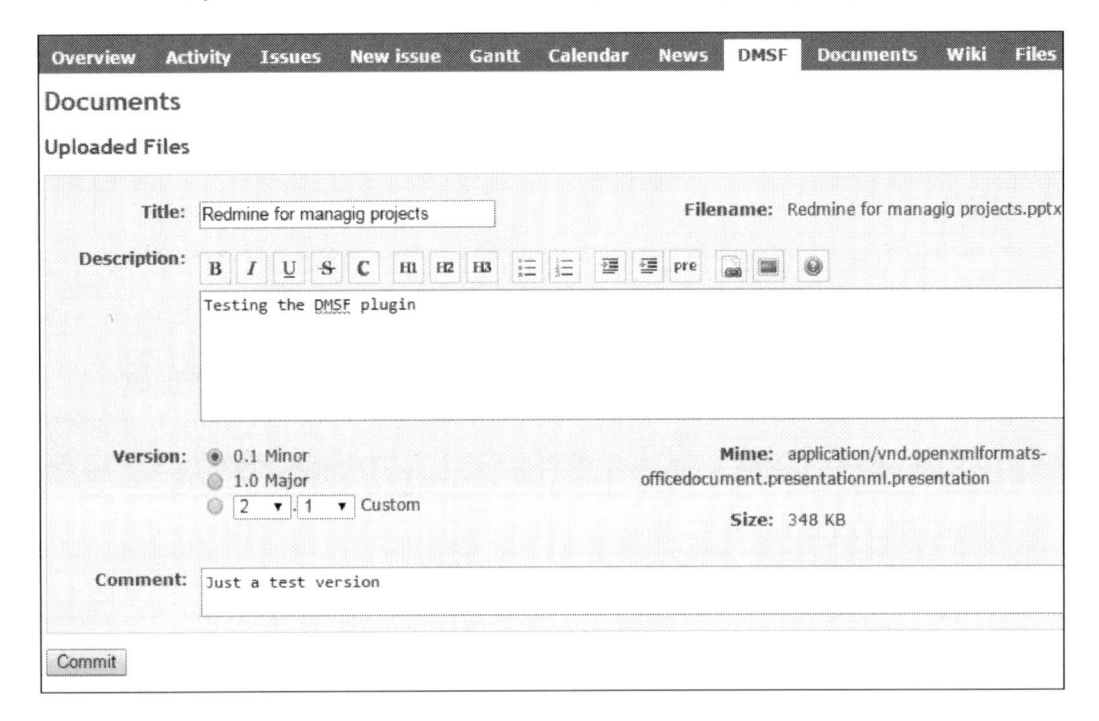

| Overview | Activity | Issues | New issue | Gantt | Calendar | News | **DMSF** | Documents | Wiki | Files |

Documents

Uploaded Files

| Title: | Redmine for managig projects | | Filename: | Redmine for managig projects.pptx |

Description: B I U S C H1 H2 H3 ≡ ≡ pre

Testing the DMSF plugin

Version:
- ● 0.1 Minor
- ○ 1.0 Major
- ○ 2 . 1 Custom

Mime: application/vnd.openxmlformats-officedocument.presentationml.presentation

Size: 348 KB

Comment: Just a test version

[Commit]

> Every time when any user updates a document through WebDAV or browser upload, its sub-version is automatically updated.

5. To start workflow on a document, after upload, just click on the check icon (last icon in the row in the document).

How it works...

At first, we installed xapian, which lets this plugin index various types of documents, such as PDF, DOC, and so on. Then, we installed the plugin as any other ordinary Redmine plugin. After optional configuration, the plugin is ready to be used on a per-project basis. This plugin is implementing most of the standard document management software's features.

There's more...

This plugin supports the WebDav protocol, which, if your server is properly configured, should enable your users to use the WebDav protocol through any of the clients, or a mapped network drive, just like they are using a folder on a local computer. To enable and map a WebDav drive and configure other settings, follow these steps:

1. Navigate to **Administration | Plugins**.
2. Find the DMSF plugin and click **Configure**.
3. On the **Webdav functionality setting**, choose **Activated**.
4. On the **Webdav strategy**, choose **Read/Write**.

On client machines use the Webdav client, or map a drive; on Windows on the command line, type the following:

```
net use X: http://your.redmine.com/dmsf/webdav/projectID/ /USER:you yourpass
```

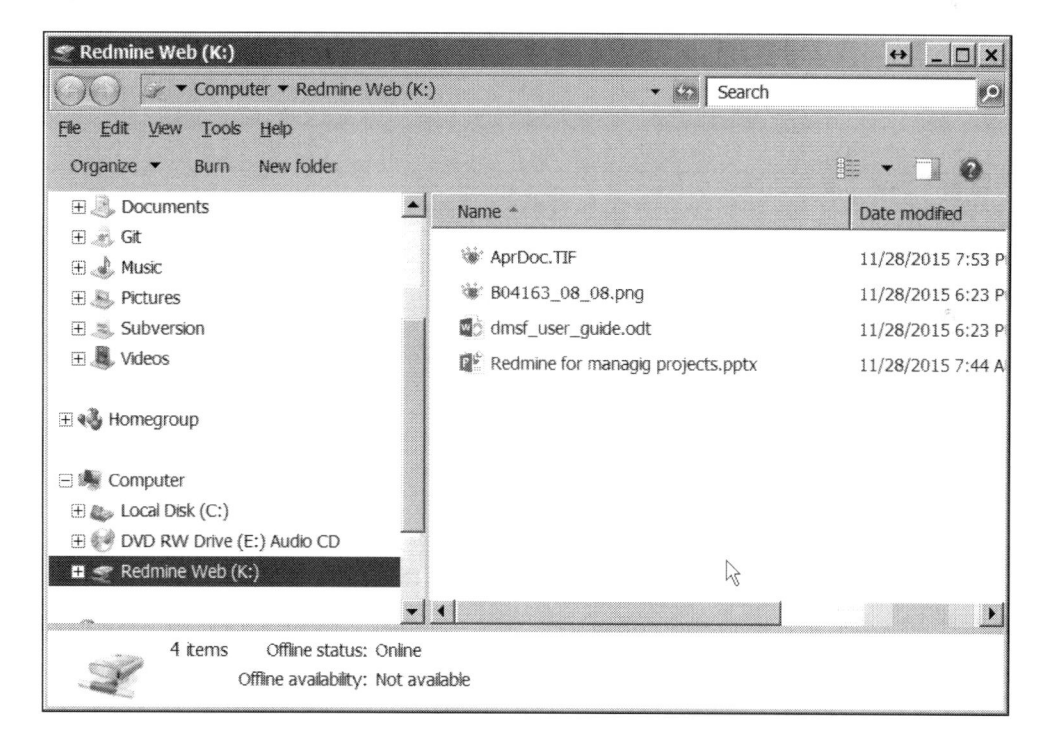

This will give you a mapped network drive of your project's documents. dding/removing or editing files will display automatically inside Redmine.

See also

Editing files directly on the Webdav mapped drive with Microsoft Office requires the creation of special files and locking their status via Webdav. Also, Microsoft creates problems with basic auth, and non-https servers. To work around these problems, either use some Webdav mapping software, such as webdrive, total commander with the Webdav plugin, or try to modify Windows keys as explained in the following article. Mapping webdav on different platforms can be found at: `http://redminecookbook.com/webdav_drive.html`.

Refer to the official Redmine DMSF plugin website at `https://github.com/danmunn/redmine_dmsf`.

Official RedmineDMSF can be found at: `https://github.com/danmunn/redmine_dmsf/blob/master/dmsf_user_guide.odt`.

Implementing and using reoccurring tasks

Reoccurring tasks is a plugin developed for Redmine, which creates a new issue in Redmine for each recurrence, linking the duplicated issue as a related issue. For example, your company may be having some kind of contract with a customer, which requires some kind of periodic activities, or any other kind of the same tasks, which require to be executed on some reoccurring schedule pattern. Redmine with reoccurring tasks plugin will make sure that you or your company fulfills its duties, as defined by a schedule.

Getting ready

Server and Redmine administrator access is required.

How to do it...

At first, we are doing a standard Redmine plugin installation using the following steps:

1. Navigate to Redmine root from the console.
2. Get the plugin code:

    ```
    git clone https://github.com/nutso/redmine-plugin-recurring-tasks.git plugins/recurring_tasks
    ```

3. Perform a database update:

    ```
    bundle exec rake redmine:plugins:migrate RAILS_ENV=production
    ```

4. Restart Redmine, as follows:

    ```
    rm tmp/restart.txt && touch tmp/restart.txt
    ```

5. Configure cron job:

```
15 */4 * * * /bin/sh "cd {path_to_redmine} && bundle exec rake
RAILS_ENV=production redmine:recur_tasks" >> log/cron_rake.log
2>&1
```

> Refer to the *Interacting with Redmine* only through e-mail recipe from *Chapter 2*, *Customizing Redmine*, for detailed instructions how to run scheduled `rake` tasks on Windows.

6. Configure the plugin's additional options by navigating to **Administration | Plugins**, find the **Recurring Tasks (Issues)**, and click **Configure**.

Plugin usage

Redmine reoccurring tasks plugin's usage is straightforward. Once installed and optionally configured, it is available for all projects, and accessible either the top menu button, or the project's main menu recurring issues item. When clicked, it opens a list of recurring issues:

#	Project	Current issue for recurrence	Recurs every	Fixed schedule?	Recur subtasks?	Next scheduled run	
494	Technical Support & Maintenance	Security logs check ()	5 days	✓		12/04/2015	Delete
475	Usamailagent	Code cleanup ()	10 days	✓		12/09/2015	Delete
514	Technical Support & Maintenance	Mail server spam blacklist check ()	1 week	✓		11/25/2014	Delete
429	Technical Support & Maintenance	Code revision ()	1 week	✓		02/07/2015	Delete
396	Technical Support & Maintenance	Server dist upgrade and security updates ()	1 month	✓		12/25/2014	Delete
312	Usamailagent	String extraction for translation ()	1 month	✓		04/03/2015	Delete
594	Usamailagent	Delete test accounts ()	2 months	✓		04/21/2015	Delete
517	Technical Support & Maintenance	Backup check & test ()	1 day			11/19/2014	Delete
824	Unival webapp	Check logs ()	1 day			11/30/2015	Delete
517	Technical Support & Maintenance	Backup check & test ()	1 day	✓		11/19/2014	Delete

To actually add a task or issue to this list, perform the following steps:

1. Create a new issue in the ordinary way by clicking **New issue** and entering its details, for example **Backup check & test()**.
2. On the issue view screen, click **Add recurrence**.

Getting the Most Out of Scripts and Plugins

3. Choose recurrence options and click **Create Recurring task**:

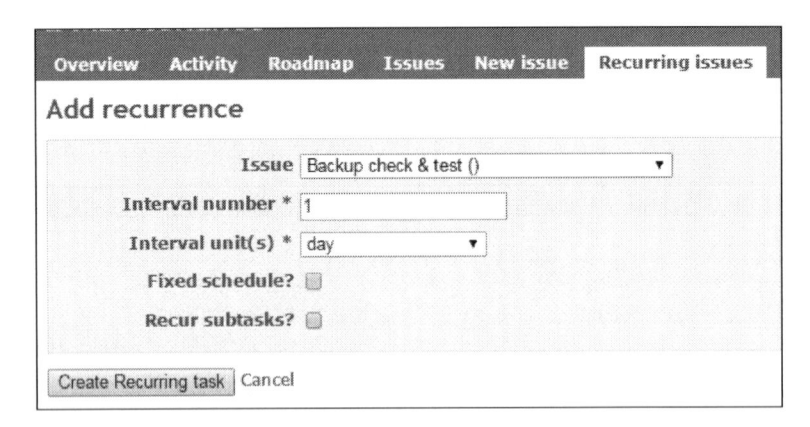

4. Once set up, your issue will have a Recurring tasks section, which will look like this:

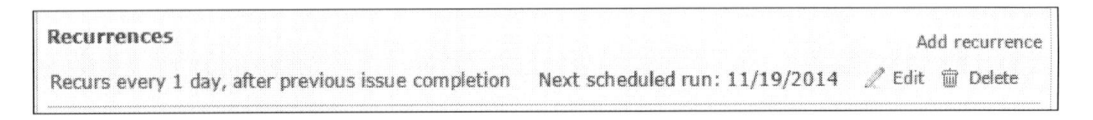

How it works...

In the first few steps, we installed reoccurring tasks, just like any other regular Redmine plugin, and at *step 5*, we configured cron job, which triggers the plugin's rake task. Plugin usage is straightforward; once it is installed, the **Recurring issues** link appears in the project's main menu, and top menu. Cron job with the rake task ensures that issues are automatically rescheduled and reopened. Adding reoccurring tasks offers schedule creation options for reoccurrence interval, which offers days, weeks, months, and years. If months are chosen, then an interval modifier dropdown appears, offering the choice of which day in month the task will reoccur.

Practicing Kanban

This book cannot teach its readers how to practice Kanban on their projects, but it can teach users how to extend Redmine's functionality to support Kanban's requirements. In this sense, this recipe deals with installation and usage of the Redmine Kanban plugin.

Chapter 8

> Originally, this plugin was developed by Eric Davis, who announced on February 14, 2013, that he will no longer maintain his Redmine plugins. So, this recipe uses the most recently updated fork, in light of maintaining the most recent Redmine version compatibility.

Getting ready

Server and Redmine administrator accounts are necessary.

Install `gem` requirements as follows:

Open the console and type the following:

```
gem install aasm block_helpers
```

Provide the sudo password if asked by installer. It may automatically install some required dependency.

How to do it...

To install the Redmine Kanban plugin, follows these steps:

1. Navigate to Redmine root.
2. Clone the repository as follows:

   ```
   git clone https://github.com/kostgr/redmine_kanban.git plugins/redmine_kanban
   ```

3. Run the following:

   ```
   bundle install
   ```

4. Migrate the plugin's database:

   ```
   bundle exec rake redmine:plugins:migrate RAILS_ENV=production
   ```

5. Restart Redmine as follows:

   ```
   rm tmp/restart.txt && touch tmp/restart.txt
   ```

Getting the Most Out of Scripts and Plugins

6. Configure the plugin by navigating to **Administration | Plugins** and clicking **Configure** in the Kanban plugin row:

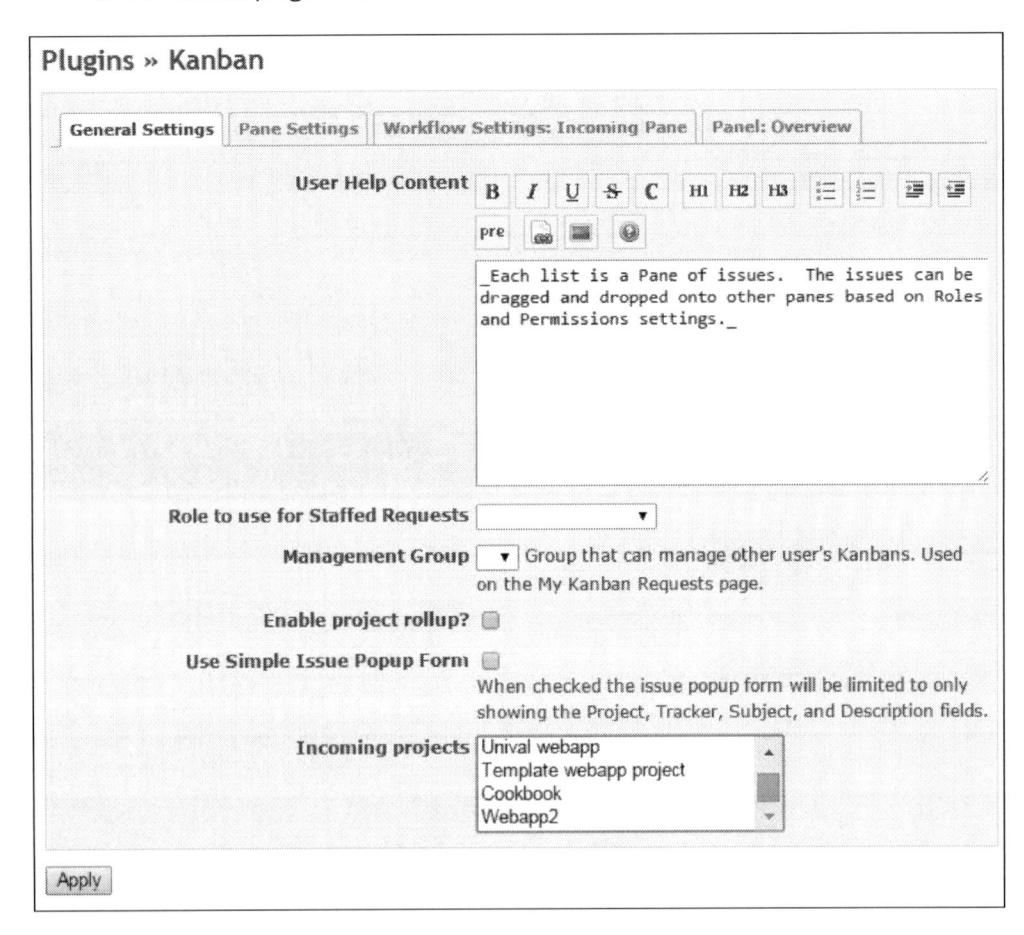

Plugins » Kanban

General Settings | Pane Settings | Workflow Settings: Incoming Pane | Panel: Overview

User Help Content

> _Each list is a Pane of issues. The issues can be dragged and dropped onto other panes based on Roles and Permissions settings._

Role to use for Staffed Requests [▼]

Management Group [▼] Group that can manage other user's Kanbans. Used on the My Kanban Requests page.

Enable project rollup? ☐

Use Simple Issue Popup Form ☐ When checked the issue popup form will be limited to only showing the Project, Tracker, Subject, and Description fields.

Incoming projects
- Unival webapp
- Template webapp project
- Cookbook
- Webapp2

[Apply]

7. You are required to configure the plugin's **Pane Settings** tab in order to display issues properly on Kanban dashboards.

Plugin usage

Upon installation, the plugin displays new links in the top menu bar, concretely: *Kanban*, *My Assignments*, *My Requests*, and *Kanban* overview. Considering that you previously configured the plugin, for example, if a plugin's pane settings are configured in the following way:

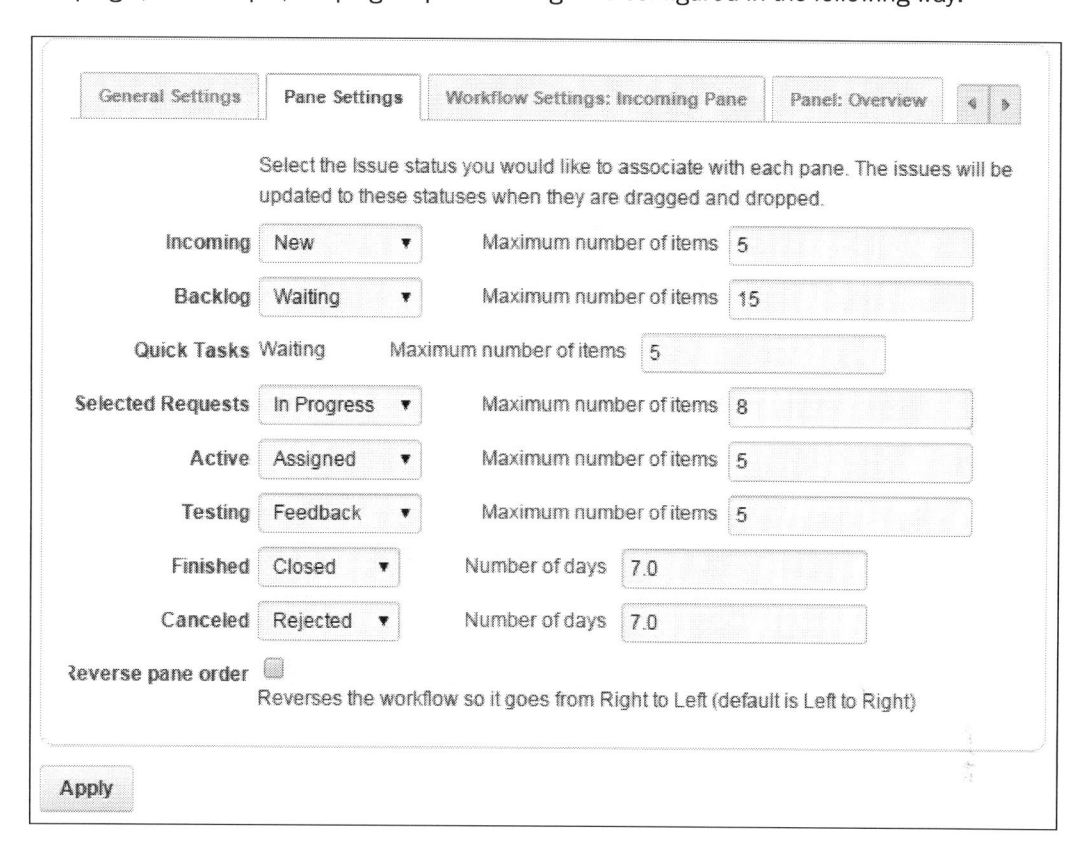

General Settings	**Pane Settings**	Workflow Settings: Incoming Pane	Panel: Overview

Select the Issue status you would like to associate with each pane. The issues will be updated to these statuses when they are dragged and dropped.

Field	Status	Maximum number of items
Incoming	New	5
Backlog	Waiting	15
Quick Tasks	Waiting	5
Selected Requests	In Progress	8
Active	Assigned	5
Testing	Feedback	5
Finished	Closed	Number of days 7.0
Canceled	Rejected	Number of days 7.0

Reverse pane order ☐
Reverses the workflow so it goes from Right to Left (default is Left to Right)

Apply

Getting the Most Out of Scripts and Plugins

It will display the Kanban dashboard like this:

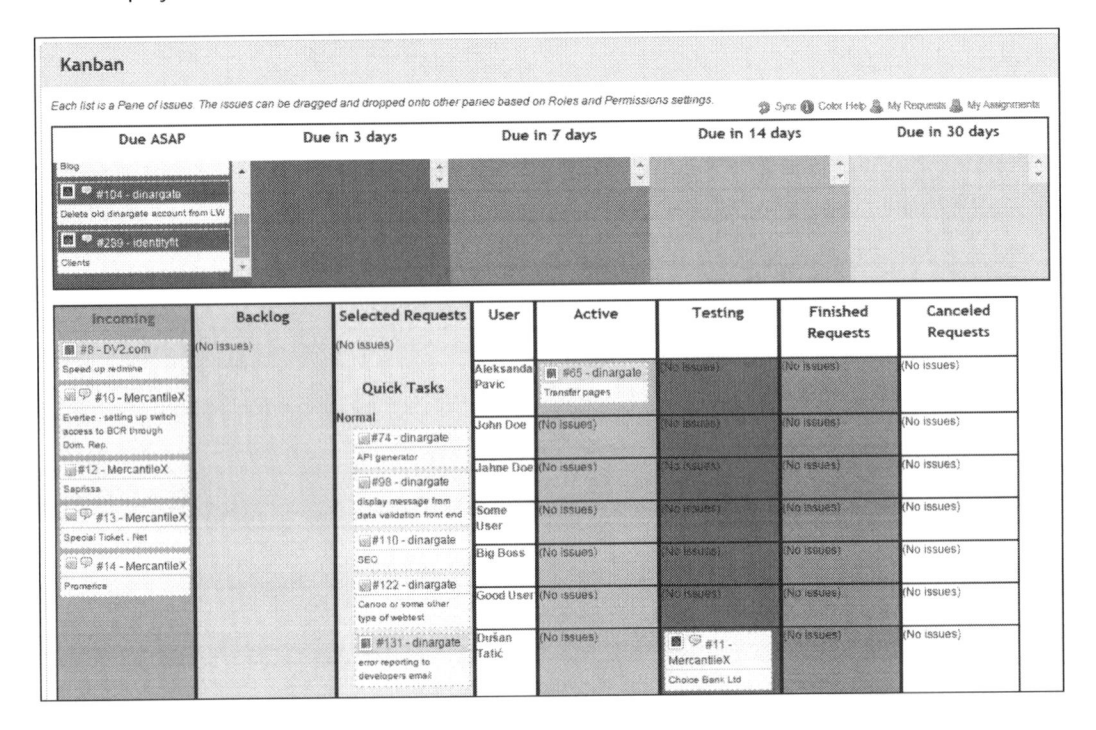

The main use-case scenario of the preceding Kanban dashboard is to drag and drop issues (cards) among users and statuses, which are preconfigured on the **Pane Settings** configuration screen. Other top menu links present additional Kanban boards that are aimed at providing better visibility of issues.

How it works...

There are many definitions of Kanban. Originally, its roots are from Japan, more specifically, Toyota's factory. You can learn more about Kanban from Wikipedia: `https://en.wikipedia.org/wiki/Kanban_(development)` and `https://en.wikipedia.org/wiki/Kanban`

Nowadays, it is widely used and adopted as a project management methodology, and applied to a wide range of projects. It belongs to Agile and lean methodologies, and it is popular in software development. Specifically, it deals with visualization of the development process and team efforts using a system of cards and backlogs, or in the case of Redmine, *issues*.

> Please keep in mind that the term *issue* can be easily changed in the language file to something more appropriate, such as *card*, or *task*.

This plugin, after the installation of requirements, installs like any other Redmine plugin, and requires some configuration in order to display issues on Kanban boards.

There's more...

This is not the only Kanban plugin available for Redmine. Some of Kanban's functionality can also be achieved even without plugins, simply by utilizing Issue filters.

You may want to spend some time researching which project management workflow is going to fit best for your needs. It is not good practice to potentially waste time just to make sure that you are doing everything by some project management methodology rules if it is not appropriate for your budget and overall project situation.

Importing issues to Redmine

This recipe covers the following scenario: the migration of existing issues and projects from other project management systems to Redmine. There are many ways to import issues to Redmine. Plugins, third-party software products, third-party scripts, and direct database import. This recipe covers the scenario of installing and using the most recent fork of the http://www.redmine.org/plugins/importer plugin.

Getting ready

Search for a way to export issues from the software that you are currently using to the CSV or Excel file format.

How to do it...

The first steps are to perform a standard Redmine plugin installation following these steps:

1. Navigate to Redmine installation root in your command line.
2. Clone the most recent fork of the importer repository:

   ```
   git clone https://github.com/mozamimy/redmine_importer.git plugins/redmine_importer
   ```

Getting the Most Out of Scripts and Plugins

3. Run the database migrate rake task:

   `rake redmine:plugins:migrate RAILS_ENV=production`

4. Restart Redmine as follows:

   `rm tmp/restart.txt && touch tmp/restart.txt`

Plugin usage

Redmine issue importer is enabled on a per-project basis. To start using it, perform the following steps:

1. Enable it for new projects on modules or for existing ones by ticking the **Settings | Modules | Importer** checkbox.
2. Once enabled, click the **Import** button in the project's main menu.
3. On the following screen, choose a file to be imported (in this case, we will import a CSV file export of issues from another Redmine):

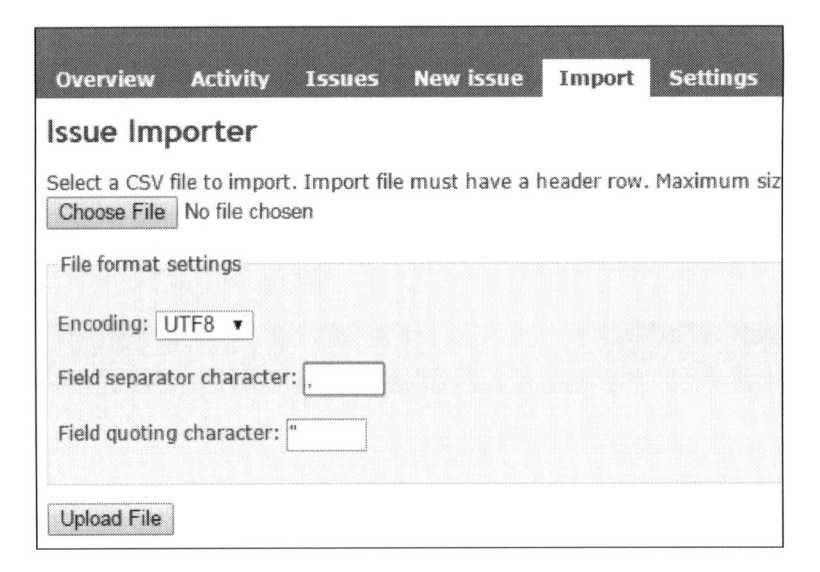

4. In the **File format settings** group box choose settings that fit your document format, and click **Upload File**.
5. On the next screen, map the issue fields from your CSV file to a Redmine's fields:

> If you are importing issues from another Redmine system, most likely, your fields will be automatically perfectly mapped.

Chapter 8

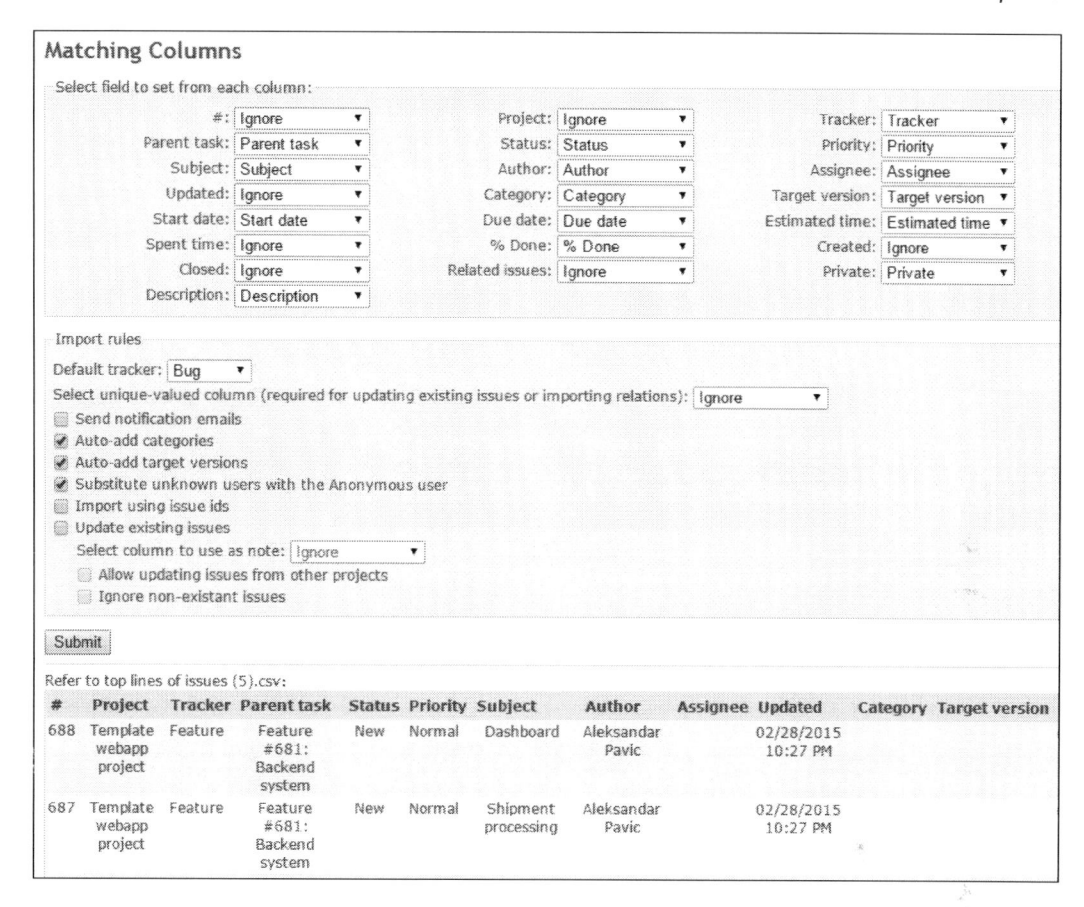

![Matching Columns configuration screenshot showing field mappings, import rules with checkboxes for Send notification emails, Auto-add categories, Auto-add target versions, Substitute unknown users with the Anonymous user, Import using issue ids, Update existing issues, and a preview table of issues to import]

6. Click the **Submit** button.
7. You will be presented with the **Import results** screen where you will see how many issues were imported and with **Failed rows** if the plugin was not able to import them.

How it works...

Redmine issue importer plugin installs just like any other ordinary plugin. Upon installation, it is available on a per-project basis, displaying a new main project menu's item **Import**. Clicking **Import** brings up the form to choose the file to upload, and configure its delimiter and quoting options. Upon clicking **Upload**, users need to configure additional importing options, and map fields from CSV to standard Redmine's issue fields. Technically, this plugin parses each row from the CSV files and inserts them directly in to the Redmine database.

There's more...

If you are migrating from Mantis or Trac, Redmine comes with two rake tasks rake `migrate_from_trac` and `migrate_from_mantis`. To perform this migration, assuming that we are testing on a blank Redmine system that we are going to use for production later, follow these steps:

1. Navigate to your Redmine root.
2. Run the rake task:

    ```
    rake redmine:migrate_from_trac RAILS_ENV="production"
    ```

3. Follow the instructions that the rake task gives you.

To perform `mantis` migration, just replace migrate_from_trac with migrate_from_mantis. You can also achieve an import of issues and projects through other plugins, third-party tools, and even paid online services.

See also

Official Redmine migrate instructions: `http://www.redmine.org/projects/redmine/wiki/RedmineMigrate`.

Using Redmine with Jenkins

Jenkins is a tool for continuous integration, often used by software development companies to provide automated workflows for building and deploying software. Usual use-case scenarios of Redmine plus Jenkins would mean that you can track Jenkins, build statuses from Redmine, and more advanced integration makes Jenkins able to create issues in Redmine automatically if a build fails.

Getting ready

A Jenkins server with active and configured jobs is required.

Redmine server administrator access and Redmine administrator account is required.

How to do it...

Once you have made sure that your Jenkins server and job that is related to your Redmine project is properly configured, proceed with the Redmine Jenkins plugin installation:

1. Open the console and navigate to Redmine installation root.
2. Navigate to plugins folder:

   ```
   cd plugins
   ```

3. Now, type these lines in the console:

   ```
   git clone https://github.com/jbox-web/redmine_bootstrap_kit.git
   git clone https://github.com/jbox-web/redmine_jenkins.git
   cd redmine_bootstrap kit/
   git checkout 0.2.3
   cd ..
   cd redmine_jenkins/
   git checkout 1.0.1
   cd ..
   ```

4. Run bundle install:

   ```
   bundle install --without development test
   ```

5. Migrate the plugin database:

   ```
   bundle exec rake redmine:plugins:migrate RAILS_ENV=production NAME=redmine_jenkins
   ```

6. Restart Redmine, as follows:

   ```
   rm tmp/restart.txt && touch tmp/restart.txt
   ```

Plugin usage

This plugin is intended to be used as a Redmine frontend to Jenkins, on a per-project basis. To start using it, follow these steps:

1. Enable the plugin by navigating to the main project's menu **Settings | Modules**.
2. Check the **Jenkins** module and click **Save**.

Getting the Most Out of Scripts and Plugins

3. You should see a **Jenkins** tab now under **Settings**, and it needs to be configured:

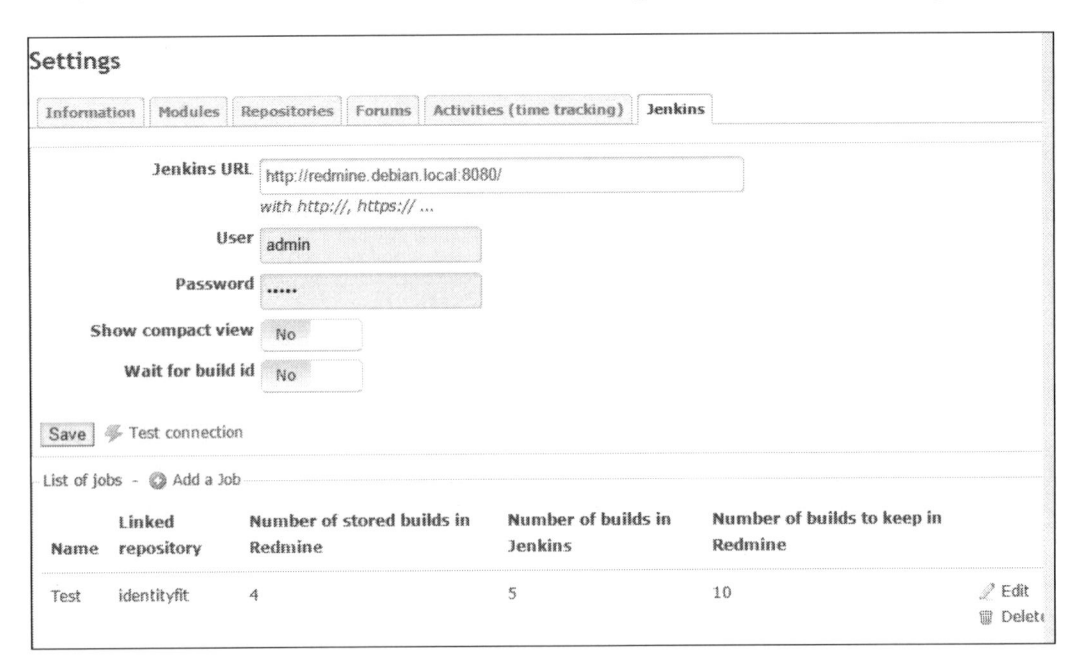

Settings
Information	Modules	Repositories	Forums	Activities (time tracking)	**Jenkins**

Jenkins URL	http://redmine.debian.local:8080/
	with http://, https:// ...
User	admin
Password	•••••
Show compact view	No
Wait for build id	No

Save   Test connection

List of jobs - Add a Job

Name	Linked repository	Number of stored builds in Redmine	Number of builds in Jenkins	Number of builds to keep in Redmine	
Test	identityfit	4	5	10	Edit Delete

In **Jenkins URL**, enter the URL of your Jenkins server; below enter credentials of the user, which is going to be used to manage Jenkins from Redmine.

1. Click **Save**.
2. Click **Test connection**, and you should get a message with your Jenkins version and the number of jobs in Jenkins.
3. Click the **Add a Job** button.
4. On the next screen, choose Jenkins job from the **Job name** dropdown, repository from the **Repository** dropdown, and how many builds to keep.
5. Navigate to **Jenkins** in the main project menu, from there you can trigger Jenkins actions, quickly view status, and review **History**:

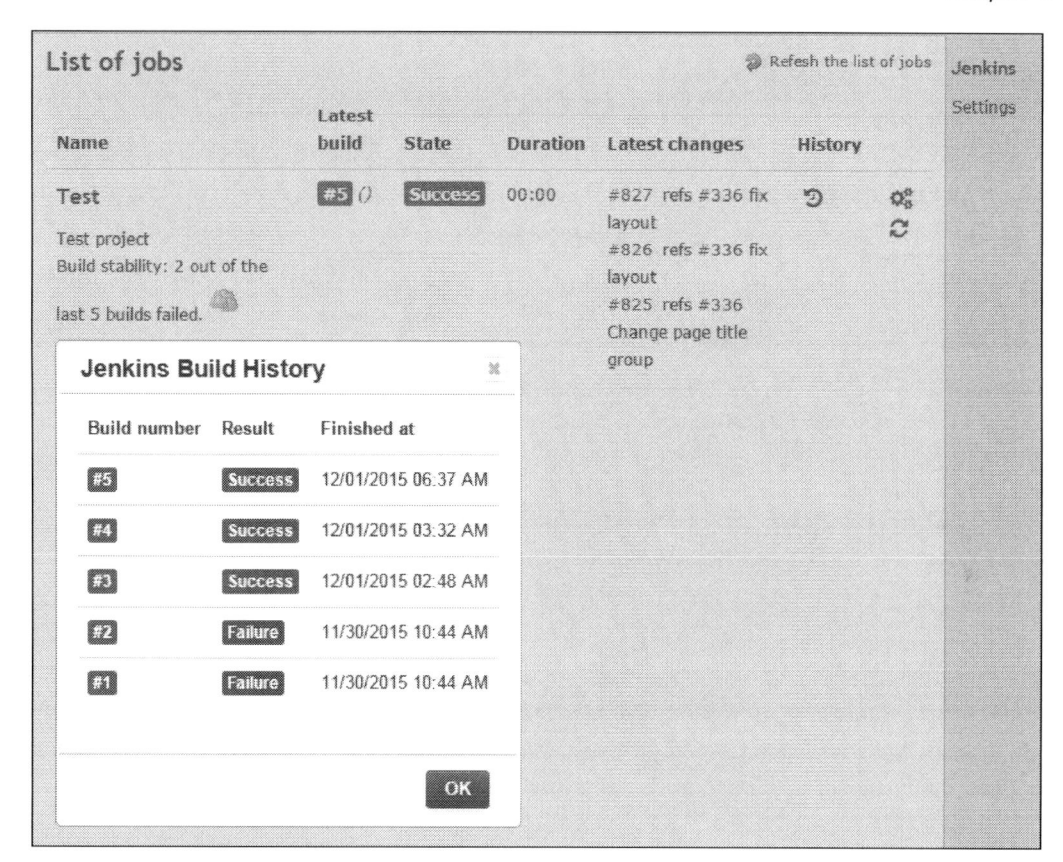

How it works...

This recipe explains how to install and use the Redmine Jenkins plugin. At first, we clone plugin repositories, checkout versions of plugins specified by installation instructions, run bundle install to complete the required gem, and restart Redmine. After this, the plugin is enabled on a per-project basis, configured to connect to Jenkins, and Jenkins jobs are added, paired with Redmine repositories. The last step of the recipe displays a sample implementation of plugin, where we can see the history and summary screens.

Getting the Most Out of Scripts and Plugins

There's more...

You can automate the workflow further. In the following image, you can see one possible scenario of Jenkins usage and workflow integrated with Redmine and source control server on a post-commit hook basis:

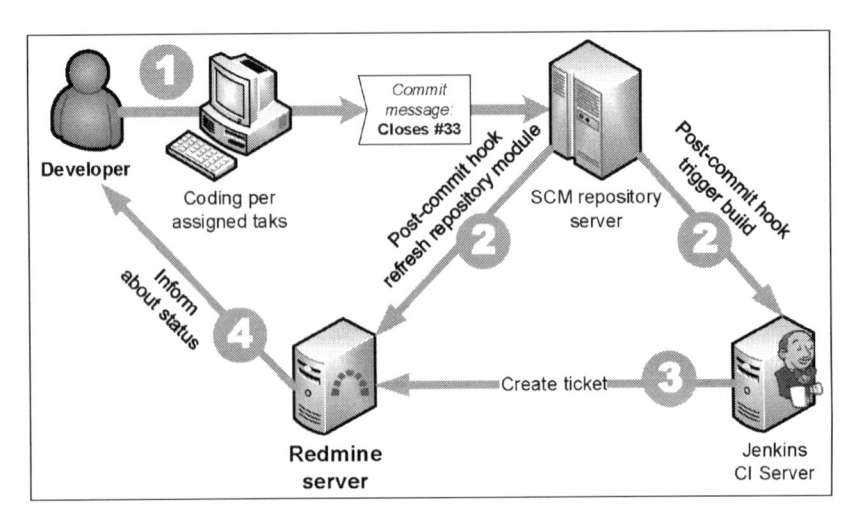

To explain in more detail, the steps on this scheme are as follows:

1. Developer codes per given task, and commits code to source control.
2. Source control triggers Jenkins build job, and Redmine repository update rake task, on post-commit hook.
3. Jenkins creates a ticket in Redmine.
4. Redmine informs user about newly created ticket.

In *Step 3*, Jenkins does not have to create a ticket in Redmine, it can be configured to send e-mails, but the goal here is the quality and traceability of work, so we can have better ETAs and statistics for the project we use these tools and workflows in, and for future projects.

See also

Check out the Jenkins cookbook from Packt Publishing:

```
https://www.packtpub.com/application-development/jenkins-continuous-integration-cookbook-second-edition.
```

Chapter 8

Using the assigned issues summary e-mail

Ideal work organization is to have your employees or team members come to work early in the morning, open Redmine or the e-mail client, a list of tasks created for them for the current day awaits them, and they start to work, task by task, promptly updating Redmine, either directly or through third-party applications. Luckily, Redmine can get you closer to this scenario by providing issues summary e-mails.

Getting ready

You need server administrator access with access to cron jobs or scheduled tasks.

You need a test user in Redmine for which you can read its e-mail, and tasks assigned for that user due within next 5 days.

How to do it...

First, we are going to test the rake task for a reminder script:

1. Open the console and navigate to Redmine root.
2. Test the following command by replacing the USER_ID with the real ID of your test user number (the default account admin is usually number 1):

   ```
   rake redmine:send_reminders days=7 users="USER_ID" RAILS_ENV="production"
   ```

3. Check the e-mail of the test user, you should get an e-mail that looks like this:

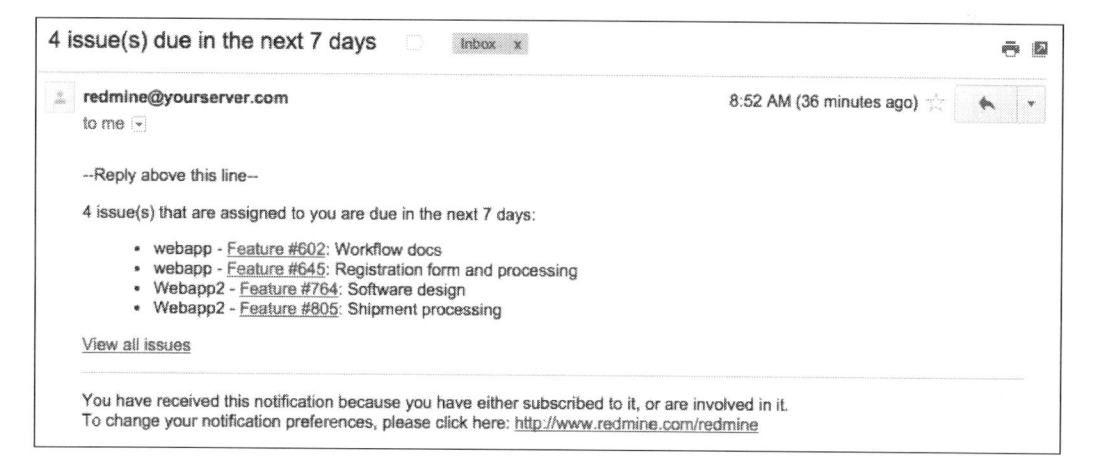

---

4 issue(s) due in the next 7 days   Inbox x

redmine@yourserver.com   8:52 AM (36 minutes ago)
to me

--Reply above this line--

4 issue(s) that are assigned to you are due in the next 7 days:

- webapp - Feature #602: Workflow docs
- webapp - Feature #645: Registration form and processing
- Webapp2 - Feature #764: Software design
- Webapp2 - Feature #805: Shipment processing

View all issues

You have received this notification because you have either subscribed to it, or are involved in it.
To change your notification preferences, please click here: http://www.redmine.com/redmine

---

237

Getting the Most Out of Scripts and Plugins

If you got an e-mail that looks similar to the preceding screenshot, it means that your system is ready, and you can proceed with adding a scheduled task or cron job.

To create a cron job, which sends e-mail reminders once per day, follow these steps:

1. Open the console as a user under, which Redmine is running and type:

   ```
   crontab -e
   ```

2. Paste the following content, replacing the variables to fit your system:

   ```
   5 0 * * * /bin/bash -c -l '/home/redmine/.rvm/gems/ruby-1.9.3-p551/bin/rake -f /home/redmine/redmine/Rakefile redmine:send_reminders days=7 RAILS_ENV="production"'
   ```

How it works...

Now, let's explain what this recipe does, and how to configure it properly to fit your needs. At step 2, while configuring the cronjob, the section, `5 0 * * *`, tells the cron job to schedule as per the following rule: mm hh dd MM yy, where * means every, and the current number means the number of these units (hours, days, minutes, and so on). After this, `/bin/bash -c -l` triggers a Linux bash shell, `-l` makes it perform, like a logged in user is performing commands and `-c` ensures that it reads our commands properly. After this enclosed in single quotes is just a bit of a differently configured command that we run in the first part of this recipe. This is changed to ensure proper paths are triggered. At first, we trigger rake, which we previously found by typing which rake, then `-f` tells it to read the file specified by path to the Redmine Rakefile, and finally, we execute a rake task to send reminders. If you want just some users to receive e-mails, specify their user IDs as explained in first part of this recipe, separated by a comma.

There's more...

Additional e-mail reminder systems are available through plugins. Some of them are: `https://github.com/Hopebaytech/redmine_mail_reminder` and `https://github.com/jkraemer/redmine_issue_reminder`. Each plugin also requires that the rake task be triggered periodically.

See also

Refer to the official instructions at: `https://www.redmine.org/projects/redmine/wiki/RedmineReminderEmails`.

Chapter 8

Text formatting with CKEditor

The default Redmine text formatting options are Markdown and Textile. Some users may have trouble learning syntax for these options. To improve user experience for non-technical users who would expect a **WYSIWYG** (**What You See Is What You Get**) text editor instead of the standard Redmine editor, you can replace it with CKEditor through a plugin.

Getting ready

Server administrator access is required.

The requirement for this plugin is ImageMagick, to install it, refer to the *Installing optional requirements* recipe from *Chapter 1, Installing and Running Redmine*.

How to do it...

Plugin installation is pretty simple, as follows:

1. Open the console and navigate to Redmine root:

    ```
    git-clone the plugin from following location: git clone https://github.com/a-ono/redmine_ckeditor.git plugins/redmine_ckeditor
    ```

2. Run the following:

    ```
    bundle install
    ```

3. Migrate the database:

    ```
    rake redmine:plugins:migrate RAILS_ENV=production
    ```

4. Restart Redmine as follows:

    ```
    rm tmp/restart.txt && touch tmp/restart.txt
    ```

5. Enable the plugin by navigating to **Administration** | **Settings** | **General**, and in the **Text formatting** drop-down menu choose **CKEditor**.

6. Click **Save**.

Getting the Most Out of Scripts and Plugins

Immediately after clicking **Save**, you will notice that default editor on the **General** tab, used to write content on homepage is replaced with CKEditor:

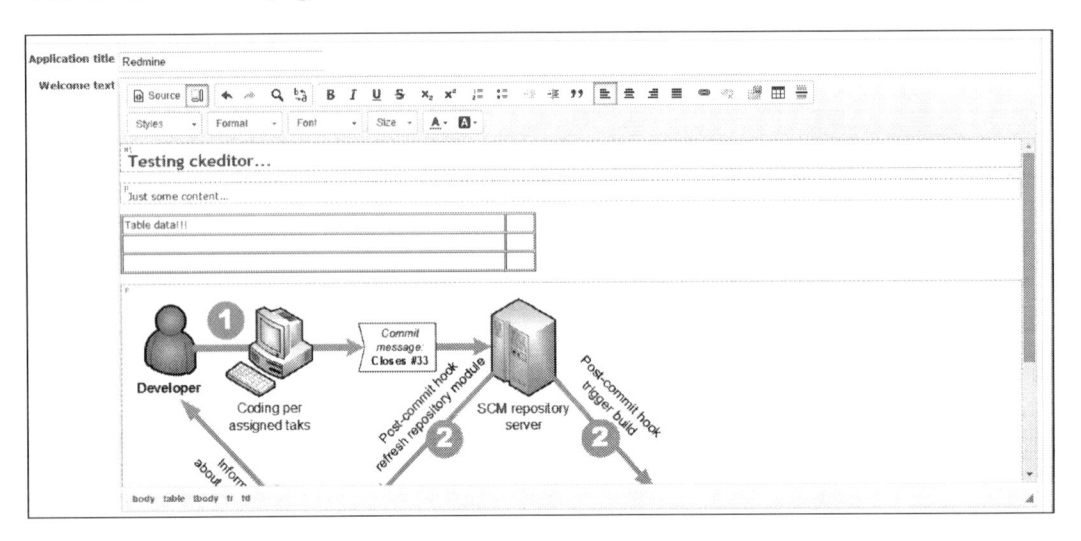

CKEditor comes with an image upload button, and the necessary codes to make it upload images to any content inside Redmine and work properly. Clicking the Image icon in the editor's toolbar brings up the image upload interface.

How it works...

This plugin replaces the default text formatting engines with the HTML formatting engine, and CKEditor replaces the default text-editor areas throughout forms across the Redmine UI. In the first steps, we clone the plugin, then run bundle install because it fetches additional gems required by the CKEditor plugin to work properly.

There's more...

The CKEditor plugin can migrate your old content across projects with the rake task executed like this:

```
rake redmine_ckeditor:migrate RAILS_ENV=production [PROJECT=project_identifier1,project_identifier2] [FROM=textile] [TO=html]
```

This plugin requires Pandoc. To install it, follow the instructions at http://pandoc.org/installing.html.

Besides migration of content, if you install a plugin from the same author from `https://github.com/a-ono/redmine_per_project_formatting`, this enables text engine selection on a per-project basis adding additional usability.

Additionally, you can install various CKeditor plugins and it can be configured by creating a custom config file, from the sample provided with the plugin. To use it, rename its configuration file to Redmine config, as follows:

```
cp plugins/redmine_ckeditor/config/ckeditor.yml.example config/ckeditor.yml
```

Being Agile with Agile Dwarf

This book dealt with Agile, Flexible, and Scrum terminology in several places. Every plugin has its own pros and cons. The Agile Dwarf plugin is definitely worth mentioning, because it drastically improves the manager's user experience by providing several dashboards to help visualize and speed up task management.

Getting ready

Server and Redmine administrator access is required.

How to do it...

Install the plugin just like any other regular plugin:

1. Open the console and navigate to the Redmine installation root.
2. Git clone the plugin's code as follows:

   ```
   git clone https://github.com/acosonic/agile_dwarf.git plugins/agile_dwarf
   ```

3. Migrate the database as follows:

   ```
   rake redmine:plugins:migrate RAILS_ENV=production
   ```

4. Restart Redmine as follows:

   ```
   rm tmp/restart.txt && touch tmp/restart.txt
   ```

Getting the Most Out of Scripts and Plugins

5. Configure the plugin by navigating to **Administration | Plugins | Agile dwarf plugin** and click **Configure**:

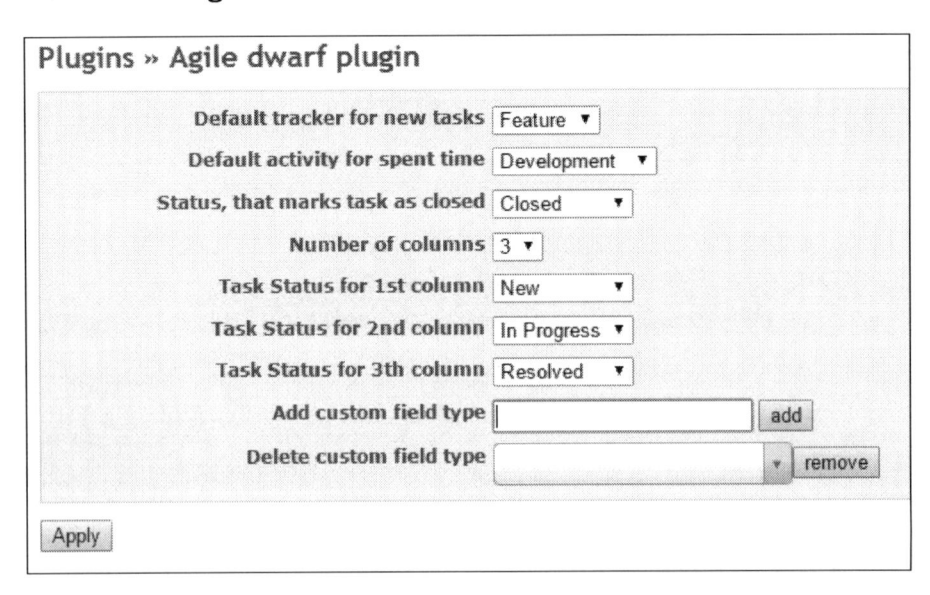

```
Plugins » Agile dwarf plugin

            Default tracker for new tasks  [Feature ▼]
         Default activity for spent time  [Development ▼]
       Status, that marks task as closed  [Closed ▼]
                    Number of columns  [3 ▼]
                Task Status for 1st column  [New ▼]
                Task Status for 2nd column  [In Progress ▼]
                Task Status for 3th column  [Resolved ▼]
                  Add custom field type  [              ] [add]
               Delete custom field type  [            ▼] [remove]

[Apply]
```

6. Give permissions for a plugin to specific roles by navigating to **Administration | Roles and Permissions** and enabling specific permissions under the **Scrum** section:

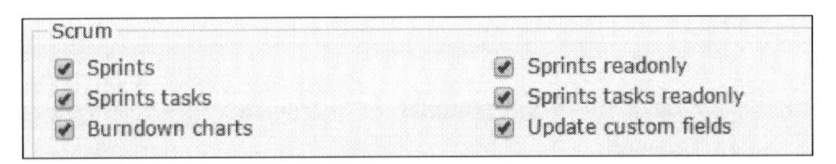

```
Scrum
  ☑ Sprints                    ☑ Sprints readonly
  ☑ Sprints tasks              ☑ Sprints tasks readonly
  ☑ Burndown charts            ☑ Update custom fields
```

7. Enable the plugin on a per-project basis by navigating to the Project's main menu **Settings | Modules** and enable **Scrum**.

> Scrum module may have a name conflict with another Scrum plugin, `https://www.redmine.org/plugins/scrum-plugin`, which is not yet corrected.

Plugin usage

At the plugin configuration, adjust the settings to match your desired workflow. Once activated on a per-project basis, it will display three additional tabs in the project's main menu **Tasks**, **Sprints**, and **Run charts**. The first tab, **Tasks**, lets you drag and drop issues across columns specified by **Number of columns** in the plugin's settings. Dragging and dropping automatically changes the plugin's status. Dragging the scale adjusts the percentage of task completion. Clicking the username offers the dropdown to change to who the issue is assigned. The same goes for clicking on other items, such as issue title and estimated time:

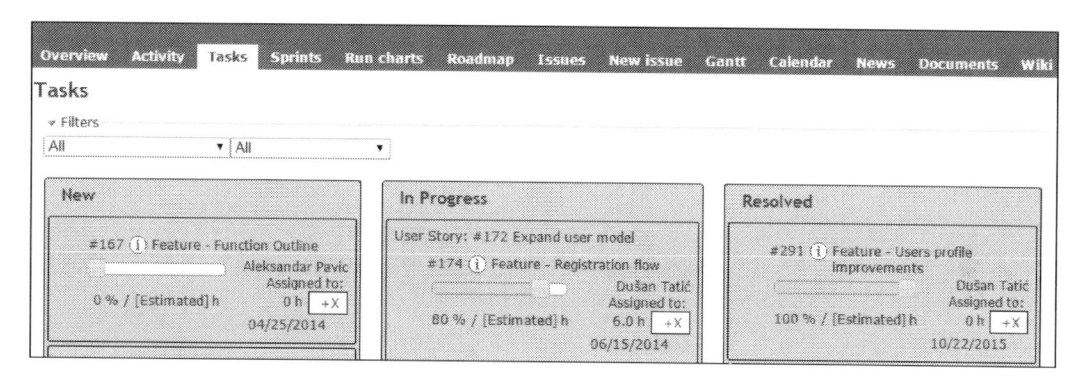

The tab **Sprints** brings up the dashboard with **Sprints** and **Backlogs**, and gives you drag and drop features across columns to drag items from **Backlog** to **Sprints**.

The **Run charts** tab displays a burn down chart of spent versus ETA time.

How it works...

The Agile Dwarf plugin installs in the usual way. After installation, it requires some additional configuration and permission settings for specific user roles. The plugin adds three new tabs to the Redmine project's main menu. Technically, the plugin extends the Redmine database and introduces new functionality through standard plugin codes.

See Also

Refer to the Agile Dwarf's original website: www.agiledwarf.com.

9
Troubleshooting

This chapter describes some common Redmine problems and how to overcome them:

- Where to get help and how to get help faster
- Troubleshooting bundler installation
- Troubleshooting Apache installations
- Troubleshooting plugin installation
- E-mail sending issues
- Incoming e-mail parsing issues
- Recovering from system failure
- Tackling a delayed response from the server

Introduction

Many users follow different tutorials found on the internet which may be outdated, or poorly written, guiding them to install Redmine as a root user or various other misconfiguration issues. Redmine version changes, underlying operating system updates, Ruby changes, Rails, gems, various required libraries, and sometimes any of just mentioned code changes can cause a Redmine installation to break. Luckily, there is an extensive list of logs that can be inspected and help administrators to resolve issues. Sometimes resolving issues is not easy due to the many variables involved in proper execution of Redmine code on the server machine.

Troubleshooting

The following image illustrates a block-scheme of logical layers, which may affect Redmine functionality in some way with the most common problems:

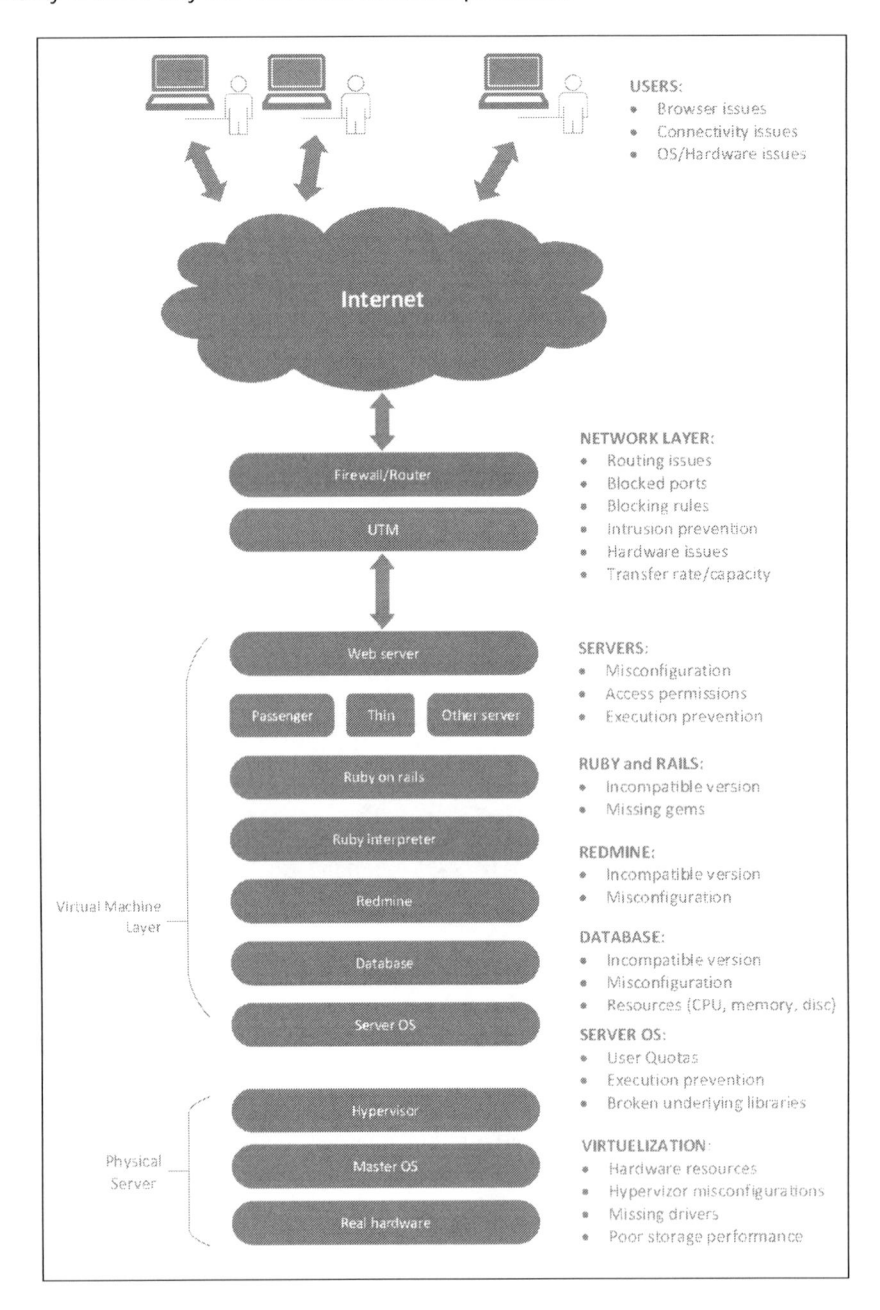

USERS:
- Browser issues
- Connectivity issues
- OS/Hardware issues

NETWORK LAYER:
- Routing issues
- Blocked ports
- Blocking rules
- Intrusion prevention
- Hardware issues
- Transfer rate/capacity

SERVERS:
- Misconfiguration
- Access permissions
- Execution prevention

RUBY and RAILS:
- Incompatible version
- Missing gems

REDMINE:
- Incompatible version
- Misconfiguration

DATABASE:
- Incompatible version
- Misconfiguration
- Resources (CPU, memory, disc)

SERVER OS:
- User Quotas
- Execution prevention
- Broken underlying libraries

VIRTUELIZATION:
- Hardware resources
- Hypervizor misconfigurations
- Missing drivers
- Poor storage performance

The recipes in this chapter are aimed at troubleshooting logs that are directly related to Redmine execution on the server machine.

Chapter 9

Where to get help and how to get help faster

If searching the web for a solution to your problem fails, the defacto place to ask for help is the Redmine community. It can be reached through the `www.redmine.org` website, and through the IRC channel #redmine on freenode.

How to do it...

Before you ask your question to the Redmine community, it is good practice to prepare data about your Redmine system because that is most likely the next question people from community are going to ask you once you submit your query. To gain information about your system if your Redmine is running, perform the following tasks:

1. Navigate to **Administration | Information**.
2. Copy the information outlined in red, and paste it with your message:

Information

Redmine 2.5.2.stable

Default administrator account changed
Attachments directory writable
Plugin assets directory writable
RMagick available (optional)
ImageMagick convert available (optional)

```
Environment:
  Redmine version            2.5.2.stable
  Ruby version               1.9.3-p551 (2014-11-13) [x86_64-linux]
  Rails version              3.2.19
  Environment                production
  Database adapter           Mysql2
SCM:
  Subversion                 1.8.8
  Git                        1.9.1
  Filesystem
Redmine plugins:
  parent_issue_filter        1.0.1
  quick_edit                 0.0.6
  recurring_tasks            2.0.0-pre
  redmine_documents          1.0.0
  redmine_email_inline_images 1.0.0
  redmine_image_clipboard_paste 1.0.0
  redmine_issues_summary_graph 0.0.9
  redmine_kanban             0.2.0
  redmine_lightbox           0.0.1
  redmine_stats              0.0.3
```

Troubleshooting

3. If your Redmine is not active, or accessible through the web browser, you can still get that information from the console by navigating to your Redmine installation root and typing the following:

   `ruby bin/about`

4. You will get the same output in the console.

Steps to resolve problems

1. Make sure that you followed the tutorials exactly as written, and adopted paths and other variables to fit your system.
2. Look into log files and console outputs– the solution may be clear or explained there.
3. Perform an Internet search (Google, Bing, and so on) about your problem, copying part of the log file that is related to your problem.
4. Search for answers on `redmine.org`.

Getting help via the Redmine forum

1. Register at `redmine.org`.
2. Click on **Forums**.
3. Click on **Help**.
4. Click on **New message**.

Submitting a bug on redmine.org

Clicking on **New issue** will present you with the bug issue submitting guidelines.

Chatting with other Redmine users and contributors

To ask for help on the IRC channel, use an IRC client or web-interface via `https://webchat.freenode.net/` and join channel Redmine. If you are using some other IRC client, here is an updated list of servers at `https://freenode.net/irc_servers.shtml`. Upon connection to the server join `#redmine` and ask your question there.

How it works...

Redmine is a web-application that is written in Ruby language and based upon the **Ruby on Rails** (**ROR**) framework. As such, it follows certain guidelines on how ROR applications are done, and as it is open source, it has a community of developers and contributors active on a daily level. This recipe instructs users how to prepare data, to get help faster, and where to look for help.

Troubleshooting bundler installation

The bundle install command is used during the Redmine installation or installation of some plugins. The most common reason for bundler installation failing is missing libraries, so gems can't compile. Usually, such problems are resolved by installing the necessary system libraries.

How to do it...

The most common error that you will get while running bundle install is as follows:

`Gem::Installer::ExtensionBuildError: ERROR: Failed to build gem native extension.`

This error indicates that installation of a gem failed, usually console output will give you exact details on which gem failed to compile, and instruction to run `gem install [somegemname]` to install this `gem` manually instead of through bundler. To see exact details about missing libs, type the `gem install [gemname]` as instructed in console output. Let's take the following example:

`An error occurred while installing mysql2 (0.3.20), and Bundler cannot continue.`
`` Make sure that `gem install mysql2 -v '0.3.20'` succeeds before bundling. ``

As you can see, the instruction indicates that you run the following code:

`gem install mysql2 -v '0.3.20'`

Running this code produces a more detailed output. At some point in your console you will see the following:

```
checking for mysql_query() in -lmysqlclient... no
-----
libmysqlclient is missing. Trying again with extra runtime libraries...
-----
checking for main() in -lm... yes
checking for mysql_query() in -lmysqlclient... no
checking for main() in -lz... yes
checking for mysql_query() in -lmysqlclient... no
checking for main() in -lsocket... no
checking for main() in -lnsl... yes
checking for mysql_query() in -lmysqlclient... no
checking for main() in -lmygcc... no
-----
```

Troubleshooting

```
libmysqlclient is missing. You may need to 'apt-get install
libmysqlclient-dev' or 'yum install mysql-devel', and try again.
```

As underlined in this output, you need to run the following installation command:

`apt-get install libmysqlclient-dev`

Therefore, the steps to resolve the problem would be as follows:

1. Examine the console output log inside console, or if unavailable, open the bundler install log from a text editor.
2. Try installing gem manually.
3. Try installing the required libraries.
4. Retry gem installation.
5. If everything fails, try bundling without that specific gem.

   You can do that by editing Gemfile in Redmine or plugin's root and adding # in front of that gemname. Keep in mind that is not recommended, but in some cases, gems might be related to functionality you are not going to use. Its better to try replacing it with different gem that compiles (see *There's more* section)

> If you are running some other Ruby on Rails applications, they may cause problems with your bundle installation by putting contents in the ~/.bundle/config file. If you run into issues with bundler, then try renaming or removing this file. Then after installation put it back or merge two config files.

How it works...

Bundler is a tool that automatically downloads and builds gem based on the specification provided with the Ruby application that you are using. Gems are pieces of Ruby software such as applications or libraries that are distributed as gems (packages containing information and files to install or compile on a target machine). They are managed by the RubyGems package manager.

In Redmine's case, the following happens:

1. When `bundle install` is typed, it reads the Gemfile specified in Redmine's home directory.
2. It starts obtaining gems from their default sources or specifically provided sources.
3. Gems are installed locally or system wide, depending on whether you run it as a root.

In this recipe we learned steps to resolve the most common bundling issue, and it is missing libraries that are required by the RubyGems manager in order to install some library specified in Redmine's Gemfile.

There's more...

Perhaps your installation will work with a different version of the required gem. This is not recommended procedure, but in some exceptional cases or custom systems, you may end up with such problem. A good example would be replacing the gem with the older version if you know that it deals with some specific feature that you are not planning to use (such as repository interaction, and so on).

Take a look at following example covering different gem specifications:

```
# Protocols: https, ssh, git
gem 'aco', git: 'https://github.com/acosonic/aco.git'
gem 'aco', git: 'git@github.com:acosonic/aco.git'
gem 'aco', git: 'git://github.com/acosonic/aco.git'

# Options tag, ref, or branch to use
gem 'aco', git: 'git@github.com:acosonic/aco.git', tag: '4.0.1'
gem 'aco', git: 'git@github.com:acosonic/aco.git', ref: 'a2b'
gem 'aco', git: 'git@github.com:acosonic/aco.git', branch: dev'

# Short version for public repos on GitHub
gem 'aco', github: 'acosonic/aco'
```

See also

- Refer to the bundler website at `http://bundler.io/`.
- Check out the RubyGems website: `https://rubygems.org/`.

Troubleshooting Apache installations

There are many tutorials available on the Internet, which are faulty or outdated. Apache version changes, Phusion Passenger changes (if used), underlying operating system changes, Ruby version, and so on. Any of these can cause Redmine to break or misbehave in some way.

How to do it...

We can group Apache problems into two groups:

- Start-up problems (usually syntax error, or misconfigurations), preventing your Apache from normal startup
- Runtime problems, and problems during Redmine startup via passenger or some other server if running as reverse proxy

Troubleshooting

To properly resolve your Apache problem, take the following steps:

1. Review the message onscreen or in console:

   > **We're sorry, but something went wrong.**
   >
   > We've been notified about this issue and we'll take a look at it shortly.
   >
   > Information for the administrator of this website
   >
   > The Phusion Passenger application server encountered an error while starting your web application. Because you are running this web application in staging or production mode, the details of the error have been omitted from this web page for security reasons.
   >
   > **Please read the Passenger log file to find the details of the error.**
   >
   > Alternatively, you can turn on the "friendly error pages" feature (see below), which will make Phusion Passenger show many details about the error right in the browser.
   >
   > To turn on friendly error pages:
   >
   > - Nginx integration mode

2. Review the logs (System logs, Passenger logs, Apache logs).
3. If using Phusion Passenger, you can turn on the `PassengerFriendlyErrorPages` by adding the following directive to your virtual host's or `httpd.conf` file:

   `PassengerFriendlyErrorPages on`

   > To monitor an Apache error log, while refreshing the Redmine page in browser, use the following command replacing the paths according to your system:
   >
   > `tail -f /var/log/apache2/error.log`

4. Correct the errors in config files.
5. Restart Apache by typing the appropriate restart command:

   `apachectl restart`

   or

   `apache2ctl restart`

How it works...

This recipe instructs users in these ways:

1. To carefully watch for error messages and console outputs.
2. Then seek for a way to fix the issue.
3. Restart the web server (in this case, Apache).

For example, one of the common Apache/Redmine issues would be:

```
App 21518 stdout:
App 21518 stderr: *** ERROR ***: Cannot execute local/rvm/rubies/ruby-
2.2.1/bin/ruby: No such file or directory (2)
[ 2015-12-14 06:30:51.0384 21486/7f586028a700 age/Cor/App/Implementation.
cpp:304 ]: Could not spawn process for applicati$
  Error ID: aa3fa373
  Error details saved to: /tmp/passenger-error-OUupoE.html
  Message from application: An error occurred while starting up the
preloader. It exited before signalling successful sta$
<h2>Raw process output:</h2>
```

Usually, Googling for complete or parts of error messages leads you to more or less good answers and resolutions. In the preceding case, we can see that Passenger cannot find the Ruby executable variable.

So, after editing the appropriate virtual host configuration, we end up with a virtual host file, such as the following (notice the updated path to Ruby):

```
<VirtualHost *:80>
  ServerName www.yourhost.com
  DocumentRoot /var/www/redmine/public
  PassengerRuby /usr/local/rvm/gems/ruby-2.2.1/wrappers/ruby
  PassengerFriendlyErrorPages on
  PassengerResolveSymlinksInDocumentRoot on
  PassengerAppEnv production
  <Directory /var/www/redmine/public>
    # This relaxes Apache security settings.
    AllowOverride all
    # MultiViews must be turned off.
    Options -MultiViews
    # Uncomment this if you're on Apache >= 2.4:
    #Require all granted
  </Directory>
</VirtualHost>
```

Troubleshooting

There's more...

The most common problems and possible causes are as follows:

- You get a directory listing instead of the Redmine homepage because of the following reasons:
    - Phusion Passenger is not being called by Apache
    - Document root is pointing to the wrong directory
    - Passenger Follow Symlinks directive is not set to on

- You get Error 403 (Forbidden) because of the following reasons:
    - Apache does not have the necessary privileges to access the Redmine directory. You followed the instructions to install for the Apache 2.2 version, but your server is the 2.4 version. Search for the following 2.2 configuration:

        ```
        Order allow,deny
        Allow from all
        ```

    - Replace this configuration with the 2.4 configuration, as follows:

        ```
        Require all granted
        ```

- You get Error 500 (Internal Error) because of the following reasons:
    - Phusion Passenger libraries are not loaded (`mod_passenger`)
    - Passenger is using the wrong version of Ruby
    - Other misconfiguration issues exist

Troubleshooting plugin installation

Plugin installations usually go without problems if you follow the general Redmine plugin installation steps or specifically written instructions from the plugin's docs. But sometimes, a plugin won't work with your Redmine installation, or even worse, it breaks your installation. This recipe deals with some common plugin installation problems.

> It is not good practice to test plugins in production environment. Redmine lets you use console value `RAILS_ENV=development` for test or development purposes. But, it is always recommended to create a full backup of your system prior to plugin installation.

Getting ready

Make sure that the plugin you are installing is compatible with your version of Redmine.

How to do it...

Usual Redmine plugin installation looks like this:

1. Git clone the plugin source or unzip it to the `/plugins` directory.
2. Optionally, run `bundle install` to pick up additional required gems.
3. Optionally, migrate the plugin's database with this command:

   `rake redmine:plugins:migrate RAILS_ENV=production`
4. Restart Redmine

The problems usually occur in *Step 3* or *Step 4* in the preceding list. To resolve plugin installation issues, use the following steps:

1. Check again whether the plugin supports your Redmine version and if there are known issues.
2. Make sure that you followed the instructions exactly as they are written and changed paths and other variables according to your system settings.
3. Follow the instructions provided onscreen, if any.
4. Analyze debug logs.
5. If a resolution is not clear from the debug log, try copying and pasting the debug log to Google search or asking on IRC or on the `redmine.org` forums.
6. Apply the resolution and restart Redmine.

How it works...

The plugin installation procedure is straightforward, as follows:

1. All plugins go to the `/plugins` folder and have their own **MVC** (**Model-View-Controller**) structure with accompanying libraries.
2. Bundle install afterward gets additional required gems and compiles them if required.
3. The rake migrate script then creates necessary database tables, if any.
4. Restarting Redmine ensures that all libraries and views are properly loaded.

Plugins may require specific gems and may fail during installation if these gems cannot be installed. They may also fail at database migration and may require additional configuration within its own config files.

Troubleshooting

E-mail sending issues

Nowadays, e-mail is still the most preferred way of electronic communication. Making sure that e-mail emission from Redmine works flawlessly and that e-mails don't end up as spam or that your mail server is not hacked or abused is very important. This recipe tries to address some of the most common e-mail configuration issues. Many problems with Redmine configuration are related to e-mail sending and properly sending e-mails so that they don't end up as spam.

Getting ready...

Make sure that you have a user account ready to send e-mail on the SMTP server. Also, make sure that your server is properly configured and secured and your reverse DNS records are entered.

> You can use a free service, such as `http://mxtoolbox.com/`, to check your e-mail server's configuration.

How to do it...

As you ensured a properly configured server to send e-mail, the next step is to configure Redmine to send e-mail. By default, after installation, e-mail notifications are turned off, until `configuration.yml` is configured to send e-mail:

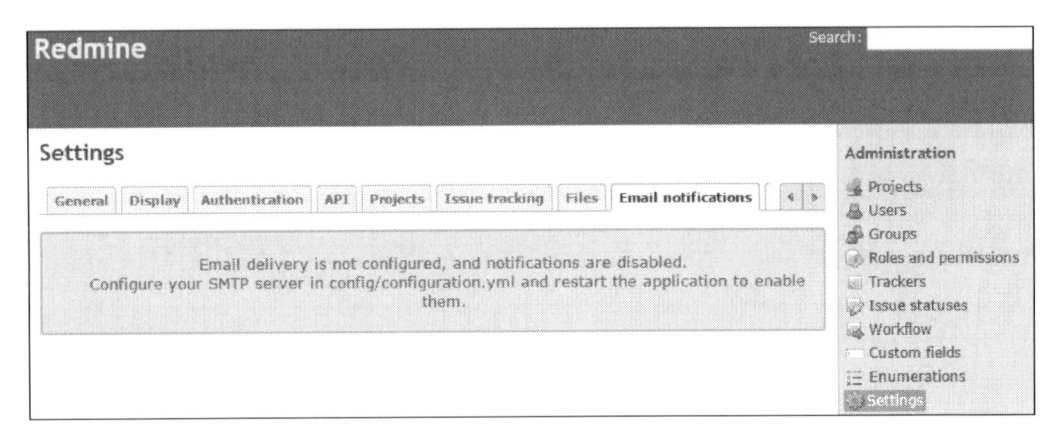

Redmine   Search:

Settings   **Administration**

| General | Display | Authentication | API | Projects | Issue tracking | Files | **Email notifications** | ◀ | ▶ |

- Projects
- Users
- Groups
- Roles and permissions
- Trackers
- Issue statuses
- Workflow
- Custom fields
- Enumerations
- **Settings**

Email delivery is not configured, and notifications are disabled. Configure your SMTP server in config/configuration.yml and restart the application to enable them.

256

Chapter 9

To configure and troubleshoot e-mail sending issues, perform the following tasks:

1. Copy `configuration.example.yml` to `configuration.yml`.
2. Open `configuration.yml` with your favorite editor.
3. Uncomment and modify settings to fit your SMTP or sendmail server.
4. For example, let's take the following configuration:

   ```
   default:
     email_delivery:
       delivery_method: :smtp
       smtp_settings:
         address: "localhost"
         port: 25
         authentication: :login
         domain: yourserver.com'
         user_name: 'redmine.yourserver '
         password: 'redmine123'
   ```

5. Restart Redmine.
6. Test e-mail by navigating to **Administration** | **Settings** | **Email notifications**.
7. Click **Send a test email** at the bottom right.
8. Troubleshooting and resolving:

   Notice the error message after *Step 7*:

   An error occurred while sending mail (hostname does not match the server certificate).

   This error will not produce an error in the log file because it is handled by the system and displayed onscreen. Thus, looking into the Redmine documentation at http://www.redmine.org/projects/redmine/wiki/EmailConfiguration and additionally to Action Mailer configuration that is specified with the link at the bottom, guides us to adding `openssl_verify_mode: 'none'` to the preceding configuration configuration. The resolution looks like this:

   ```
   default:
     email_delivery:
       delivery_method: :smtp
       smtp_settings:
         address: "localhost"
         port: 25
         authentication: :login
         domain: yourserver.com'
         user_name: 'redmine.yourserver '
         password: 'redmine123'
         openssl_verify_mode: 'none'
   ```

Troubleshooting

9. After applying the preceding patch, restart Redmine, and redo test. Sending of e-mail should now work.

How it works...

Redmine relies on the Action Mailer component, which is configured through the `configuration.yml` file from Redmine's config directory. It's rich with features, and enables Redmine to deliver e-mail through several ways. In this recipe, we covered a basic example of e-mail delivery troubleshooting with the advice to use a properly configured e-mail server so that Redmine e-mails don't end up as spam.

See also

Refer to the Redmine official mail notifications configuration guide at http://www.redmine.org/projects/redmine/wiki/EmailConfiguration.

Additional configuration options for the Action Mailer component can be found at http://guides.rubyonrails.org/action_mailer_basics.html#action-mailer-configuration.

Incoming e-mail parsing issues

Redmine can accept e-mails sent to it through a rake task (client pull) or through a web service (server push). Troubleshooting, in this case, can apply to configuration problems and runtime problems.

How to do it...

To troubleshoot configuration problems, first make sure that your configuration works by testing it manually from the console prior to configuring cron job or scheduled tasks. Scheduled tasks and cron jobs need to execute proper environment (production) and perform as expected.

An example problem would be, as follows:

```
rake redmine:email:receive_imap RAILS_ENV="production" host=demo.redminegit.com username=redmine.demo password=redmine
rake aborted!
Net::IMAP::NoResponseError:  Authentication failed.
```

It is clear from the console that our credentials are not good.

> In order to view potential errors with cron jobs, you can always log them in `/var`, or somewhere else, instead of pointing output to `/dev/null`.

The second part of potential trouble is a case when Redmine is not parsing incoming e-mails properly. This can be due to the following reasons:

- The e-mail of the sender does not exist in Redmine
- The sender's client (Outlook, Apple Mail) is generating some unparsable content
- The issue to which the e-mail is related is deleted
- Mistyped keywords, such as project, tracker, and so on

> Occasionally, log in to your server as a Redmine user and check for potential e-mail problems.

How it works...

Redmine comes with additional scripts, which lets it process incoming e-mail. When reading an e-mail from the server, Redmine uses the address of sender to find the corresponding user in its database. If the e-mail subject contains something such as `"Re: [xxxxxxx #123]"`, the e-mail is processed as a reply and a note is added to issue #123. Otherwise, a new issue is created:

> *In order to create an issue, all required custom fields must be provided. Without them, issue creation will fail. As an alternative you can ensure that every custom field has a default value which is then used during issue creation.*
>
> *Quoted from:* `http://www.redmine.org/projects/redmine/wiki/RedmineReceivingEmails`

See also

Refer to the official guide on parsing incoming e-mails at `http://www.redmine.org/projects/redmine/wiki/RedmineReceivingEmails`.

Troubleshooting

Recovering from system failure

Your hardware malfunctioned, server got hacked, or Redmine does not work after upgrade, and of course, backup is unavailable for some reason. System failure does not necessarily mean that you have lost all your Redmine data and files.

Getting ready

Prepare a new system with a blank Redmine installed or hard drive space to save Redmine data, which will be used after reinstallation.

How to do it...

Recovering from system failure should not be too hard considering that you can still access the hard drive on which Redmine data is stored. The steps to recover from failure would be, as follows:

1. Export the database or at least copy its files; usually for MySQL databases, data is stored in the `frm` and `ibd` files located in `/var/lib/mysql` or elsewhere depending upon system configuration.
2. Copy everything from the Redmine installation `root/files` directory.
3. Copy configuration files `database.yml`, `configuration.yml`, and `environment.rb`.
4. Copy `plugins` folders.
5. Install blank Redmine, the same version as you had on your crashed machine.
6. Restore everything to the target system (copy files from *step 2*, *step 3*, and *step 4*), import SQL files to database.
7. Configure configuration files (`database.yml`, `configuration.yml`, and so on).
8. Reinstall plugins by typing commands required for their installation.
9. Re-run bundle install to ensure no missing gems are required by plugins or another part of your old configuration.
10. Restart the server.
11. After the previous steps, your server should be fully recovered maintaining its users, files, projects, and issues.

> It is important to keep the same URL as your crashed server so that content written inside wiks, documents, and issues won't direct users to a nonexisting website.

How it works...

Redmine is a Ruby On Rails application, storing user's files in a files directory, and the database is managed by an RDBMS system, such as postgreSQL or MySQL, which store databases in their own internal formats. If your server crashed, this recipe teaches you to perform the following fixes:

1. Install the new version of Redmine, the same as that of your crashed server.
2. Restore database, files, and configuration, overwriting newly created Redmine files.
3. Restart a server and check whether everything is moved and running as expected.

Tackling a delayed response from the server

As time goes by your user base growing or simply daily usage can produce lots of issues and content inside Redmine. Depending upon your server choice and configuration, you might notice decreased performance. However, this does not necessarily need to be the cause of Redmine's slowdown. Generally, something else might be using your server, or causing the database, memory, or CPU to perform poorly.

How to do it...

The best way to monitor your server's capacity usage is to do it when it's maximally loaded. This is probably during work days. If you run webalizer statistics or something similar, you will get an hourly average usage log, like the following:

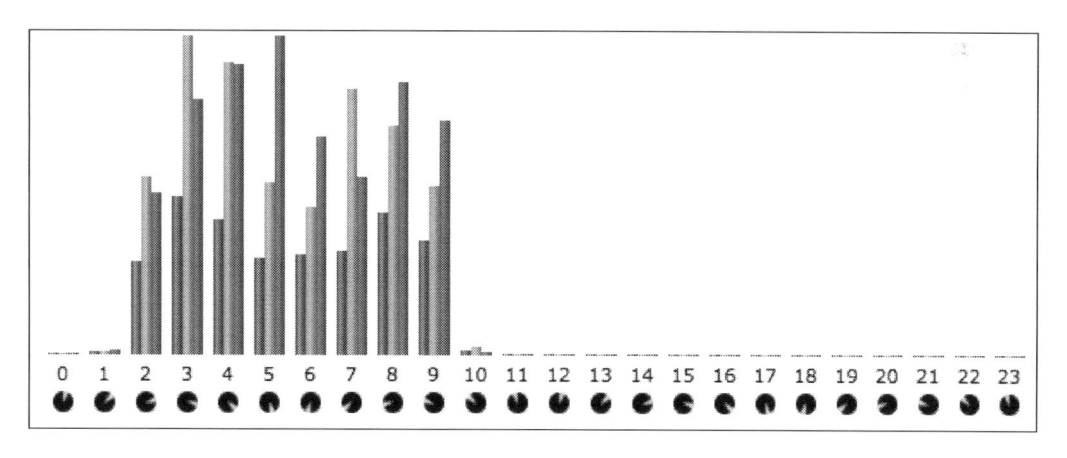

Obviously, the proper time to analyze CPU usage, database, and so on is between 2 and 9 hours.

Troubleshooting

> Please keep in mind that your server may be in a different time zone and adjust the time difference between your time zone and the time zone displayed on the server's logs.

To actively monitor log (on Unix) on Windows, you can use BareTail, or tail through minigw, in the following way:

1. Navigate to your Redmine installation root.
2. Type the following command, replacing `production.log` to `debug.log`, depending upon which environment are you analyzing:

   ```
   tail -f log/production.log
   ```

3. The output should produce a similar output:

   ```
   Started GET "/issues/4471" for 213.253.121.11 at 2015-12-22 05:45:18 -0500
   Processing by IssuesController#show as HTML
     Parameters: {"id"=>"4471"}
     Current user: redmine.test (id=7)
     Rendered issues/_action_menu.html.erb (3.1ms)
     Rendered issue_relations/_form.html.erb (1.3ms)
     Rendered issues/_relations.html.erb (2.3ms)
     Rendered issues/_history.html.erb (4.2ms)
     Rendered issues/_action_menu.html.erb (63.8ms)
     Rendered issues/_form_custom_fields.html.erb (6.6ms)
     Rendered issues/_attributes.html.erb (42.3ms)
     Rendered issues/_form.html.erb (54.9ms)
     Rendered attachments/_form.html.erb (1.6ms)
     Rendered issues/_edit.html.erb (65.9ms)
     Rendered issues/_sidebar.html.erb (3.9ms)
     Rendered watchers/_watchers.html.erb (3.2ms)
     Rendered issues/show.html.erb within layouts/base (171.2ms)
   Completed 200 OK in 252.3ms (Views: 172.4ms | ActiveRecord: 25.3ms)
   ```

4. In the preceding code, you can see how much time exactly which part of the requested controller action took.

> If you are using Phusion Passenger and have delayed response only at the beginning of your or your user's Redmine usage, it means that the delay is occurring because of Passenger startup. To get rid of such problems, try tweaking the Passenger config values, such as: `PassengerPreStart`, `PassengerMaxPoolSize`, `PassengerConcurrencyModel`, `PassengerThreadCount`, and `PassengerMinInstances` values.

If the previous process does not provide enough information for you because it does not provide statistics over some period of time, you can install `rails` request log analyzer in the following way:

1. Navigate to Redmine code root, and edit Gemfile by adding the following:

   `gem "request-log-analyzer"`

2. Run the following:

   `bundle install`

3. Execute request log analyzer by typing the following:

   `bundle exec request-log-analyzer --format rails3 log/production.log`

4. It will create a very detailed report, which can be used as a starting point for further analyses. To see a complete example output of production Redmine instance, go to `http://redminecookbook.com/request-log-analyzer-report.html`.

Apart from what's just mentioned, you should analyze logs from your database to see what improvements can be achieved there.

The previous process only indicates that a problem exists. To improve your Redmine performance, read *Chapter 6, Performance and System Tuning*.

How it works...

As explained already, delayed response can be caused by many factors, such as hardware problems, other processes using CPU and database, server misconfiguration, and so on. This recipe teaches users to look into log files, and try to identify bottlenecks:

1. At first, we analyzed the `production.log` file of a live Redmine installation during its peak usage time.
2. Later, we installed an additional gem called `request log analyzer`.
3. We ran this gem on our `production.log` file, which created a combined report file that was available for further analyses.

Troubleshooting

4. Additionally, in the *There's more...* section, we will add Rack Insight toolbar, which displays debugging information inside Redmine's UI.

There's more...

Now, let's do something really cool. As Redmine is an ROR application, Rack Insight (one of debug toolbars for Ruby on Rails applications) can be used.

To install and use it, follow these steps:

1. Navigate to Redmine's installation root and open gemfile with your favorite code editor.

2. Simply add the following line:

   ```
   gem "rack-insight"
   ```

3. Then, edit `Config/envrionments/production.rb` or `development.rb` depending upon which configuration you use, and add the following content:

   ```
   config.middleware.use 'Rack::Insight::App',
       :secret_key => 'someverylongrandomstring',
       :ip_masks   => false, # Default is 127.0.0.1
       :password   => "yourpassword"
   ```

4. From the command line, run the following:

   bundle install

5. Restart Redmine.

6. After Redmine restart, you should see a debug bar like a small dash at the top-left corner. Hovering over it with the mouse will display the following:

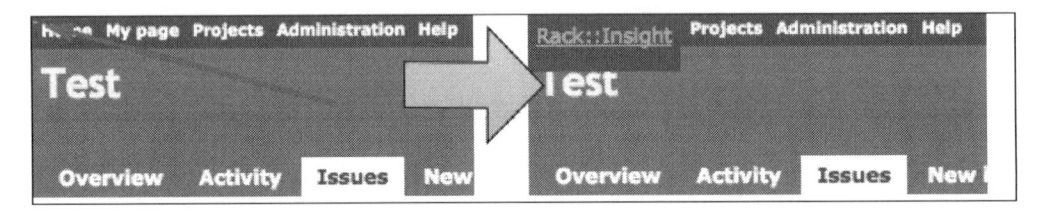

7. Then, clicking **Rack::Insight** will ask you for a password, which will, after the proper password is entered, display the Insight bar at the top. To move it to bottom, like in the following example, just click **Rack:Insight**:

Chapter 9

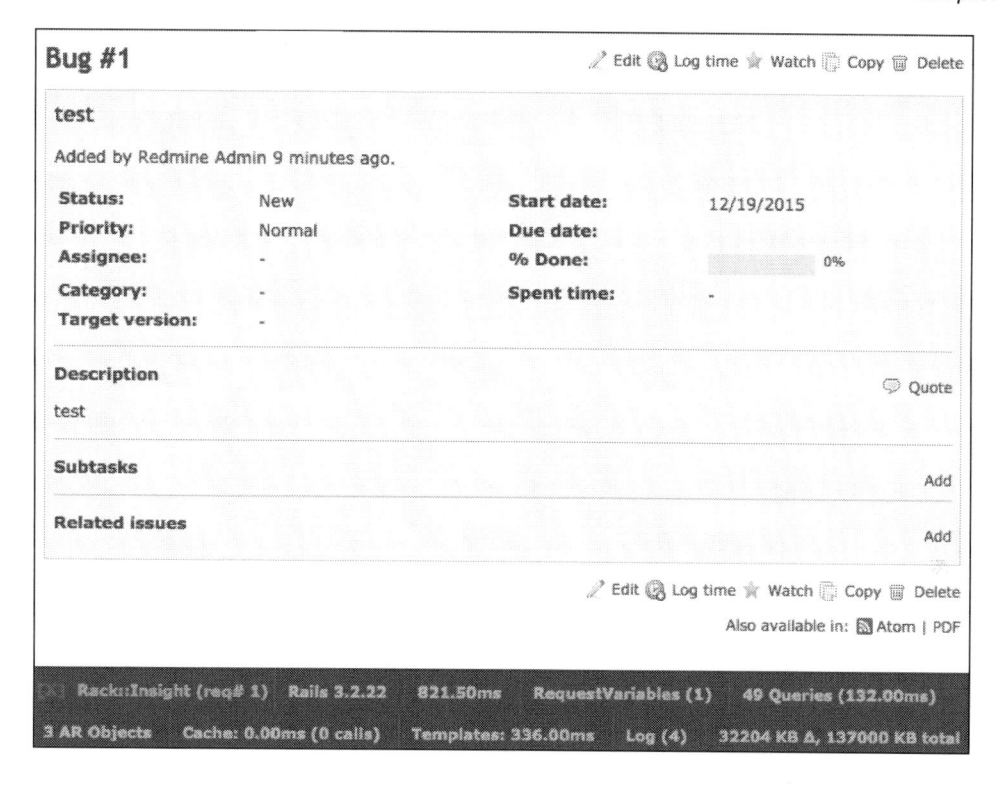

8. As you can see on the green bar at the bottom, various debug-related information is displayed. Here, you can see how much time exactly which action took. Queries took 132 ms, and templates 336 ms.

9. Even more details are available by clicking any of links displayed on the **Rack Insight** bar, for example, clicking the **Log** tab will display the following:

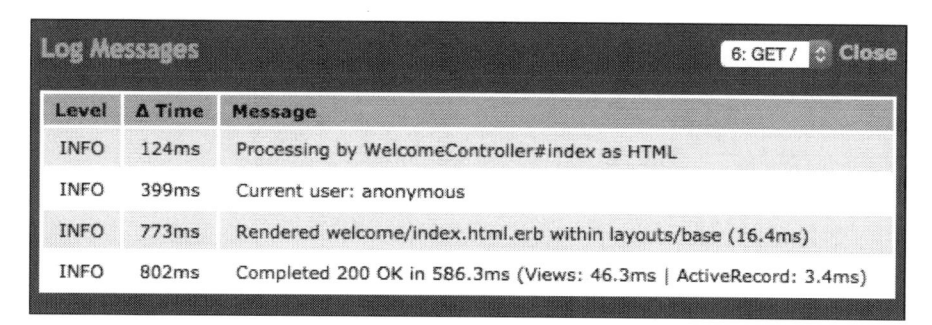

See also

Refer to the Request log analyzer instructions at `https://github.com/wvanbergen/request-log-analyzer/wiki`.

10
Making the Most of Redmine

This chapter deals with some advanced or alternative uses of Redmine, and it is more business-oriented while keeping some particular configuration how-tos. The recipes that we will learn in this chapter are as follows:

- How to convince management to use Redmine
- Redmine as a Helpdesk with auto-responder
- Using Redmine as a service desk platform
- Improving Redmine Security for ISO 27001
- Redmine and SLA
- KPIs inside Redmine
- Using Redmine with ITIL

Introduction

Due to its flexibility in nature, considering the fact that it's open source and widespread, having more than 600 plugins developed over time makes Redmine a credible and trustworthy choice to fulfill some other duties than just basic project management for small teams of software developers.

In a modern business world, flexibility is highly desirable, and applications, such as Redmine, which can quickly adapt to change in your business process without the need to pay to update your old application or buy a new one. This can mean a huge difference in terms of expenses, incomes, and the company's ability to quickly adopt and respond to the new challenges in the business environment or on the market.

Making the Most of Redmine

So, considering the fact that one of Redmine's main modules is Issue tracker, there is only the question of what are we going to track with it—projects or processes—because the main difference between project and process is repeatability, which is a characteristic of process versus uniqueness, which is characteristic of projects.

Observing both projects and processes from the software's standpoint, both represent collection of tasks. Logically, project's tasks are unique, oriented to a certain goal, usually but not necessarily with a strictly defined start and end of project, while processes tasks are usually repetitive tasks or a collection of repetitive tasks. For example, daily customer support operations are a process, while creating a customer support department is a project.

Considering this fact, we can clearly replace the word *Project* with a *Word* process, and we have a free process tracker application. Process tracker applications are usually a part of some big ERP where they track production of some products, or whatever their business is related to.

In any case, Redmine implementation can help us organize our work in a way that we know in any moment: *who* did or is going to do *what*, *when*, and *why*, which we can call the 3W.

So, from 3W we get a *traceability of work*, and a transition toward knowledge-oriented enterprise. Based on previous experiences, for example, if we did one project through Redmine, and tracked work (tasks and hours), we can immediately know, for the next similar project, a good ETA for how long the project is going to take to be completed, and how long is it going to last. In addition, new employees can study what has been done in past by other more-experienced workers, and learn the job that way.

How to convince management to use Redmine

Transition to Redmine can occur if a management realizes that they need to organize work differently and migrate from paper-based business to computer supported, or from one form of computer-supported business to another (from text documents and table sheets to a web-based application, or from desktop and single user to a web-based application and multiuser environment). Sometimes, they may not realize that change is required, or simply, they do not know how Redmine can help them and your company benefit in everyday work. This recipe can help you prepare a good demo or presentation for them.

Getting ready

Fetch information about other departments of your company, its short- and long-term plans, and its strengths and weaknesses.

How to do it...

Sometimes, management may have a hard time realizing that migration is necessary, or a hard time deciding to use Redmine in favor of some other highly-marketed product, and you may need to convince different layers of management.

Convincing low-level management

Low-level management are usually team-leads, project managers, human resource department, people on public relation positions, line boss, and shift boss. The characteristic of this position is that they are most likely going to use Redmine more than other users. What they are interested in most is that everything is organized, and they can provide necessary reports to their superiors. They are not going to be easily convinced, and they are usually afraid that they will lose important data or spend too much time entering data somewhere else than Excel sheets. To convince them, follow these steps:

1. Create a demo installation of Redmine.
2. Enter real users and projects (processes) to the demo.
3. Assign real tasks to real users with different statuses, and progress, which will help them realize how Redmine is used on a daily level.
4. If possible, convince your colleagues first to support your demo, and interact (collaborate) with them on a few sample tasks.
5. Finally, ask your boss to present them with a demo or to prepare for them a presentation of your implementation and your vision of future Redmine use inside the company.

Middle management

They are most likely not going to use Redmine on a daily basis, but rather interact with it through some other channel, such as Atom feeds, a smartphone app, and so on. They are most likely going to be interested in the following questions: how much is it going to cost the company, what are you going to do when it breaks or when you leave the company, and how are you and them going to benefit from usage. Convincing them should occur after convincing your immediate superior; for them, it is enough to prepare a presentation, answering the above questions, and if requested, show them a demo.

Top management

They are most likely going to be interested in the following: are you going to use it, are other employees, including other levels of management going to use it? Who will educate new employees to use it? Does it support growth of the company? Will it support migration to something else if required? Does it support the company's long-term vision, and does it complies with international standards, such as ISO or ITIL?

How it works...

In order to convince management and colleagues to use Redmine, this recipe teaches you to prepare a demo with projects and issues as realistic as possible and presentations for all levels of management.

There's more...

If you need inspiration, it is enough to type the following keywords in Google: Redmine `filetype:ppt`, or just Redmine presentation, you will get hundreds and thousands of results with people using Redmine for various different purposes.

See also

Refer to the sample presentation from this recipe that is available as LGPL on `www.redminecookbook.com/redmine_convince_management.html`.

Redmine as a Helpdesk with auto-responder

A typical Helpdesk can effectively perform several functions. It provides a single (or multiple) point of contact for users to gain assistance in troubleshooting, get answers to questions, and solve known problems. A Helpdesk generally manages its requests through the use of software, such as issue tracking systems. These systems often involve the use of a *bug tracker*. A tracker allows the Helpdesk to track and sort user requests with the help of a unique number, and it can frequently classify problems by user, computer program, or custom-defined categories. There are many software products available to support the Helpdesk function. Some target the enterprise-level Helpdesk and some target departmental needs.

Redmine can also be used as a Helpdesk application, out of the box, and due to its flexibility in nature, it can serve one or several functions of a standard web-based Helpdesk. It can be used as a Helpdesk app standalone or as a separate project within a larger Redmine implementation.

Getting ready

Define your helpdesk processes and workflows.

The helpdesk can be customer-oriented or employee-oriented, it can provide help for one product, multiple products, or wider range of products, and services. Typical Helpdesk software has the two following major components:

- Knowledge base
- Issue tracking

Usage and Helpdesk features are determined by process flow and use-case requirements. A typical Helpdesk management process workflow looks like this:

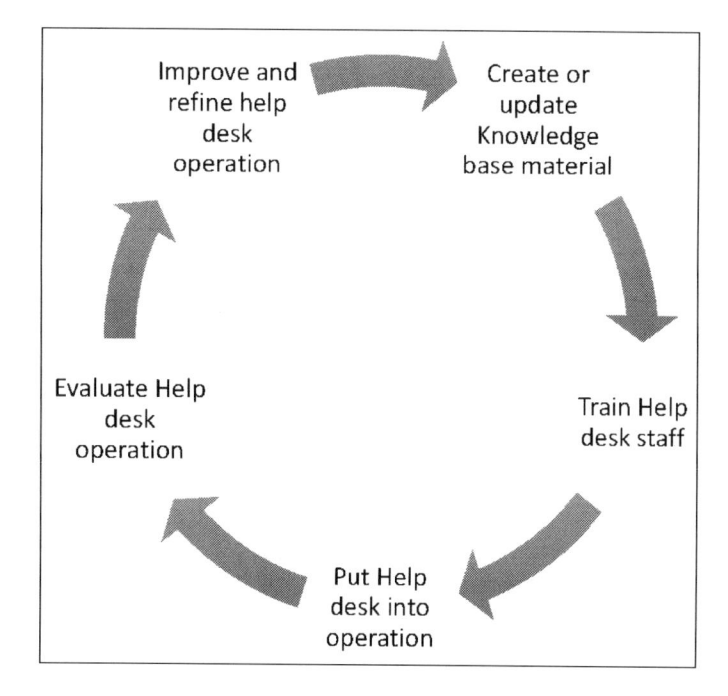

- Improve and refine help desk operation
- Create or update Knowledge base material
- Train Help desk staff
- Put Help desk into operation
- Evaluate Help desk operation

Whereas the typical workflow of a Helpdesk operation looks like this:

1. Receive request from the user.
2. Optionally, automatically respond to user.
3. Assign the user's ticket to the operator automatically or the first available operator reviews user's ticket.
4. Resolve the ticket or prioritize it and assign it to another operator.

In terms of Redmine adoption to this simple but usual flow, we would perform the following steps:

1. Determine and create user roles (Operator, Manager) and their permissions.
2. Determine issue types (the default ones are bug, feature, and so on).
3. Determine custom fields (such as customer's telephone).
4. Update terminology (replace term project with term process or Helpdesk).
5. Create projects or categories (desks).
6. Create users and test the flow.

Making the Most of Redmine

7. Install Helpdesk plugin and/or integrate Redmine with the company's contact form or other third party form.
8. Out of all of the preceding steps that we covered already in previous chapters, what we have not covered is installation and usage of the Helpdesk plugin.

How to do it...

To install and use the Helpdesk plugin, perform the following steps:

1. Navigate to Redmine root.
2. Run the following:

   ```
   git clone git://github.com/jfqd/redmine_helpdesk.git plugins/redmine_helpdesk
   ```

3. Install additional dependencies (`codeclimate-test-reporter`) by running the following:

   ```
   bundle install
   ```

4. Run a `rake` task to migrate plugin's database, as follows:

   ```
   rake redmine:plugins:migrate RAILS_ENV=production
   ```

5. Restart Redmine, as follows:

   ```
   rm tmp/restart.txt && touch mp/restart.txt
   ```

6. Ensure that the plugin is installed by navigating to **Administration | Plugins**.
7. On a project that you want to use the plugin on, navigate to the project's main menu, **Settings | Information**, and fill in the following values:
   - **email-first-reply**: This is an e-mail response that your customers will get. It is usually something such as *Dear user, your request is received and will be fulfilled within XY...*.
   - **helpdesk-email-footer**: This is footer content.
   - **helpdesk-sender-email**: This is the e-mail of helpdesk support (from which an e-mail of the answer will be sent). It may be different from Redmine's default e-mail emission address defined in **Administration | Settings | Email notification**.
   - **helpdesk-send-to-owner-default**: This if set to no, automated replies won't be sent.
8. Check the **owner-email checkbox**.

9. Configure cron job to pull the message automatically for this particular project, or configure server push, as explained in the following:

   ```
   */5 * * * * redmine /usr/bin/rake -f /path/to/redmine/Rakefile
   --silent redmine:email:receive_imap RAILS_ENV="production"
   host=mail.example.com port=993 username=username password=password
   ssl=true project=project_identifier folder=INBOX move_on_
   success=processed move_on_failure=failed no_permission_check=1
   unknown_user=accept 1 > /dev/null
   ```

10. If you are using Pop 3, the command will look different, as follows:

    ```
    rake redmine:email:receive_pop3 RAILS_ENV="production" host=
    mail.example.com username=user password=pass project=test no_
    permission_check=1 unknown_user=accept
    ```

> In order to have a working auto-responder, you must have e-mail sending options properly configured and tested under **Administration | Settings | Email notification**.

The best way to test this is just to use a `rake` task from the console, which will be triggered later by a cron job, and send an e-mail to yourself. A properly configured Helpdesk looks like the following:

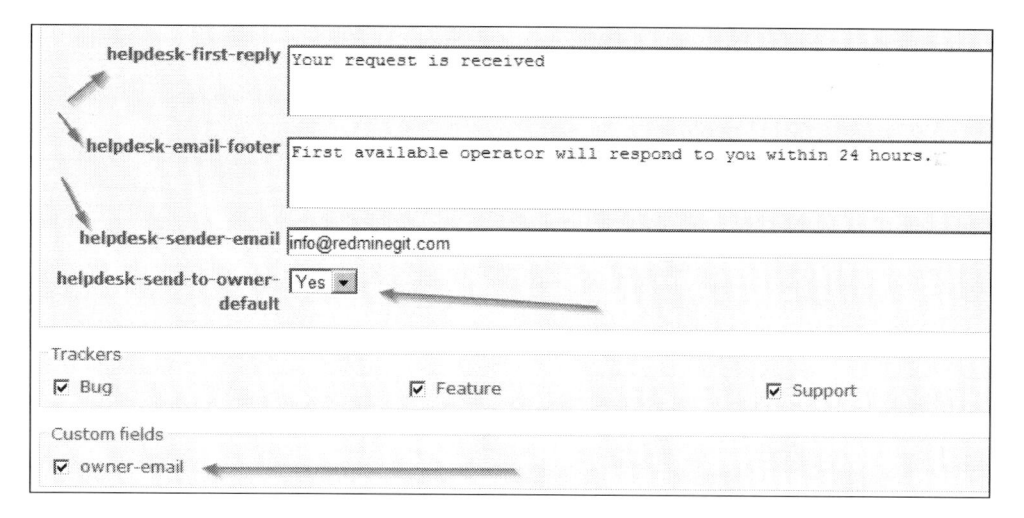

helpdesk-first-reply	Your request is received
helpdesk-email-footer	First available operator will respond to you within 24 hours.
helpdesk-sender-email	info@redminegit.com
helpdesk-send-to-owner-default	Yes

Trackers
☑ Bug   ☑ Feature   ☑ Support

Custom fields
☑ owner-email

Making the Most of Redmine

How it works...

The following image illustrates the current workflow of the Redmine Helpdesk plugin, which is basically a workflow that most web-based support helpdesks are using, and it is a behavior of support systems that customers would expect:

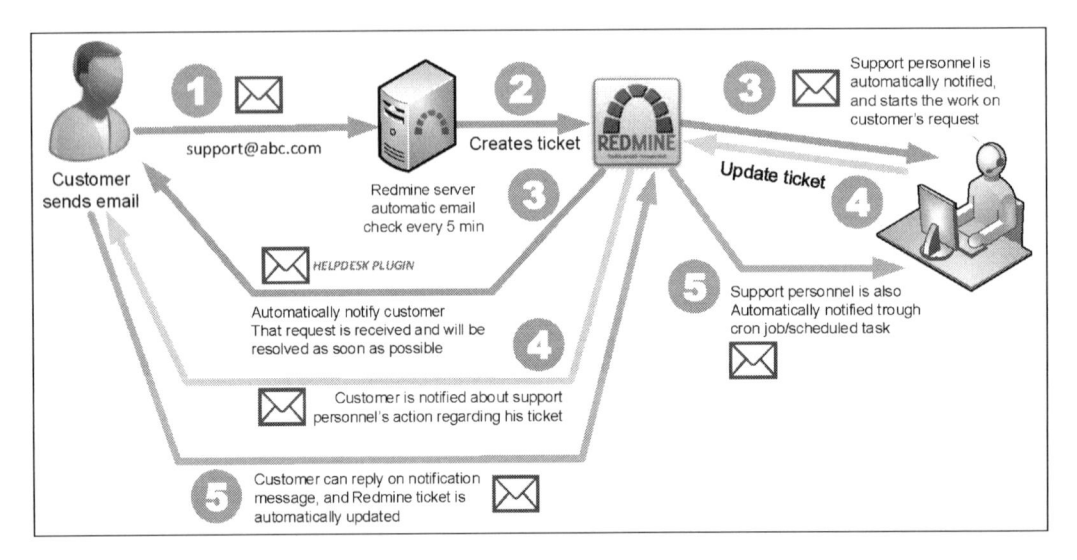

One way of accomplishing this behavior is by installing the Redmine Helpdesk plugin and configuring it together with automated parsing of incoming e-mails.

See also

Refer to Plugin's website `https://github.com/jfqd/redmine_helpdesk`.

> Please keep in mind that there is usually many forks of some plugin, and you may find some changes in forked versions that can maybe suit your needs better. Take a look at the following image to see how to find the most recent fork:

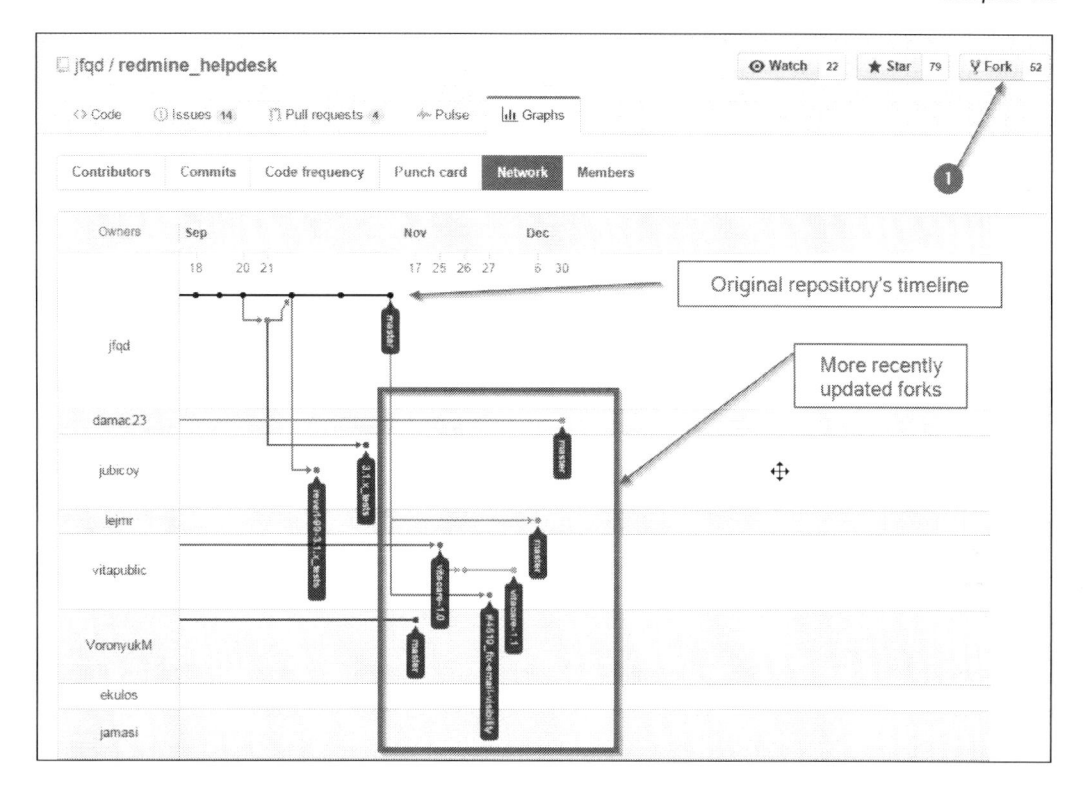

Using Redmine as a service desk platform

Service desk in ITIL is a broader term than a Helpdesk. Actually, Helpdesk is supposed to be just a part of service desk. Redmine can support different ways of service desk organization, such as the following:

- Single centralized service
- Multiple decentralized services

For example, if you run a large international customer service, you may have teams in different time zones, and operating in different languages because operators are supposed to receive requests and respond to customers in their own language. Unbelievably, Redmine is capable of supporting such a use-case scenario out of the box.

Making the Most of Redmine

Possible scenarios of Redmine usage include the following:

- Managing users (operators) through Redmine or through the company's Active Directory, or some other LDAP, depends upon other aspects of your company's IT organization
- Connecting a company's website (contact form) through the API with the appropriate Redmine's subproject
- Implementation of the Helpdesk plugin as explained in the previous recipe
- Having local branch users use Redmine in their native language

Organizational requirements mean the following:

- Keep all global stuff (how-tos, formal documents) in their parent project
- Daily operations for each country as a subproject, connected directly to the communication channels, such as third-party CRM, the company's contact us form

Getting ready

Define and accept (company-wide) business processes that ensure that each customer or employee's request is created as a ticket in Redmine regardless of how this request came in, then categorize this ticket, determine SLAs (Service Level Agreement), and resolve the request. The following image illustrates all communication channels converging at Redmine:

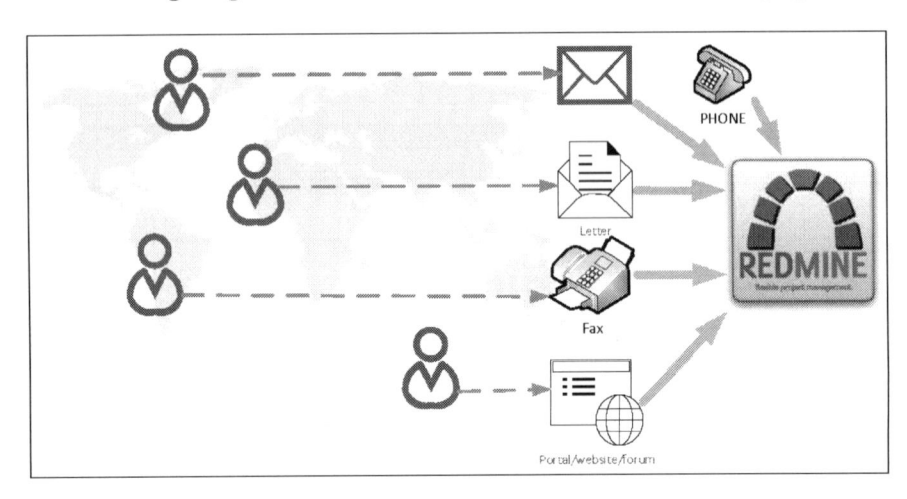

If you need to connect Redmine with your customer contact form, take a look at *Chapter 7, Integrating Redmine with Other Software*. Here, you will find examples of code to connect to the Redmine API from C# and PHP, which are most commonly used on websites.

Take a look at the previous recipe, *Redmine as a Help desk with auto-responder*, to automate issue creation from a customer's e-mail.

> If you let your operators enter issues from e-mail to Redmine instead of having Redmine fetch and create issues automatically, you are risking failing to comply with SLA because your employee may overlook e-mails, have a technical problem, be out of the office, and so on.

How to do it...

Service desk is supposed to serve as a single point of contact, single point of entry, and a single point of exit. Redmine can in the same time serve as a centralized and as a decentralized service desk, serving operators in their own language. If your company is not multilanguage, simply skip this step, or modify it according to your needs:

1. Create a parent project that is not supposed to contain any issues to prevent issues from accidentally being entered. So, uncheck the Issues module while creating a project. Let's name it `Support for our great IoT products`.
2. Create sub-projects for branches such as in the following image:

Projects

★ **Support for our great IoT products**
Main project

    IoT support Germany
    Requests from German website.

    IoT support US
    LA Office support requests

3. Define issue categories and additional custom fields for issues; for example, a set of categories could be: *Asset Acquisition, Asset Move, End User Support,* and *End User Move*. Additional custom issue fields could be: *Problem Type, Problem Area,* and *Problem Detail*. To change them, navigate to **Administration | Custom fields**.
4. Define priorities (a basic set of issue priorities is already defined in Redmine, to change it, navigate to **Administration | Enumerations**, and edit values under **Issue priorities** section).
5. Define roles for staff.
6. Define workflows.
7. Enter the main know-how documentation in a main project.
8. Train your staff.
9. Put a service desk into operation.

Making the Most of Redmine

How it works...

ITIL considers the service desk as a wider concept than a Helpdesk, actually, quoted from *Business Service Management,* Michael Johnson, eISBN-13: 9781743044452:

> The service desk is one of four ITIL functions and is primarily associated with the Service Operation lifecycle stage. Tasks include handling incidents and requests, and providing an interface for other ITSM processes. Features include:
>
> **Single Point of Contact** *(SPOC)* and not necessarily the **First Point of Contact** *(FPOC)*
>
> > Single point of entry
> >
> > Single point of exit
> >
> > Easier for customers
> >
> > Streamlined communication channel
> >
> > Primary purposes of a service desk include:
> >
> > Incident control: life-cycle management of all service requests
> >
> > Communication: keeping a customer informed of progress and advising on workarounds

Redmine fulfills the duties of service desk, by serving as:

- *SPOC*: This is when one department or job type is responsible for resolving the ticket or giving it to another worker or department.
- *Single point of entry*: This is when the customer's request is accepted only if it is entered in Redmine (data is entered directly to Redmine through operators over the phone or directly by customers through a contact form, e-mail, or through some third-party application, for example, a mobile application communicating through API).
- *Single point of exit*: This is when workflow is completed only when a task is closed in Redmine. Also, customers are always informed in the same way about the status of their request, as such Redmine streamlines communication, and ensures no request passes by unattended.

Benefits of such an organization include the following:

- Customers don't have to determine who to call
- It enables all incidents to be logged in a centralized and standard manner, making it possible to identify, predict trends, and react more quickly
- It provides customers with a single point of contact for support services
- It's more efficient and cost-efficient than having every branch of the company having its own IT department taking care of additional assets
- It centralizes and formalizes processes and tools while reducing inefficiencies and costs

Improving Redmine Security for ISO 27000

ISO 27000 is a growing set of standards that is oriented towards information security. It covers more than just privacy, confidentiality, and IT or technical security issues. In addition, it is applicable to organizations of all shapes and sizes. Redmine can be implemented in companies certified for ISO 27000 or those preparing to get the certificate.

> It is always good to increase security of the production system which is in any way related to your business. It may store important data or be business critical.

Nowadays, hackers do not just make planned attacks to certain entities, they rather utilize various tools, such as bots and web crawlers to collect information about vulnerable servers and websites, and they run known exploits to hack them. The more users there are on a website, the more sensitive data is present, such as credit card numbers, credentials of some kind, and the more likely hackers will attack. So, apart from this recipe and techniques described in this book, make sure you are using the most recent versions of operating systems and Redmine. If you, for some reason, cannot update your system, then make sure that all known security holes are taken care off.

Getting ready

Make sure that your server is properly installed, updated, and there are no unnecessary ports and services exposed to the Internet.

To get free and valid SSL certificates that can be used with Redmine, install the Let's Encrypt tool. You don't have to do it as a root, but then you will have to use sudo for this tool.

Making the Most of Redmine

To install it, follows these steps:

1. Clone it from GitHub:

   `git clone https://github.com/letsencrypt/letsencrypt`

2. Run the following:

   `cd letsencrypt && ./letsencrypt-auto -help`

> The let's encrypt certificate is valid only for 3 months, but it is great for testing and setting the server up properly. After or during the free months, obtain a proper SSL certificate or set up the auto-renewal script for the Let's Encrypt certificates.

How to do it...

To prevent hackers from gathering your data by recording traffic to and from your Redmine server, it needs to be properly secured in the following ways:

1. All users must connect and use Redmine through SSL
2. All e-mails must be read and sent through SSL

Install and use SSL certificates

1. To install and use free SSL certificates from Let's encrypt:
2. First grab the let's encrypt certificate using the following command:

   `./letsencrypt-auto certonly -webroot -w /home/redmine/public_html/ -d redmine.biz`

3. Configure Apache virtualhost or another type of web server to use the let's encrypt certificate, considering that you run the previous command with the `redmine.biz` example domain, your SSL certificates part should look like the following:

```
SSLEngine on
SSLCertificateFile /etc/letsencrypt/live/redmine.biz/cert.pem
SSLCertificateKeyFile /etc/letsencrypt/live/redmine.biz /privkey.pem
SSLCACertificateFile /etc/letsencrypt/live/redmine.biz/fullchain.pem
```

Enforce all traffic to go through SSL

To make sure that your users cannot make a mistake by typing a Redmine URL without HTTPS, follow these steps:

1. Navigate to the Redmine installation root, subfolder `public`:

    `cd /home/myUser/redmine/public`

2. Create a `.htaccess` file with the following content:

    `RewriteCond %{HTTPS} off`

    `RewriteRule (.*) https://%{HTTP_HOST}%{REQUEST_URI}`

Use only secure mail authentication and transfer

Mail is configured through `redmine/config/configuration.yml`, and typical secure sending settings look like this:

```
email_delivery:
      delivery_method: :smtp
      smtp_settings:
         enable_starttls_auto: true
         address: "smtp.gmail.com"
         port: 587
         domain: "smtp.gmail.com"
         authentication: :plain
         user_name: "your_email@gmail.com"
         password: "your_password"
```

Typical incoming mail is triggered via console (cron job), and should look similar to the following command:

```
rake redmine:email:receive_imap RAILS_ENV="production" host=mail.example.com port=993 username=username password=password ssl=true project=project_identifier folder=INBOX move_on_success=processed move_on_failure=failed no_permission_check=1 unknown_user=accept
```

> Please keep in mind that you need to adjust hosts, users, passwords, and domains to match your system's settings.

Making the Most of Redmine

How it works...

This recipe addresses some of the basic techniques of web-application hardening. It instructs users to force encrypted (SSL) traffic from and to the server. Using SSL, you are hardening the application security in such a way that hackers who record traffic to and from your Redmine server will only get garbage contents, which won't be easy to turn into data without utilizing some more complex hacking and decrypting techniques. The *There's more* section of this recipe presents some additional techniques, such as masking the footprint of your web server, enforcing password policy, and hiding sensitive information onscreen. Please keep in mind that certifying for ISO 27000 or any of its sub-standards standards is a large endeavor, and it is a continual process. This means that you need to keep up with standard changes, recommendations, and recertify every few years.

There's more...

Additionally, it is good to hide details about your server. Having server details visible in the header makes it easier for hackers to run the proper exploits and gain unauthorized access to your system.

One way to hide problematic headers is as follows:

1. Enable `mod_headers` for Apache:

    `a2enmod headers`

2. Add the following command to your virtual host's directive:

    ```
    # Hide/Remove the Passenger Headers
    Header always unset "X-Powered-By"
    Header always unset "X-Runtime"
    ```

3. Restart Apache, as follows:

    `service apache2 graceful`

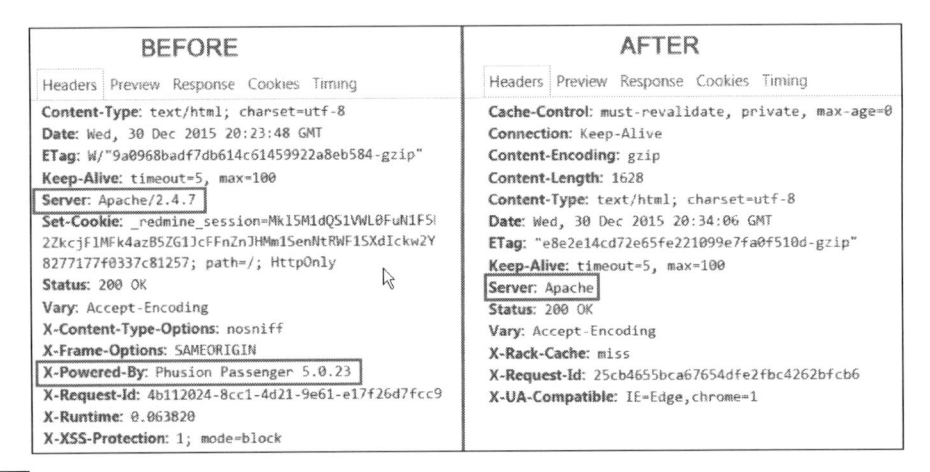

BEFORE	AFTER
Headers Preview Response Cookies Timing	Headers Preview Response Cookies Timing
Content-Type: text/html; charset=utf-8	**Cache-Control:** must-revalidate, private, max-age=0
Date: Wed, 30 Dec 2015 20:23:48 GMT	**Connection:** Keep-Alive
ETag: W/"9a0968badf7db614c61459922a8eb584-gzip"	**Content-Encoding:** gzip
Keep-Alive: timeout=5, max=100	**Content-Length:** 1628
Server: Apache/2.4.7	**Content-Type:** text/html; charset=utf-8
Set-Cookie: _redmine_session=Mk15M1dQS1VWL0FuN1F5!2ZkcjF1MFk4azB5ZG1JcFFnZnJHMm1SenNtRWF1SXdIckw2Y8277177f0337c81257; path=/; HttpOnly	**Date:** Wed, 30 Dec 2015 20:34:06 GMT
	ETag: "e8e2e14cd72e65fe221099e7fa0f510d-gzip"
Status: 200 OK	**Keep-Alive:** timeout=5, max=100
Vary: Accept-Encoding	**Server:** Apache
X-Content-Type-Options: nosniff	**Status:** 200 OK
X-Frame-Options: SAMEORIGIN	**Vary:** Accept-Encoding
X-Powered-By: Phusion Passenger 5.0.23	**X-Rack-Cache:** miss
X-Request-Id: 4b112024-8cc1-4d21-9e61-e17f26d7fcc9	**X-Request-Id:** 25cb4655bca67654dfe2fbc4262bfcb6
X-Runtime: 0.063820	**X-UA-Compatible:** IE=Edge,chrome=1
X-XSS-Protection: 1; mode=block	

Enforce password policy

One important aspect of security is password complexity. Currently, there is no official support for password complexity, or a developed and mature enough plugin to be used in production, so you would have to rely only on Redmine's password length enforcement. However, you can enforce password policy through the LDAP tool, and connect Redmine to LDAP to overcome this shortage of enforcement.

Protect sensitive data visible on screen

In ISO information security standard, you should not have sensitive data such as passwords visible onscreen because somebody may take a photograph of your screen and exploit this data. To ensure that sensitive data in Redmine is protected, install the plugin to hide or show passwords on click. This plugin is called wikicipher. To install it, follow the instructions from `https://github.com/thorin/redmine_wikicipher`.

Additional tips

Here are some additional tips that can also be applied to Redmine servers, They are general web-server protection strategies:

- Make sure to protect access to your database ports from access outside of your server, consult your database and server's manual
- Make sure that Redmine is not running as root user; to install and run Redmine properly, refer to *Chapter 1, Installing and Running Redmine*
- If you are using Apache, consider installing the "mod-security" plugin and configuring it, but be advised that sometimes it can create problems with Redmine, such as the following:
    - Blocking some files to be uploaded
    - Blocking some text to be created inside wiki or issues, and so on
- Additionally, consider putting your Redmine server behind some firewall or intrusion detection filter, which may even have DDOS protection capabilities

See also

- Refer to **Open Web Application Security Project** (**OWASP**) at `https://www.owasp.org/index.php/Main_Page`.
- ISO 27000 standards family can be found at `https://en.wikipedia.org/wiki/ISO/IEC_27000-series`.
- Redmine security advisories can be found at `https://www.redmine.org/projects/redmine/wiki/Security_Advisories`.

Redmine and SLA

SLA stands for Service Level Agreement and it can play a significant role in service-oriented business. It is not mandatory or required for a business to function, but using this can bring intangible value to the organization, help establish good work routines, and increase productivity and company's results as time goes by, projecting also positively on the overall company's wellbeing.

Getting ready

SLAs are *agreements*, sometimes they can become a part of the contract with your clients, but they should not be treated as a tool of enforcement, but rather as a good will and practice from your side to meet client's requests on an agreed level. So in this sense, prepare SLAs that are going to be used with Redmine.

How to do it...

Redmine does not have all the built-in functionalities required for SLA. Some of the SLA requirements can be achieved through custom fields, and they can even be mandatory when entering an issue. However, Redmine lacks some important functionality, such as automated warnings of an upcoming SLA violation. There are feature requests for such functionality, and compared with other solutions available on the market, Redmine still provides more than enough functionality to be very useful in this type of organization as well. To instantly start using SLAs on a per-project basis, you can install plugin Redmine SLA, as follows:

1. Navigate to Redmine root and type the following:

   ```
   git clone https://github.com/undx/redmine_sla.git plugins/redmine_sla.git
   ```

2. Then migrate DB, as follows:

   ```
   rake redmine:plugins NAME=redmine_sla RAILS_ENV=production
   ```

3. Restart Redmine as follows:

   ```
   rm tmp/restart.txt && touch tmp/restart.txt
   ```

4. Once installed, you should see the plugin under **Administration | Plugins**.
5. Plugin is enabled in each project per default, there is no need to turn it on or off like some other plugins, which work as a module. To use it on per-project basis:
6. Define issue categories by navigating to the project's main menu **Settings | Issue categories**.

7. Click **New category**.
8. Enter values that are required for **Name** and **Default SLA**; optionally, you can have some user chosen per default if that issue category is selected. Let's take the following screenshot as an example:

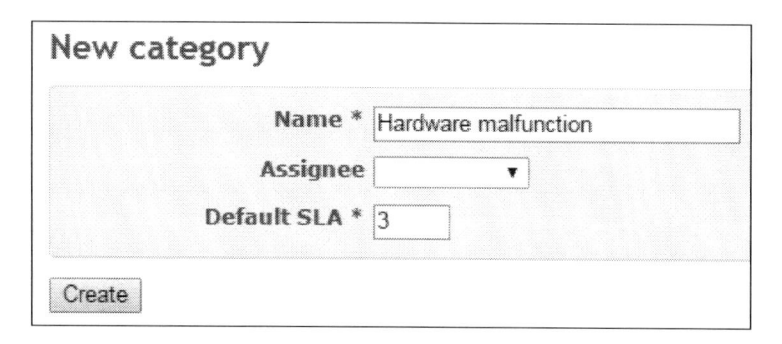

> **New category**
>
> Name * [Hardware malfunction]
> Assignee [▼]
> Default SLA * [3]
>
> [Create]

9. Here, the SLA field value is expressed in days!
10. While entering a new issue and choosing the appropriate category, the plugin will automatically set **Due date** for you based on defined SLA and prevent Due date from being changed regardless of the user's permissions.

How it works...

The Redmine SLA plugin uses issue categories to enforce due dates based on Default SLA defined for that particular issue category. Once the category is set and the issue saved, it automatically enters the due date that is based on the value entered as Default SLA for this issue category.

There's more...

This plugin can be combined with the same author's VIP plugin. In this case, you can define different SLAs for VIP clients. This plugin can be obtained from https://github.com/undx/redmine_vip.

Additionally, this plugin can also be combined with another Redmine issue SLA plugin from a different author, which enables SLA on a per-hour basis.

Making the Most of Redmine

KPIs inside Redmine

With KPIs, the situation is not so good, there are not many options available, mainly due to the fact that KPIs are usually different and calculated in a different way for each company.

One method of displaying KPIs directly within Redmine's project would be by combining two plugins. The first plugin lets you display custom SQL on the wiki page, and the second plugin lets you apply permissions on this particular page so that no users with a particular role can access this page.

> This recipe was tested on the 2.5 version of Redmine. At the time of writing this book, plugins were not upgraded to support 3.x version. Readers are advised to monitor this book's website www.redminecookbook.com because plugin updates used in this book will be announced there.

Getting ready

Ensure server access or make your Redmine server administrator to do this.

Prepare the SQL querying tool, which you will use to create and test the KPI's SQL query. It will be something such as phpMyAdmin or HeidiSQL depending upon your database system.

Key Performance Indicators are a business intelligence metric that are oriented towards a company's declared goals. So in order to determine KPIs, the company must first declare its goals, define business processes, ways to measure the quantity and quality of process outputs, and then identify key performance indicators. For example, a good KPI example would be: measurement of average time required from customer's request to completing request with customer satisfaction. Good goals for KPIs for a certain period such as month or year would be: reduce the time required to successfully complete a customers request by 10%.

How to do it...

First, we are going to install Redmine Wiki SQL plugin, as follows:

1. Navigate to the Redmine installation root.
2. Type the following:

   ```
   git clone https://github.com/kabutoya/redmine_wiki_sql.git plugins/redmine_wiki_sql
   ```

3. Restart Redmine because DB migration is not required:

   `rm tmp/restart.txt && touch tmp/restart.txt`

4. To verify that this plugin is installed properly, go to a wiki page of some project that already has some issues and type the following:

   `{{sql(select id as 'ID', subject as 'Subject', DATE_FORMAT\ (issues.due_date , '%d/%m/%Y'\) AS 'Due Date' from issues)}}`

5. The output should look somewhat like this:

ID	Subject	Due Date
6	Malfunction of elevator	05/01/2015
7	Broken window	05/01/2015
8	Water leaking	05/01/2015
10	Door won't close	05/01/2015
11	HOUSEMAN	05/01/2015
13	MD	05/01/2015
14	Paint job required	05/01/2015
15	MD	05/01/2015
16	MD	05/01/2015
17	MD	05/01/2015

> This plugin allows execution of any SQL query, which means that users can abuse it or accidentally cause damage to the database. To prevent damage, carefully assign wiki editing roles.

Now that we have installed the plugin and verified it, it's time to install the wiki page permissions plugin so that we can ensure that nobody unauthorized can read the wiki page with KPI reports. To install it, follow these steps:

1. From the Redmine installation root, type the following:

   `git clone https://github.com/stpl/manage_wiki_view_page_permission.git plugins/manage_wiki_view_page_permission`

2. Migrate the plugin's DB, as follows:

   `rake redmine:plugins NAME=manage_wiki_view_page_permission RAILS_ENV=production`

Making the Most of Redmine

3. Restart Redmine:

    `rm tmp/restart.txt && touch tmp/restart.txt`

4. Verify that the plugin is installed by navigating to **Administration | Roles** and **Permissions | Wiki**, and there should be a new permission, unchecked by default, called **View protected pages**.

For example, we are going to create an actual KPI for a company, which uses Redmine to deal with their customer requests. We will measure the average time between issue creation in Redmine, and time when this issue is closed.

To create and protect this report, perform the following steps:

1. Create a wiki page called Redmine KPI by navigating to the main project menu | **Wiki**.
2. Click **Edit** and paste the following contents:

    `[[RedmineKPI]]`

3. Click **Save**.
4. Click the **RedmineKPI** link.
5. Then click on **Edit**
6. Paste the following content:

    ```
    h1. Average time in hours between issue opening and closing:

    {{sql(select floor((avg(TIME_TO_SEC(TIMEDIFF(closed_on,created_on)))/60)/60) as "hours per task" from issues limit 0,1000)}}
    ```

7. Click **Save**.
8. Click the Lock icon.

So, the preceding code produces the following output:

Average time in hours between issue opening and closing:

hours per task
130

This indicates **130** hours from issue opening until issue closing, this is not bad for a janitor company, considering the fact that it's 5 working days. This janitor company can claim in their advertising materials that they resolve almost all issues within 5 working days. However, a good KPI improvement would be to reduce time to 4 working days, and drill-down and advanced SQL queries and reports can discover which task took longer than 5 days, and notes inside issues that can be served to the company's owner to identify issues which caused delay on these tasks so that they can improve their service in future.

How it works...

This recipe combined two plugins wiki SQL queries and wiki protect pages, to run SQL code inside a wiki page and protect it against unauthorized users. After installation of the two mentioned plugins, we created a wiki page, and ran an SQL query inside it. SQL queries need to be enclosed within `{{sql()}}` to get executed. Errors inside the query will display in a red box. The proper way to work with this plugin would be to paste queries which are confirmed to work through some database management software.

The clarification of a sample KPI query is as follows:

```
select floor((avg(TIME_TO_SEC(TIMEDIFF(closed_on,created_on)))/60)/60)
as "hours per task" from issues
```

- `timediff`: This calculates the difference in time format from `closed_on` and `created_on` for every issue
- `time_to_sec`: This converts the difference in seconds
- `avg`: This calculates average value in seconds from `closed_on` and `created_on`, converted by `time_to_sec` to seconds
- `/60)/60`: This converts seconds to hours, which are then converted to the next least integer value by the `floor` function, and named `"hours per task"`

The protection of the created page is accomplished with roles, so you should take care which roles can see protected pages, and which cannot.

See also

If this is too complicated for you, there are commercial offerings of plugins for KPI, such as http://rmplus.pro/en/redmine/plugins/kpi KPI plugin, which is very well documented, and lets you create KPIs based on several predefined templates.

Using Redmine with ITIL

ITIL, an acronym for Information Technology Infrastructure Library, is a set of best practices for **IT Service Management** (**ITSM**). It is very similar to ISO 20000. ITIL describes processes, procedures, tasks, and checklists, which are not organization-specific and can be applied by an organization to establishing integration with the organization's strategy, delivering value, and maintaining a minimum level of competency. It allows the organization to establish a baseline from which it can plan, implement, and measure. It is often used to demonstrate compliance and to measure improvement.

Making the Most of Redmine

Getting ready

Familiarize yourself with ITIL, read some ITIL books, or take courses, and see how your company can adopt ITIL.

How to do it...

Redmine can support ITIL within your organization at multiple points. Considering that ITIL covers the following:

- Service Strategy
- Service Design
- Service Transition
- Service Operation
- Continuous Service Improvement

Redmine can find its role in many places.

Probably, the best way to start is by creating a specific project, which will be named `ITIL implementation at our company`. This project should serve as a central hub to store all ITIL-related documentation, presentations, and so on. This is also to collaborate and share ideas with your colleagues regarding ITIL implementation in your company.

A typical Redmine role, and a good starting point is a service desk, which handles incidents and service requests, as well as providing an interface to users for other ITSM activities, such as the following:

- Incident management
- Problem management
- Configuration management
- Change management
- Release management
- Service-level management
- Availability management
- Capacity management
- Financial management
- IT service continuity management
- Security management

Covering of all these aspects and roles of usage exceeds the frames of this recipe and chapter. So for example, take a look at the *Redmine and SLA*, and *Using Redmine as a service desk platform* recipes from *Chapter 10, Making the Most of Redmine*, for examples on how Redmine can serve in an ITIL-oriented organization.

How it works...

The primary goal of every ITIL and ITSM implementation is to know exactly, in every moment, how much something costs your company, and how much does it cost your user. For example, large companies with multiple internal users (departments), can spend millions on licenses, support contracts, hardware renewals, maintenance and electricity for datacenters. Financial leaders of the company may decide to cut costs or often argue with IT leaders regarding these costs. The goal in this case is to know who is using what of your services and software or hardware resources, and how much does it cost. Such data can provide valuable insights, and discover resources, which are not properly used, maintained, and of course, drastically cut the costs.

Redmine, in this case, can provide valuable data, depending upon your use-cases and workflows. For example, if you are a software company, and you are using Redmine, among other things for Release management, you can use its built-in milestones/versions. For a good example on how it is used, visit `http://www.redmine.org/projects/redmine/roadmap` where you will see which features are planned for which upcoming releases. In this book, you will also find various recipes, regarding this topic, and other topics related to ITIL and ITSM.

See also

- `https://en.wikipedia.org/wiki/ITIL`
- `https://en.wikipedia.org/wiki/IT_service_management`

Index

A

Action Mailer component
 URL 258
Active Directory (AD)
 Redmine, integrating with 174-177
activity monitoring
 through atom feed 190, 191
Agile Dwarf plugin
 about 241, 242
 URL 243
 using 243
Apache
 running with, as mod_fcgid 20, 21
Apache installations
 troubleshooting 251-254
atom feed
 activity monitoring through 190, 191
authentication
 tuning 159-161
auto-login features 159-161

B

backing up
 configuring 138
 database 139
 files 139
 files, restoring 140
 restoring 139
backlogs plugin
 about 92
 improving 125-128
 URL 93

browser plugins
 Redmine, using through 185-187
bundler installation
 troubleshooting 249-251
 URL 251

C

C#
 REST API, using with 200-204
 URL 204
Center for Business Practices (CBP)
 URL 109
CKEditor
 Pandoc, URL 240
 text, formatting with 239-241
clamav
 installing, on Windows 142, 143
clients
 tracking 215-217
 URL 215
clipboard plugin
 images, pasting from 212-214
 URL 214
CORS Request
 URL 196
custom Ruby
 Cent OS servers, preparation for 32
 RVM installation 32
 Ubuntu servers, preparation for 31
 using, for Redmine 31

D

database
   migrating 147-151
   upgrading 147-151
data dirs
   checking, for malware 142
   clamav, installing on Linux 142
   clamav, installing on Windows
      users 142, 143
Desktop clients
   URL 204
DevKit
   URL 14
DMSF Plugin
   documentation, URL 222
   URL 98, 222
document management
   about 217, 218
   using 219, 220
Drupal module
   URL 199

E

Eicar test string
   URL 144
e-mail
   incoming e-mail, parsing issues 258, 259
   incoming e-mail parsing, URL 259
   issues checklist, URL 259
   notifications configuration guide, URL 258
   sending, issues 256-258
   URL 257
e-mail reminder systems
   URL 238
e-mail servers configuration
   URL 256

F

Facebook
   URL 101
file upload size
   increasing 173, 174
First Point of Contact (FPOC) 278

G

git-clone
   URL 108
Global Roles
   URL 46
gravatars
   URL 101
   using 99, 100

H

help
   bug, submitting on redmine.org 248
   getting 247, 248
   getting, via Redmine forum 248
   issues, solving 248
   users and contributors, chatting with 248
Helpdesk
   installing 272-274
   URL 274
   using 272-274
   with auto-responder, Redmine as 270-272
homepage
   layout, customizing 50-52

I

IIS
   configuring 18, 19
   URL 18
   using, on Windows 16
ImageMagick 29
images
   pasting, from clipboard 212-214
incoming e-mail configuration
   URL 57
information
   sharing 101
**Information Technology Infrastructure
      Library (ITIL)**
   about 289-291
   URL 291
IRC channel
   URL 248

ISO 27000
   additional tips 283
   password policy, enforcing 283
   screen, sensitive data protecting 283
   secure mail authentication and transfer, using 281, 282
   security, improving 279, 280
   SSL certificates, installing 280
   SSL certificates, using 280
   traffic to go through SSL, enforcing 281
   URL 283
issue and time
   relating, between 81-83
issue-code relation
   advanced issue-code relationships, applying 121-124
   using, via source-control 85
   per tracker workflows, configuring 84
   using 83-88
issues
   assigning, to groups 102, 103
   assigning, with watchers 102
   relations, managing 69-71
issues importer plugin
   about 229, 230
   URL 229
   using 230-232
issues summary e-mails
   using 237, 238
IT Service Management (ITSM) 289

J

Java PMD
   URL 120
Jenkins
   cookbook, URL 236
   plugin usage 233-236
   Redmine, using with 232, 233

K

Kanban plugin
   about 224
   defining 228, 229
   installing 225, 226
   URL 228
   using 227, 228
kbsalis library
   URL 197, 199
Key Performance Indicators (KPI)
   about 81
   in Redmine 286-289

L

landing page plugin
   URL 52
LGPL
   URL 270
log analyzer
   URL 263
log level
   setting 164, 165
logo customization
   URL 39
LogRotateWin
   URL 166
Long Term Support (LTS) 3

M

metrics
   project issue metrics 106
   time metrics 107
   used, for improving team performance 106
   user metrics 107
   version metrics 107
Microsoft Project
   data, importing 181-185
   exporting to 180, 181
Microsoft SQL Server (MSSQL) 11
migration
   about 145-147
   database 147-151
   instructions, URL 232
mobile applications
   configuring 188, 189
   installation 188
   using 188, 190

mod_fcgid
   Apache, running with as 19, 20
   URL 21
modules
   customizing, per project 39, 40
   existing projects 40, 41
multicultural teams
   in different time zones, managing 118
   Redmine multilanguage, setting up 119, 120
   time zone features 119, 120
MVC (Model-View-Controller) structure 108, 255
My page
   customizing 36, 37

N

Navicat Premium
   URL 151
Nginx
   configuring 26, 27
   installation, testing 27, 28
   Redmine, running with 24

O

OpenID connection string
   URL 161
OpenSSL Developer Package
   URL 17
Open Web Application Security Project (OWASP)
   URL 283

P

package
   URL 201
PHP
   REST API, using with 197-199
PHP mess detector
   URL 120
Phusion Passenger
   Redmine, restarting under 130
   Redmine, running with 21-24
   status checking, under Linux 135
   URL 134, 170

plugin installation
   troubleshooting 254, 255
plugins
   for KPI, URL 289
   URL 108
PortQuery tool
   URL 177
PostgreSQL
   URL 169
project entry page
   layout, customizing 49, 50
project management
   URL 103
projects
   multiple projects, managing simultaneously 74-77
   new project creation. fine-tuning 158, 159
   splitting, into phases 60-62
   URL 77
providers
   URL 161
Puma
   configuring, to start with Windows 18
   Redmine, restarting 131
   testing 17, 18
   URL 19, 134
   using, on Windows 16, 17

R

Redmine
   about 2, 60
   accessing 5, 6
   active Redmine processes, checking on server 134
   and Service Level Agreement (SLA) 284, 285
   built-in features, URL 118
   community, URL 247
   configuring, for sub-uri 27
   custom Ruby, using 31
   documents, URL 98
   e-mail configuration, URL 152
   embedding, into web application 192-195
   extensions and plugins, URL 187
   homepage, URL 7
   ImageMagick 29
   installing, from source on Ubuntu 7, 8

installing, on Ubuntu server 3-5
installing, on Windows servers 11-16
instances, URL 73
integrating, with Active Directory 174-178
interacting with, from Visual Studio 208-210
interacting with, only through e-mail 52, 53
Issues Checker extension, URL 185
issues importer plugin, using 230-232
issues, importing 229
Issue wiki, URL 71
KPIs 286-289
mobile applications, using 188
new version downloading, URL 146
optional requirements, installing 29
plugins, installing 211, 212
plugin, URL 37
project management software tools, URL 73
relevant documentation, keeping 96-98
restarting 130
restarting, on another application
    server 132, 133
restarting, on Puma 131
restarting, under Phusion Passenger 130
Rmagick 29
running, with Ngnix 24
running, with Phusion Passenger 21-24
running, with Thin 24
scaling, across multiple servers 170-173
SCM binaries, installation 30
sourcefiles, obtaining 8
starting 130
upgrade, URL 147
URL 2
using, as service desk platform 275-279
using, through browser plugins 185-187
using, with Information Technology
    Infrastructure Library (ITIL) 289-291
using, with Jenkins 232
views, editing manually 38, 39
website installation instructions, URL 153
wiki HowTos, URL 31
redmine.org
  bug, submitting 248
Redmine source files
  downloading 8
  extracting 8

installation 9-11
SVNcheckout method 9
Redmine, usage
  low-level management, convincing for 269
  management, convincing for 268
  middle management, convincing for 269
  top management, convincing for 269, 270
re-occurring tasks plugin
  implementing 222, 223
  using 223, 224
reports
  creating, on spent time 77-79
repository module
  code differences of particular folder,
    viewing 116
  revisions per folder, viewing 115
  two repository revisions, differences
    viewing 115
  two versions of same file, differences
    viewing 116, 117
  used, for displaying code
    differences 114, 115
REST API
  URL 204
  using, with C# 200-204
  using, with PHP 197-199
Rmagick 29
roadmap
  and versions 89-91
  defining, to release plan 88, 89
Roles Shift plugin
  URL 46
Ruby
  upgrading, safely 153-155
  URL 13
RubyGems
  URL 251
Ruby on Rails (ROR) application
  about 30, 248
  tutorials, URL 39
Ruby Version Manager (RVM)
  about 31, 33, 153
  patchsets, URL 170
  URL 33
Ruby web servers
  URL 29

S

Scrum
  meetings, improving 125, 127
  URL 128
scrum plugin
  URL 242
security
  advisories, URL 283
  enhancing 151-153
  improving, ISO 27000 used 279, 280
server push
  URL 124
servers
  checking, under Linux 137
  checking, under Windows 136
  delayed response, handling 261-265
  URL 248
service desk platform
  Redmine, using as 275-278
Service Level Agreement (SLA)
  and Redmine 284, 285
Single Point of Contact (SPOC) 278
Single point of entry 278
Single point of exit 278
single server
  about 166
  CPU & RAM for database, allocation
      increasing 168, 169
  number of threads/processes,
      increasing 168
  usage, planning 167, 168
software development methodologies
  URL 88
Source Control Management (SCM) binaries
  installing 30
SourceForge
  URL 114
SSL version
  URL 17
subprojects
  creating 62-65
  using 62-65
subtasks
  tasks, splitting into 66-68

sub-uri
  Redmine, configuring for 27
  URL 24
Subversion Client (SVN) 7
Sysinternals process explorer
  URL 134
system failure
  recovering from 260, 261

T

tasks
  splitting, into subtasks 66-68
TCP IP connectivity
  URL 12
team members
  access, limiting 104, 105
  roles, shifting 104
  user accounts, deleting 105
  users, locking 104
team performance
  analyzing, through code repository 110-114
template projects
  creating 72, 73
  using 72, 73
text formatting
  CKEditor used 239-241
Textile markup
  URL 98
Thin
  configuring 25
  Redmine, running with 24
timeline
  gravatars, using 99, 100
  project activity, tracking 99
  using 98-101
time logging
  URL 83
Tortoise GIT
  integrating with 205-208
  URL 205
Tortoise SVN
  integrating with 205-208
  URL 205
TurtleMine plugin
  URL 205

U

Ubuntu
 database configuration 8
 Redmine, installing from source 7
 Redmine, installing 3-5
upgrading
 database 147-151
User groups
 creating 47, 48
 using 47, 48
User Interface (UI) elements 35
user profiles
 extending, with additional data 41-44
user roles
 customizing 45, 46

V

Visual Studio
 interacting, with Redmine 208-210
 vsix, URL 208

W

watchers
 used, for assigning issues 102
web application
 Redmine, embedding 192-195
WebDav protocol
 about 221
 mapping, URL 222
wikicipher
 URL 283
Wiki SQL plugin
 installing 286, 287

Windows
 IIS, using 17
 Puma, using 17
 Redmine, installing on 11-16
windows set command
 URL 15
workflows
 tuning 161-164
WYSIWYG (What You See Is What You Get) text editor 239

Thank you for buying
Redmine Cookbook

About Packt Publishing

Packt, pronounced 'packed', published its first book, *Mastering phpMyAdmin for Effective MySQL Management*, in April 2004, and subsequently continued to specialize in publishing highly focused books on specific technologies and solutions.

Our books and publications share the experiences of your fellow IT professionals in adapting and customizing today's systems, applications, and frameworks. Our solution-based books give you the knowledge and power to customize the software and technologies you're using to get the job done. Packt books are more specific and less general than the IT books you have seen in the past. Our unique business model allows us to bring you more focused information, giving you more of what you need to know, and less of what you don't.

Packt is a modern yet unique publishing company that focuses on producing quality, cutting-edge books for communities of developers, administrators, and newbies alike. For more information, please visit our website at `www.packtpub.com`.

About Packt Open Source

In 2010, Packt launched two new brands, Packt Open Source and Packt Enterprise, in order to continue its focus on specialization. This book is part of the Packt open source brand, home to books published on software built around open source licenses, and offering information to anybody from advanced developers to budding web designers. The Open Source brand also runs Packt's open source Royalty Scheme, by which Packt gives a royalty to each open source project about whose software a book is sold.

Writing for Packt

We welcome all inquiries from people who are interested in authoring. Book proposals should be sent to `author@packtpub.com`. If your book idea is still at an early stage and you would like to discuss it first before writing a formal book proposal, then please contact us; one of our commissioning editors will get in touch with you.

We're not just looking for published authors; if you have strong technical skills but no writing experience, our experienced editors can help you develop a writing career, or simply get some additional reward for your expertise.

Mastering Redmine

ISBN: 978-1-84951-914-4   Paperback: 366 pages

A comprehensive guide with tips, tricks and best practices, and an easy-to-learn structure

1. Use Redmine in the most effective manner and learn to master it.
2. Become an expert in the look and feel with behavior and workflow customization.
3. Utilize the natural flow of chapters, from initial and simple topics to advanced ones.

Redmine Plugin Extension and Development

ISBN: 978-1-78328-874-8   Paperback: 114 pages

Build stunning extensions quickly and efficiently by leveraging Redmine's plugin facilities.

1. Gain access to powerful and useful features by hooking into Redmine's underlying infrastructure.
2. Real-world examples that will help you in building cross-platform applications using Redmine.
3. Full of illustrations, tips, and tricks to facilitate the development of plugins and extensions.

Please check **www.PacktPub.com** for information on our titles

Symfony2 Essentials

ISBN: 978-1-78439-876-7　　　　Paperback: 158 pages

A fast-paced developer's guide to using Symfony2 to make your everyday web development work more efficient

1. Build web applications with the latest features of Symfony2.

2. Focus on common tasks such as creating CRUD, creating an API, and providing a login.

3. Install and configure Symfony2 and evaluate it for your everyday needs.

Bazaar Version Control

ISBN: 978-1-84951-356-2　　　　Paperback: 402 pages

A fast-paced practical guide to version control using Bazaar

1. Gain an understanding of what version control is, and how you can benefit and effectively use it to collaborate with other people.

2. Place any project under version control and track the history of changes easily.

3. Understand all the core operations and the most common workflows through practical examples and clear explanations.

Please check **www.PacktPub.com** for information on our titles

Printed in Great Britain
by Amazon